The Writing Strategies Book

With **300** strategies

JENNIFER SERRAVALLO

The Writing Strategies *Book*

YOUR **EVERYTHING GUIDE** TO DEVELOPING SKILLED WRITERS

HEINEMANN • Portsmouth, NH

Heinemann
361 Hanover Street
Portsmouth, NH 03801–3912
www.heinemann.com

Offices and agents throughout the world

The author and publisher wish to thank those who have generously given permission to reprint borrowed material:

Planning Your Week form and Class Profile form from *Independent Reading Assessment: Fiction* by Jennifer Serravallo. Copyright © 2012 by Jennifer Serravallo. Published by Scholastic Inc. Reprinted by permission of the publisher.

Engagement Inventory form from *The Literacy Teacher's Playbook, Grades 3–6: Four Steps for Turning Assessment Data into Goal-Directed Instruction* by Jennifer Serravallo. Copyright © 2014 by Jennifer Serravallo. Published by Heinemann, Portsmouth, NH. All rights reserved.

Credits continue on page 410.

Library of Congress Cataloging-in-Publication Data
Names: Serravallo, Jennifer, author.
Title: The writing strategies book : your everything guide to developing skilled writers / Jennifer Serravallo.
Description: Portsmouth, NH : Heinemann, 2017. | Includes bibliographical references.
Identifiers: LCCN 2016040461 | ISBN 9780325078229
Subjects: LCSH: English language—Composition and exercises—Study and teaching (Elementary) | Creative writing (Elementary education) | Language arts (Elementary)
Classification: LCC LB1576 .S343426 2017 | DDC 372.62/3—dc23

LC record available at https://lccn.loc.gov/2016040461

Editors: Zoë Ryder White and Katie Wood Ray
Production: Victoria Merecki
Cover and interior designs: Suzanne Heiser
Typesetter: Gina Poirier, Gina Poirier Design
Manufacturing: Steve Bernier

Printed in the United States of America on acid-free paper

21 20 19 18 17 VP   2 3 4 5

For Lucy and Carl.
I'm a writer and a
teacher of writing
because of you.

Contents

Goal
5

162

Organization and Structure

x

Acknowledgments

Any time I asked a teacher, "Would you mind piloting a few lessons and giving me feedback? Maybe make a chart?", my question was met with an enthusiastic "Yes." This book's lessons have been vetted, and samples of real student work and real teacher-created charts grace its pages thanks to these educators from Connecticut to California:

John Acampora

Jack Awtry

Andrea Batchler

Anna Bennett

Kathryn Cazes

Jamie DeMinco

Caitlin Dudley

Diana Erben

Cassie Foehr

Jennifer Frish

Brooke Geller

Merridy Gnagey

Tara Goldsmith

Barb Golub

Berit Gordon

Betsy Hubbard

Megan Hughes

Elizabeth Kimmel

Wendy Koler

Sara Lazration

Erica McIntyre

Mindy Otto

Alisa Palazzi

Samantha Pestridge

Robin Sheldon

Tiana Silvas

Laurie Smilak

Lauren Snyder

Lindsay Stewart

Courtney Tilley

Mary Ellen Wallauer

Chelsie Weaver

Jackie Yehia

A million thanks to my editors: for finding ways to make the book better from the global to the minute, for pushing my thinking, and for your patience. This book wouldn't be without you:

Zoë Ryder White

Katie Wood Ray

Thanks to the Heinemann team, from production to design to marketing, for working through the piles of figures and permission forms, for making the book visually stunning and easy to navigate, and for making sure the book gets a hearty launch out into the world:

Amanda Bondi

Eric Chalek

Suzanne Heiser

Victoria Merecki

Brett Whitmarsh

And to my family: Jen, Lola, and Vivian. My inspiration, my heart.

Getting Started

A Very Brief Introduction to Principles, Research, and Theory, and How to Use This Book

The idea for a book of writing strategies exists many times over. This one is possible only because of the great books that have come before it. There are books suggesting writing strategies meant for professional writers and college students, such as those by Noah Lukeman, Roy Peter Clark, and Janet Burroway, among others. There are countless examples of excellent compilations of writing strategies in books written for teachers of writing, such as Fletcher and Portalupi's Craft Lessons Series, Barry Lane's *After "The End"* (1993), Carl Anderson's Strategic Writing Conferences series (2008–2009), Donald Graves' many books, Katie Wood Ray's *Wondrous Words* (1999) and other titles, Katherine Bomer's books, Georgia Heard's books, Nancie Atwell's *In the Middle* (2014) and other resources, Lucy Calkins' Units of Study series, and many more. My aim in this book is to offer my favorite, most useful collection of strategies that span all aspects of the writing process, all genres and modes of writing, and that will work well with students in grades K–8. I want to offer you a little bit of everything. I streamlined the language and examples, and I present the strategies in a format that is organized so that the busy teacher can find just the right strategy at just the right moment. Of course, you'll elaborate on the streamlined language and make it your own.

But wait—before you dive in, I'm so glad you're taking the time to spend a few moments with this "Getting Started" introduction. In this introduction, you'll gain a helpful overview of the thinking that undergirds this book's ideas as well as an overview of its organization. You'll learn about strategies and all the aspects that I chose to include to elaborate on them—mentor texts, prompts, lesson language, teaching tips, and more. You'll learn how to navigate the pages of the book so you can find what you're looking for quickly and easily, for this is not a read-every-single-page kind of book (unless you want it to be). You'll get a quick crash course on some important terminology and concepts that will help you use this book to its fullest— thoughts about writing as a process, and modes and genres of writing, for example. And finally, you'll learn how to adapt what's in the book to fit your students' writing time in the classroom, no matter what form that time takes.

◎ Navigating the Book

You're holding a book that's more than 400 pages, but I want to tell you that once you understand how it is organized and how to navigate its pages, you will be able to find what you're looking for in a minute or two.

When I began work on this book, on the heels of its sister *The Reading Strategies Book* (Serravallo 2015a), I thought long and hard about how to organize the chapters. I considered organizing the book by stages in the writing process, because I believe so strongly in teaching writers not only how to write strong pieces but also how to work through a process to develop the ideas within them. When looking for helpful writing strategies, many writers and writing teachers might think, "Where am I in the development of my piece?" and perhaps want to search for ideas that would support their work during that phase. But then, I thought, "Aren't there strategies that fit in multiple points across the process?" Does a writer only think about spelling when editing? No, of course not. Does a writer only consider the lead of a piece when drafting? No, it could also be in planning or revision. When does a story writer add in dialogue? It could be thought about during planning, but could be written during drafting or revision. And so, I scrapped the idea to organize by process. (But don't worry—every strategy still has a process recommendation alongside it in the margins—read more about process beginning on page 9.)

Then, I considered organizing the book by genre. Lessons to teach memoir in one chapter, fiction in another, personal narrative in another. I imagined a separate chapter for how-tos, and still another for nonfiction research reports. There would be a section on poetry and another on essay. But then, I figured there were a number of problems with that, as well. Sometimes the lines are blurred a bit—a poem can be written to tell a story, for example, or to teach about a topic. A nonfiction piece can take a narrative form (biography) or expository (*All About Whales*) or be a hybrid of the two (historical accounts). Not to mention, there are strategies that I'd use for a variety of genres—thinking of an important place, for example, can lead me to write a story about something that happened there, or a nonfiction piece giving information about the place, or even a poem inspired by the mood of that place.

In the end, I came back to organizing the book by *goal*. It should come as no surprise, because anyone who has read something I've written or listened to a talk I've given in the last five years has heard me talk about Hattie's (2009) research into effective classroom practices and how convinced I am that helping kids to articulate clear goals for their work, and supporting them with strategies and feedback to accomplish those goals, makes a huge difference in their ability to succeed. Some of the goals are terms you may otherwise know as qualities of good writing (Anderson 2005; Calkins 1994), craft (Fletcher and Portalupi 2007; Ray 1999), or writing traits (Culham 2003, 2005) such as organization, elaboration, word choice, and conventions. Others are more about habits of writing such as writing engagement or generating ideas. Still others fall outside those two categories: composing with pictures, for example, or working with writing partners and clubs. The ten goals I've arrived at are those that I've found to be most common in supporting writers in grades K–8.

How Do I Choose Which Goal to Begin With?

Each chapter in this book focuses on one of ten possible goals. The first few pages of each chapter offer a quick overview of what the goal is and why it's important and a brief section on how to determine if it's the right fit for the student you're considering teaching it to. I can't say enough about how important it is to spend time making sure you're choosing the right goal to focus on for each writer in your classroom. Choosing an appropriate goal requires that you have a deep knowledge of your students, developed through assessments of course, but also through talking to your students and getting to know them as people. You'll likely plan to spend time observing them as they write and meeting with them in conferences to learn about their interests and hopes for their writing. You'll also likely do more formal assessments such as asking them to write "on demand" (completing a piece of writing in one sitting) and looking at those pieces for qualities of writing that you hope to teach. For more information on formative assessment, and expectations to have for writers grade-by-grade, I recommend Anderson's *Assessing Writers* (2005), Calkins' *Writing Pathways* (2014), and my Literacy Teacher's Playbook series (2013–2014).

The ten goals for teaching writing are arranged in a sort of loose hierarchy. Think of it not as a hierarchy of most important to least, or from simplest to most sophisticated. Instead, this is a hierarchy of *action*. For example, if I notice a child could use support in two areas—say, structure and elaboration—I'm inclined to start at the one that's closest to the top (structure) and work my way down (elaboration). Think of that example. Why teach a child to fill her page with details if the details are disorganized and it will make the writing difficult to follow? The hierarchy is largely influenced by my studies with Carl Anderson and his book *Assessing Writers* (2005).

Determining Where to Start: A Hierarchy of Possible Writing Goals

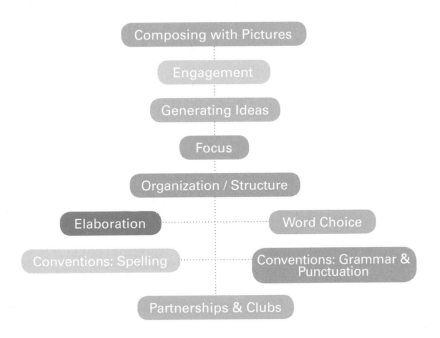

The first goal is composing with pictures. It's a goal centered around teaching children to use sketches and illustrations to tell stories, teach, and/or persuade. The idea behind this first goal is that even before children are able to write conventionally with words, they can compose pieces of work using what they *can* do—draw pictures. Also, as children get older, using pictures as a way to practice qualities of good writing, and as a way to plan their writing, has lots of value. Teachers may therefore find this is a helpful goal to focus on for young writers, and also for more experienced writers who would benefit from focusing on the pictures they draw alongside the words they write.

Engagement comes next because unless students see themselves as writers, have the stamina to sit and write, and want to write, it'll be hard to focus on qualities. They've got to practice to improve.

Generating ideas is a goal that's close to the top of the list because it's crucial to help children come up with their own topics and ideas for their writing. An inability to do so could also be a root cause of disengagement with writing. Although there are certainly instances where students will need to write from a prompt, I would argue it shouldn't be all they do. This chapter will help you create writers who have a never-ending bank of things to write about.

Focus is the next goal category because when a writer sets out to write a piece, there should be something that helps it to be cohesive. It could be an idea, it could be a thesis statement, it could be a focus on a period of time (as is sometimes the case with some stories). But it can't be wandering all over the place. Without focus, it's hard to know what details to add and what to take away, and it's hard to have a purpose or meaning behind the writing.

Next: structure. A piece needs to be organized so that a reader is able to follow the story, the argument, or the categories of what's being taught. Having a clear structure, and having solid parts within that structure (lead, middle, ending, for example), helps a writer to know how to use detail effectively.

The next two goals—elaboration and word choice—appear side by side on the hierarchy. Each goal will help writers fill out the structure they've created. Elaboration is about helping children to add the right amount and the right types of details to connect to the meaning, genre, and structure of their piece. Word choice is about the careful decisions a writer makes on the word level. The two goals are closely related, but when working with students you'll probably find it more effective to work on one at a time.

The next two goals are about conventions—one on spelling and one on grammar. These live side by side in the hierarchy as well. They are toward the bottom of the hierarchy not because I think they are less important, but because I'm more apt to help a student with one of the other goals before these if the others aren't solid. Students will have more energy for editing their spelling, or considering their punctuation choices, or looking over their piece to correct dangling modifiers if they care about what they wrote and there are sufficient, well-organized details included in the piece.

The final goal focuses on partnerships and writing clubs. This is one that you'll likely weave throughout your whole year for every student, if you choose to get partnerships and writing clubs up and running (and I hope you do!). And there may be some students who would benefit from a particular, personalized focus on how to collaborate within a group.

Just as I feel sure enough that this hierarchy is largely what drives my decision making when I work with student writers, I'd be lying if I said there aren't exceptions. Perhaps, for instance, the reason a student's writing volume is low is because she doesn't have any ideas. Well, in that case, I'd start with the goal on generating strategies. Or maybe a student needs help with structuring his writing, but there are so few details that there isn't much to put a structure around. In that case, I might help him brainstorm what else he could say, and then we could go back to organize it.

Some of you may be noticing the absence of the words *voice* and *craft*. Although you won't see these two terms as the titles of chapters or as goals, the lessons within many of the chapters will help your writers to create pieces with voice and craft. A writer's voice is communicated through many aspects of writing including syntax decisions (which would fall under the punctuation and grammar goal) or the vocabulary she chooses to use (which falls under the word choice goal). A writer makes craft decisions at many points of the process and in many aspects of the piece, including the details she chooses to include (this is included in the elaboration chapter) and how the piece flows (organization and structure). In a way, to me it seems like writing well is all about craft and voice, and so you'll see those words mentioned again and again throughout many chapters.

How Do I Find the Right Strategy Within the Chapter? Part I: Levels

Strategies are arranged within each chapter from those that are best for less-experienced writers to those that are best for more-experienced writers. All strategies have a recommended range of grade levels, though using grade levels is tricky, and correlations should be considered a loose guideline. The grade levels alongside each strategy represent the grade levels in which I'd be most likely to teach the strategy, assuming that the students within that grade level are somewhat typically developing, on-benchmark, standards-meeting kids. Of course we know there is probably not a single classroom in the United States where we could say that about every student in any class. So my advice is that for less-experienced writers, or those who are writing below expected grade-level benchmarks, you'll need to find strategies that are appropriate for writers marked for lower grade levels than what you teach; if you're working with especially advanced writers then you can go to strategies marked for higher grade levels than what you teach (for example, a more-advanced-than-is-typical second grader might benefit from a strategy marked as "fourth grade through eighth grade"). In fact, even within a grade level you'll see a range of abilities of what a child can do in September through June, so a kindergarten teacher may be leaning more toward the "emergent" strategies in the beginning of the year and a mixture of those appropriate for grades K and 1 by the end.

Find grade-level correlations for each strategy at a glance on the overview table at the opening of each chapter.

Strategies for Collaborating with Partners and Clubs

	Strategy	Grade Levels	Genres/ Text Types	Processes
10.1	Use a Partner to Hear More Sounds in Words	K–1	Any	Editing
10.2	Using Partners to Make Writing More Readable	K–2	Any	Revising, editing
10.3	Storytelling from Sketches	K–3	Narrative	Rehearsing, developing
10.4	Talk Around the Idea, Then Write	K–8	Any	Rehearsing, generating and collecting, developing, drafting
10.5	Make Promises (You Can Keep)	K–8	Any	Any
10.6	Partner Inquisition (to Get Your Thinking Going)	1–8	Any	Revising
10.7	Tell Me: Does It Make Sense?	1–8	Any	Revising
10.8	Partner Space	2–8	Any	Any
10.9	Help Wanted/Help Offered	2–8	Any	Any
10.10	PQP (Praise, Question, Polish)	2–8	Any	Developing, drafting, revising, editing
10.11	Tell Me: Does It Match My Intention?	3–8	Any	Revising
10.12	Interrupt Your Partner	3–8	Narrative	Rehearsing, developing
10.13	Dig for Fictional Details with a Partner	3–8	Narrative	Developing, drafting, revising
10.14	Form a Club	4–8	Any	Any
10.15	Storytelling to Figure Out Point of View and Perspective	4–8	Narrative	Developing, revising
10.16	Tell Me: How Does It Affect You?	4–8	Any	Revising
10.17	Code the Text	4–8	Any	Revising

How Do I Find the Right Strategy Within the Chapter? Part II: Genre

In addition to levels, I've included advice about which genres each strategy will work best for. In some cases, you'll find the strategy marked "any," meaning that with slight tweaks to the language, you can make the strategy work for any writing mode: informational/nonfiction, opinion/persuasive, narrative, poetry. For example, "Write a Poem to Try on a Focus" (page 145) is a strategy you'll find early on in the chapter about focus. The heart of the strategy is that students take their long-form writing (informational, opinion, or narrative) and try to condense the essence into a poem, causing them to consider the most important words and the most important meaning they are trying to get across. This works for any genre!

Other strategies are really unique to the genre, such as strategy "Uh-Oh… UH-OH…Phew" in the structure chapter (page 175), which is really leading children to learn about how to structure a narrative with a central problem that gets worse until the solution or resolution at the end. Another genre-specific example is the lesson about crafting a thesis statement, which will really only work in the persuasive mode of writing.

All this said, there are numerous genre-bending examples, and at times dividing things by genre is artificial. Fiction can teach us about life, the world, and people—it's not strictly informational writing that teaches. Poetry can be narrative (consider stories in poetry such as *Love That Dog* by Creech [2001]) or informational (such as some of Douglas Florian's animal or insect poems [1998]). Narrative can be used to elaborate within an informational text (consider the way Seymour Simon uses narrative in many of his informational picture books.)

Identifying the kind of writing your student(s) are choosing to make, or the type you're teaching as a class study, will be important to help match your writers to the right strategies. In the graphics on pages 7–9, I am offering examples of writing modes, genres, and definitions to help you with your planning and to help you categorize and contextualize the strategies.

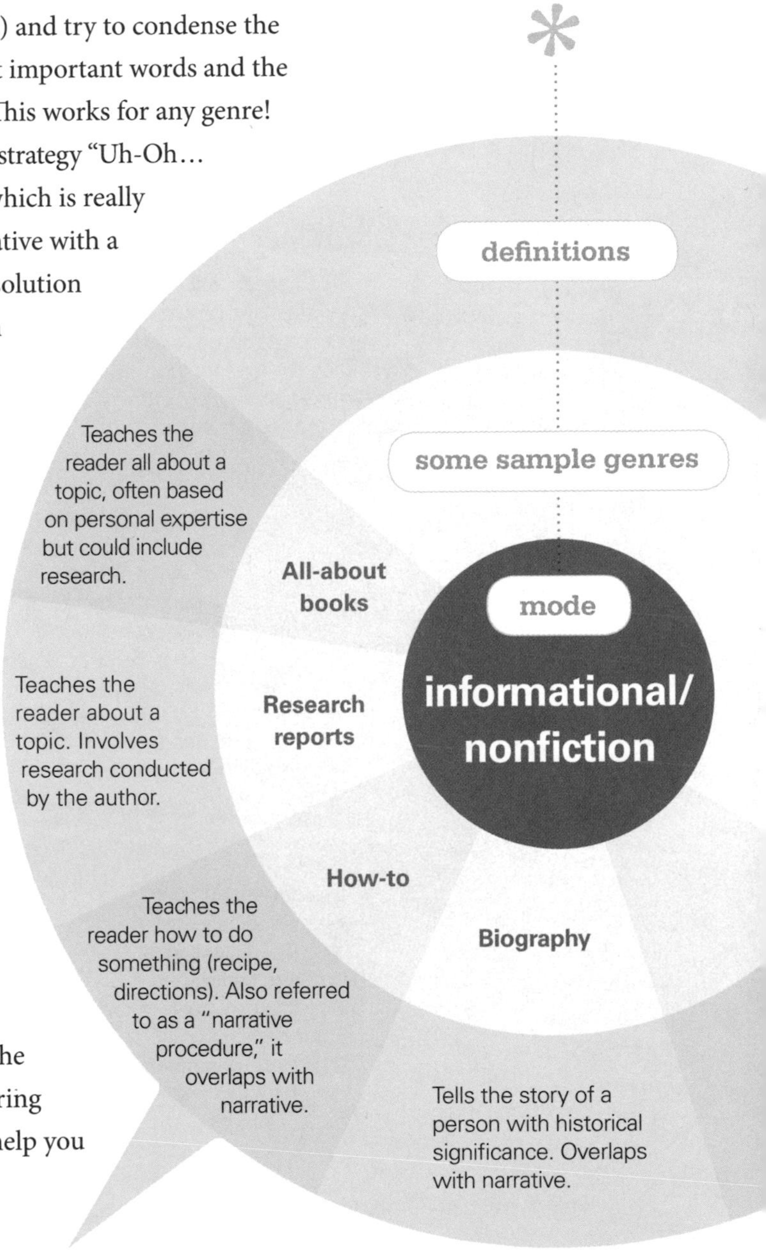

definitions

some sample genres

mode

informational/ nonfiction

All-about books
Teaches the reader all about a topic, often based on personal expertise but could include research.

Research reports
Teaches the reader about a topic. Involves research conducted by the author.

How-to
Teaches the reader how to do something (recipe, directions). Also referred to as a "narrative procedure," it overlaps with narrative.

Biography
Tells the story of a person with historical significance. Overlaps with narrative.

some sample genres

mode

narrative

Personal narrative

A true story from the author's life. When focused in time, it can also be referred to as a "small moment."

Realistic fiction

A created story with fictional characters, plot, and/or setting.

Memoir

Overlaps with informational because the story is true, and possibly with opinion if the author is presenting the memoir in essay form or is trying to persuade the reader about an idea about his or her life.

Historical fiction

A created story with some historically accurate details.

An article authored by an editor or on behalf of the editor that often appears in newspapers. The author gives a viewpoint or opinion on a topical issue.

A form of criticism in which the author judges the merits of the subject being reviewed based on subject-appropriate criteria. For example, a restaurant review would include notes about ambiance, food, and service.

The writer makes a claim and then defends that claim with information from credible sources. Writers offer evidence and explain how the evidence supports the claim. Counter-claims are often also included.

Editorial

Argument

Review

opinion/ persuasive

A journey of thought, often with a clearly articulated slant, idea, or thesis statement. Possible overlap with informational or narrative, depending on the form the essay takes.

Essay

mode

Speech

A formal address, meant to be delivered orally to an audience.

some sample genres

8

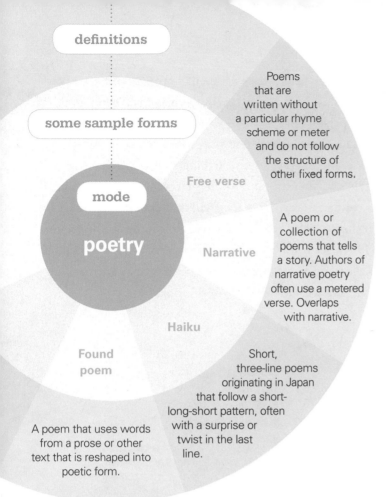

some sample forms

definitions

mode

poetry

Free verse — Poems that are written without a particular rhyme scheme or meter and do not follow the structure of other fixed forms.

Narrative — A poem or collection of poems that tells a story. Authors of narrative poetry often use a metered verse. Overlaps with narrative.

Haiku — Short, three-line poems originating in Japan that follow a short-long-short pattern, often with a surprise or twist in the last line.

Found poem — A poem that uses words from a prose or other text that is reshaped into poetic form.

How Do I Find the Right Strategy Within the Chapter? Part III: Process

There is no single writing process. Read or listen to author interviews, and when asked to talk about how their books come to be, you'll hear a range of responses. Some just draft. Some draft and revise many times over. Others plan extensively before drafting. Some take long walks, rehearsing and rehearsing in their minds until they are ready, and then they sit down and it all comes out on the page. Writers will also use a variety of terms to talk about the same process work—for example, *prewriting*, *rehearsing*, and *developing an idea* can all be synonymous. Regardless of the differences, I think you'd be hard-pressed to find a writer who doesn't follow a process, for, as Donald Murray points out, "Thinking of writing as a process is an acceptance of the idea that writers are doing more than recording. They are thinking on the page, discovering what they want to say, and messing around with their words as they write. What results is almost never what was planned out. This means that writing is a subject that needs to be taught, not just assigned" (1985, 4).

For developing writers, it's often helpful to teach them *a* process, with the knowledge that over time they will adapt what you've taught them and will develop a process that works for them personally.

Many children in grades K–2 are taught to follow a process whereby they begin to plan by generating a topic, and then spend time talking and/or sketching to further plan out what they'll say. After that, they draft their writing, often first in sketches and then later by adding words. Often they will draft many examples of the type of writing they are trying to make, before going back to choose one or two to revise and edit (Calkins 1994). See below for a visual example of process. I find that children's stamina at this age is greatest during the phases where they are making new pieces—either planning out what they'll write or drafting.

The process many K–2 students follow when creating writing.

In early elementary grades, most teachers help each child set up a writing folder and offer students lots of choices of paper to support their work during writing time. Students will independently choose single pages or prestapled booklets. (For more on managing paper choice, see the section on writing centers, beginning on page 20.)

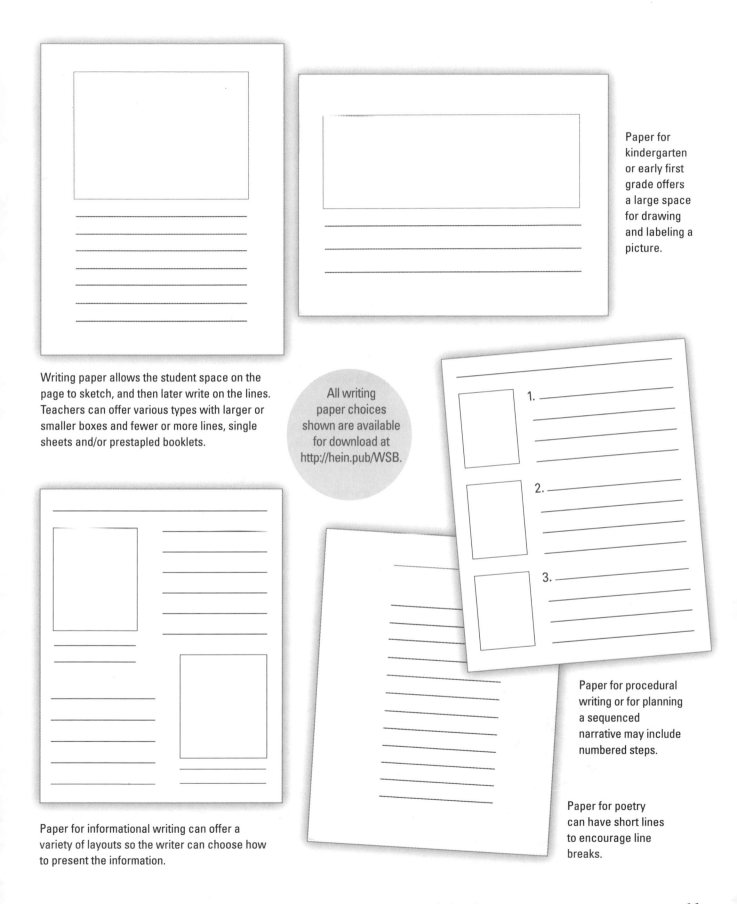

Paper for kindergarten or early first grade offers a large space for drawing and labeling a picture.

Writing paper allows the student space on the page to sketch, and then later write on the lines. Teachers can offer various types with larger or smaller boxes and fewer or more lines, single sheets and/or prestapled booklets.

All writing paper choices shown are available for download at http://hein.pub/WSB.

1.

2.

3.

Paper for procedural writing or for planning a sequenced narrative may include numbered steps.

Paper for informational writing can offer a variety of layouts so the writer can choose how to present the information.

Paper for poetry can have short lines to encourage line breaks.

In addition to the writing folder, some teachers of grades K–2 encourage children to keep a very simple and small notepad—made from a small stapled stack of paper or a pocket-sized notepad from the drugstore—for the purpose of collecting or listing writing ideas/topics.

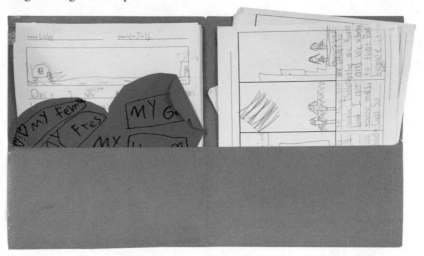

This writing folder from a first-grade student shows a side for work in progress and a side for work that's finished for now. Students independently get more paper when they are ready to start a new piece, and collect their work for future revision and editing in the folder. A red "map of the heart" (Heard 2016) is tucked inside to remind her of possible topics for writing.

Beginning in grade 3, teachers will often choose to introduce more-formal writing notebooks. Notebooks are a place for students to house their developing ideas and collect possibilities, yes, but they are also places for them to play around with their ideas before moving to a draft. Many writers use notebooks to keep lists of possible writing topics, to collect bits of language they may plan to use later, and to experiment with aspects of their writing such as writing multiple possibilities for outlines to structure their writing, trying different possibilities for leads, or creating webs to develop characters (Fletcher 2003). Typically, children younger than third grade (and truthfully even some third graders) aren't developmentally ready for the tinkering in a notebook that will further delay the stage of the writing process where they begin to draft. These younger writers will more often benefit from the support that writing across pages in a booklet offers, and they might have difficulty moving chunks of text from notebook to draft when the time comes.

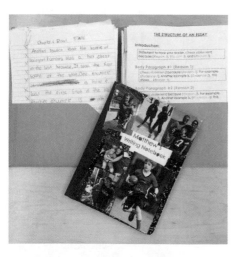

A fourth-grader's writing notebook houses collections of ideas, plans, and try-outs before drafting. A folder holds drafts in progress.

For grades 3 and above, therefore, the process will be slightly different than in the early elementary grades, looking something like what's shown in the figure on page 13.

Keep in mind that the process you introduce to students may not always be exactly what they follow—what's more important is that they follow some process to get ideas, work on them, and work on them some more. In the wise words of Murray, "The process is not linear, but recursive. The writer passes through the process once, or many times, emphasizing different stages during each passage. There is not one process, but many" (Murray 1985, 4).

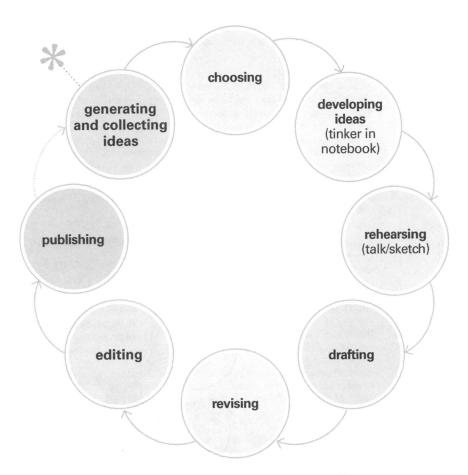

Many students in grades 3 and above will follow a process similar to this one.

6.33 How Does Y[...]

Who is this for?

LEVELS
4–8

[...]TYPE

Strategy Think of the characters you create as being real people. Think about the details of how they talk (voice, cadence, slang, dialect, accents). Plan for or revise for details in the dialogue to help make your character unique.

Lesson Language *Each of the characters in your story should have a distinct voice. So clear, so different, that a reader may be able to tell who said what even without the dialogue tags. You can think about different aspects of your character's speech to develop this. One aspect is the speaker's cadence. Think about if your character would talk in short, simple sentences or long, run-on sentences. Another aspect is slang. Think about what expressions your character might use, or a word or phrase they use in common situations. You could also consider any accent or dialect your character might have and include some words spelled phonetically to reflect how they talk.*

Teaching Tip Note that this could be broken up to be several different lessons—one on cadence, one on slang, one on dialect, and so on.

Using a Mentor

One example of note is the Judy Moody series. Point out to children that Judy always says, "Rare!" when she likes something. It's something the author created for just that character, and it isn't something we've seen in other books or even heard in our lives, most likely (McDonald 2007).

Prompts
- Think about how your character will speak.
- Look back at the dialogue you've written.

Hat Tip: *Breathing In, Breathing Out: Keeping a Writer's Notebook* (Fletcher 1996)

244

How does[...]

what is his tone of vo[...]
loud
serious tone

Does he have an accent? Dialect?
NJ accent
"wooder" (water)
"hoagie"

Does he speak in slang?
"aint"
"bae"

➤ Think of your character as a real person. How does he/she talk?
- voice
- slang
- cadence
- dialect
- accents

Chelsie Weaver

Strategy Read other narratives th[...] about. Note the vocabulary and/or ma[...] When creating dialogue in your piece, try to incorporate the same speech patterns and vocabulary to give your characters authenticity.

Using a Mentor Be sure to choose a mentor text with dialogue and where the dialogue clearly gives away the time period. For example, notice this selection from *Going to School in 1876* by Loeper.

> "I ain't afraid of her," Tommy says.
> "She's just a weak old lady," Billy add[...]
> "She's no bigger than a post rail," say[...]
> anyone!"
> The boys laugh together.
> "What are you boys carrying on abou[...]
> the new teacher. "Get to your seats[...]
> and behave yourselves," she shouts[...]
> rapping them on their heads with a
> stick. "I won't tolerate any nonsense.
> And if I catch you at any, I'll whale
> the daylight out of you!" (1984, 69)

A writer studying this passage may notice words like *ain't* as well as the comparison to a *post rail* or the teacher's threat to *whale the daylight* out of the children who

---

In the **Margins** you'll find guidance about who the strategy is best for. I've included a typical grade-level range where I'd be most likely to teach this strategy, although children's levels of writing development will likely vary within and across grade levels, and this should be treated as a loose guideline. I've also included recommended steps of the writing process and possible genres. For more information on choosing the right strategy for each student, see pages 16–18.

A section titled **Using Mentors** offers suggestions of mentor texts that can show students examples of the craft technique in action. Feel free to use the ones I suggest, or choose some of your own favorites! For more information on mentor texts, see the section beginning on page 25.

Visuals are included for all lessons. Depending on the lesson, I've sometimes included an anchor chart, other times a personalized goal card meant to be left with the student. In other cases, I've offered an example of student work or even photographs of a student in the process of practicing the strategy. Teachers from all over the country have generously opened up their classrooms to pilot lessons and send in what they've made. For more information on charts and tools, please see pages 23–25.

You'll find a **Hat Tip** on almost every page of this book. These are references to the roots of the ideas included in the strategies and/or the authors by whom the ideas were inspired.

Hat Tip: *Finding the Heart of Nonfiction: Teaching 7 Essential Craft Tools with Mentor Texts* (Heard 2013)

Who is this for?

LEVELS
4–8

GENRES / TEXT TYPES
narrative nonfiction, historical fiction

PROCESSES
developing, revising

Elaboration

245

◎ Teaching Writing Goals over Time

Once you've established a student's writing goal, perhaps by looking at several examples of her writing or by studying a more formal piece of writing that was created "on-demand" in a prompt situation, you will next need to consider how supporting the student's goal will look over time. In the following sections, I'll explain strategies and feedback/prompting in more detail to help you envision how strategy instruction may play out in the classroom.

On Strategies

You can think of the goals as the *what* and the strategies as the *how*. Each strategy is phrased in a way that it breaks down the work of the skill or craft technique into a series of actionable steps. Strategies help to take something that proficient writers do naturally, automatically, and without conscious effort, and make it visible, clear, and doable for the student writer. Choosing to teach strategies means that we are deliberately teaching the *writer* not the *writing*—we are not fixing the particular piece, but rather are empowering the student with knowledge to work on this piece, and future pieces, himself (Calkins 1994; Graves 1983). Instruction into strategies for writing has been shown to be among the most effective instructional practices in the teaching of writing and in writing remediation (Graham et al. 2012; Duke 2014).

Think of a strategy as a temporary scaffold to enable student practice. The how-to will often be offered to a student during a lesson, then practiced alongside the teacher. After learning a strategy, children should understand that they need to continue to practice it independently. Therefore, it's important that a strategy is phrased clearly enough that it is portable, and general enough that it is transferrable: a student can take it back to his seat with him, and use it today, but also tomorrow, on this piece, and on the next piece he tries. After using it many times, we can hope that the steps of the strategy become automatic so that the student no longer needs to apply conscious attention to it. That is, the strategy goes underground and the skill remains.

Any writer could come up with hundreds of strategies for any writing skill, habit, behavior, or craft technique. Three hundred of my favorites are included in this book, but once you get the hang of the language and phrasing, I have no doubt you'll be crafting your own.

As students work on one goal over time, you'll no doubt be offering them multiple strategies to practice it. To say it another way, any one strategy won't be all they'll need to accomplish a goal. Really being secure with a goal means having a variety of strategies to use and apply in different circumstances.

For example, consider a child who could use support with elaboration. (By the way, most will.) The student has strong ideas and writes with organization, but the writing is short, and thin, and as a reader you feel like the student is leaving out lots of important information. You'll likely work with that student to show him a variety of ways to add detail to the piece he's currently working on, and then maybe even the next one, which might be in a new genre. Consider the example below, which shows one student's journey to develop a repertoire of strategies in the goal of elaboration over the course of six weeks.

Week 1	Working on a fictional narrative. Learned and practiced strategies 6.33 ("How Does Your Character Talk?") and 6.14 ("Show, Don't Tell: Emotions").
Week 2	Working on a fictional narrative. Learned and practiced strategies for developing setting details, strategy 6.26 ("Exploring Options for Setting") and strategy 6.13 ("Show, Don't Tell: Places").
Week 3	Working on fictional narrative. First conference this week revisited the strategy for setting details. Later in the week, learned and practiced a strategy for developing character traits, strategy 6.20, "External Character Description."
Week 4	Finished up fictional narrative, revising for all strategies learned with support from the teacher. Began working on an informational essay. Learned and practiced strategy about adding partner facts, strategy 6.23.
Week 5	Continuing informational essay. Learned and practiced strategy for supporting facts with additional information, strategy 6.22.
Week 6	Continued informational essay. Worked on using narrative/anecdote as an elaboration technique, strategy 6.41.

So as you can see, one student's experience with a goal can cut across many strategies, and even across genres. This won't always be the case—that a student who needs support elaborating in narrative will also need that same goal in informational writing—but it may be. When teaching a student to work on a goal, the teacher will be involved with ongoing assessment to determine when the student is able to independently practice the previous strategy introduced and can handle taking on a new one.

Prompting and Guiding Writers

Within each lesson, a student or students will benefit not only from a demonstration or example of the strategy, but also from some feedback, prompting, and support as they try—right then and there—to have a go at the strategy themselves. According to Hattie's (2009) research, feedback that is connected to a goal has the potential to bring about enormous positive growth for the student. So, it's not enough to just tell students what to do, or even just how to do it. We need to support them as they practice, letting them know how their approximations hold up to the expectation, and to help them troubleshoot as they encounter difficulty when practicing the strategy.

When prompting writers and giving feedback, I'm careful to say only as much as I need to. There's a temptation to jump in and take over, talking in paragraphs or doing a lengthy demonstration, but I have found that when I can put the student in the driver's seat to practice, and I restrain myself and only say short phrases or brief sentences, I can get her to do more work—and consequently enjoy more learning. As you coach and prompt your writers and offer them feedback on their work, be mindful of the ultimate goal to create independent writers who don't need you next to them to use the strategies you're teaching.

Prompts are not only brief, they are also clearly connected to the strategy. I want to make sure that I'm giving support for the strategy I just taught. So, when a student is practicing a strategy for generating ideas in his notebook, I'm not going to start coaching him to spell a word that is tricky. In addition to keeping the language tied to the strategy, I'm also careful to not get too mired in the specific content of the piece the child is writing. It's tempting to go there, but then I'm really just fixing the child's particular piece, and many students won't make the connection that the process we followed to do it is something they can do in other pieces as well. For example, instead of saying, "I agree you could write about your family dog. Are there some specific memories you have? Like, maybe the day you got her or maybe something happened on a walk one day?" instead say, "Now that you have a topic, think about specific memories connected to the topic." Both examples prompt for the strategy of generating ideas based on something important to you, but the second example is phrased in a way that the child can take it and apply it to the next topic, and the next, and the one after that.

◎ Setting Up the Classroom to Support Independence

Children will need lots of time to practice writing and working through the writing process. They'll need support from you in the form of whole-class instruction, small-group lessons, and individual conferences. In classrooms where volume, energy, and productivity are high, the teacher is freed up to meet with students based on their writing goals, and students are industriously working. This won't happen by accident: The teacher must carefully plan for the writing environment, must set clear expectations for what is to happen during writing time, and must make resources and materials available to students to allow them to independently problem solve. When children aren't taught to be self-directed, they tend to get much less writing done and are often waiting in line at the teacher's desk for approval, correction, or problem solving.

Making Goals Visible

Once you have in your mind what a student's goal will be, I recommend having a "goal-setting conference" to discuss it with the student (Serravallo 2012, 2013a, 2013b, 2014). To conduct such a conference, you may put an example of the student's writing on the table in between the two of you, and through a series of guided questions, ask the student to reflect on what he notices are his strengths and possible next steps. Students may need examples of other authors' work for the purpose of comparison, or even a rubric or checklist of the qualities of good writing as they pertain to the genre of the piece being reflected upon. Or, if you want to work with a child on a goal of writing stamina or volume, you may offer the student the opportunity to look at an engagement inventory (see page 58). The point is, you'll carefully select what you put in front of the student to help him see what you saw. If you can get the student to articulate the strategy

The feedback I offer students takes a few predictable forms:

- **compliment:** names something the student does well (e.g., "You checked the word wall to help you spell that sight word without sounding it out!")
- **directive:** directs or commands the child to try something (e.g., "Reread the ending. Make sure it leaves your reader with something to think about.")
- **redirection:** names what the child is currently doing, and redirects the child to do something slightly different (e.g., "You're listing specific facts you know. Let's try to first list the names of the chapters you might write, then we'll get to the facts.")
- **question** (e.g., "Can you write a definition to give more detail?")
- **sentence starter:** offers the child language, which is especially helpful when coaching a child through oral storytelling, or when working with partners or writing clubs; the student will repeat the sentence starter and then verbally complete the sentence (e.g., "Once . . . And then . . . Later . . .").

(rather than come out and tell him what he needs to work on), research says he will be more likely to be motivated to work toward it (Pink 2011).

During this goal-setting conference, you can offer the child an inaugural bookmark or goal card of some sort to signify the beginning of the new work the student will take on. This card can be a place to articulate the student's goal (i.e., "Work on adding more purposeful details"), and it can also house strategies you offer the student over time, as you support her with this new goal. The teacher may record the new strategy, or in some cases the student may.

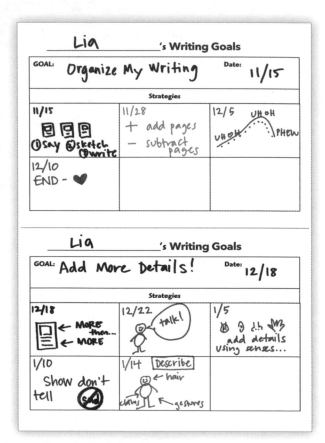

Making goals and strategies visible to students during their writing time helps to set them up for independence and success.

Writing Centers

You can equip children to independently access the materials they'll need, and troubleshoot some of their own problems, by setting up a writing center in your classroom. This writing center is not the place where the students do the writing, but is instead a bookshelf or ledge where all the writing materials a writer might need can be kept. What you'll choose to include may vary based on what you've taught your children to use and their age and level of writing development. Here are some options to consider:

- various types of writing paper (see page 11 for some thumbnails of K–2 examples; in grades 3–5 you may want to include yellow notepads for drafting, loose-leaf paper for revised second drafts, and/or fancy publishing paper with borders or decorations)
- materials for making book covers (construction paper, etc.)
- staplers
- glue sticks or rubber cement for rearranging a cut-up draft, or gluing illustration boxes or other features to drafting pages
- revision strips (thin pieces of paper with a few lines that can be taped or glued to a margin or bottom of a page to allow for more writing space)
- dictionaries
- thesauruses
- iPad or laptop with access to online resource sites and URLs clearly posted or bookmarked in the Internet browser
- past charts archived in a spiral-bound resource book
- books for writers such as Fletcher's *A Writer's Notebook* (2003) or *Seeing the Blue Between*, edited by Paul Janeczko (2006)
- highlighters
- scissors
- different-color pens for revising or editing
- sticky notes
- lists of places to publish writing and/or announcements for submissions to student magazines
- about the author template pages
- wallpaper or other decorative paper for making covers
- colored duct tape for making spines of books
- different-size labels for adding titles and author names to decorated covers or pages
- paper fasteners
- blank books
- three-hole punch
- checklists and other reminders of previously taught strategies.

First-grade writing center

A chart from the current unit of study reminds students of some strategies so they can write with independence.

Writing tools such as checklists and graphic organizers that have been introduced are available to students to grab as they need them.

Students have access to a variety of writing paper choices including single sheets and stapled booklets, some with large boxes and few lines and others with a small picture box and more lines for writing.

Staplers are made available so students can independently add new pages or revision flaps.

Writing materials such as green and blue pens for revision and editing, scissors for cutting apart drafts, and markers and crayons for adding color to published pieces are all made available so children can access them independently.

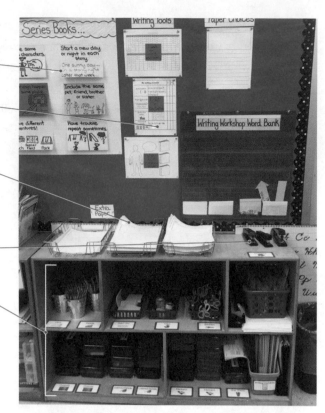

Fourth-grade writing center

Student drafting folders are organized by table grouping.

Paper choices for various parts of the writing process are organized in labeled bins.

Writing tools such as different-color pens for editing and revising, as well as sticky notes for adding in revisions allow students to independently move through the writing process.

Writing toolbox of miniversions of past charts and helpful reminders supports independent problem solving.

Tools for fancying up and publishing writing are accessible—markers, colored pencils. Scissors and tape for cutting apart and reconfiguring drafts.

Mentor texts, reference materials to aid with editing, and books to inspire writing.

Charts and Tools

In their Smarter Charts book series (2012, 2014) and Digital Campus course (2014), Marjorie Martinelli and Kristi Mraz offer compelling evidence that when a person provides visuals to accompany any written text or speech, the receiver is more likely to remember it. Think about that, and you'll probably admit that it's true for you. Inspired by them, I've worked to include visuals alongside every strategy in this book—some are student work examples, others are charts, still others are tools or strategy cards you may leave with a student during a conference. My intention is twofold. One, I want to help you, my reader, to be able to flip through the book quickly accessing what you need with a ready-made memorable visual example to better help you understand what *you're* learning from this book. My second reason is that I hope these visuals serve as examples—of the kind of writing your kids will make, or of the kind of charts you may hang in your classroom, so that your children will be better able to access and remember what *they're* learning from *you*.

If you're new to charting or creating visuals in your classroom, I can't recommend Kristi and Marjorie's work highly enough. For a quick primer, I want to spend just a bit of time explaining what makes charts and tools helpful and to provide some examples of the types of charts and tools you'll find in this book.

Characteristics of a Helpful Chart or Tool

Dozens of generous teachers sent me their classroom charts, snapped photos of their writers in action, piloted my lessons and made stuff to go with them, and had after-school pizza-eating-and-chart-making parties to send me some ideas. I am so grateful, and their names appear in the acknowledgments of this book. Of all the stuff I collected, the ones I chose to include have a few things in common:

- They are very clear, and visually simple.
- Whenever possible, they are low on text.
- They have icons, pictures, and/or color-coding to help the person using it navigate it easily, and get the essential information quickly.
- They are appropriate for the age (and reading level) of the intended user.
- They have a clear heading to tell the user what the chart is about.

Feel free to borrow or be inspired by the charts and tools that are included in this book, and, as soon as you're ready, adapt them to make them your own. For example, consider adding in your own students' writing as exemplars in place of the student writing that appears in the samples. Mention the mentor texts your class knows well. Change up the visual imagery so it better fits your grade level. The more you take on the chart-making so that it lives within the context of your classroom and it is created in the company of your children, the more the children will

Draw with circles and Sticks

Exemplar charts. These charts will include an annotated piece of text, such as an excerpt from the work of a mentor author, a page of writing from a student in your class, or your own demonstration writing. The callouts or annotations you add can highlight the use of a strategy. They can be created with the students—the teacher can prepare the chart with the selection, and students can suggest annotations that the teacher writes.

Alphabox Topic: Ballet

A	B	C	D
Arabesque	Ballet Baryshnikov Barre	Choreography	Développé
E	F French Fondu First position	G	H
I	J Jeté	K	L
M	N	O	P plié Pointe Pas Pirouette
Q	R Relevé Russian	S Second position	T tutu turn out
U	V	W Working leg	X, Y, Z

Tools are made with the intention of leaving something with students to support their continued practice with the strategy. Students may tuck them into their writing folder or the front cover of a notebook, and retrieve them when they are practicing independently or with a partner or group. You could create tools ahead of time, or make them with the student during your conference.

"Phone" A Friend...

① Ask ② Discuss ③ Write

A **process chart** is a helpful reference of the steps of the strategy. It's often helpful to include pictures and/or icons alongside the words of the strategy. Most teachers will select key words from each step of the strategy instead of writing the entire, wordy, multisentence strategy on the chart.

use it. For more inspiration when creating your own, see Kate and Maggie Roberts' *DIY Literacy* (2016) (they even say you don't need nice handwriting!).

Types of Charts and Tools

Take a look at some of the types of charts and tools that are included across the 300 strategy pages in this book. You'll see a variety of types, but regard each one as just an example. On a page where I've included a process chart, you could very easily teach the lesson and make a content chart instead. The types of charts and tools included in this book fall into six categories. Examples and descriptions of each can be found across the top of this page and page 25. They are:

- exemplar charts
- tools
- process charts
- repertoire charts
- content charts
- demonstration notebooks.

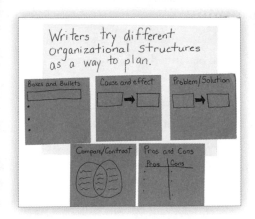

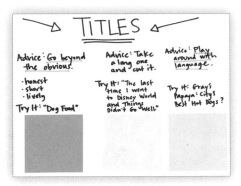

A **repertoire chart** is a collection of strategies with a heading of the genre and/or quality of good writing being studied ("Writing Well-Organized Essays") or the stage of the writing process ("When We Create Characters for Fiction . . ."). These serve to remind students of the strategies they've learned over time to hold them accountable for incorporating the strategies when appropriate. These types of charts can also be helpful when the classroom is getting very full of paper on the walls—more-detailed single-use charts can be "retired" and synthesized into a repertoire chart.

Content charts offer students a way to reference information they would use in their own writing, such as a bank of commonly used symbols in favorite mentor texts that they may want to incorporate in their own writing, or a graphic organizer to show how to organize the genre that is being studied.

Demonstration notebooks offer a ready-made visual reference and quick demonstration and/or practice text on the page (Roberts and Roberts 2016).

Mentor Texts

After I completed and turned in my first book, my editor asked if I wanted to include an acknowledgments page. Yes, of course I did! There were so many people to thank. But truthfully, I had never written one before. I got a stack of five or so Heinemann books off my shelf and read the acknowledgments that began each. I was reading not to borrow their list of people to thank, but to figure out *how they were written*. I studied the structure, the length. I read for tone and pacing. After reading a few, I identified some key traits of a professional book acknowledgments page, and got to work on my own.

"Writing well involves learning to attend to the *craft* of writing, learning to do the sophisticated work of separating *what it's about* from *how it is written*" (Ray 1999, 10). If this is something that writers do in the real world, doesn't it make sense to teach this to children, too? When we help them to study the work of other authors ("mentor authors") who have written something similar in form or genre to what they want to write, they can study it, "reading it like a writer," to learn about the craft techniques and strategies the writer must have employed to write it, and then they can transfer those discoveries to their own writing. As Frank Smith writes, "Teachers must also ensure that children have access to reading materials that are relevant to the kind of writer they are interested in becoming at a particular moment. Teachers must recruit the authors who will become the children's unwitting collaborators" (Smith 1988, 26).

Throughout the strategy pages in this book, I've offered suggestions of mentor texts that you may lean on as you work to teach your student writers strategies connected to their goals. There are many examples of entire books devoted to matching up writing qualities and craft techniques to exemplar children's literature, such as *Wondrous Words* (Ray 1999), *The Writing Thief* (Culham 2014), *Mentor Texts* and *Nonfiction Mentor Texts* (Dorfman and Cappelli 2007, 2009), and many others.

As you plan to use mentor texts, consider a few different instructional methods as possibilities to explore them with your students. One option is to state the strategy that you plan to teach, then show the example from the mentor text, and then do a quick demonstration of how you use the strategy and the example to make your own. A second option is to use inquiry as a method. To use inquiry, you'd show your students one or multiple examples of a craft technique and ask the students to explore them with a question in mind such as, "How does it seem this author uses commas? What are the purposes for including them where she does?" or "Look at the way the authors of these three newspaper articles crafted a lead. What can we say are the elements of a strong, effective beginning?" Students can then work collaboratively in pairs or groups, side by side with you, or independently to discover, notice, and name. Through this discovery and naming, students will often develop a deeper understanding, and possibly even a deeper appreciation for, the particular writing technique (Ray 1999).

These mentor texts are ones you'll likely refer to again and again—you may have a special place for them in your writing center, carry some around with you when you meet with students in conferences and small groups, and have some sitting on a ledge near where you sit to teach, so they are on-hand for demonstrations.

◎ How the Strategies in This Book Might Fit into Your Classroom

I am a dedicated reading and writing workshop teacher, à la Nancie Atwell, Donald Graves, Donald Murray, and Lucy Calkins and the Teachers College Reading and Writing Project. I also believe that a writing workshop works best within a balanced literacy framework. I would fit the content of this book into all of the components—minilessons, shared writing, interactive writing, and so on—and also to fuel my differentiated instruction as I support students with individual goals through conferring and small-group instruction. If you want to learn more about this approach to teaching writing, I recommend you pick up a copy of the classic *The Art of Teaching Writing* (Calkins 1994), take a peek at Lucy Calkins' *Units of Study for Teaching Writing, Grades 3–5* (2006), or read up on the roots of the writing workshop approach in books such as *Writers: Teachers and Children at Work* (Graves 1983), *A Writer Teaches Writing* (Murray 1985), or *In the Middle* (Atwell 2014).

If you're similarly inclined, the next two sections will help you imagine ways to craft units of study and manage differentiated instruction. If you've got a different approach to writing than workshop, check out the table in the "Using the Strategies Alongside a Variety of Literacy Frameworks" section beginning on page 31, to learn about some of my suggestions for other ways to make use of the strategies in this book.

Planning a Unit of Study

During the course of the school year, students in your class will benefit from structured units in which you introduce a genre, quality of good writing, or writing habit through a series of lessons organized around common goals. Each unit will typically last around four weeks, or 16–20 teaching days, and will help students to work through the writing process one or more times. By the end of the unit, students will be able to celebrate at least one finished piece of writing that shows evidence of what they've learned.

To design a unit, it's helpful to begin with a few things.

- First, try to articulate what it is you want the students to learn. These learning outcomes can be stated as goals, essential questions, enduring understandings, and/or skills (Wiggins and McTighe 2011).

- Second, select example(s) of mentor texts that will serve as models for students. For more information on mentor texts, see the section earlier in this chapter on pages 25–26.

- Third, I advise you to work through the process with the genre you'll be teaching or to practice the behavior or qualities of good writing you'll highlight in the unit. This will serve you in many ways including these two: (1) you'll get a sense for what the potential challenges are so that you can better explain how to troubleshoot when your children encounter them, and (2) you'll have your demonstration texts ready to go.

- Fourth, design a pre- and postassessment, which can be as simple as a prompt to ask students to write in the genre you'll be practicing, in one sitting. This will help you notice trends in your students' skills and understandings to better design your whole-class lessons. Also, with this information you can pinpoint individual needs to support during conferences and small groups.

Your next step will be to create a map of the process you want your writers to follow, and the pace at which you'll introduce strategies for each new step of the process. If you're a fourth-grade teacher, your starting map may look something like this:

Week 1	Generating and collecting	Generating and collecting	Generating and collecting	Generating and collecting	Choosing
Week 2	Developing	Developing	Rehearsing and drafting	Drafting	Revising
Week 3	Revising	Choosing	Developing	Developing	Rehearsing and drafting
Week 4	Revising	Editing	Editing	Publishing	Celebrating!

In the example above, I'm going to lead children through a series of lessons that will help them generate and collect lots of ideas for topics. Then, by day 5 they'll choose one they want to work on. They'll spend a couple days in their notebook tinkering with the ideas, then a couple days drafting. I'll teach a couple revision lessons and encourage them to try those and others they know for improving their writing. Some kids will still be drafting, others will be ready to revise. Then, I'll ask them to choose a second idea to take through the process again—developing, rehearsing, drafting, revising. Now they'll have two pieces on which to practice the strategies they've learned,

Week 1	Generating and collecting 3.1 Important People	Generating and collecting 3.2 Moments with Strong Feelings	Generating and collecting 3.5 Mapping the Heart	Generating and collecting 3.10 Scrapbook Your Life (to Write About It Later)	Choosing 4.7 Ask Questions to Focus
Week 2	Developing 5.8 Uh-Oh . . . UH-OH . . . Phew	Developing 5.29 Multiscene Storyboarding	Rehearsing and drafting 6.4 Act It Out . . . Then Get It Down	Drafting 6.9 "What *Else* Happened?"	Revising 6.13 Show, Don't Tell: Places
Week 3	Revising 6.33 How Does Your Character Talk?	Choosing 4.15 Focus on an Image	Developing 5.35 Coming Full Circle	Developing 5.36 Seesaw Structure	Rehearsing and drafting 5.39 Write the Bones, Then Go Back to Flesh It Out
Week 4	Revising 6.43 Lie (To Tell the Truth)	Editing 8.18 Turn to Spell-Check	Editing 9.8 Guess What! Complete Sentences	Publishing 4.4 Write a Title	Celebrating! (see Appendix)

and two pieces on which to try the editing suggestions I offer. On the final day, we'll spend time making a cover, choosing a title, maybe illustrating a picture to go with the piece. The day after, we'll celebrate our hard work.

Once you've planned the shape of your unit, you can look through this book, and your other writing resources, to find lessons that are a perfect fit. For example, if I want to teach a unit on writing fictional narratives, I might follow the plan on the bottom of page 28.

Managing Conferring and Small-Group Instruction

As you set your students up for independent writing time, you'll be free to move about the classroom to work with students in one-to-one conferences or in groups when a few have a common goal and would benefit from the same strategy. These meetings with individuals and groups allow you to differentiate what you're teaching, match the strategies to individual students' goals, and give students opportunities for guided practice with you by their side.

You may find it's helpful to have two things in place to help you: first, a schedule to ensure you'll be able to meet with every student at least once or twice each week, and second, a system for anecdotal records.

Creating a Conferring and Small-Group Schedule

My first step when creating a schedule is to make a class list where I can see the students, their goals, and possible strategies I plan to teach at a glance. This will help me notice which students can be grouped together because they have the same goal and would benefit from a common strategy and which students are outliers (because they are working in a different genre, they have a unique goal that doesn't align with others' goals, or because they are writing at a different level and a need a simpler or more sophisticated strategy). See the figure on the top right for an example.

Once I have a sense of who I can work with in a group, I will put their names on my schedule for group work (see the figure on the bottom right). I budget about ten minutes of my

Class Profile

Name		Goal and Notes
Alex	✓✓	Engagement (stamina)
Kezia	✓✓	Organization
Lateesha	✓	Elaboration (ch. devel.)
Meiling	✓	Elaboration
Joana	✓	Organization
Vanessa	✓✓	Focus (meaning/idea)
Jackson	✓	Elaboration (ch. dev.)
Mark	✓	Engagement (stamina)
Caroline	✓✓	Engagement (volume)
Shanique	✓	Elaboration
Mercer	✓✓	Focus (meaning/idea)
Mateo	✓✓	Word choice
Eliot	✓	Elaboration
Nick	✓✓	Word choice
Francine	✓	Elaboration
Rachel	✓	Elaboration
Rajiv	✓✓	Elaboration
Jasmine	✓	Organization
Isabelle	✓✓	Word choice
Kamala	✓	Meaning/Focus
Sunniva	✓✓	Focus
Theo	✓✓	Focus

A class profile page allows the teacher to look for patterns to inform whole-group and small-group instruction.

Planning Your Week

	Monday	Tuesday	Wednesday	Thursday	Friday
Mini-lesson	Story mountain	leads	Slow down storytell	dialogue	setting description
Strategy Lesson (10)	Nick Mateo Isabelle	Kamala Mercer Vanessa	Kezia Joana Jasmine	Lateesha Jackson	
Strategy Lesson (10)	Alex + Mark	Meiling Shanique Eliot	Francine Rachel Rajiv		TBD
Conference (5)	Caroline	Nick	Rajiv	Sunniva Vanessa	Theo TBD
Conference (5)	Isabelle			Joana	Caroline TBD
Partner/Club		Sunniva + Theo		Mercer + Mateo	Alex Kezia
Other					

A weekly conferring and small-group schedule allows me to maximize my time to differentiate instruction while students write independently.

time for each group of about three students. The other students will be on my schedule for conferences. Each conference typically takes about five minutes. For more information about conferring with writers, see *How's It Going?* by Carl Anderson (2000).

In truth, it's rare that this schedule is followed 100 percent to the letter. In fact, in many cases I need to make revisions to my weekly plan because something comes up—for example, I notice a child could use more supported practice with a strategy, or someone ends up not needing the strategy I was planning to teach because they've shown they can do it in their writing. Making revisions to my plans means I'm staying attuned to the needs of my class. Even though I know I'll want to plan to be responsive, I find that having something written down ahead of time helps me be more efficient and effective during the time students are writing independently. If a student is absent, or a group runs long, I can just pen in the changes I need to make to the following day to get back on course. I usually plan for a five- to ten-minute buffer each day to be able to respond to the unexpected.

Establishing a System of Anecdotal Records

Unless you have a photographic memory like Cam Jansen, it's going to be next to impossible to remember every detail and nuance from every conference and small group, each strategy you taught each student, and how the students responded. I strongly recommend you have some way to keep track of it all.

The figure on the left shows an example of the simple form I used to use in my own classroom. Each student had her own page, so that I could see an individual's progress over time. The student's goal would go at the top of the page. As I worked with a student, I'd write down the date and notes about what that student was demonstrating as strengths (on the left) and the things I noticed the student could use support with (on the right). Whatever I ended up teaching that day would be marked by a *T* in a circle. At the end of conference or small group, I'd draw a horizontal line. During the next conference or small group, I could quickly reference my past notes and follow up on the strategy previously taught to see if the student needed additional support with it or if he was ready to move on to new learning. You can keep these notes in anything that makes sense to you—if you're comfortable with digital formats, you could use Evernote or GoogleDocs. If you are

A sample note-taking form allows me to track student progress over time as I introduce new strategies and support the student with ongoing practicing of strategies that I've previously taught.

old school, use a binder, notebook, or two-pocket folder for each student. What's most important is that it's portable and not too cumbersome and that it works for you so you'll actually use it.

Using the Strategies Alongside a Variety of Literacy Frameworks

Whether your school uses a nonworkshop approach to writing, you have a workshop-based curriculum already created, or if you have a program that you must follow, the strategies in this book will still be extremely helpful in setting up independent, skilled writers. In the table that follows, I've brainstormed a short list of ways that you might use what's in this book to enhance your writing time, no matter what form it takes:

Writing Approach or Program	How You Might Use This Book
Units of Study for Writing	The units of study will be an invaluable guide to your whole-class teaching, with some ideas built in for conferring and small-group instruction that aligns to the unit objectives. But no author of a curriculum knows the current set of kids sitting in front of you, or what their most recent assessments have shown about the ways they need help and support. This book can help you to plan for responsive, differentiated instruction based on individual goals.
Daily 5 "Work on Writing"	During this highly independent time when students are writing to continue pieces they started during another time of day or to work on projects of their own choosing, the strategies and visual reminders in this book will help them to practice and transfer the skills you've previously taught.
Complete writing programs such as Schoolwide, Being a Writer, Empowering Writers, or Traits Writing	In a highly supportive workshop-inspired program, a teacher follows clear unit plans with lessons and activities and can make use of the mentor texts provided. Some teachers find that supporting students with strategies that are broken down into clear concrete steps can help them to better access the objectives of the lessons. Other teachers may appreciate alternate mentor text suggestions to highlight the craft techniques in the lessons. In these programs, many of the writing assignments offer students a limited choice or a strong suggestion of a topic to write about—this book, especially the chapter on generating ideas, will help students tap into some of the ideas they may have inside them. The main way I'd probably use this book alongside these programs is as a master collection of strategies to inform my differentiated instruction—small-group work and conferring—during the independent writing time.

continues

Writing Approach or Program	How You Might Use This Book
Writing to prompts or assignments, or based on themes	If you tend to assign students writing topics and prompts, this book might offer some ideas for strategies to help break down the assignment into more concrete, manageable steps. For example, instead of asking kids to "craft a thesis statement for a literary essay," you might search the book for a strategy that offers step-by-step advice for *how* to do it. In addition, the prompt is usually just the beginning of *what* to write about. There are lots of strategies in the book that will help students to improve the quality of what they write.
Writing exercises included within the context of textbook-based literacy programs	Often the writing exercises included within textbook programs are meant to offer the children ideas for what to write about, more than how to write. The strategies in this book will support you in teaching them the "how." It may also be that the writing they do connect to the textbook is largely drafting with a bit of revision and/or editing. The strategies in this book may help to expand your students' horizons in terms of writing process, especially with strategies for how to generate their own writing topics.
Daily journals	If you have a daily practice where students write in journals, consider taking a look at the kind of writing they are doing and the quality of that writing to see if you can offer them strategies to lift the level of it. Often, without instruction, a student's journal entries will be similar in style, structure, and craft from the beginning of the year until the end. With some strategies from this book, the students could write using more varied topics, alternate structures, diverse types of detail, and more purposeful conventions.
Writing in the content areas and/or guided research	When choosing to include writing as part of science, social studies, or math, the focus is so often on the content itself (the Revolutionary War, the water cycle, the Pythagorean theorem) that writing skills and strategies take a backseat. Consider using the ideas in this book to balance the teaching of the content with the teaching of how to craft a well-written piece of writing so that your understandings about the content shine through.
No formalized approach to writing	Maybe you occasionally include a writing exercise, offer your students a graphic organizer, or give them time to "freewrite." This book will help you to support your writers as you design a course of study (see "Planning a Unit of Study," pages 27–29) or teach them strategies that they can incorporate into their independent projects.

Strategies help to take something that proficient writers do naturally, automatically, and without conscious effort, and make it visible, clear, and doable for the student writer.

—*Jennifer Serravallo*

Composing with Pictures

◎ Why is this goal important?

Writing instruction can begin before students can write a letter or spell a word. And, as many have argued, it should. By teaching children to compose with pictures, they can be freed up to create texts in any genre and to understand that meaning comes first, long before they are ready to spend lots of mental energy hearing the sounds in words and writing down what they hear (Ray and Glover 2008; Glover 2009; Ray 2010). Some may call this stage of development *emergent writing*, a time when "children begin to understand that writing is a form of communication and their marks on paper convey a message" (Mayer 2007, 35).

Those of you who work with very young children may be wondering, "What does this look like in the classroom for a student to be composing *exclusively* with pictures? Is that really *writing*?" The short answer is that it looks just like what writing time may look like in upper elementary classrooms in terms of lesson structures—and even the qualities of good writing and writing habits that can be taught. For example, the teacher may begin the writing time with a focus lesson to help the children get started, or to pick up from where they left off the day before. Sometimes this lesson may take the form of a short minilesson where a strategy (like those in this chapter) is demonstrated. Other times, the teacher may choose to revisit a favorite read-aloud picture book to discuss what the illustrator did to tell the story or to teach about the topic. Still other times, a teacher may share a student's work and explain the strategy the child used to get his ideas down on paper, drawing the best he can. Then, students get time to compose new pieces (drawing pictures to tell a story, teach about a topic, or convince the reader) or return to a piece in progress to make changes. In short, children are planning their writing, drafting, and revising—but the work is primarily (or exclusively) in pictures. Teachers support children with focusing their writing on a topic or story idea, teach them about adding in details, and even work with them to make their drawings "readable" to others.

To successfully compose with pictures, children need to learn how to represent what they see with marks on the page that communicate their meaning to their readers (i.e., I am telling the story of a time I went to the zoo with my mom and my reader can see a mom and a child at a zoo) and to make drawings that they can then "read back" to share with others or to revise. Spending time on some drawing lessons for primary elementary students will also help them feel empowered to compose independently and avoid frustration as they work on their pieces. Some of the lessons in this chapter, therefore, are meant to support students' representational drawing.

Once students have become fluent writers, there may still be reasons to support their composition with pictures. For example, sketching is used throughout the primary grades as a planning tool, so when children have automaticity getting their ideas down on the paper in pictures, they will be better set up to refer to the pictures as they draft, will be able to get more details down as they write, and will be able to have more time freed for the other parts of the writing process.

So, the strategies in this chapter will support students in pre-K through any age where they will still compose with pictures (usually around grade 2).

◎ How do I know if this goal is right for my student?

Many pre-emergent or emergent readers would be good candidates for this as a first goal. Children who may not know many letters and sounds, or who are just beginning to develop this awareness, can be taught to create, compose, storytell, and teach through sketches and drawings. Then, when it's time for labeling and writing sentences, they will understand that first and foremost, a writer writes to communicate something. To learn about your students' letter-sound awareness, you may administer an assessment that asks them to identify letter names and letter sounds.

There are also strategies throughout this book for children who are in the early, mid, and late emergent stages that, with minor simplifying/adapting, can be used for emergent writers. For example, the engagement chapter (Chapter 2) includes strategies that support students who could use practice blocking out distraction and concentrating on their work. The focus chapter (Chapter 4) includes strategies that ask students to make sure all the pages connect to their topic. The structure chapter (Chapter 5) includes strategies that can teach children to organize a three-page story into a beginning, middle, and end. The elaboration chapter (Chapter 6) includes strategies that teach students different types of details to include in their writing (which, of course, if you're teaching emergent writers, you'd explain to mean *include in their pictures*). There is an entire chapter devoted to spelling (Chapter 8), which includes beginning strategies like using an alphabet chart, appropriate for children once they know many of their letters and sounds. So, if you decide to start in this chapter, I would encourage you to also look across the remaining nine chapters for other ideas to support your writers' composing.

In fact, I struggled with the idea of separating the strategies in this chapter from those in the other nine chapters because I believe that the process and qualities of good writing that we teach to older students can be taught to younger students as well (Ray and Glover 2008). Still, I thought it may be helpful to have all of the strategies that involve composing with pictures in one place, with the caveat that teachers of children composing with pictures will find other relevant strategies across the book—and teachers of children writing conventionally will find relevant strategies here.

As mentioned earlier, this goal may also be important for students who do know their letters and sounds and may already be writing words and sentences, but their words and sentences are disconnected from meaning. Children across the primary grades can benefit from spending time sketching their ideas before moving to writing the words. Before they are fluent writers, children often have to focus very hard and deliberately on hearing the sounds in words and writing down what they hear, so much so that sometimes they forget what they wanted to say or end up with a text that is much more simplistic than what they wanted to write. For some students in kindergarten, first, or perhaps even second grade, spending time on communicating ideas or composing a story in pictures first can help them to front-load meaning and then compose with words to match that meaning.

Strategies for Composing with Pictures

Strategy	Grade Levels	Genres/Text Types	Processes
1.1 Talk (as You Draw)	Emergent	Any	Drafting
1.2 Point Around the Pictures	Emergent	Any	Reading writing aloud, revising
1.3 Reread Your Pictures So It Sounds like a Storybook	Emergent	Narrative	Storytelling
1.4 Reread Your Pictures to Teach	Emergent	Informational/nonfiction	Reading writing aloud
1.5 Add Detail to Make Pictures Easier to Read	Emergent–K	Any	Drafting, revising, editing
1.6 Label Your Pictures	Emergent–K	Any	Drafting
1.7 Look Back and Say, "How Can I Make This Clearer?"	Emergent–K	Any	Revising, editing
1.8 Make Your Picture Look like the Picture in Your Mind	Emergent–1	Any	Rehearsing, drafting, revising
1.9 Left to Right	Emergent–2	Narrative, informational/nonfiction	Drafting
1.10 You Can Come Back to a Piece and Do More	Emergent–2	Any	Drafting, revising
1.11 Drew the People? Draw the Place!	Emergent–2	Narrative	Drafting, revising
1.12 Writing Across the Pages	Emergent–2	Narrative, informational/nonfiction	Rehearsing, drafting, revising
1.13 A Series of Pictures to Show Change	Emergent–2	Narrative, informational/nonfiction, procedural	Drafting
1.14 Circles and Sticks	Emergent–2	Any	Rehearsing, drafting
1.15 Drawing with Shapes	Emergent–2	Any	Drafting
1.16 Touch, Then Draw	Emergent–2	Any	Drafting
1.17 Draw (the Best You Can) and Move On!	Emergent–2	Any	Drafting
1.18 Imagine It, Make It!	Emergent–2	Any	Rehearsing, drafting

Who is this for?

LEVEL
emergent

GENRE / TEXT TYPE
any

PROCESS
drafting

Strategy When you write, you don't need to be quiet! You can say what you're writing about (or drawing) out loud to yourself. As you say a new part aloud, you can add that new part to your picture.

Teaching Tip You'll find that allowing children to talk to themselves during your writing and reading time will often help them to be more productive and more engaged. They will need the feedback that hearing themselves think out loud provides. As you work with students, you can prompt them to add more, clarify their details, and/or explain what they've written using some of the prompts below.

Teaching Tip You'll want to figure out what type of writing the child is making, and then adapt your prompts accordingly. For example, "What else happened?" works well for narrative, but "What else do you know about that?" works better for informational/nonfiction.

Prompts
- And what else happened?
- Oh, wait. Who's that?
- What will she do next?
- Oh, I see. And then what?
- What does he say?
- Where are they, I wonder?
- So, you said _____. *(Retell story the student recounted to you, pointing to the parts of the pictures.)*

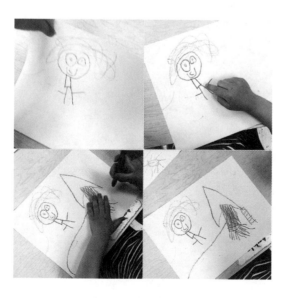

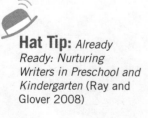

Hat Tip: *Already Ready: Nurturing Writers in Preschool and Kindergarten* (Ray and Glover 2008)

Strategy When you read back your writing to someone else, try to point around the picture. When your finger lands on a part, say all you can about that part.

Teaching Tip This strategy is one that helps the child to verbalize, and perhaps elaborate, on his picture and is marked as appropriate for "any" genre. It's likely that you'll adapt your prompts based on what it seems like the child has made. It's important to figure out first, through asking questions about what has been written or drawn, what it seems like the child is trying to do with his writing. Does it seem like a story? Does it seem like it's teaching about something (information)? Does it seem like the child is listing things? When a child is aiming to draw or write a story, be mindful that you're coaching into storytelling language, not just listing and labeling, as she points around the picture (the difference is a child who says, "Zoo. Mom. Me. Where we go in" and a child who says, "I went to the zoo with my mom. We walked under the big archway to get inside.").

Prompts

- It's a story? Tell what happened first, next, and after that.
- I see your picture is teaching me something. Tell me all about it.
- What's that?
- What's over here?
- Can you point to another part and tell me what you wrote or drew?
- You have a lot of information in your picture!

Who is this for?

LEVEL
emergent

GENRE / TEXT TYPE
any

PROCESSES
reading writing aloud, revising

Hat Tip: *Already Ready: Nurturing Writers in Preschool and Kindergarten* (Ray and Glover 2008)

Who is this for?

LEVEL
emergent

GENRE / TEXT TYPE
narrative

PROCESS
storytelling

Watch a video of a student rereading pictures:

http://hein.pub/WSB

Hat Tip: *Already Ready: Nurturing Writers in Preschool and Kindergarten* (Ray and Glover 2008)

Strategy Point to the picture or part of the picture that shows the beginning of your story. Tell it like a story using what the characters say and do. Touch or turn to the next part. Tell it like a story. Turn to the end. Tell it like a story.

Lesson Language *When I read my writing to someone, I need to think about what story my pictures tell. When I wrote my story, I included characters (people, animals) and I was thinking about what was happening, what the characters do and say. When I read my writing, I can make it sound like a story. I won't say, "This is me. This is the ice-skating rink. These are my skates."* (Point to your demonstration picture, and give a nonexample, simply labeling the parts of the picture.) *I'm going to tell it like a story, listen: "Once I went to an ice-skating rink with my mom. We laced up our skates and went out on the ice. It was slippery! I said, "Hold my hand, mom! Don't let me fall!" Do you hear the difference? When I say what my characters do and say, it sounds like a story!*

Teaching Tip You may want to record what a child says in her storytelling in your anecdotal records. Some teachers record students' speech right on their writing/pictures, but many believe this negatively impacts a student's agency and confidence for writing words when she is ready. When an adult writes on a child's paper, this may communicate that the child's attempts at making meaning don't make sense without the teacher's written words, which may undermine her future attempts at writing with pictures and/or with words (Ray and Glover 2008).

Prompts

- You told me what the characters did. Let's add in what the characters said!
- Tell it like a story.
- What else happened in this part?
- Find the picture that starts the story.
- How does it end?
- Don't just end it with one quick sentence! Storytell it. What did your characters do? Say?

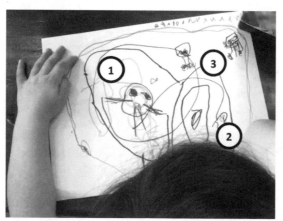

(1) Jake's going to help Izzy. "I'm coming!" That's his feet and that's his eyes. "I'm coming!" Jake says.

(2) And he flew into there to help Izzy out. But he was too stuck. So, she have a hook. And this hook was magic. It maked her come out. And it was pixie dust! Away!! And she comes out.

(3) Let's make another Izzy. There. She's out! She can fly! She has pixie dust and if she gets trapped again she will get out. And then she goes all the way down and there's a ghost. A nice ghost.

Strategy Go back to your picture(s). Point to the part or picture that teaches something important about your topic. Touch or turn to the next part. Tell what new fact about your topic this part of the picture or this page teaches.

Lesson Language *If I wrote or drew to teach, then when I read my writing back I'm going to make it sound like a teaching book. I'm going to tell my reader the facts I wrote about. Let me show you. I drew a picture of a big T. rex. I know a lot about them so I added a lot of details in my picture. I'm going to touch one part and teach what that part says. "The T. rex had very large jaws with big sharp teeth." Now I'm going to touch a new part and teach what that part says. "The T. rex had very short arms. It would only run using its hind legs."*

Teaching Tip Please see the Teaching Tip in strategy 1.3 (Ray and Glover 2008) for advice on transcribing students' retellings of their writing from pictures.

Prompts

- What does this picture teach about?
- Point to a part and tell me what I can learn from that.
- Do you know other facts?
- What does this part of the picture teach?
- Sound like a teacher.
- Your drawing teaches a lot of facts about the topic!

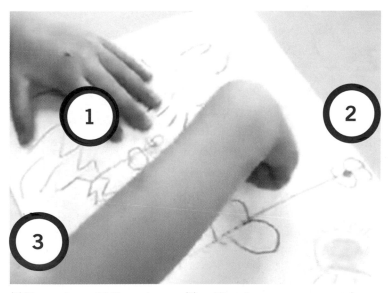

(1) The sun keeps this flower to grow (2) and then the sun moves over and keeps this flower to grow (3) and then the roots dig under the ground.

Who is this for?

LEVEL
emergent

GENRE / TEXT TYPE
informational/ nonfiction

PROCESS
reading writing aloud

Watch a video of a student teaching about a topic from his writing:

http://hein.pub/WSB

Hat Tip: *I Am Reading: Nurturing Young Children's Meaning Making and Joyful Engagement with Any Book* (Collins and Glover 2015)

Who is this for?

LEVELS
emergent–K

GENRE / TEXT TYPE
any

PROCESSES
drafting, revising, editing

Strategy Look carefully at your picture. Think about any details (small parts) you can add to it. Add those details.

Teaching Tip In the chapter on elaboration, there are a variety of strategies meant to encourage children to add different sorts of details (speech bubbles [strategy 6.3], setting [strategy 6.26], characters [strategy 6.40]). Emergent writers who are ready to add those kinds of details may be helped by modified versions of those strategies. This strategy is intended to support complexity in students' representational drawings—for example, if a student draws one circle and two lines to represent a person, can you nudge her to include eyes? Arms? If a student represents a house by drawing an oblong shape around a person, can you encourage him to add a roof or a door so that it looks more like a house?

Prompts

• What's that? Can you add something?
• What details might you add?
• I see a _____ and _____. What else does a _____ have?
• You added more details and now I can tell what you drew!
• I see you added more details. Do you think it helped your picture?

Hat Tip: *Writing for Readers: Teaching Skills and Strategies* (Calkins and Louis 2003)

Strategy Point to something in your picture. Say what it is. Say it again, slowly. Write down each sound you hear next to the picture on the page.

Teaching Tip This strategy is one that you'd use once children have had plenty of practice with the meaning making of illustrating their stories and ideas, and storytelling or teaching from those pictures. Pushing the conventional writing/print too soon could overly focus the child on getting down words rather than other qualities of good writing such as structure and elaboration. To determine readiness for this strategy, you may consider administering a letter-sound identification assessment. Once you've determined children have a sense of letter-sound correspondence, there are a variety of other strategies in the chapter on spelling (Chapter 8) to help children hear the sounds in the words and record the letters on the page.

Prompts
- What sounds do you hear?
- Say the word slowly.
- What letter makes that sound?
- Write that letter down, and say the word again.

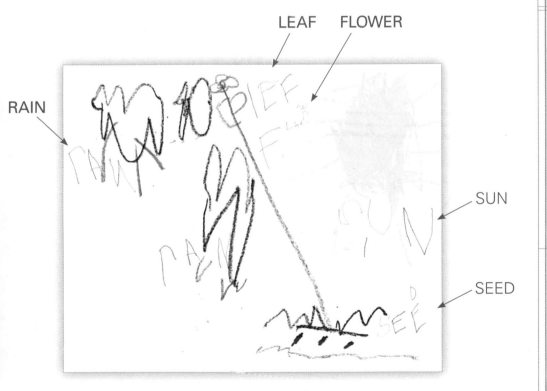

LEAF   FLOWER

RAIN

SUN

SEED

Who is this for?

LEVELS
emergent–K

GENRE / TEXT TYPE
any

PROCESS
drafting

Hat Tip: *One to One: The Art of Conferring with Young Writers* (Calkins, Hartman, and White 2005)

1.7 Look Back and Say, "How Can I Make This Clearer?"

LEVELS
emergent–K

GENRE / TEXT TYPE
any

PROCESSES
revising, editing

Strategy Look at your drawing (or writing). Think, "What does it look like I drew here? Can I make it any clearer?" Point to the parts of your picture to say what you drew. See if you can add or change anything so someone else can read it, too.

Teaching Tip This strategy is helpful for students who have the fine motor skills to be able to draw conventionally, yet sometimes wander back to marks on the page that seem to be more random. This strategy nudges them to revise and edit their work for a clear purpose: so others can read what they intended to mean! Chances are that relooking will also help them to add in more details.

Prompts
- Tell me what you drew.
- What is each part of your picture about?
- Let's look at this part. Can you make it clearer?
- Let's look at this part. Does it look like how you want it to look?
- Do you think someone else will be able to figure out what this is? What might you change or add?

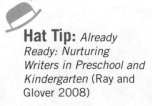

Hat Tip: *Already Ready: Nurturing Writers in Preschool and Kindergarten* (Ray and Glover 2008)

Strategy Close your eyes and picture what you're writing about. Open your eyes and try to put the details of what's in your mind onto your paper. When you have added all you can, close your eyes again and think, "What else am I missing?" When you open your eyes, see what you can add to your work.

Lesson Language *I'm trying to imagine my story.* (Model thinking with eyes closed.) *I see myself at the beach with my dad and sister. Let me open my eyes.* (Model drawing a simple sketch of waves, sand, and two stick figures.) *Let me close my eyes again to see what else there is that I don't have on my paper yet.* (Model closing eyes and thinking aloud.) *It was a hot day and we decided to sit under the umbrella. Let me get those details in my picture, too!* (Open eyes and model drawing a large sun in the sky and a beach umbrella.)

Prompts
- Close your eyes and picture what you want to write about.
- What do you see in your mind?
- Let's check your picture. What can you add?
- What are you going to draw?
- Is anything missing?

Who is this for?

LEVELS
emergent–1

GENRE / TEXT TYPE
any

PROCESSES
rehearsing, drafting, revising

Hat Tip: *One to One: The Art of Conferring with Young Writers* (Calkins, Hartman, and White 2005)

LEVELS
emergent–2

GENRES / TEXT TYPES
**narrative,
informational/
nonfiction**

PROCESS
drafting

Hat Tip: *One to One: The Art of Conferring with Young Writers* (Calkins, Hartman, and White 2005)

Strategy Write the way a book goes so your readers can read it! When you are drawing a series of things that happened, try to draw from your left to right. When you are writing across pages, start at the first page, then the next, and then the next.

Lesson Language *I want to tell a story about a time I built a sand castle but the wave knocked it over. I have to think about what happened first: I got my bucket and used it to build the castle. So I'm going to draw that all the way over here on the left. Next, the wave came! I'm going to draw that over here on the right. Now my reader will know to start over here* (Point to the left side of the page.) *and move over here* (Point to the right side of the page.).

Teaching Tip To assess whether children understand how books work, you may want to administer the Concepts About Print assessment as described by Clay (2000). Although it's typically regarded as an assessment of emergent reading knowledge and skills, it can also inform your writing instruction. The assessment looks at whether children understand concepts such as the cover, back cover, title page, where to begin reading, the difference between a word and letter, the purpose of punctuation, and more. Reinforcing an understanding of left-to-right directionality in both reading and writing will allow you to support students across the day as they practice these new understandings.

Prompts

- Show me where you'll start writing.
- That's the middle page, which is for the middle of your story. Where is the first page?
- Let's make sure we start on the left side. Left is here.
- You just started your story on the starting page! Now show me where you'll go next.
- You wrote your story in the same order as you'd see it in a book! The first thing is on the first page, the next thing is on the second page, and the last thing is on the last page! That'll make it easy for your readers to read it.

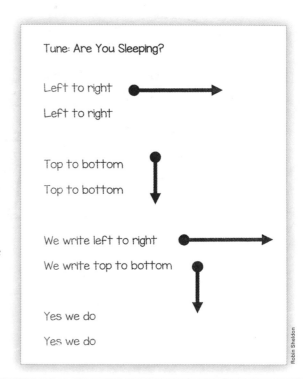

Tune: Are You Sleeping?

Left to right
Left to right

Top to bottom
Top to bottom

We write left to right
We write top to bottom

Yes we do
Yes we do

Robin Sheldon

Strategy Reread and look at a piece you worked on the last time you wrote. Think, "Is there anything else I want to do? Is there anything I want to change?"

Lesson Language *When I come back to a piece of writing, I have so many choices! I don't just have to say, "I worked on this the other day so it's done." I can decide to change something. Some of the ways I can change what I wrote are to add something on a page, change something on a page, move things around, take something out, or add on a whole new page.*

Teaching Tip Note that in the Lesson Language, I include a list of different revision "moves" that should be taught to students, one at a time. I wouldn't introduce five different revision moves in one lesson. So, if these ways to revise are new to your students, you may choose to unbundle this strategy and teach some in isolation first, drawing from other strategies in this chapter, perhaps.

Teaching Tip This lesson helps students to build stamina for returning to a writing piece and working on it over time, across more than one sitting. This strategy may be tricky for some writers because students who are in the emergent stage of their writing development, not yet writing words to hold meaning, don't always read their writing back as the same piece each time they read it. Students who are beginning to write words or even sentences may use invented spelling that is too hard for them to read back. Consequently, one day the three-page booklet may tell a story about a princess who left her castle and found a horse. The next day it might be a list book. And then another day it might be about a firefighter, depending on how representational (or not!) the pictures are. Students who have some memory of their intention, have some interest in returning to a piece, and can reread based on representational drawings and/or writing are the best candidates for this strategy.

Prompts

- Let's start by rereading. *(Reading can be pointing at pictures to say what the writer wants to communicate, not only reading words.)*
- You realized you didn't finish what you meant to write. Adding on makes sense!
- Do you remember what you wrote?
- What was this part about?
- You're the author in charge of this piece! If you want to add something or change something, it's up to you.

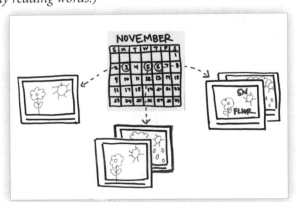

LEVELS
emergent–2

GENRE / TEXT TYPE
any

PROCESSES
drafting, revising

Who is this for?

LEVELS
emergent–2

GENRE / TEXT TYPE
narrative

PROCESSES
drafting, revising

Strategy Don't let your characters float on the page! Make sure you show *who* is in your story and *where* they are. Check to see that you have the people and the place!

Lesson Language (Draw as you think aloud.) *I want to tell the story about the time I went to the river and flipped over rocks to find what was underneath. So I need to make sure I put my characters in the picture. Let's see. There's me (Draw.) and there is my sister. (Draw.) Now I need to make sure we aren't just floating! Let me see if I can put in details about the place. There is a river. (Draw.) And I want to add the details of the rocks in the river. (Draw.) I used to go there in summer so I'll add a sunshine to show it's hot. (Draw.) Let me look back at it and see if there's anything I missed about the who or the where.*

Using a Mentor You may consider pulling any picture book that is a class favorite to show children how illustrators include the setting as they tell their story.

Prompts
- Who is in your story?
- Draw the person.
- I see you have three people in your story.
- You started to draw the place. Are there other details you want to add in about the place?
- Where did this story happen? Can you picture it?

Robin Sheldon

Hat Tip: *In Pictures and in Words: Teaching the Qualities of Good Writing Through Illustration Study* (Ray 2010)

Strategy As you write a book, all the pages need to be about the same topic. But from page to page, there needs to be something different. Draw the first page. Then think, "What's going to be different on this next page?" Continue until you've written your whole book.

Teaching Tip This strategy can be adapted to work for either narrative or informational texts. If the student is writing narrative, then the whole book needs to be about the same topic (my trip to the beach, the time I found a dinosaur bone) and each page will tell the next, next, next event in the story—each page is a new event. If the student is writing informational texts, then the whole book is going to be about the same topic (dinosaurs, ballet, New York City) and each page will be different because it'll teach about a different fact about the topic. Be on the lookout to support children who are new to booklets and either recopy the same thing on every page or write about different topics on each page.

Prompts
- What will change from this page to the next?
- What happens on this page? What happens on this page? How will you show what's different?
- You said this page was about _____. So this page needs to be something different.
- You told me you're teaching all about _____. So on this page, remind me what you wrote. And on this page, what did you write? And what will this page be?
- You wrote three pages. Each one is different, but they are all about the same topic!

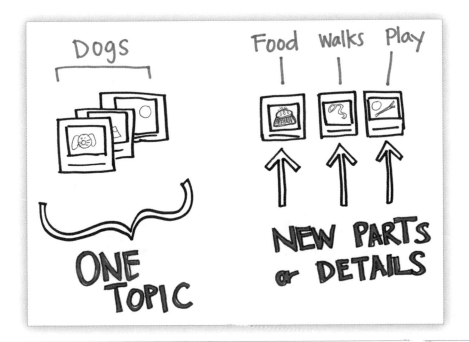

1.13 A Series of Pictures to Show Change

Who is this for?

LEVELS

emergent–2

GENRES / TEXT TYPES

narrative, informational/ nonfiction, procedural

PROCESS

drafting

Strategy Think about something in your picture that moves or changes in real life. Draw a picture to show what it looks like when it starts. Draw a picture to show how it changes. Draw a picture to show how it changes again.

Lesson Language *I want to show how a plant grows from a seed to a flower. I am going to show a different thing that changes on each page. On this page, I'm going to draw a seed, underground. On this page, I'm going to show it starting to sprout. It changed in life, so it's going to change in my pictures. On this page, I'll show it above ground as a plant. And on my fourth page, I'm going to show the plant with the picture.*

Teaching Tip You may find that giving some children a three-page (or more) booklet helps them to internalize the structure of a story or procedure and to grasp the concept of things happening over time, with one event per page. When other children are given a multipage booklet, they write about different topics on each page. This strategy offers support to those writers, allowing them to show narrative or action in a series of pictures that either stay on the same page or stay connected across pages.

Using a Mentor You may find a simple book in your classroom library that can help to demonstrate the idea that something changes or moves on every page. For example, *Laundry Day* by Karen Hjemboe (2000) shows a sequence of actions a family takes to wash clothing. *Eat It, Print It* by Stephanie Vernali (2000) is a list book that shows a fruit or vegetable whole, then cut, then printed with paint on a page.

Prompts
- Who's that? What's happening?
- What did she do next?
- Can you draw that next part in a new picture?
- What's the next thing she does?

Hat Tip: *Nonfiction Craft Lessons: Teaching Information Writing K–8* (Portalupi and Fletcher 2001)

Strategy Imagine what you're trying to draw as simply a combination of sticks (lines) and circles or ovals. With your eyes closed and finger in the air, draw circles and sticks to follow the shape of what you see in your mind. Open your eyes, and draw using circles and sticks on your page.

Teaching Tip This strategy is one that definitely will warrant a demonstration the first time it's introduced. Draw while thinking aloud, "Should I draw a circle or a stick for the head of the bunny rabbit? I'll draw a circle for that part. How about the arm? Hm. That looks more like a stick."

Prompts
• Put the image in your mind. Now use your finger to draw on top of your imaginary picture.
• What's the next part you see? Would it be a circle or a stick?
• Now open your eyes and draw it on the paper.
• You can close your eyes again if you need to remember what you were going to do.
• I can tell what you drew there! The circles and sticks worked!

Merridy Gnagey

Who is this for?

LEVELS
emergent–2

GENRE / TEXT TYPE
any

PROCESSES
rehearsing, drafting

1.15 Drawing with Shapes

Who is this for?

LEVELS
emergent–2

GENRE / TEXT TYPE
any

PROCESS
drafting

Strategy Look at one part of the larger thing you're trying to draw. Ask yourself, "What shape does that look like?" Then, draw that shape. Then, look at the next part and the next until you have all the shapes down. Look back at the whole and add anything you need so that it looks like what you want it to be.

Lesson Language *When I think about something I want to draw, I sometimes get worried about being able to draw it. But I have learned to look at it part by part. I can now see the shapes in what I want to draw. For example, if I want to draw a person I can say, "I don't know how to draw that!" or I can say, "Well, a head is just a circle. Let me put a circle down." Then, I can look at the neck as a small rectangle and draw that. Then, the body is one bigger rectangle, and so on. (Proceed with a demonstration, drawing in front of the students you're teaching.)*

Teaching Tip This lesson can be phrased to encourage children to look at something in front of them (an object, drawing, or other illustration) or to look at something in their mind ("Close your eyes and imagine . . .").

Prompts
- What shape do you see?
- What part are you going to draw first?
- You drew a circle for that part. It does look like a _____.
- You can't tell what shape it is? Trace it with your finger.

Sara Lazration

1.16 Touch, Then Draw

Strategy Touch what you want to draw. As you touch think, "What is the shape? How big is it? How is it connected to another part I have drawn?" Once you have felt what you're going to draw, pick up your pencil and draw it.

Teaching Tip This is my favorite strategy for teaching children how to draw people representationally. It helps them go from a person with arms coming out of the head to a person with arms coming out of shoulders. Many children notice their neck for the first time when they realize that there is something below their head but above their body. Also, students who draw ten or more fingers on each hand, after feeling and noticing each finger, realize that each hand gets five! It also helps students to draw with some sense of proportion—the body is bigger than the head, for example.

Teaching Tip This strategy will only work with three-dimensional things, and it'll be important to remind children that they can't touch other people without asking their permission first.

Prompts
- As you touch, what shape do you feel?
- What do you notice about it?
- Now try to draw that same shape on your paper.
- You've drawn the _____. What is connected to that?

1. Touch

2. Shape?

3. Draw

LEVELS
emergent–2

GENRE / TEXT TYPE
any

PROCESS
drafting

Who is this for?

LEVELS
emergent–2

GENRE / TEXT TYPE
any

PROCESS
drafting

Strategy Picture what you want to write. Draw as best you can. Try not to erase or worry about it looking perfect. Move on to add more details or start a new piece.

Lesson Language *Writers need to work to get their ideas down, and sometimes that means letting go of trying to make everything perfect. When you draw pictures, try to draw them as best you can, so that you can "read" the story or book back to your partner or to me. Nobody is expecting you to be a professional artist.*

Teaching Tip I don't want to communicate to children that it's OK to be sloppy or careless. However, this strategy is "just right" for children who feel held back by a need to make everything perfect. Which they won't be able to do because they are four or five or six years old! (Hey, could most adults, even?) What we're going for at this stage of writing development is representational drawing, which means that the image is recognizable by both the writer and the reader.

Prompts

- See it in your mind. How do you think you can draw that?
- I see you got down a _____ and a _____. I can tell that's a _____!
- You drew _____ so I can tell that's a _____ and not _____.
- You can do this. Just draw the best you can.

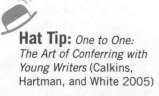

Hat Tip: *One to One: The Art of Conferring with Young Writers* (Calkins, Hartman, and White 2005)

Strategy Think of all the places you've seen writing in the world: signs, directions, stories, information books, shopping lists, and more. Think, "What kind of writing do I want to make?" Choose your paper from the writing center and get working!

Teaching Tip Providing your students with access to a wide range of paper choices gives them many writing options. Small rectangles can become signs, pages with lines on the bottom can be stories, paper with a series of boxes can be a recipe or directions, pages stapled together in a booklet can become stories or informational books all about one topic. Modeling writing during shared writing or interactive writing will help to reinforce for students that different paper types can match different writing purposes, genres, types, or modes. You may also consider creating a bulletin board above or near the writing center with the sample of paper choice and an example of a real-world piece of writing that would match that choice.

Prompts
- What do you think you might make?
- Maybe the paper choices will help to give you an idea.
- Hm. Let's think about what kind of paper you'd choose for that project.
- It sounds like you have a project in mind! Time to pick some paper.
- A booklet is a great choice for making a story. You can write the beginning on page 1, the middle on page 2, and the end on the last page.

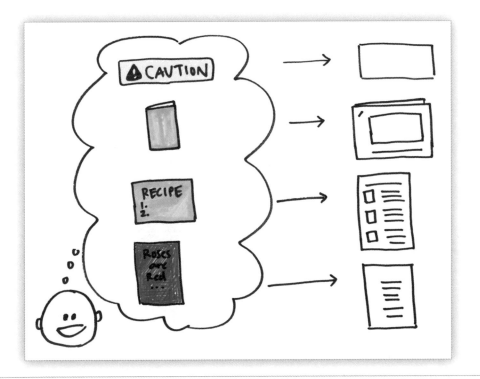

Who is this for?

LEVELS
emergent–2

GENRE / TEXT TYPE
any

PROCESSES
rehearsing, drafting

Hat Tip: *Interactive Writing: How Language & Literacy Come Together, K–2* (McCarrier, Pinnell, and Fountas 1999)

Engagement

Independence, Increasing Volume, and Developing a Writing Identity

◎ Why is this goal important?

Anyone who has written will tell you that writing can be hard, sometimes drudging work. As Dorothy Parker famously said, "I hate writing, but I love having written." Of course, not all feel that way, but I think as teachers we need to acknowledge that the act of writing itself is not immediately enjoyable for all children, and even successful professional writers sometimes find it hard to sit still and get words on the page.

To be successful at writing takes a huge amount of mental focus and discipline. You have to love, and be engaged with, some part of it. Perhaps it's the creativity and creation aspect that gets a writer excited. Maybe it's the act of writing to find out what will happen next, to write to discover, rather than to write to record. Or for others, it's about the excitement of having their writing read by others, by having an audience.

Writers also need to take initiative. They start writing projects even when they aren't told exactly what to write about, or what genre to write in. They have ways to generate topics, they understand reasons for writing, and they understand the power their words can have (Calkins 1994; C. Anderson 2005).

The question is, is this a teachable goal? Can we teach children to have more energy for their writing? Can we teach them to connect with it, to feel engaged with it—not just in an "I'm doing what the teacher told me and behaving" way, but in a real "getting into the flow" way? Can we support children in regarding themselves as writers, understanding their own distinct writing styles, and working in a way that feels joyful? I think yes.

◎ How do I know if this goal is right for my student?

My favorite tool for figuring out who needs support with engagement is the engagement inventory (see the figure on page 58; Serravallo 2010, 2013b, 2014, 2015a). Some may be familiar with this tool as a way to understand student on- and off-task behavior during reading, but we can learn a tremendous amount when we use it for writing, too. For those unfamiliar with it, the engagement inventory is essentially a kid-watching tool. For one entire writing period, the teacher will watch and record student behaviors and signs of engagement (instead of the usual conferring or pulling small groups). I may record things like students getting up to sharpen pencils, or asking to use the bathroom or to get a drink of water. I may note how much students write, or how much time they spend writing before they start to lose steam. I might notice how much time is spent planning their writing and how much time is spent drafting. I then can look across the information I collect for patterns within the class to discover how I can best support student engagement.

Students' writing volume can teach us a lot about their level of engagement. Just as we study reading volume by tracking progress on a reading log, we can study writing volume by noticing how many lines or pages students fill in an allotted time. A low amount of volume one day may just mean a student did a lot of work rehearsing or thinking. But if a child consistently generates very little writing during the writing period, it could be a sign that the student isn't very invested in her writing, or that she is getting distracted often during writing time. And when we are trying to improve student writing, volume can matter as much as teaching any of the qualities of good writing. As Stephen King writes in *On Writing: A Memoir of the Craft*: "You cannot succeed unless you read a lot and write a lot. It's not just a question of how-to, you see; it's also a question of how much to. Reading will help you answer how much, and only reams of writing will help you with the how. You can learn only by doing" (2000, 173).

Name	Time/Environment 10a–10:10 quiet	Time/Environment 10:10–10:20 quiet	Time/Environment 10:20–10:30 announcements, noise in hall	Time/Environment 10:30–10:40 quiet	Time/Environment
Marcus	SET	✓	✓	✓	
Tara	Plan	✓	✓	P	
Michael T	✓	✓	P	✓	
John	✓	✓	WC	✓	
Ana	✓	P	✓	✓	
Andrew	✓	HR	✓	D	
Maya	✓	D	D	D	
Jonas	✓	✓	✓	✓	
Jaclyn		✓	✓	P	
Chelsie	P	P	✓	✓	
Michael R.	WC	✓	✓	✓	
Ella	SET	✓	✓	✓	
Kim	SET	✓	P	✓	
Vivian	✓	✓	P	✓	
Merridy	✓	✓	✓	P	
Jesus		✓	✓	P	
Katherine	Plan	✓	✓	✓	
Lia	✓	Plan	✓	✓	
Jack	✓	✓	✓	✓	

Teacher Name: Ms. McNally   Date: 10/20

WC – @ writing center
SET – setting up, sharpening pencils, arranging papers
P – meeting w/ partner
✓ – writing
HR – hand raised
D – distracted, disengaged
Plan – planning

Engagement Inventory

So, what should we expect of student volume? Many factors come into play, but below you will find a general sense of the volume of writing I'd expect after a block of writing time, stage by stage. Of course, this amount of volume is most likely as students freewrite in a notebook or draft; revision and editing are often times when writers are returning to previously-written work and making changes rather than creating new pages of writing. Estimates are based on handwritten, not typed, pages and are adapted from *Writing Pathways* (Calkins 2014).

Stage/Grade	Volume Expectations
Kindergarten	Beginning of the year, 1–2 pages that include a picture with some labels and/or a short line of text in about twenty minutes of writing time
Late kindergarten	One three-page booklet with a sketch and a sentence on each page in twenty-five minutes
Early first	One three-page booklet including three sketches, approximately 1–3 lines of writing in twenty-five minutes
Late first, early second	Half of one five-page booklet including sketches and 2–5 lines of print in thirty minutes

Mid to late second	Half of one five-page booklet including small quick sketches and 5–8 lines of print in thirty minutes
Third	1–1.5 pages in thirty-five minutes
Fourth	1.5–2 pages in thirty-five minutes
Fifth to eighth	2–4 pages of writing in thirty-five to forty minutes

Finally, just as we ask students to reflect on their lives as readers—the good times and bad, the favorite books and those they turn away, when and where they read and so on—we can do the same in writing. Check out the forms in Jim Vopat's *Micro Lessons in Writing: Big Ideas for Getting Started* (2007a) or Nancie Atwell's *In the Middle: A Lifetime of Learning About Writing, Reading, and Adolescents* (2014) or make your own! The figure to the right has some suggested questions culled from both sources.

Name _____

What do you do to get ready to write?
_____

What are your favorite writing materials?
_____

What do you do to put off writing?
_____

What inspires you to write?
_____

What advice would you give to other young writers?
_____

How do you (or others) learn to write?
_____

What are your most and least favorite genres to write? Why?
_____

Where do you like to write? Where do you get your best writing done? Why?
_____

What are your greatest strengths as a writer?
_____

What would you like to get better at as a writer?
_____

Adapted from *Micro Lessons in Writing: Big Ideas for Getting Started* by James Vopat and *In the Middle* by Nancie Atwell. Download this and other forms at http://hein.pub/WSB.

Strategies for Supporting Writing Engagement

Strategy		Grade Levels	Genres/Text Types	Processes
2.1	Create Your Best Environment	K–8	Any	Creating a writing space, preparing to write
2.2	Picture the End! (Or, Imagine It Done)	K–8	Any	Any
2.3	Listen. Praise.	K–8	Any	Any
2.4	Use the Room	K–8	Any	Any
2.5	Decide a Piece Is "Finished" (for Now)—and Self-Start a New One	K–8	Any	Generating and collecting, revising, editing
2.6	Writers Are Problem Solvers	K–8	Any	Any
2.7	The Pen Is Mightier Than the Sword	K–8	Any	Any
2.8	Keep Your Pencil in Your Hand/Fingers on the Keyboard	K–8	Any	Any
2.9	Partners Can Give Gentle Reminders to Stay on Track	K–8	Any	Any
2.10	Silence the "It's No Good" Voice	K–8	Any	Generating and collecting, drafting
2.11	Make a Plan for Writing Time	1–8	Any	Developing
2.12	Reread to Jump Back In	1–8	Any	Any
2.13	Keep Objects Close	1–8	Any	Creating a writing space, preparing to write
2.14	Set a "More" Goal for the Whole Writing Time	1–8	Any	Generating and collecting, developing, drafting
2.15	Break Up Your Writing Time into Smaller Chunks	1–8	Any	Generating and collecting, developing, drafting
2.16	Stuck with Writing? Read.	1–8	Any	Generating and collecting, developing, drafting
2.17	Imagine Your Audience	2–5	Any	Developing, drafting, revising
2.18	Keep a Side Project	2–8	Any	Any
2.19	Consult a Fellow Writer	2–8	Any	Any
2.20	Experiment with Change	3–8	Any	Revising
2.21	Why Do You Write?	3–8	Any	Any
2.22	One Bite at a Time	3–8	Any	Any
2.23	Your Aim: Black on White	3–8	Any	Any
2.24	Make It a Habit	3–8	Any	Any
2.25	Live Like Someone Consumed by a Project	4–8	Any	Developing, drafting, revising
2.26	Write to Vent, Then Turn to Your Project	4–8	Any	Preparing to write
2.27	Be Realistic	4–8	Any	Any

Can we support children
in regarding themselves
as writers, understanding
their own distinct writing
styles, and working in a
way that feels joyful?
I think yes.

—*Jennifer Serravallo*

2.1 Create Your Best Environment

Who is this for?

LEVELS
K–8

GENRE / TEXT TYPE
any

PROCESSES
creating a writing space, preparing to write

Strategy Think about places where you've gotten your best writing done. Imagine what that space looked like. Jot notes or sketch to describe the qualities of that space. Try to create a space for yourself with those same qualities in school and at home.

Teaching Tip I'm the kind of writer who can't stand too much clutter—it seems to clutter my brain as well. I like a visually pleasing environment, organized sensibly, that has what I need within arm's reach. In college, I wrote every paper in my dorm room and had friends who would never dream of writing anywhere but the library. A writer's physical space helps her be optimally productive. This lesson is a great one to teach children who need support in creating an environment at their home to help them get writing done outside of school, and you also might consider how flexible you can be within the classroom to allow for kids to sit in places other than their desks.

Using a Mentor Share the writing environments of some of the authors your students know and love. Many will have online author pages where they will describe or show a picture of themselves in their writing space.

Prompts
- What do you think you need in a writing space?
- Are you someone who likes quiet or background noise?
- What would the space look like?
- Describe it.
- You're telling me where you'd like to write. Describe what the space would look like.
- Sketch it!

Hat Tip: *Independent Writing: One Teacher— Thirty-Two Needs, Topics, and Plans* (Cruz 2004)

Strategy When your energy and attention starts to fade, refocus by envisioning what it will be like when your piece is finished. Imagine your project completed, being read by a member of your intended audience. "See" what it looks like, and work toward that.

Using a Mentor Sometimes it helps students to "see" the end by choosing a text that's like the one they want to write. This may mean a book that is in a similar genre, maybe even a book on a similar topic. Looking at an example of a finished, published piece might help them feel inspired. "I want mine to start like this," they may say, or "I can imagine using text features like this." Chances are, they will not only be inspired by the finished product in their hands, but they may also pick up some revision tips along the way! The more control you can give to students in choosing their own mentors, the more motivating this process will be. Imagine a first grader saying, "I'm going to make speech bubbles just like my favorite author Mo Willems does!"

Prompts
- Let's look together at this book to see what inspires you.
- Is there a book you are so glad was written? Go grab it. Let's use it as inspiration.
- What is it you love about this book?
- Imagine your book being done like this one. Describe what you imagine.

Barb Golub

Who is this for?

LEVELS
K–8

GENRE / TEXT TYPE
any

PROCESS
any

Hat Tip: *A Quick Guide to Reviving Disengaged Writers, 5–8* (Lehman 2011)

Who is this for?

LEVELS
K–8

GENRE / TEXT TYPE
any

PROCESS
any

Strategy Read your writing aloud to your partner. His job is to listen for the engaging parts. When your partner finds a spot he enjoys, he will interrupt you and together you can mark the margin next to the powerful spot.

Lesson Language *Sometimes when we write, a voice of doubt starts to creep in. "Who's ever going to want to read this?!" you might think. "There's nothing here worth keeping," you might tell yourself. It is at this moment that you need to reach out to a friend for some help. Not the kind of help to "fix" the things you think are wrong, but the kind of friend to cheer you on to keep going.*

Teaching Tip Having a regular partnership or writing club routine in a classroom helps children to be held accountable to each other. This peer influence is often more powerful than any you could impose! See Chapter 10 for more suggestions on helping writers work together to support all steps of the writing process.

Prompts
- Go ahead and read aloud to your partner.
- As the partner, you should be listening for what you can praise.
- Tell him, what did you like best?
- Tell him, what seems to work in this draft?
- Tell him, what feels powerful about the writing?

Hat Tip: *A Quick Guide to Reviving Disengaged Writers, 5–8* (Lehman 2011)

2.4 Use the Room

Strategy When you feel stuck, scan the walls of the classroom. Search for a chart or piece of work that shows the same thing you're working on as a writer. Think about the step of your process, and the work you're trying. Take a tip from one of the charts, and get back to work!

Lesson Language *It's natural that at times, a writer's attention will drift or your energy will start to fizzle. When that happens, the first thing to do is to catch yourself. Notice that you're not giving your attention to your writing. Then you can use the classroom environment to help to jump-start yourself out of a daydream state or a state of frustration.*

Teaching Tip The decision to offer this strategy means that your classroom is one that is filled with helpful charts. Generally speaking, charts that chronicle your whole-class instruction around particular genres or steps of the writing process, and that were created with your students, are ones that are meant to be referred to by students to support their independence. (See Martinelli and Mraz 's *Smarter Charts* series for more information on charting.)

Prompts
- What's causing you to get stuck?
- Think about where you could look in the room to help you with that.
- I notice you caught yourself daydreaming! That's the first step. Now what will you do?
- What step of the process are you working in? So, what chart might help?

Merridy Gnagey

Who is this for?

LEVELS
K–8

GENRE / TEXT TYPE
any

PROCESS
any

Hat Tip: *Smarter Charts, K–2: Optimizing an Instructional Staple to Create Independent Readers and Writers* (Martinelli and Mraz 2012)

2.5 Decide a Piece Is "Finished" (for Now)— and Self-Start a New One

2.5

Who is this for?

LEVELS

K–8

GENRE / TEXT TYPE

any

PROCESSES

generating and collecting, revising, editing

Hat Tip: *One to One: The Art of Conferring with Young Writers* (Calkins, Hartman, and White 2005)

Strategy When you feel a piece is finished (you've written all you can, checked it over, and don't have any changes to make), then turn a page or get new paper, and start a new one. Check the charts in the room for reminders of how to get started.

Teaching Tip The word *finished* is in quotes in this strategy because many writers will tell you that writing is only done when it's due—there is always something to tweak. Still, teaching children to independently put a piece aside and turn to something new to keep up their productivity does not mean that what goes in the "finished" pile will never be touched again. As you teach your students a variety of ways to revise and edit their drafts, you'll likely archive the lessons on charts. These can serve as checklists, helping writers to know when to try a few more strategies before they put the piece aside, and when to move on, declaring a piece "finished," at least for now. This list will likely evolve throughout the year as students learn new strategies for revision and editing. The list will need to be appropriate developmentally and also reflect the teaching and learning that's happened in the classroom. In other words, don't put things on the chart unless you're sure the children can do them independently! The sample on this page came from an early first-grade classroom.

Prompts

- Tell me what you've checked.
- Let's go back to your piece to see if it feels done.
- Now that you're done, what will you do?
- Where in the room can you look for help with getting started on a new piece?
- I noticed you decided this piece is finished for now and you've moved on to something new. You're a writer with plans!

Think you're done? Be sure to check…

	YES!
It's a small moment.	
I have good details. (about what I did, said, and felt)	
I checked my snap words.	
I checked my tap words.	
I have capitals. One day	
I have endmarks. . ! ?	

Ok! You're done! Start a new piece.

Merridy Gnagey

2.6 Writers Are Problem Solvers

Strategy First, identify the problem you're having. Then, check the spot in the room, a resource, or a friend that might help you solve the problem. Try a solution. If it doesn't work, try something else.

Lesson Language *Writers know to expect problems. That's part of the process of writing! We'll run into challenges not knowing what may happen next in our piece. Or sometimes, we realize the organization we have isn't working and it needs to be reworked. Or we feel like we have writer's block, at a loss for new ideas. The exciting thing about problems is that we can solve them! And then, we are not only writers but we are also problem solvers! We don't give up! We don't quit.*

Teaching Tip This strategy, like "Use the Room" that appears earlier in this chapter, assumes that there are things in the room that can be helpful, and that you've taught children how to use them. For example, in a primary classroom a word wall may help a writer to spell high-frequency words. If you've introduced and used mentor texts, then having these available for children to reference on their own could help them. Sometimes the problem might be that they need to work in a new spot in the room because of the amount of distractions at their current spot. Brainstorm possible problems with your students, and come up with a list of resources and solutions. Or, this strategy can be like a culmination of past teaching from this and other chapters.

Prompts
- What in the room can help you solve that problem?
- I agree! That chart can help.
- Be a problem solver. What can you try?
- I see you're stuck. Let's think together about what your options are for solutions.

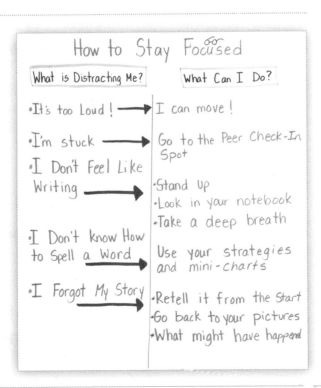

How to Stay Focused

What is Distracting Me?	What Can I Do?
• It's too Loud ! ➡	I can move !
• I'm stuck ➡	Go to the Peer Check-In Spot
• I Don't Feel Like Writing ➡	• Stand Up • Look in your notebook • Take a deep breath
• I Don't know How to Spell a Word ➡	Use your strategies and mini-charts
• I Forgot My Story ➡	• Retell it from the Start • Go back to your pictures • What might have happened

Hat Tip: *One to One: The Art of Conferring with Young Writers* (Calkins, Hartman, and White 2005)

Who is this for?

LEVELS
K–8

GENRE / TEXT TYPE
any

PROCESS
any

Strategy Try out a variety of pen and pencil types. Notice how they glide on the page. Notice how the marks look on the paper. Make a choice about which tool will help you get your best writing done.

Teaching Tip You may wonder why I'd devote an entire page to a strategy about pens. When I read what Don Murray wrote about how important his writing implements are to him, I reflected on myself as a writer. A new writing project rarely commences without a trip to my local stationery store to purchase some new pens. Teachers can relate to this—the excitement of back-to-school shopping, the thrill of getting new office supplies. Well, don't you think student writers could be excited by this, too? Think about your writing center and what materials you offer. Does everyone in your class have to use the same felt-tipped pen or wooden pencil? Might some students be more excited to write when given the option of gel pens, colored pens, or smooth-flowing ballpoints? The materials matter when considering some of the hard work of revision and editing, which some children are reluctant to jump into with both feet. For example, Lucy Calkins and Pat Bleichman in *The Craft of Revision* suggest giving children "revision pens" (perhaps green! Or purple!) to get them excited for the work of making changes to their writing (2003).

Prompts

- Is the pen/pencil you've chosen helping you write?
- Are you comfortable when you write?
- What kind of writing tool might help you feel more comfortable?
- Check out the writing center to see if there's something else you'd rather work with.

Keep Your Pencil in Your Hand/Fingers on the Keyboard

Strategy Pick up your pencil to begin writing (or place your fingers on the keyboard and don't move!). Even when you pause, keep the pencil in your hand, ready to write (or fingers on the keyboard). Only drop the pencil (lift your fingers) at the end of writing time.

Teaching Tip This may sound strange, but many children will put their pencil down every time they pause—to think of what word to write next, to figure out a spelling, to take a break. Every time they do this, picking the pencil back up to get back in writing position slows them down and affects their volume. It's like driving your car with one foot on the brake, stop-stop-stopping after each time you accelerate. Keeping your foot on the gas pedal—or the pencil in your hand—helps to encourage momentum and volume.

Prompts
- Keep the pencil up!
- It's OK that you're pausing to think, but keep your hand and pencil ready to catch an idea when it comes.
- I'm going to stick around and watch you write for a moment.
- You can do it—keep that pencil in your hand!

Jackie Yehia

Who is this for?

LEVELS
K–8

GENRE / TEXT TYPE
any

PROCESS
any

Hat Tip: "Pump Up the Volume" (Moore 2013)

2.9 Partners Can Give Gentle Reminders to Stay on Track

Who is this for?

LEVELS
K–8

GENRE / TEXT TYPE
any

PROCESS
any

Strategy If you find your attention sometimes wanders or your energy sometimes wanes, you can ask your partner to give you a helpful nudge to get you back on track. You can ask them to notice when you aren't getting your best writing done and to give you a gentle reminder such as "Keep going!" or "You can do it!" or "I can't wait to see what you wrote today!"

Lesson Language *During writing time, I want you to sit near your writing partner. This will help us transition quickly to partner time, and it will also mean that you each have a support nearby. Sometimes, knowing that you're accountable to someone other than yourself can help you stay on track. If you notice that you are the kind of writer who sometimes finds his attention wandering, you might ask your partner to keep an eye on you. They will have their own writing to do, of course, but if they notice, out of the corner of their eye, that it's been a while since you've written, or that you're starting to fall asleep at the desk, they can give you gentle reminders to keep going. Or, so as not to interrupt their own writing, they might take a moment's break from their own work, glance over to see how it's going with you, and give you a nudge.*

Prompts

- Remind your partner.
- What can you say to help your partner keep going?
- Say this: "_____ (name), you can do it! Reread what you wrote and jump back in."
- Say this: "_____ (name), it's almost partner time! I can't wait to see what you wrote today."

Hat Tip: "Pump Up the Volume" (Moore 2013)

> Partners support and encourage each other!
>
> They might say...
>
> * "You can do it! Re-read what you wrote and jump back in!"
>
> * "It's almost partner time! I can't wait to see what you wrote today!"

Jackie Yehia

Strategy Be aware of a voice in your head that keeps you from starting (or continuing) your writing. Write without stopping the pencil or pen. When you hear the voice urging you to stop, silence it. Redirect your energy back to the page.

Lesson Language (This sample language is geared toward students collecting in notebooks, but you could also adapt it to work with students who are hesitant to get their words down during the drafting phase of the writing process.) *Your first, most important audience is yourself, writes Ralph Fletcher (1996). The notebook can be a place where you can collect ideas without fear of others' judgment. You can write, freeform, knowing that some of what you write down is just the beginnings of something greater. Getting something down is far better than getting nothing down. You don't have to keep what you write, or turn it into anything grand. Just writing helps you to think, and you never know what might come out of you as you do!*

Using a Mentor Stephen King, in *On Writing: A Memoir of the Craft*, says, "You can, you should, and if you're brave enough to start, you will" (2000, 270).

Prompts
- Your writing is a safe place. Just get down whatever is on your mind.
- I can see you thinking. Don't edit; just get it down.
- Let's have a go at the page. Write without letting any doubt creep in.
- I'll sit beside you as you try this.
- You're on a roll! That's it, get the words down without worrying if they are perfect.

Barb Golub

Who is this for?

LEVELS
K–8

GENRE / TEXT TYPE
any

PROCESSES
generating and collecting, drafting

Hat Tip: *Breathing In, Breathing Out: Keeping a Writer's Notebook* (Fletcher 1996)

Who is this for?

LEVELS
1–8

GENRE / TEXT TYPE
any

PROCESS
developing

Strategy Think about the project you're working on, and what you want to accomplish. Speak a promise aloud to your partner, or jot down a quick list in the margin of your page to identify what your plans are for yourself as a writer today. Check in on your plans as you go.

Teaching Tip For students who have a hard time generating a list of ways they may improve their own writing, you may offer them past writing charts in the classroom, or any tools you've given them as individuals during conferring. Some children may benefit from a short partner conversation at the beginning of writing time to set their expectations and get into the zone. Other students may benefit from a nudge in a one-on-one conference during which either the teacher or the student could jot down the plan for writing time they discussed.

Prompts
- What are you hoping to accomplish today?
- List three things you want to try to do with your piece today.
- Jot your plan in your margin.
- Speak your plan to your partner. Once you say it aloud, it's like a promise!
- Your plan will keep you focused!

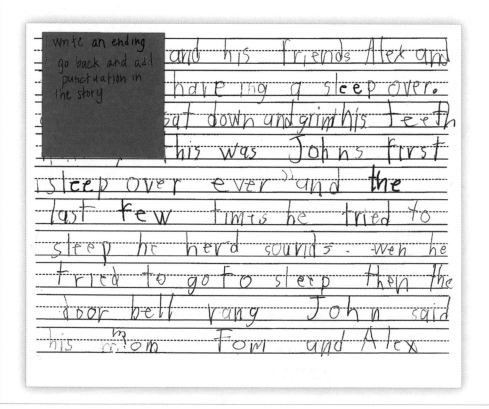

Hat Tip: *One to One: The Art of Conferring with Young Writers* (Calkins, Hartman, and White 2005)

2.12 Reread to Jump Back In

Strategy Reread what you've written so far. Get your mind back into your piece. Pick up your pencil and continue writing as if you'd never stopped.

Teaching Tip Notice the students who spend endless minutes transitioning into writing. Pencil sharpening, bathroom breaks, a walk around the classroom the longest way possible to finally arrive at the bin of paper. These are students who may need some help with jump-starting themselves to get back to the "zone" they were in when writing ended last time. This strategy is just for them! An added benefit here is that not only student engagement but also writing quality will improve. By reminding yourself of what you last wrote, your writing will be more seamless and clear. This is also a really helpful strategy to use in combination with any revision strategy. As you reread, you're not only going to pick up where you left off and add on to the end, but you'll also likely notice places where you can make changes to what you've already written.

Prompts
- Reread.
- Remind yourself of what you wrote last time.
- Now that you've reread, what do you think you'll do first?
- Do you remember where you left off last time? Reread to remember.
- Are you having a hard time getting back into your "zone"?
- As you reread, imagine yourself writing it again and then pick up your pencil and keep going.

REREAD ... & JUMP IN!

① REREAD ②REMEMBER ③ WRITE

Hat Tip: *One to One: The Art of Conferring with Young Writers* (Calkins, Hartman, and White 2005)

Who is this for?

LEVELS
1–8

GENRE / TEXT TYPE
any

PROCESSES
creating a writing space, preparing to write

Hat Tip: *Breathing In, Breathing Out: Keeping a Writer's Notebook* (Fletcher 1996)

Strategy Think about the objects that you find soothing (to put you in the right mind-set for writing) or stimulating (to spark new ideas). Examine these objects to help you get started.

Teaching Tip On the day I first started to write this book, I cleared off my desk, framed a current picture of my children, clipped hydrangeas from the garden, and gathered up a stack of my favorite books about the teaching of writing. The stuff we keep as visual inspiration and within our reach can help us as writers to get into the writing zone. In the classroom, it may be challenging to have children bring in stuff to scatter about before writing begins each day, but you can consider having children create something that can be tucked into their desk and brought out during writing time. For example, you could invite children to decorate the cover of their writing notebook or folder with photographs and images that inspire them. You could also ask them to list or sketch what they want to have out in their writing space at home, to set them up for success there, as well.

Prompts
- What objects might help you to get new ideas?
- Think about the objects you find comforting.
- What objects might help you to get writing?
- What items do you need in the space?
- If you can't have those objects here, can you use pictures?

Mindy Otto

Strategy Think about how many lines you tend to write in one writing period. Set a goal for yourself to write more. Run your finger down the margin of your page, and place a dot to indicate your "finish line." See if you can write up to—or past!—that goal in today's writing time.

Teaching Tip Hear it from Zinsser: "You learn to write by writing. It's a truism, but what makes it a truism is that it's true. The only way to learn to write is to force yourself to produce a certain number of words on a regular basis" (2001, 49). In most classrooms, children compose with pen or pencil rather than using a word processor with a word count function. Therefore, I find making a goal based on the number of lines they want to push themselves to write is a visual, yet quantitative way of helping them write more. The age of the children you teach, and what their paper looks like, may change how many lines is an "appropriate" goal. If you want to help kids make a realistic rough estimate, try gathering them to your meeting space and asking them to get their "pens on fire!" for five minutes. No stopping. Then, have them count how many lines they can write. Then, have them multiply that number by 5, 6, 7, or 8 depending on the total length of your writing time (25–40 minutes). Ask them to count how many lines more that would mean and put a dot in their margin. Of course, no one likely writes with "pens on fire" for an entire forty-minute period, but it can be a motivational goal to get going down the page.

Prompts

- Check your goal. You've been writing for fifteen minutes and have fifteen to go. Are you about halfway there?
- You put your dot there, but I wonder if we could slide it down the page just a little more.
- Challenge yourself! Put the dot a little farther than you think you can.
- You met your goal! Now let's set another one.

Who is this for?

LEVELS
1–8

GENRE / TEXT TYPE
any

PROCESSES
generating and collecting, developing, drafting

Hat Tip: *A Quick Guide to Reviving Disengaged Writers, 5–8* (Lehman 2011)

2.15 Break Up Your Writing Time into Smaller Chunks

LEVELS
1–8

GENRE / TEXT TYPE
any

PROCESSES
generating and collecting, developing, drafting

Strategy Break up your total writing time into smaller chunks. Set a goal for yourself (numbers of lines or words). Set a timer or watch the clock. Write! Consider if you've met your goal or you need to adjust it for the next five minutes. Challenge yourself to outgrow your best each time.

Lesson Language *At times, the writing period can seem long and daunting. When it does, it helps to set short-term goals that make it feel more manageable. You can set a clock or count the number of lines or pages you want to reach before you take a short break, then get back to writing time with another short break.*

Prompts
- How many minutes do you want to stick to writing before taking a break? How many lines or pages do you think you can write in that time?
- Let's try out one minute and see how much you write.
- Let's decide how many breaks you'll want in the next thirty minutes. How many lines will you try to write in each chunk of time?

Hat Tip: *A Quick Guide to Reviving Disengaged Writers, 5–8* (Lehman 2011)

Strategy If you find yourself at a loss for words, unable to write, it might be worthwhile to step away and do something else. You can pick up a text in the same topic or genre as what you're trying to write, and read. You can get inspired by what the author said, or how the author said it. As soon as inspiration strikes, return to your writing.

Using a Mentor Having a basket of mentor texts in your writing center can help students to independently visit and use their resources during times of struggle. Of course, these mentor texts are most helpful as writing examples if they have been read aloud and studied together prior to being placed in the center.

Prompts

- What's a text you might turn to while you're stuck?
- What is causing you to get stuck?
- Are you stuck for ideas? What books might help with that?
- Are you stuck on structure? What mentor could you turn to?
- Who is an author you might want to read?
- That author would be a great person given what you want to write about.

Writer's BLOCK ?? Here are some texts you can turn to for inspiration!

Genre	Books	Sample lines
Realistic Fiction	"Each Kindness"	That afternoon, I walked home alone When I reached the pond, my throat filled with all the things I wish I would have said to Maya. Each kindness I had never shown.
Non-Fiction	"Polar Bears in Danger"	The **Artic** is home to the polar bear, the world's biggest land **predator**. In the Arctic Circle, a large part of the sea remains frozen all year. This area is called the ice cap. In winter, the sea around the ice cap freezes, too. Polar bears spend the fall, winter, and spring hunting on the frozen sea.
Historical Fiction	"Scarlet Stockings Spy"	Uncertainty settled over the city like soot. Suspicions skulked through the cobblestone streets like alley cats. Rumors multiplied like horseflies. Spies were everywhere. Some spied for the British, loyal to the king. Others spied for the Patriots, loyal to Washington's army.
Poetry	"Water Music"	Reflection Water is a magic mirror Showing earth and sky, Revealing the fairest to the careful eye What is up is down, What is far is near; A truth so fragile Only eyes can hear. "Reflection" by Jane Yolen (1998)

Jackie Yehla

Hat Tip: *What You Know by Heart: How to Develop Curriculum for Your Writing Workshop* (Ray 2002)

2.17 Imagine Your Audience

Who is this for?

LEVELS
2–5

GENRE / TEXT TYPE
any

PROCESSES
developing, drafting, revising

Strategy Think about who you're writing for, or who you hope or expect will read your piece. Draw a quick sketch of that person or those people, an image to represent your audience, or put up a photograph in front of you on your desk as you write (if it helps!). As you write, pretend like you're speaking to that person.

Teaching Tip If the student's audience is more abstract than a person or group of people in a single photograph or sketch, the student can simply envision and remind herself of the audience during writing. Younger children tend to like the tangibility of actually looking at the "audience" when writing.

Prompts

• Who are you hoping will read your piece?
• Keep that person in mind as you write.
• You can try pretending to speak to that person. It may help you get words out that you can use in your writing.
• Keep your audience in mind.
• When you wrote that, it sounded just like how you'd speak to that person!
• I can hear your voice come out more, because you're thinking of your audience as you write.

2.18 Keep a Side Project

Strategy Think about the topics that matter most to you, and the genres you're most drawn to. Start your own project about that topic and/or in that genre, regardless of what the class is studying at that time.

Lesson Language *Sometimes we work on writing because we are assigned it, and other times, we work on writing because we are passionate about it. As a student in school, there will be times when you don't have complete and total choice of what you have to write. There may be times when trying out something new is great for you because you find a genre you didn't know about before that now clicks with you. Other times, you won't be as excited by the project as you would if the class were studying something else. These are great times for side projects, to keep your writing energy up and writing life going outside of the classroom.*

Teaching Tip Jane Yolen once said: "I never get writer's block because I write on a number of things at the same time. If one is not going well, I turn to another." Encouraging your students to keep side projects will maximize productivity!

Using a Mentor
Because this suggestion is for students to operate very independently with their writing, it would be helpful for them to have access to possible mentor texts they could use to serve as their teachers, in the absence of any formal lessons.

Prompts
- What's the genre you feel most passionate about?
- What's a topic that you really care about?
- Think about what writing project you might keep on the side.
- Let's talk about how you'll work on your writing project outside of school.

> **Writing Project Mix & Match!**
>
> **Choose 1** Topic | **Choose 1** Genre
>
> - An animal
> - A foreign country
> - A social issue
> - Current events
> - An embarrassing memory!
> - An exciting moment
> - Your favorite celebrity
> - A hobby
>
> - Persuasive Review
> - Persuasive Letter
> - Fantasy Story
> - Realistic Fiction
> - Memoir
> - Research Report
> - Diary Entry
> - Friendly Letter (or Email!)
> - Informational Book
>
> You can write anything about anything!
> ↳ What will you write?
> ↳ When will you write it?
> ↳ How will you publish it?

Diana Erben

Who is this for?

LEVELS
2–8

GENRE / TEXT TYPE
any

PROCESS
any

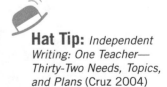

Hat Tip: *Independent Writing: One Teacher—Thirty-Two Needs, Topics, and Plans* (Cruz 2004)

Who is this for?

LEVELS
2–8

GENRE / TEXT TYPE
any

PROCESS
any

Hat Tip: *A Writer Teaches Writing* (Murray 1985)

Strategy For whatever part of the process you're in, if you feel stuck you can consult with another writer who may be able to get you jump-started. Discuss what you think you might write about, the challenges you're having, or how you think it might go. Listen to yourself as you talk. Once you feel like you said aloud what you want to say on the page, go back to your writing.

Teaching Tip Setting up formal partnerships, and/or the flexibility for writers to pull another writer aside, perhaps to a specially designated spot in the room, can be a lifesaver. Which one of us hasn't gotten stuck before, and used our "phone a friend" card to get out of trouble? This strategy works in any part of the writing process, from students who are trying to figure out what to write about, to students who need a reader to check for craft, to someone who needs help with edits. See Chapter 10 for more ideas on how to structure peer collaboration and support in writing.

Prompts

- Is there someone in the room who might be able to help with that?
- Why don't you and _____ go find a quiet spot to see if you can't help each other.
- Did you say something aloud to her that helped you figure out a possible solution?
- Listen to yourself as you share your concerns.
- Describe why you're stuck and what help you might need.

2.20 Experiment with Change

Strategy Find a spot in your draft that isn't working well. On a strip of new paper, try to imagine that part being very different. Write it. Then, get a new strip and try that part in another entirely new way. Look back at your experiments to choose which fits best with your final piece.

Lesson Language *Perhaps you used to be the kind of writer who would go back to a draft and just change a word here or there. Instead of describing the coat as "white," you'd write "snowy." Instead of writing, "My sister yelled," maybe you'd change it to, "'Get out of here!' My sister yelled." Changes like that can help your writing, but at the heart of the revision process is re-visioning, or reseeing your writing. Trying to imagine it in a totally new way. One thing that helps is to say, "Well, what if . . . ?" to yourself and really think of revision as a time to experiment.*

Teaching Tip Some children may come to you saying, "OK, I'll do an experiment. But I don't know what kind of experiment to do." In this case, you'll want to refer children to any classroom charts that may serve as reminders for the sorts of developing and revision ideas you've shared with them for this, and past pieces. Lesson ideas for types and purposes for revision can be found across Chapters 4, 5, and 6.

Prompts

- What part are you thinking of experimenting with?
- Let's try it in a different way.
- You can try it first aloud, then jot it down.
- Looking back at your options, which one works best?
- Think, "What if . . . ?" when looking at your draft.

Who is this for?

LEVELS
3–8

GENRE / TEXT TYPE
any

PROCESS
revising

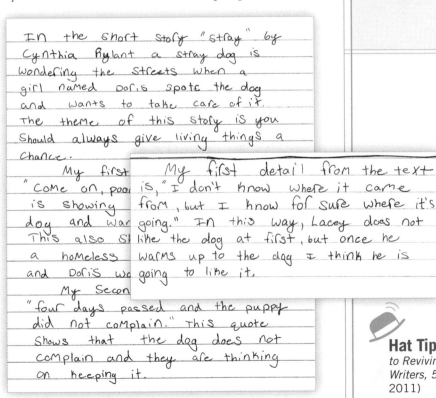

In the short story "Stray" by Cynthia Rylant a stray dog is wondering the streets when a girl named Doris spots the dog and wants to take care of it. The theme of this story is you should always give living things a chance.

My first [detail from the text] "Come on, poor [dog] is, "I don't know where it came is showing [...] from, but I know for sure where it's dog and war[...] going." In this way, Lacey does not This also s[...] like the dog at first, but once he a homeless [...] warms up to the dog I think he is and Doris wa[...] going to like it.

My Secon[...]
"Four days passed and the puppy did not complain." This quote shows that the dog does not complain and they are thinking on keeping it.

Hat Tip: *A Quick Guide to Reviving Disengaged Writers, 5–8* (Lehman 2011)

Why Do You Write?

Who is this for?

LEVELS
3–8

GENRE / TEXT TYPE
any

PROCESS
any

Strategy Think about the piece you're working on. Think about why you're writing it. Try to tap into what it is that you care about in the piece, and why you want your writing out in the world.

Lesson Language *Writing can feel hard sometimes. It takes energy! So it's important for any writer to stay focused on intentions and passions and maybe do a little self-talking during the writing to remember the why. If you can think about your writing eventually going someplace, that may help. If you can imagine the message you have to send and why others need to hear it, that may help. But if you only feel like you're writing it because it was assigned, or because your teacher told you to write, well, that may be at the heart of the issue. Try to find a purpose for what you're currently working on or start a new piece, thinking about your intentions from the beginning.*

Teaching Tip This strategy is a harder sell for times when students are assigned writing. Consider using this strategy with "Their Topic, Your Idea" (page 148) in those cases.

Prompts
• Think about what you care about in your piece.
• Why do you think you chose to write about this topic?
• What is it about this topic that speaks to you?
• Think about if you want to continue with this piece.

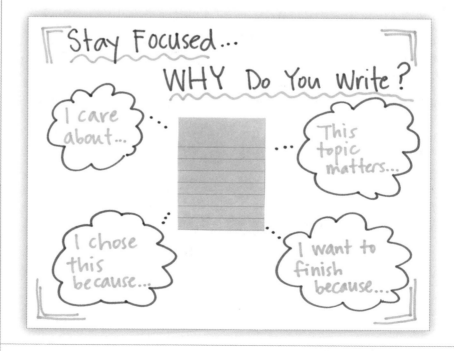

Hat Tip: *A Quick Guide to Reaching Struggling Writers, K–5* (Cruz 2008)

2.22 One Bite at a Time

Strategy Don't focus on the whole piece, just focus on one part. Try to write that part. Once it's done, think about the next part you want to write. Write just that part. Before you know it, you'll have the whole thing done!

Teaching Tip To many people I know, the thought of writing a book is so overwhelming that they seem stuck getting started. My advice is to stop thinking of the whole book, and instead think of a chapter. Then, outline that chapter, and then just write one part. Then the next. Then the next. If you think of the whole book, you're sometimes crushed under the weight of the task ahead. If you set your sights on something doable, you'll end up outdoing yourself! Even though our students aren't trying to write 200-page books, the idea of a whole essay or a whole two-page story can seem overwhelming. Thinking of parts and taking it on one part at a time can help quell writer's block.

Using a Mentor Children may enjoy hearing stories of writers' processes, many of which you can find by visiting authors' own websites.

Prompts
- What's one (maybe small) part of what you're trying to make?
- Can you break up the whole thing into pieces?
- You don't need to do it all today. Think about what may come first.
- Just focus on one part.
- Think about what you'll do next.
- I see you set your sights on something doable for today, given the time you have.

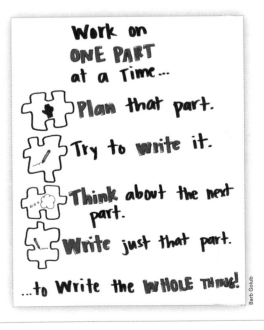

Barb Golub

Who is this for?

LEVELS
3–8

GENRE / TEXT TYPE
any

PROCESS
any

Hat Tip: *Bird by Bird: Some Instructions on Writing and Life* (Lamott 1994)

Who is this for?

LEVELS
3–8

GENRE / TEXT TYPE
any

PROCESS
any

Strategy If you feel blocked, try to clear your mind of skills and strategies that you feel shaky on. Focus on just one thing: getting "black on white" (marks on the page). You can go back to your writing later to try out the other skills and strategies.

Lesson Language *You've all learned a lot of strategies that writers use to make their writing more focused, structured, and detailed. Your mind might be swimming with rules of the English language, words you're trying to learn how to spell, and the knowledge that using precise verbs and nouns makes writing more powerful. But here's the thing: All that knowledge can work against you if it's blocking you from actually getting some words down. Revision and editing can happen later. Maybe you'll be glad to hear this quote from C. J. Cherryh: "It is perfectly okay to write garbage—as long as you edit brilliantly."*

Prompts
- Try to get something down.
- Be less concerned with how perfect the writing may be and more concerned with just getting something down today.
- Set a goal for how much you'll get down. Let's focus on quantity now, and quality later.
- You're doing it! Getting marks on the page is going to help you generate inertia!

Hat Tip: *A Writer Teaches Writing* (Murray 1985)

Strategy Create a habit of writing regularly, perhaps by promising yourself a certain amount of writing each day, done at a consistent time, created in a consistent place. Give yourself a challenge. Chart your progress.

Teaching Tip This strategy helps students imagine a writing life outside of the regular writing time you've carved out in class during the school day. Students who write regularly, ideally both at school and outside of school, will become immersed in their project, which will yield greater engagement.

Using a Mentor

10 Steps to Becoming a Better Writer

Write.

Write more.

Write even more.

Write even more than that.

Write when you don't want to.

Write when you do.

Write when you have something to say.

Write when you don't.

Write every day.

Keep writing.

—Brian Clark

Prompts

- How much writing will you try to do each day?
- Let's make a plan.
- If you were to set up a routine, what would that routine look like?
- Is there a place where you can plan to get writing done?
- Is there a consistent time each day that works for you?
- Challenge yourself.

Chapter Title	GOAL	10/20	10/23	11/9
Composing with Pictures	20	1	6	6
Engagement	28	18	18	20
Generating Ideas	40	26	27	34
Focus	35	7	9	10
Organization and Structure	34	18	21	23
Elaboration	40	16	17	29
Word Choice	25	10	12	12
Conventions	53	9	13	32
Partnerships and Clubs	25	6	6	8
TOTAL STRATEGIES	300	111	129	174

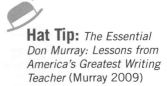

Hat Tip: *The Essential Don Murray: Lessons from America's Greatest Writing Teacher* (Murray 2009)

LEVELS
4–8

GENRE / TEXT TYPE
any

PROCESSES
developing, drafting, revising

Strategy Think about the topic you're writing about, not just during writing time but away from your desk as well. See if anything in your everyday life helps you to make connections to your topic or helps you think more about your topic. Bring the connections back to your writing desk to consider during writing time.

Lesson Language *When a writer's project really matters, he lives in such a way that the whole world is filtered through the lens of the writer's topic. A song comes on the radio and it is as if the DJ knew you were writing about the topic that connects to the song. You pick up a newspaper, and there on the front page in glaring print is something that connects to your topic. Your friends start talking about a viral video on Facebook, and there again is your topic! The reason this happens is that a writer's brain is often so consumed by the project that it will start to make connections to anything and everything. To do this, though, you have to be thinking about your project even when you're away from writing time. Doing so helps to bring energy back to your project when you have time to write.*

Prompts
- How can you keep this idea alive, as you leave writing time and the classroom today?
- What might you think about after writing time?
- Was there anything that happened yesterday that caused you to make connections to your writing project?

Hat Tip: *What You Know by Heart: How to Develop Curriculum for Your Writing Workshop* (Ray 2002)

Strategy If you're coming to writing time distracted by other events in life, take the first five minutes to do a quick write, venting and dumping all of that on the page. Then turn the page (literally and metaphorically) and begin on your writing project for class.

Teaching Tip This idea was suggested to me by a middle school teacher during a roundtable conversation at the 2015 National Council of Teachers of English conference in Minneapolis. This wise teacher said that his students often walked into his classroom with some social drama that had just occurred in the halls, and instead of telling them to buckle down and get to work, he honored their need to process what they were dealing with to enable them to focus on the writing work ahead of them for the day.

Prompts

- Go ahead and write for a few minutes to get what's on your mind out on the page.
- Now that you've spent a bit of time getting that out on the page, do you feel ready to continue on?
- You've spent a few minutes venting, now it's time to turn to your writing project.
- Vent now, then you can focus later.
- I can tell you've calmed down. I think you're ready to join us, and turn to your writing project.

Who is this for?

LEVELS
4–8

GENRE / TEXT TYPE
any

PROCESS
preparing to write

Hat Tip: *Micro Lessons in Writing: Big Ideas for Getting Started* (Vopat 2007a)

Who is this for?

LEVELS
4–8

GENRE / TEXT TYPE
any

PROCESS
any

Strategy If you're feeling writer's block, it may be because you have an expectation for what you're going to make that is unrealistic. Say to yourself, "I'm going to write the best I can today, and that is good enough for now." When you've written, you can go back to see how you'd like to make it better.

Lesson Language *Sometimes a writer feels a block because she is so concerned with making everything perfect or getting it right on the first draft that she is paralyzed. Setting goals that are more realistic can help you feel like the task ahead of you for the day is doable. Also, a little self-talk to set aside the doubt can help you accept that whatever you make today is OK because it's your best work, and there is always revision you can do to make it better.*

Prompts

- Tell me about what you're expecting to accomplish today as a writer.
- Do you think your expectation is realistic?
- How can you set a more realistic expectation?
- Let's think about what you could do for today.
- Do you think there's something standing in the way of getting your writing done?

Hat Tip: *A Writer Teaches Writing* (Murray 1985)

Tapping into personal

passions and interests

is a crucial part of

becoming an independent,

self-directed, lifelong writer.

—*Jennifer Serravallo*

Generating and Collecting Ideas

◎ Why is this goal important?

As Roy Peter Clark writes in his book *Help! for Writers: 210 Solutions to the Problems Every Writer Faces*, inertia is a crucial aspect of being a productive writer (2011). No writing leads to no writing. But once a writer gets started, *some* writing often leads to *more* writing.

Some would argue that many writers do not have to seek ideas—the ideas for what to write next will find them, mainly because they live a wide-awake, writerly life (Murray 1985). In case your student writers don't already have that disposition, many of the strategies in this chapter will help them to be on the lookout for possible topics and ideas. These strategies will help them develop an awareness of their surroundings and an ability to be keen observers.

Writers also rely not only on their present encounters with the world, but on their ability to recall their past (Murray 1985). Some of the ideas in this chapter are about finding writing possibilities in your memories.

Writers benefit from collecting what might later be forgotten, even when they don't know when it might become helpful or relevant to their writing (Fletcher 2003). Some of the strategies in this chapter will nudge your student writers in grades 3 and above to keep their own notebooks as a sort of idea storage and as a place to respond and react. When writers do this, they'll have a ready-made bank of ideas to return to again and again.

In a writer's lifetime, there will undoubtedly be times when someone gives an assignment or prompt: college term papers, a reporter on a beat, a standardized testing situation. However, many writers are able to generate their own topics for writing based on what they care most about. Tapping into personal passions and interests is a crucial part of becoming an independent, self-directed, lifelong writer.

◎ How do I know if this goal is right for my student?

Research has shown that when students have the opportunity to choose their own topics, they have ownership over their writing and their writing improves (Thomas 2016). However, choosing topics won't come easily to everyone. Writers who have a hard time getting starting during free writing time, writers who complain of writer's block, and writers who flat out tell you "I don't know what to write about" are ideal candidates for this goal and the strategies in this chapter. If you ever find yourself conferring with a student writer who looks to you longingly to give them their topic-of-the-day, you'll "teach a man to fish" when you offer a strategy for generating ideas rather than giving them the short-term "fish" of a topic for the day. To find candidates for this goal, notice students who, after a class lesson on ways to gather ideas, sit stymied, or end up with a very short list of what to write about.

Strategies for Generating and Collecting Ideas

Strategy		Grade Levels	Genres/Text Types	Processes
3.1	Important People	K–8	Any	Generating and collecting
3.2	Moments with Strong Feelings	K–8	Personal narrative, memoir, poetry, opinion/persuasive	Generating and collecting
3.3	Observe Closely	K–8	Any	Generating and collecting, drafting
3.4	Photo Starts	K–8	Any	Generating and collecting, developing, drafting
3.5	Mapping the Heart	K–8	Any	Generating and collecting
3.6	Reread and Look for Patterns	1–8	Any	Generating and collecting
3.7	Writing to Change the World!	1–8	Opinion/persuasive (letters, speeches, signs, etc.)	Generating and collecting
3.8	Walk Your World	1–8	Any	Generating and collecting
3.9	Interview to Dig for and Uncover Topics	1–8	Opinion/persuasive, narrative	Developing, drafting, revising
3.10	Scrapbook Your Life (to Write About It Later)	1–8	Any	Generating and collecting
3.11	Mine Mentor Texts for Topics	2–8	Any	Generating and collecting
3.12	These Are a Few of My Favorite Things	2–8	Any	Generating and collecting
3.13	Start with a Character	2–8	Fiction, mostly	Generating and collecting, developing
3.14	Listen for (and Write!) Music	2–8	Poetry, mostly	Generating and collecting, drafting
3.15	Jot Today, Write Tomorrow	2–8	Any	Generating and collecting
3.16	Give Yourself Exercises/Assignments	3–8	Any	Generating and collecting
3.17	Get Sparked by Setting	3–8	Any	Generating and collecting
3.18	Tour Your Home	3–8	Narrative (personal narrative, memoir, fiction)	Generating and collecting
3.19	Always Times, One Time	3–8	Personal narrative, memoir, poetry	Generating and collecting

07/29/2019
Items checked out to: p13336721

TITLE The writing strategies book :
BARCODE   31333046356935
DUE DATE   08-12-19 00:00AM

SUMMER READING CHALLENGE

Sign up the week of June 3rd to get
your map, and enjoy activities at the
Library throughout the summer.

A UNIVERSE
of Stories

for Kids and Teens

Sign up the week of June 3rd to get
your map, and enjoy activities at the
Library throughout the summer.

Strategy	Grade Levels	Genres/Text Types	Processes
3.20 Ideas for Other Genres Might Be Hiding (in Plain Sight!)	3–8	Any	Generating and collecting
3.21 Borrow a (Spark) Line	3–8	Poetry, narrative, essay	Generating and collecting, drafting
3.22 Found Poems	3–8	Poetry, narrative, essay	Generating and collecting, drafting
3.23 Over and Over	3–8	Poetry, mostly	Generating and collecting, drafting
3.24 Wonder, "What If . . . ?"	3–8	Fictional narrative	Generating and collecting
3.25 Mix and Match Story Elements	3–8	Fiction	Generating and collecting
3.26 Word Mapping	3–8	Any	Generating and collecting, developing
3.27 If It Could Go on Facebook, You Can Jot It in a Notebook	4–8	Any	Generating and collecting
3.28 Ask Yourself Questions (and Then Answer Them)	4–8	Any	Generating and collecting
3.29 Collect Triggers	4–8	Any	Generating and collecting, revising
3.30 Subtopics Hiding in Topics	4–8	Any	Generating and collecting
3.31 Purposefully Wander	4–8	Any	Generating and collecting
3.32 Abstract Issues, Specific Examples	4–8	Any	Generating and collecting, drafting
3.33 Scan the Newspaper	4–8	Fictional narrative	Generating and collecting
3.34 Read Something on an Unfamiliar Topic	4–8	Any	Generating and collecting
3.35 Person vs. Nature	4–8	Narrative	Generating and collecting, developing
3.36 Find Characters and Ideas in the World	4–8	Any	Generating and collecting
3.37 Defining Moments	4–8	Narrative	Generating and collecting
3.38 Start with an Outlandish Claim	4–8	Opinion/persuasive, memoir	Generating and collecting

Who is this for?

LEVELS
K–8

GENRE / TEXT TYPE
any

PROCESS
generating and collecting

Strategy Make a list of the people in your life that matter most to you. Starting with one person, list memories you have with that person. Choose one and write the memory bit by bit.

Teaching Tip Just about any generating strategy can be used to springboard a writer into just about any genre. As described above, this strategy clearly sets children up to write personal narrative or memoir. However, by changing the language slightly you could easily shift to realistic fiction ("Make a list of the people who matter most to you. Use that person to create a character. Write a story that could realistically happen.") or even historical fiction ("Think of a person who matters to you. Imagine this person in another time, or maybe even another place. Consider the challenges they'd face. Create a story set in that time."). The strategy could also work to support different modes of writing in a variety of genres. An important person could be written about in an essay ("Think of a person who matters to you. Consider an idea you have about that person. Jot down reasons the person matters, which can serve as a quick outline."), or a biography ("Think of a person who matters. Create a timeline of the important events from that person's life. Write about each event on a separate page.").

Using a Mentor In *Grandpa Green* (Smith 2011) the title character creates topiaries in the shapes of people and places of his memory. Each sculpture sparks a memory about a time or part of his identity.

Prompts
- Name some people in your life who matter to you.
- List some memories of these people.
- Which memory is clearest in your mind? Turn to a new page and start writing it.

Hat Tip: *Launching the Writing Workshop* (Calkins and Martinelli 2006)

3.2 Moments with Strong Feelings

Strategy Choose a strong feeling (worry, fear, embarrassment, excitement, joy, etc.). Think about memories you have that connect to that feeling. Try to use details that show the feeling of that moment.

Teaching Tip Katherine Bomer (2016) in *The Journey Is Everything* shares a related strategy of starting with "hot spots" and allowing students to think on the page. To try Bomer's idea, have students start with strong emotions, and then have them freewrite about why they feel that way about their topic. This is helpful for generating ideas for opinion/persuasive pieces, such as essays or speeches.

Using a Mentor Read aloud a picture book where the character has strong emotions, especially emotions that change, to show how an author can be inspired by those feelings, and also how the author shows the feelings in the story. Check out Bonny Becker's *A Visitor for Bear* for one example (2008).

Prompts

- Start with one strong emotion. Now list times you remember feeling that emotion.
- That is a strong feeling! Try to think of a time you felt that way.
- You've got a few ideas for stories/poems connected to that feeling. Let's pick a new feeling.
- What strong feelings might spark good ideas for writing?

FEELING	IDEA
CHEERFUL	When we had chocolate chip cookies for snack
WORRIED	When I thought Sam wasn't my friend anymore
SCARED	When I couldn't find my mom at the store
SAD	When Jesse made fun of my shoes
ANGRY	When I dropped my clay pot and it broke

Merridy Gnagey

Who is this for?

LEVELS
K–8

GENRES / TEXT TYPES
personal narrative, memoir, poetry, opinion/persuasive

PROCESS
generating and collecting

Hat Tip: *Explore Poetry* (Graves 1992)

3.3 Observe Closely

Who is this for?

LEVELS
K–8

GENRE / TEXT TYPE
any

PROCESSES
generating and collecting, drafting

Strategy Find an object that matters to you. Examine it closely, looking at it part by part. Describe what you see literally, using all of your senses. Describe what you see by comparing it to other things. Describe how it makes you feel.

Teaching Tip Students may not have meaningful objects at the ready in the classroom. To use this in class, consider asking students to bring in meaningful objects from home. You could also teach this strategy to set your writers up to get ideas when they are away from the classroom—at home at night, on the weekends, or during vacations.

Prompts
- Go part by part.
- Describe it, don't just tell what that part is called.
- Linger on that part a bit longer, using more words to say what you see.
- Think about using other senses. What can you add?
- What does it remind you of?

Hat Tip: *What You Know By Heart: How to Develop Curriculum for Your Writing Workshop* (Ray 2002)

Strategy Collect photographs (ask your family for help and permission!). Look closely at a photograph and try to reexperience the moment it was taken, thinking about what you see, hear, feel, smell, and so on. Write the moment as you remember it, using as much detail as you can.

Teaching Tip This strategy could be angled to support a specific genre study. For example, if a student is working on historical fiction or narrative nonfiction, you could teach the student to look at a historical photograph that features a person or people. Look closely at the picture, thinking about who the person might be, what his life might be like, what it might be like to be in the environment in which he is pictured. Try writing a scene featuring him using first person or third person.

Prompts
- Look closely at the picture.
- What do you remember?
- Storytell that moment for me, so I can imagine it like I was there.
- Can you imagine being there, back in that moment?
- I wasn't there with you—tell me about everything you remember.

Who is this for?

LEVELS
K–8

GENRE / TEXT TYPE
any

PROCESSES
generating and collecting, developing, drafting

Hat Tip: *A Quick Guide to Reaching Struggling Writers, K–5* (Cruz 2008)

3.5 Mapping the Heart

Strategy Draw a large heart on a notebook page or large piece of paper. Write the names of topics, or sketch pictures to remind you of topics that are close to your heart. You can think about people, places, things, and so on.

Teaching Tip It's a good idea to equip your writers with a bank of ideas they can return to, independently, when they feel like they are at a loss for how to get started. Mapping the heart and even allowing kids to create photo collages on their folders or notebooks offer them a well to return to again and again.

Prompts
- What feels closest to your heart? Write a word in the center.
- Let's think together about some of the places that are important. As we think of them, we can jot them down.
- You can sketch it, or you can write a word to remind you.
- That's a big topic. See if there are some smaller topics within that topic you can list.

Hat Tip: *Awakening the Heart: Exploring Poetry in Elementary and Middle School* (Heard 1999); *Heart Maps: Helping Students Create and Craft Authentic Writing* (Heard 2016)

Strategy Reread your notebook, drafts, and/or published work. Think about what patterns you see in your work. Think about whether you have any other ideas for stories, poems, or essays that have the same topic that you tend to write a lot about.

Using a Mentor Nancie Atwell (2014) talks about the importance of a writer's "territories"—the topics he returns to again and again. One topic can offer a lifetime of possibilities for writing—in different genres, by narrowing or broadening the topic, by looking at the topic from a new perspective. Look at the body of work from one author who is a class favorite and talk about what that writer's territories might be. Discuss with students how the author returns to common themes, topics, ideas, or characters but makes each work feel new. For example, Patricia Polacco often writes stories about family inspired from her own childhood. Roald Dahl mixes in a bit of magic to most of his stories. He also often kills off the parents on the first page (*James and the Giant Peach, Charlie and the Chocolate Factory, The Witches*), or creates parents/adults who are miserable (*Matilda, The Twits*) and good, sweet children who often triumph.

Prompts
- When you reread your notebook, what topics seem to keep coming up again and again?
- You noticed some topics you write about a lot. What are you thinking about those topics?
- Do you have an idea for another piece that is about that same topic?
- Sure! You could try a different genre. What are you thinking of?

Merridy Gnagey

Hat Tip: *A Quick Guide to Reaching Struggling Writers, K–5* (Cruz 2008)

3.7 Writing to Change the World!

LEVELS

1–8

GENRE / TEXT TYPE

opinion/persuasive (letters, speeches, signs, etc.)

PROCESS

generating and collecting

Strategy Think about something you want to see happen, or that you want to change. That can give you an idea for a topic. Then, think about who has the power to change it. That can help you to keep your audience in mind from the beginning.

Using a Mentor *Click Clack Moo: Cows that Type* offers beginning writers an example of writing to persuade, though the persuasion is less for changing the world and more for changing their own circumstances (Cronin 2000). It's a funny story about some cows that demand blankets from Farmer Brown (it's cold in the barn at night, after all!). This story will help children understand the power their words can have when their writing is persuasive—and when it gets to the right person/audience. *All the Water in the World* by George Ella Lyons starts off informational, but ends with a persuasive plea to the reader to consider the value of water and not waste or ruin our earth's supply (2011). Political speeches by members of Congress or past or future presidents can be great examples, as can some op-eds.

Prompts

• Name a few things you want to see change.
• What do you wish was different in the world?
• You thought of an idea for a piece of writing. Who do you think has the power to make changes? That's who you might want to read it.
• You can start, "I wish . . ."
• You can start, "I would change . . ."
• What kind of writing do you think you'll make (letter, speech, sign, etc.)?

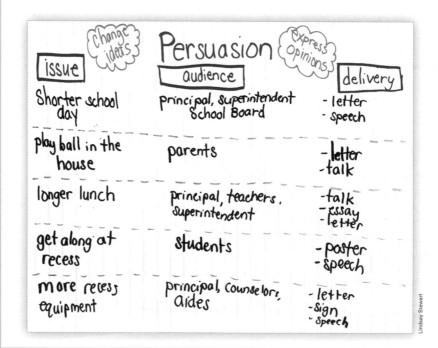

Lindsay Stewart

Hat Tip: *For a Better World: Reading and Writing for Social Action* (Bomer and Bomer 2001)

3.8 Walk Your World

Strategy Go on a walk (through your school, your neighborhood, your home) carrying a notebook. Be ready to see what is, and also what could be. Jot your observations in a notebook. Use the observations to start some writing.

Teaching Tip If you are teaching this strategy in the context of a unit with an already established genre, you can spin the language of the strategy to clarify what "what could be" could mean. In fiction, students will likely be thinking of a story that could happen in that place or witnessing an event and changing the facts to make the narrative more compelling. If the class is working in a persuasive writing unit, the "what could be" might mean writing to change someone's mind about something or convince someone of something based on an observation (for example, walking into the school cafeteria and seeing the poor-quality lunch could prompt them to write to convince the principal to provide healthier choices). Writers in informational writing studies could walk their world to find possible topics they are inspired by and that they want to teach others about. If you're teaching a child without a genre in mind, this strategy could be left somewhat open-ended, encouraging her to record observations and then riff off those observations to generate ideas for her own pieces.

Prompts

- Since you've been walking, what have you seen?
- You named what you saw. Now, let's imagine what could be.
- You named what you saw. What would you like to be different?
- From all that you've noticed about your neighborhood, what would you like to change?
- Look back across your possible topic ideas. Which one inspires you most?

Who is this for?

LEVELS
1–8

GENRE / TEXT TYPE
any

PROCESS
generating and collecting

Observation Exercise!

* Look around you.
* Focus in on one object or area.
* Think: What could be?
* Create the same image in your mind.
* Record your observation in your notebook! WRITE!!! WRITE!!!

Betsy Hubbard

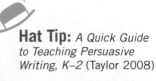

Hat Tip: *A Quick Guide to Teaching Persuasive Writing, K–2* (Taylor 2008)

Who is this for?

LEVELS
1–8

GENRES / TEXT TYPES
opinion/persuasive, narrative

PROCESSES
developing, drafting, revising

Hat Tip: *A Quick Guide to Teaching Persuasive Writing, K–2* (Taylor 2008)

Strategy Find people you want to help who are important to you. Ask them questions about what help they need and what you can do. Jot their answers down. Reread their responses to see if there is a topic you care about.

Lesson Language [angled toward persuasive writing; see Teaching Tip for other genre spins] *Here are some questions you can ask of people in your family, community, and/or school:*

- *Do you have any problems that I can help you solve?*
- *Can you think of something you wish was different? Something you'd like to change?*
- *Can you think of something that I can help you with?*

Teaching Tip There are all kinds of reasons you might interview someone. In terms of strategies for generating ideas, the strategy as written above will help a writer who is working to write a persuasive piece (letters, speeches, editorials, signs). You might also choose to interview someone because you are curious about their story or something they experienced, and you think that learning more about it could give you an idea for your own narrative (for example, interviewing a grandparent about something from their childhood). There is a different spin on interviewing included in the chapter on elaboration (Chapter 6), which might help a writer to include more details because of an interview.

Prompts

- Who might you interview?
- Let's think of some questions to ask that person.
- It's important to choose questions that the person could actually answer.
- Looking across your interview responses, what interests you as a writer? How do you want to help?
- What are some ways you might see if you can help?

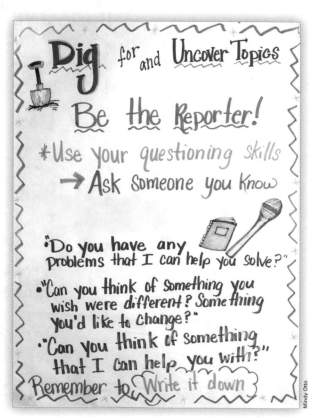

Mindy Otto

Scrapbook Your Life (to Write About It Later)

Strategy Collect important items and photographs that will help you recall moments. Later, return to them to rekindle the memory. Write what you remember.

Lesson Language *As writers live their lives, they often try to collect moments that they'll return to later to spark writing. One way to collect and save a moment is to "scrapbook" in a small, physical piece that will remind you of that time. The items you choose to glue into your notebook or on the cover of a writing folder may be things like ticket stubs to a concert or sporting game, a note your mom wrote you and left for you in your lunchbox, snapshots, or pictures cut from a magazine that remind you of objects, people, or places important to you and your own life.*

Teaching Tip In the younger grades, this would likely be done on the cover of their writing folder or on a piece of paper that would be tucked inside. In grades 3 and above, students may scrapbook the cover of their notebook or include a few pages within.

Prompts

- What are some "scraps" that you may have at home that could spark a memory during writing time?
- What things can you collect in your notebook to hold on to some of these events?
- Make a plan for some of the stuff you'll collect in the weeks ahead.

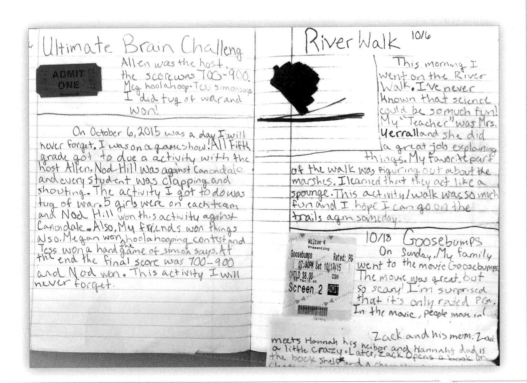

Who is this for?

LEVELS

1–8

GENRE / TEXT TYPE

any

PROCESS

generating and collecting

Hat Tip: *Breathing In, Breathing Out: Keeping a Writer's Notebook* (Fletcher 1996)

LEVELS
2–8

GENRE / TEXT TYPE
any

PROCESS
generating and collecting

Strategy Reread a text you love. Think about the things in it that you connect to, because you have had similar experiences or know about similar topics. Think about the things that are points of disconnection because your experiences are very different, or your knowledge is about the other side of what's being presented. As you read, keep a list of the topics and ideas that the other author's work has sparked in you.

Lesson Language *Many authors will tell you this true fact: the best writers are readers first. There is so much to learn from published authors, and the authors in our classrooms. We often talk about how we can learn a lot about the craft of writing, but the truth is that we can also learn so much from even the topics that authors write about! As we read a book, we can try to think about ways in which we connect to the text (I could write about that topic, too! That same thing happened to me! That reminds me of a story I could write that happened in a place like that! I have a person in my family like that, I could write the stories about that person! I know a lot about this topic!), and the points of disconnection (My experience is opposite. I could write about that! I don't know about the topic X that this author is writing about, but I know about topic Y!). These can help to uncover the topics that we can write about from our own lives.*

Prompts
- What can you connect to?
- What topics in this piece do you also know a lot about?
- Is there anything in this piece that you disagree with? What might you write about?
- List some ideas for topics based on what you read.

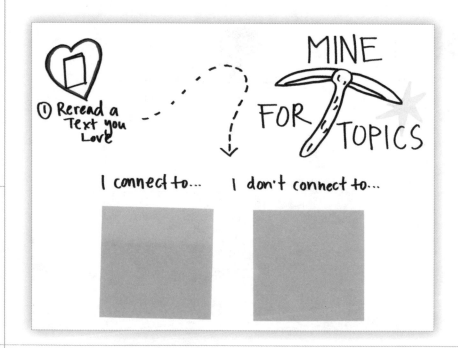

Hat Tip: *A Quick Guide to Reaching Struggling Writers, K–5 (Cruz 2008)*

Strategy In your mind, visualize an object that is important to you. You may even want to sketch it. Use this object to begin a writing entry. You could write about it (information), write about why it's important or the ideas it brings up for you (opinion), or write a story about a time that features the object (narrative).

Using a Mentor *Wilfred Gordon MacDonald Partridge* is a touching story about a boy who befriends some residents of a home for the aged. One resident has "lost" her memory, they all say, until Wilfred collects objects to help her "find" it again. Each object he collects help to spark memories that she shares with him (Fox 1989).

Prompts

- Sketch the object you're thinking of.
- How do you want to write about this object?
- What does this object make you think/feel/remember?
- List a few ideas you have for writing based on this object.
- You thought of two ideas for stories from just this one object!

Who is this for?

LEVELS
2–8

GENRE / TEXT TYPE
fiction, mostly

PROCESSES
generating and collecting, developing

Hat Tip: *Time for Meaning: Crafting Literate Lives in Middle & High School* (Bomer 1995)

Strategy Create a character. You can base your character on someone you know, a combination of people you know, or someone in your world you observe. Think, "What kind of problems, issues, and wants would this character have?"

Teaching Tip You may want to provide your students with a list of prompts to help them think about their character, such as:

- Wants? Needs?
- Likes? Dislikes?
- Strengths? Weaknesses?
- Physical description?
- Who else is in this character's life? How do they impact him?
- Places he feels safe? Scared?

Prompts

- List out some of the traits your character would have.
- You can get ideas from your imagination, or from what you know about people like this character.
- Thinking about the character, make a list of some problems he would have.
- That's a realistic problem/want based on the traits you've created.
- You've listed some ideas about the character. Take it a step further: Ask yourself *why*.

Strategy Listen to the sounds in your everyday world: machines, moving things, falling leaves, traffic, and so on. Use the sound as the rhythm of the poem, attaching your own words to each beat.

Teaching Tip This strategy is not the same as one that teaches children to elaborate with sound words or onomatopoeia, which you'll find in the chapter on elaboration (Chapter 6). The idea behind this strategy is that the sounds help to create a rhythm, which becomes the internal beat of the poem itself.

Using a Mentor Gwendolyn Brooks' poem "We Real Cool" (1999) reads just like a jazz beat that could have been playing in the pool hall that the narrators are speaking from. *Drum Dream Girl* by Margarita Engle (2015), about a Chinese-African-Cuban girl who broke the Cuban taboo against female drummers, echoes the rhythms of the instrument.

Prompts

- What do you hear?
- Tap out the rhythm of the sounds.
- How would you write that sound?
- Think about the rhythm and pattern of that sound.
- If you wrote that into a poem, what would repeat?
- What additional details would you include?

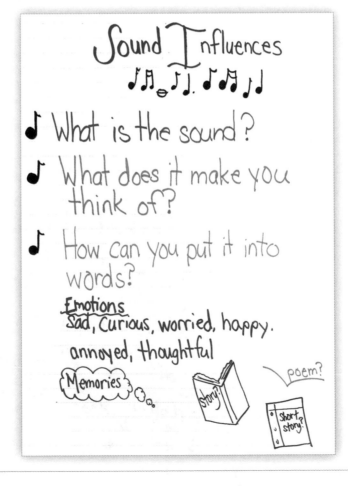

Who is this for?

LEVELS
2–8

GENRE / TEXT TYPE
poetry, mostly

PROCESSES
generating and collecting, drafting

Hat Tip: *Explore Poetry* (Graves 1992)

3.15 Jot Today, Write Tomorrow

Who is this for?

LEVELS
2–8

GENRE / TEXT TYPE
any

PROCESS
generating and collecting

Strategy Make a plan for where you'll keep ideas as they occur. Carry around what you need to get the ideas down. Come back tomorrow with some ideas to try out during writing time.

Lesson Language *If you feel like you sometimes sit down for writing and feel empty-handed (or -headed), without an idea of where you're going for the day, it might be good to try to fill up your notebook with ideas everyday so that there is always the spark of something waiting for you when you have time to sit down and really write. Many writers find it helps to carry a tiny, pocket-sized notebook around with them to jot down just a key word or phrase when something strikes them in the moment. Then, when they have more time to explore the topic, they will have a huge menu of options from which to choose.*

Teaching Tip This one, like a few others in this chapter, is meant to help children to write outside of the time given in school. "Living like a writer" means thinking about writing and trying to write during more than just the forty minutes allotted at their desk each day.

Using a Mentor Share *What Do You Do with an Idea?* for inspiration to take time to nurture the ideas you have (Yamada 2014).

Prompts
- Let's think about where you'll collect these ideas so you have them ready to go tomorrow.
- Can you think of a time when you had an idea away from your desk?
- Let's plan out what you could do if that happens.
- Imagine yourself in that place where you had the idea. What do you think sparked it?
- Hold on to your thought by repeating it again and again in your mind.

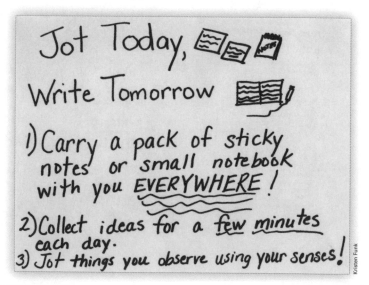

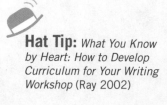

Hat Tip: *What You Know by Heart: How to Develop Curriculum for Your Writing Workshop* (Ray 2002)

3.16 Give Yourself Exercises/Assignments

Strategy Give yourself an assignment to stretch your observation or thinking. Start with a specific verb (*describe, compare, react*) and specific language of what your task is. Try to write without stopping for 5–10 minutes, focused on the assignment.

Teaching Tip Many writing books with adult/professional audiences offer exercises. Often meant as short warm-ups, these exercises can sometimes awaken something in a corner of a writer's brain that has been asleep or free some language that wouldn't have otherwise been used. You may need to give students some examples and options here, and after some time many will be able to generate them on their own. Some ideas to get you going:

- Describe the smells/sights/sounds of your home/beach/favorite place.
- Compare some specific everyday thing to something abstract; a specific person A to person B; two specific things/people/places that are similar; two specific things/people/places that are very different.
- React to the feeling you get when you hear about a specific person/place/thing or to a specific event.

Using a Mentor

"Inspiration is for amateurs—the rest of us just show up and get to work" (Fig 2009).

Prompts

- What's your assignment going to be?
- Try to write without stopping.
- You really stayed focused on that job you gave yourself!

> React to the feeling you get when you hear about Camp.
>
> When I hear about camp I think about a vast sanctuary. A place where I can be worry free, unlike my school year which consists of nights until 11 pm and then mornings starting at 6am. Camp brings me a new perspective on our world for I befriend girls from all around the globe. I meet girls who make me comfortable in my own skin, and we are all able to share who we are without feeling awkward about telling one another about our weird qualities.
>
> When I think of camp I think of a place of eternal happiness. You are free to explore what is around you, allowing for more insight into the environment. With an abundance of things to do, so many inspiring people, and opprutunities you would never dream of having, it feels as if nothing can go wrong. Everything at camp is so simple, it makes you realize how the little things in life have a big impact. Like the nights where my friends and I lie in our bunks talking until midnight, and then wake up early in the morning to run to breakfast, or just walking down the pond path in our squeaky flip flops, talking about whatever comes to mind.
>
> Camp is the place that makes me feel most at home. I'm able to express who I am without feeling self concious and mainly, it is where I can find hapiness anywhere in the simplest ways.

Hat Tip: *Breathing In, Breathing Out: Keeping a Writer's Notebook* (Fletcher 1996)

3.17 Get Sparked by Setting

Who is this for?

LEVELS
3–8

GENRE / TEXT TYPE
any

PROCESS
generating and collecting

Strategy Sit still, quietly, in a place (or imagine a place in your mind or look at an illustration or photograph of a place, imagining yourself there). Jot down what it's like there, using all of your senses. Think about the emotions it brings up for you, and what might be important about the place you're in. When you feel inspired, start writing!

Teaching Tip If you want students to experience being in a place, this strategy can work as a class field trip or can be advice you give to writers to use for their writing life outside of school. Photos, illustrations, and copies of paintings with striking settings can also be a nice addition to your writing center.

Using a Mentor Consider sharing examples of books with children where the place is such a crucial part of the story, it is almost a character. And think together about how the writer may have been inspired first by the place. See, for example, *Sarah Plain and Tall* or *Skylark* by Patricia MacLachlan (1985, 1994).

Prompts
- Where do you plan to observe?
- Let's observe right here. Say what you notice.
- What feelings does this place bring up for you?
- Try not to get distracted. Be here, and notice your environment.

> ### Get Sparked by Setting
>
> I'm sitting here on the booth in the kitchen. The smell of my mom's bran muffins baking wafts through my nose. The crinkle of aluminum foil as my mom gets her vitamin, and the relaxing sound of the running water as my mother does the dishes fill my ear. I can almost feel the soothing warm water on my hands. My brother's toys are dotted around the kitchen — puzzles, trucks, cars. The kitchen brings me happiness, because my family is always in it. My kitchen is important because it provides us food, and brings our family together.
>
> But my kitchen doesn't just bring me happy memories and feelings. There's the hopeful looks at the clock above the oven, seeing if our family's late (which we almost always are). There's the high-pitched screams of my little brother as he enters his meltdown mode. The smell of burnt toast that we never take out soon enough.

Hat Tip: *Help! for Writers: 210 Solutions to the Problems Every Writer Faces* (Clark 2011)

3.18 Tour Your Home

Strategy Start at a place in your childhood home. Guide the reader through a slow tour of your home, writing with lots of detail about what you see and what memories each spot brings up for you.

Lesson Language *Ideas for stories often hide in physical spaces. The sights, smells, and sounds of your environment can help you to remember important one-time events, or things that happened "all the time" in that place. I'm going to share with you a tour of one room of my childhood home. Notice how I am describing the place, but also tucking in memories that happened in that place:*

> In my sister's and my bedroom, there is carpeting on the floor. There might be a spot here or there where an art project went wrong, or a little nail polish spilled. Our closet is amazing—huge and racks galore. If you open up the door at the back of the closet, you can get to a small attic space, where my mom is always setting and collecting mousetraps. My sister and I are on twin beds, right across from each other. I can remember chucking pillows at her in the darkness when her snoring would wake me up.

Teaching Tip You could use this same strategy but change the place—a favorite vacation spot, the spot where you hang out every day after school, your grandparent's house, and so on.

Prompts

- Pause. What do you see in that place?
- Imagine the stories that would come up in that spot.
- Thinking back in time, stay in that place, and jot some story ideas down.
- Now that you have a few ideas from that spot, try to move on to another spot in your home.
- Isn't it amazing how many story ideas are tied to a place?

Who is this for?

LEVELS
3–8

GENRE / TEXT TYPE
narrative (personal narrative, memoir, fiction)

PROCESS
generating and collecting

Tour Your Home

my muted ~~PRP~~ purple front-door, which I opened for the first time to welcome my first best friend when I was six. ~~MY~~ My two white couches, parallel to one another, each with their own markings from messy toddlers, or immaculate projects that might have been a little bit too crafty. The hard wood steps that creak even under the slightest pressure are not my best friend when I want to sneak upstairs and sleep without anyone realizing in my parents bedroom is their king size bed, complete with a tempur-pedic mattress, making it the perfect place to rest on during thunder storms or those nights where I feel it is impossible to go upstairs into my bed. In my sisters room are two twin beds, one that I used to occupy, facing one another. This made the perfect set up for early Sunday mornings, jumping from one bed to the other ~~seat~~ shouting "avada-kedavra" or "Imperio" as we would take the roles of Harry Potter and the infamous Voldemort.

Hat Tip: James Howe, personal communication

LEVELS
3–8

GENRES / TEXT TYPES
personal narrative, memoir, poetry

PROCESS
generating and collecting

Strategy Think about life events that have happened again and again. Think about one of those times that stands out because of something that happened, something that someone said, or something that you felt. Write the story of that one time bit by bit.

Lesson Language *Many people have events in their lives that happen again and again. Sometimes it's tradition—we always have a Feast of the Seven Fishes dinner for Christmas Eve, for example. When I was little, I always spent two weeks at my grandparents' house each summer. My sister and I always seemed to fight on long car trips when we were kids. I can start by making a list of these "always times" in my notebook. Then, I can focus in on one and replay those times in my mind, thinking if any stands out from a single one. That will often make for a great story!*

Using a Mentor *When I Was Young in the Mountains* by Cynthia Rylant is a list memoir of some "always times" (1982). This strategy nudges children to list first, then take one off the list and write the story of that time. You might look to another narrative that is a clearly focused "one time" such as Marla Frazee's *Rollercoaster* for an example of the second part of this strategy (2003).

Prompts
- Think of some things you remember happening over and over again.
- Think about things that repeat year to year.
- Think about routines you have day to day.
- Take one of those "always times" and focus on it. Replay them in your mind.
- What is one specific time that stands out?

Hat Tip: *Writing a Life: Teaching Memoir to Sharpen Insight, Shape Meaning—and Triumph Over Tests* (Bomer 2005)

Your Life Matters!
Consider Your Life's Events, and:

1. Think of ones that have happened again & again.

2. Think of one that stands out:
   what happened?
   what was said?
   what did you feel?

3. Write that time bit-by-bit.

Barb Golub

Strategy Reread your notebook looking at the topics you've written about. Think about the new genre you plan to write in. Reimagine a previous entry written in the form of a new genre. Turn to a clean page and start a notebook entry exploring how it might go.

Teaching Tip In some curricula, one unit may focus on writing fiction and another, right on its heels, may focus on a completely different genre, such as writing persuasive letters. For some students, this abrupt shift is jarring, and they may feel empty-handed when it comes to getting started. This strategy is just right for them; helping them to see that the ideas in their notebooks have potential for other genres will empower them to ground the new experience and genre in the familiar and known.

Using a Mentor Find an author who writes across genres, and show students how the same ideas and topics in one genre end up in another. For example, Eloise Greenfield's book of poems *Honey I Love* (1995), her memoir *Childtimes: A Three-Generation Memoir* (1979), and her novel *Koya Delaney and the Good Girls Blues* (1992) all deal with themes of childhood and family.

Prompts
- What are some topics in the entry you're looking at? List them.
- Imagine how that topic might work in the new genre.
- Look at that! You found three new topics in that one story.
- Find something you wrote that you care about. What other topics might be in that entry that you care about?

Who is this for?

LEVELS
3–8

GENRE / TEXT TYPE
any

PROCESS
generating and collecting

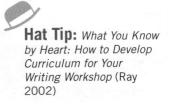

Hat Tip: *What You Know by Heart: How to Develop Curriculum for Your Writing Workshop* (Ray 2002)

3.21 Borrow a (Spark) Line

Who is this for?

LEVELS
3–8

GENRES / TEXT TYPES
poetry, narrative, essay

PROCESSES
generating and collecting, drafting

Strategy Start with a suggested trigger line or a borrowed line (from your notebook, another author's work, something you overheard). Listen to the line as you write it down, and let it jump-start the rest of your piece.

Teaching Tip Some suggested "sparks" are listed in the figure below. Encourage children to also go back through their notebooks to find single sentences or phrases that might make a good first line of a poem or to a notebook entry where they may have collected bits of language to inspire just this thing.

Using a Mentor "Where I'm From" by George Ella Lyon (1993) offers a great springboard for many children. Her website has a plethora of ideas of other places starting with this poem can take you (www.georgeellalyon.com/where.html).

Prompts

- Try to finish the line. What does that start make you think of?
- Now that you have a bunch of lines down, look back at them to see if you've figured out a topic you'd like to write more about.
- What will your next line be?
- Listen to that first line. Try to keep writing without picking up your pen (or judging yourself!). For this first draft, just get it down.

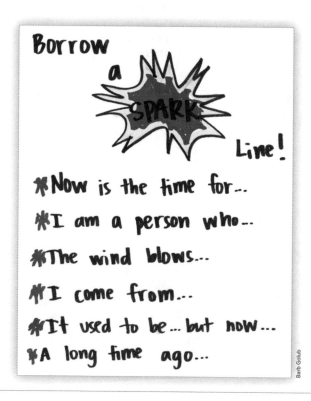

Hat Tip: *Explore Poetry* (Graves 1992)

3.22 Found Poems

Strategy Find something with print (a package of food in your kitchen, a sign, an article in the newspaper, a piece of mail). Look for some words that can begin a poem. Try rearranging the words and/or riffing off of certain lines.

Teaching Tip Beginning by creating a found poem can feel like a comfortable start for some writers because they are using existing words to get started. Sometimes the poem they create is the piece they end up wanting to work more on. Other times, this found poem can springboard the student into a narrative or even an essay. A more sophisticated spin on this strategy is to teach students to be aware of, and responsive to, the source material. For example, if it's a newspaper article, the poem might have something to do with the article's topic or feeling.

Prompts
- Start by writing down some of the words you find.
- Pause and think about what you've written down. Can you add on some of your own words or thinking?
- Feel the rhythm of the words. What could you write next to keep it going?
- You can ask yourself a question about what you've written so far to spark some new thinking and new words of your own.

Organic

Are they safer?
More nutritious?

It isn't clear.
Check the label. Get the facts before you shop.

Pesticides.
Food additives.
Environment.

Dilemma in the produce aisle.

"Found" from: Organic Foods: Are They Safer? More Nutritious?
Mayoclinic.org

Hat Tip: *Explore Poetry* (Graves 1992)

Who is this for?

LEVELS
3–8

GENRE / TEXT TYPE
poetry, mostly

PROCESSES
generating and collecting, drafting

Strategy Listen during your day for the lines you hear over and over again, or the actions you repeat again and again. Use this repetition from your day as a repeated line in your writing. Think about what you want your poem to be about, and add in your own words and details in between the repetition.

Lesson Language *When I think about my day and the lines I hear over and over that others say, I think about everyday niceties: "How are you?" "I'm good, and you?" and "Nice weather we're having today, huh?" I could write a poem with "How are you today?" as the first line of each stanza, and the rest of the stanza exploring what I might really want to say one day or another, if it didn't break with social norms to do so ("Just OK / If you want to know the truth. / Got some disappointing news. / How about you?"). Also, I think about the things I say to my children again and again, like "C'mon! Hurry up! We're going to be late," which I sometimes regret. I could write a poem using that line again and again with images of what would happen if I didn't rush them ("I see you there / glancing at the rainbow swirl / in the puddle").*

Prompts

- Think back across your day. Is there something you find yourself saying again and again?
- Think about a part of your day, say, every morning. Is there something you hear or do repeatedly?
- Now that you have your repeated line, what do you think you want your poem to be about?

Hat Tip: *Explore Poetry* (Graves 1992)

3.24 Wonder, "What If . . . ?"

Strategy Think of something you know to be true and real from your own life. Imagine, "What if . . . ?" and let your imagination take you to a new idea for character, plot, or theme.

Using a Mentor *Nothing Ever Happens on 90th Street* (Schotter 1999) is the story of a girl with an assignment from school to write about what happens in her neighborhood. She starts off feeling like this is a problem because nothing happens, but then she starts using her imagination, wondering "what if?" and creates fiction! It all starts when she imagines taking the Danish in her hand, breaking it into pieces and scattering it. What would happen? Maybe dozens of pigeons would swoop down, the baby in the carriage would get excited, and his ball would drop out of his hand. The ball would then roll into the street where a pizza delivery person on a bike would fall, and so on.

Prompts
- Let's start with a true story. Tell me something that happened.
- Now let's imagine "what if . . . ?" Try changing one of the characters.
- Let's imagine a change in the problem. What new problem might happen?
- Let's imagine a change in the setting. If that story took place somewhere else, what might have happened next?
- What is the real-life lesson from that event? Let's change it and imagine how the story would have unfolded differently.

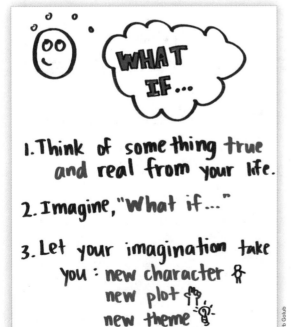

Barb Golub

Hat Tip: *Help! for Writers: 210 Solutions to the Problems Every Writer Faces* (Clark 2011)

Who is this for?

LEVELS
3–8

GENRE / TEXT TYPE
fictional narrative

PROCESS
generating and collecting

Who is this for?

LEVELS
3–8

GENRE / TEXT TYPE
fiction

PROCESS
generating and collecting

Strategy Make a three-column chart—one for characters, one for settings, and one for theme. List ideas in each column. Take one from each column and imagine "What if?" Write a blurb of a story idea. Repeat!

Prompts
- What ideas do you have for characters you might create?
- Let's start with realistic characters who are similar in age to you.
- Go back into your notebook and look for observations you've made of people. Those might make good characters!
- What settings can you think of?
- List some possible themes.
- You can think of themes that have come up in your life, or ones you've read in books.

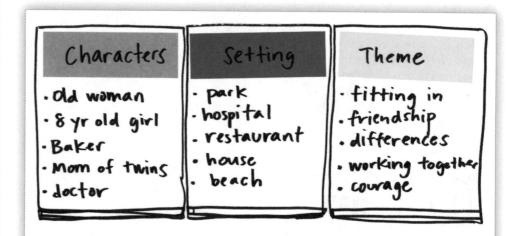

Hat Tip: Kate Messner, NCTE Workshop (2015b)

3.26 Word Mapping

Strategy Put a word related to your topic in a circle in the middle of your page. Draw lines out to other words that connect to the word in the circle. What branches out can be other single words that are related to the topic or details that support the topic. Look back at your map to see what surprises you and what connects. Then, move to your draft and include some of what you mapped.

Prompts

- Just do some free association. Start adding words that connect.
- Think of words or phrases.
- Try not to overthink it. The idea here is to brainstorm.
- Look back at all the words and phrases on your map.
- What surprises you?
- What connections can you make?
- What are you now thinking about your topic?
- What might be an angle your topic can take?

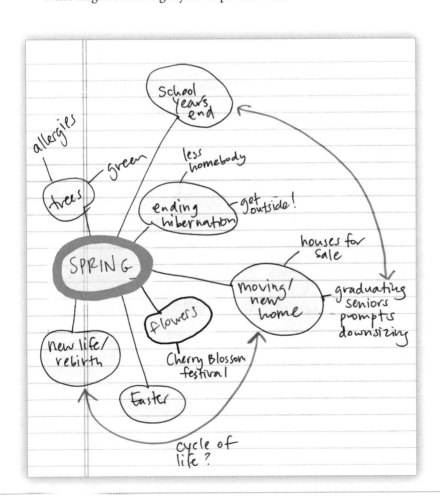

Who is this for?

LEVELS
3–8

GENRE / TEXT TYPE
any

PROCESSES
generating and collecting, developing

Hat Tip: *A Writer Teaches Writing* (Murray 1985)

Who is this for?

LEVELS

4–8

GENRE / TEXT TYPE

any

PROCESS

generating and collecting

Strategy Catch yourself in a moment of life where you realize there's something important, or something worth sharing. Jot down the kernel of an idea on anything you can find. Bring your kernel back to explore during writing time.

Lesson Language *Think about the spark that makes you take out your cell phone to snap a picture and share it on Instagram, Snapchat, or Facebook, or the one that nudges you to log in to Twitter to compose your 140-character insight. There's probably something in that moment that makes you say, "This is important. This matters." (Maybe, as long as you're not the kind of person that tweets about what you had for lunch!) There may also be something that makes you think, "There's an audience for this. I'm expecting a response." When you're out and about, living your life, you may meet a new person or see a new setting or have a strong feeling evoked that makes you say, "There's something to this. I need to write it down." You may just grab a napkin or gum wrapper, or you have your notebook in your backpack. Those small kernels you collect from being out in the world can be the beginnings of stories, poems, articles, or more later on.*

Prompts

- You'll practice this as you go about your day today, but just to give it a quick try now, let's think back on the last few hours. What was worth sharing?
- What moment happened that others (an audience) might be interested in hearing about, too?
- What kernel can you capture?
- Just from the last few hours, you've got three new possible writing starts. Try to carry this strategy with you into your afternoon and evening.

#Instagramworthy

What makes a moment worth capturing?

What was worth sharing today?

How can you capture the moment?

How might you be able to use this to share with others?

Can you write it in a story? A poem? An article?

Try it out!

Strategy If you have the beginning of an idea—a topic, maybe—but don't know where it's going or what to do with it, you can try to interview yourself, on paper. Try to explore all the corners of your idea by questioning why the idea matters, what might it lead to, what would happen if, what else you might be forgetting here, and so on.

Teaching Tip The questions you'd propose to students who want to try this strategy might change depending on the genre, and possibly also the audience. For example, if you wanted to explore a topic for an informational text, you might ask yourself, "What else is important here? What other details do I know that fit with this idea? How else can I explain it?" If you were working on a memoir, on the other hand, you might ask, "What else do I remember about this moment? What significance am I trying to bring out?"

Prompts

- Reread a bit. Ask yourself a question.
- If you were interviewing yourself, what would you ask yourself about this piece?
- Let's try to explore this idea a bit together.
- That question helped! You got some new ideas for where to go with the topic.

Self interview
FOR....
What did the Declaration say?

Q. What do I want to say about the independence?
A. I want to tell my readers to know why the concept of independence was important to the colonists, because now, independence is something people don't thing twice about, but back then, independence was a radical idea. I also want to say that independence was a risky idea, but it was so important that people didn't care

Q. Why did they take their anger out on the King?
A. I want to explain how despite the fact that it was British Parliment creating laws that the colonies opposed to, King George III is the one everyones outrage is being taken out on. This would be significant because it shows how despite the fact that they had a clear goal, they still had some mislead ideas.

Q. What message do I want to send?
A. I want to send the message that the Declaration of Independence was a radical idea, and that it was risky, but many people wanted independence too deeply to care.

Who is this for?

LEVELS
4–8

GENRE / TEXT TYPE
any

PROCESS
generating and collecting

Hat Tip: *Breathing In, Breathing Out: Keeping a Writer's Notebook* (Fletcher 1996)

3.29 Collect Triggers

Strategy Have your eyes and ears open to tidbits that may have no current practical purpose to your writing. Collect them for later use to jump-start a writing piece or to add in to something when you're revising.

Lesson Language *In Ralph Fletcher's* Breathing In, Breathing Out: Keeping a Writer's Notebook *(1996), he suggests the following types of "triggers":*

- *Odd Facts—from a radio interview, a newspaper clipping, or something your father mentions at breakfast.*
- *Questions—Go about your life with a sense of wonder. When you have questions, especially the sort that feel unanswerable, jot them down.*
- *Odds and Ends—memories, something funny your little brother said, a description of how the cicadas sound on an August evening. This is the "stuff" that is maybe uncategorizable.*
- *Lists—of names of potential characters, places you've been, possible titles for the future.*
- *Lines and Insights—one-liners from other authors' writing or something you overheard. These could also be one-liners you make up (even if you don't know how they'd apply to a piece of writing you've written or want to write).*

Teaching Tip Each of the bulleted items above could be its own lesson/strategy. You may consider teaching them as a "string" of lessons for various types of ways to use a notebook.

Prompts
- Can you think of some triggers?
- What kinds of things do you plan to write down?
- At first, it may help to focus on something as you go about your life. Which type do you want to focus on?

Hat Tip: *Breathing In, Breathing Out: Keeping a Writer's Notebook* (Fletcher 1996)

3.30 Subtopics Hiding in Topics

Strategy Think about a writing project you worked on in the past that you were really on fire about. List out some of the topics and ideas that were a part of that writing project. Work alone or with a partner to think about how some of those subtopics might become a writing piece.

Lesson Language *Say I wrote a story about a day at a baseball game with my dad. Within that story, there are many subtopics that may be worth returning to: baseball, competition, fandom, spending time with my dad, and so on. Maybe I want to take on one of those smaller topics, or take on the original topic in a new way.*

Using a Mentor By studying across an author's body of work, you're likely to find connections. For example, you can look at Patricia Polacco's work and see that she is a writer of realistic fiction, with stories that often stem from real events in her childhood—her relationship with her own grandmother (Babushka), for example, inspired her to create young characters who interact with elderly ones in almost all of her books. Every story is different, but the themes are the same. Or, look at some of Kate Messner's nonfiction: She wrote *Up in the Garden and Down in the Dirt* (2015c), a book about life above and below ground, and she also wrote *Over and Under the Snow* (2011), about life above and below ground during winter.

Prompts
- What's a project you can remember loving to work on?
- What was it about that project that you loved?
- List some of the topics and ideas that were a part of that project.
- Yes, that's one main thing that the project was about. What are some others?
- Name some subtopics.

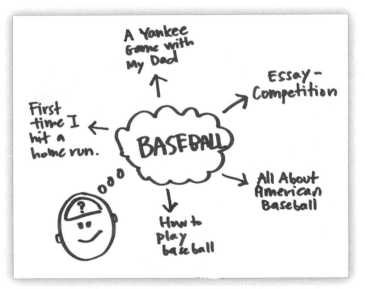

Who is this for?

LEVELS
4–8

GENRE / TEXT TYPE
any

PROCESS
generating and collecting

Hat Tip: *A Quick Guide to Reaching Struggling Writers, K–5* (Cruz 2008)

3.31 Purposefully Wander

Strategy Start with any idea that is interesting to you. Start writing, trying not to let your pen stop. Don't force yourself to focus on the idea that started the piece; instead, let your mind wander to explore new corners and tangents of the idea. Look back across your entry and circle or underline new ideas for topics that came up in the midst of writing.

Prompts
- Let yourself go off to a new topic.
- Think about what that reminds you of. Where might you go next?
- Look back at all you've written. Do you see new ideas hiding?
- Let yourself get off-topic. Reflect, wonder, wander.

> It's a beautiful spring day and I can't help thinking about how brown and gray the world was just a couple weeks ago—and now everything is bright, green, and alive. This makes me think about resilience and how living things have an ability to bounce back. Like that time I was in a bike race and fell, and then the race was over, a hospital visit, and later instead of giving up, I still tried to do the race (although by myself). Lots of memories happened at that lake – swimming in the summer, walking our crazy dog. Oh! That time she ran away off-leash and we didn't find her til sundown.
>
> *Transition from observation to big idea.*
> *Transition from idea to "one time" story*
> *Wander to other memories in same setting*
> *Focus in on one, different memory*

Hat Tip: *What You Know by Heart: How to Develop Curriculum for Your Writing Workshop* (Ray 2002)

Strategy Think about some abstract concepts and issues that are important in our world. Think about a specific example that would allow you to explore the bigger concept or issue. Choose a genre and write an entry trying it out.

Prompts
- What does this issue bring to mind for you?
- When you think about this issue, what do you think about?
- List some possible topics that connect to this issue.
- What's a specific example?
- Can you imagine what genre you may want to be writing in?

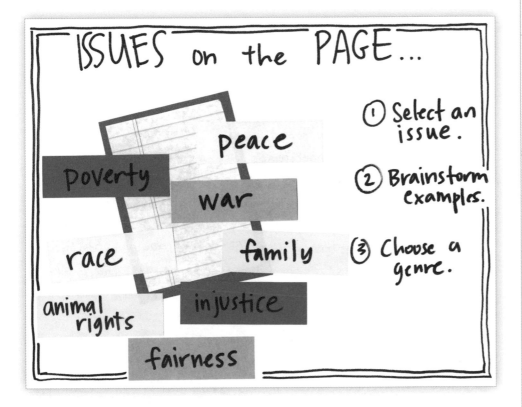

Who is this for?

LEVELS

4–8

GENRE / TEXT TYPE

any

PROCESSES

generating and collecting, drafting

Hat Tip: *For a Better World: Reading and Writing for Social Action* (Bomer and Bomer 2001)

Who is this for?

LEVELS
4–8

GENRE / TEXT TYPE
fictional narrative

PROCESS
generating and collecting

Strategy Look through each section of the newspaper or online news site for kernels of story ideas. Take something true (a missing pet, a fire a few blocks away, a wedding) and spin it into a possible idea for a fictional story. Think about what true details you'll keep and what elements of the story (character, setting, problem) you'll fictionalize.

Prompts

• Let's look together at the stories in today's newspaper. As we scan this first page, let's just jot down single words that jump out as possible topics.
• What's something you read about? How can that become a story idea for you?
• Don't forget the often-forgotten sections. Wedding announcements? Police blotter?
• Within one article, there may be many ideas hiding. Let's list them.

Scan the Newspaper

Words/ for possible story topics:
stories in newspaper

• How no one wants to be Trump's vice president —This could lead to a story about a bully who was team captain for a kickball team in school, but no one wanted to be on her team.
• There was a young woman who was forced to join the FARC rebels in Colombia — This can lead to a story about a boy/girl who was in a popular group at school, and the leader of the popular group was controlling and made her/him to crazy things
• There was an article about a prototype for a super-sonic vaccum, but it was really expensive. This can lead to a story about a new spacecraft that everyone is bidding for, but is $100,000,000,000.

Hat Tip: *Help! for Writers: 210 Solutions to the Problems Every Writer Faces* (Clark 2011)

Strategy Find a book, magazine, or newspaper article on a topic you know almost nothing about. Read about the topic with an open mind, allowing the information the author writes about to spark a new idea for your own writing.

Prompts

- What are some topics you know nothing about, but that you're interested in learning about?
- As you read what you've chosen, try to list some possible ideas for your own writing.
- Based on what you've read so far, what ideas do you have for your writing?
- You came up with several ideas just from that first chapter!
- What kind of writing do you think you'll make?

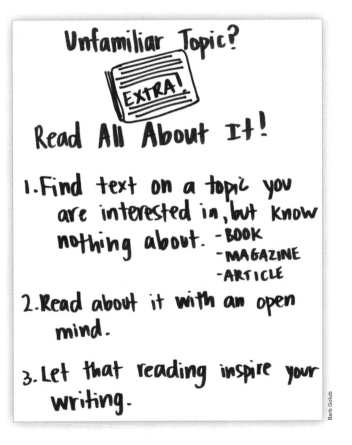

Barb Golub

Who is this for?

LEVELS
4–8

GENRE / TEXT TYPE
any

PROCESS
generating and collecting

Hat Tip: *Help! for Writers: 210 Solutions to the Problems Every Writer Faces* (Clark 2011)

3.35 Person vs. Nature

Who is this for?

LEVELS
4–8

GENRE / TEXT TYPE
narrative

PROCESSES
generating and collecting, developing

Strategy Think of a character and something in nature (a storm, an animal, a landform) that could pose a conflict. Imagine the change that would happen in the character if she faced that conflict.

Teaching Tip In a series of lessons, you may also introduce person vs. person conflicts, such as *Romeo and Juliet* and person vs. self conflicts such as *Ish* by Peter Reynolds (2004) about a boy who starts to doubt his own art abilities and finally comes to terms with his art looking like an approximation (-*ish*) of what he's making, and share examples of these types with children.

Using a Mentor *Brave Irene* by William Steig (1986) and *Hatchet* by Gary Paulsen (1987) are good examples of texts that pit a person against nature as the original conflict or problem. You would only need to share short excerpts, or even a summary, of the book for students to get the idea! You could then return to the texts to discuss with children how the writer elaborates to tell us both the "outside story" of the storm or the harsh conditions of the forest, and then the "inside story" of how the character is dealing with the challenges, growing, and changing.

Prompts

- You've got a clear idea of your character.
- Let's think now about obstacles. List some.
- What type of obstacle might that character face?
- Consider that obstacle. What change would the character experience when dealing with it?

Hat Tip: *Nonfiction Craft Lessons: Teaching Information Writing K–8* (Portalupi and Fletcher 2001)

Strategy Decide on a new place to visit. Go there with no more than a notebook and a set of listening ears and observing eyes. Let yourself pick up on conversation and details of the person. Jot down what you observe, and also what you imagine, about the people you see.

Teaching Tip This strategy will take you outside of the classroom, so it would work well as a whole-class lesson followed by a field trip, or as a suggestion to a student, group, or class for independent writing outside of the school day.

Prompts

- When you're in that new place, try to notice the people. See if any might make a good character.
- In that place, listen in on bits of conversation. Record conversation you think you might use.
- What will you be listening for?
- What details in the place might you want to capture for your own writing?

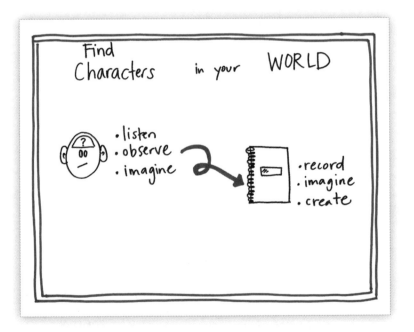

LEVELS
4–8

GENRE / TEXT TYPE
any

PROCESS
generating and collecting

Who is this for?

Hat Tip: *Help! for Writers: 210 Solutions to the Problems Every Writer Faces* (Clark 2011)

Who is this for?

LEVELS
4–8

GENRE / TEXT TYPE
narrative

PROCESS
generating and collecting

Strategy Think back to small moments in your life that are full of meaning and importance (a first or last time, a time when something changed, a time when you conquered something, and so on). Make a list, then choose one to try out writing the story.

Teaching Tip This strategy could be tweaked to include genres beyond personal narrative or memoir. Students might change details about their experience to create a fictional piece. Also, the significant moment and reflections on the moment could help students develop a thesis statement, which then could lead them to essay.

Using a Mentor Share with children a story that you know is inspired by an author's true life. For example, Patricia Polacco's *Thank You Mr. Falker* (1998), which tells the true story of Tricia's struggles with reading and the teacher who helped her to overcome them.

Prompts

- Can you think of a moment in your life that is full of meaning?
- Think about a first time, or a last time.
- How about moments with strong feelings? Name a feeling and start brainstorming.
- Try to get a few ideas down on the page; you can consider which one will work in a moment.
- You've got a list full of ideas. Choose one to start trying it.
- When you try it, storytell it.

Hat Tip: *Writing a Life: Teaching Memoir to Sharpen Insight, Shape Meaning—and Triumph Over Tests* (Bomer 2005)

Defining Moments

Small Important Moments
- The first time I walked into town with my friend, not my parents
- The fist time I bought something with my own money
- The first time I gave a gift to someone that I worked really hard on
- When my sister moved out of our room.
- A time when I had homework from every subject and two tests the next day in 6th grade, and I realized middle school was gonna be a lot harder than elementary school.
- When I jumped off the second tower at the pool

I told myself not to look down, but my eyes seemed magnetized towards the bottom of the pool. My breath catched. There was something so downright terrifying and magnificent of looking down at the people watching me, instead of being one of the people at the bottom, watching people jump. 'Just one step forward.' I thought, 'That's all you have to do.' But it was more than one step forward. It was throwing myself off this platform, not knowing where the wind was going to take me, or how it would feel when I hit the water.

3.38 Start with an Outlandish Claim

Strategy Start a notebook entry with a strong claim. Feel free to be outlandish, and use strong words and phrases such as *always, no one, everyone, never,* or *for sure.* Use that claim as a springboard to start freewriting, and see where your pencil takes you!

Teaching Tip To aid in freewriting, you may remind students of sentence starters that help to keep conversation going, and ask them to use the sentence starters to bridge between one idea and another on the page. Phrases such as "I'm not sure, but maybe . . ." or "On the other hand . . ." or "Some people think . . . But I think . . ."

Prompts
- Make that claim stronger—use a word like *everyone, for sure, never.*
- It's OK if you don't believe it 100 percent. Start with the claim and see where it takes you.
- Start freewriting.
- Write, "On the other hand . . ." and explore where that takes you.
- Try to write without judging yourself. Just keep your pen moving.

> Parents are always responsible for their children's behavior.
>
> So much is said about a parent's responsibility to raise responsible, caring people who will make an impact on the world. Of course, people who do horrible things often wind up on the news and people find themselves asking, "But what kind of parents would raise that!?" The question suggests that parents are at fault for a stupid mistake, or horrible act, but is that always really true? At what point does a child's free will take over and leave behind the morals the parents work to instill? On the other hand, there are parents who neglect or abuse children and the children end up being not only ok, but people determined not to repeat the mistakes of the ones who raised them. So how does it happen? Who's to blame?

Who is this for?

LEVELS
4–8

GENRES / TEXT TYPES
opinion/persuasive, memoir

PROCESS
generating and collecting

Hat Tip: *The Journey Is Everything: Teaching Essays That Students Want to Write for People Who Want to Read Them* (Bomer 2016)

Goal
4

Focus/Meaning

◎ Why is this goal important?

Readers usually expect that a piece of writing is about something and that the author communicates a point. For example, if you were to read an op-ed about a candidate for a presidential election, you'd expect that the author wouldn't use half his allotted space to discuss penguins stranded in the arctic. Also, because the piece is an op-ed, you would expect that it not only covers the candidates but also the author's opinion—in this case, which candidate would better lead the country. When we read a David Sedaris memoir, we expect to laugh, and we also expect that the story he tells us fits in to the larger narrative he's sharing about his life, or that he is making a point about the experience he shared so that readers can take away something and learn from it. Even our youngest writers who tell and draw stories can learn to focus their work so that the story doesn't go on and on and on. For example, we can teach them to find the part of the story that's the most interesting and tell just that part.

When in the writing process do writers figure out a focus and decide on the point they want their writing to make? Interview a room of writers and you'll likely get a range of responses. Some writers can develop a focus before writing, but that doesn't mean it'll always go as planned. Writing is itself an "act of discovery" and it's possible that through the process of writing, a new focus, angle, meaning, or perspective will emerge (Murray 1985, 18). So, for some, reading over what they've written, reflecting on what it is they truly want to say, and revising with that in mind will make more sense. It is often helpful to teach student writers that it's important to have a focal point in mind when they begin to write—wandering aimlessly on the page is not too helpful, except occasionally during the phases when writers generate or develop ideas—but they should also be open to discovering new possibilities as they write. The strategies in this chapter will help writers to discover and plan for focus before, during, and after drafting—across the many phases of the writing process.

It's also true that the strategies in this chapter will work together with strategies in other chapters. After all, meaning isn't just communicated in one single statement—an author maintains her focus on a piece's meaning by choosing to include or leave out particular details. As Ralph Fletcher (1993) writes, "Every part, every *word*, depends on its relationship to the whole" (4). Also, the genre the author chooses and the structure within that genre also help to support the intended focus and meaning. As mentioned earlier, an opinion piece needs to be focused not only on a topic but also on an opinion about the topic. An informational piece may be focused broadly on a topic or more narrowly on a subtopic. Stories can be focused by time (telling just one scene or a small moment) or meaning (centered around a message or theme).

◎ How do I know if this goal is right for my student?

You may be able to determine if students could use support with this goal by reading their writing and talking to them about it. Ask, "What is it you think your piece is mostly about?" and consider their response in the context of their age, the level of writing development, and the genre they've chosen. For example, a student who is writing a narrative can choose to focus in time (i.e., writing about just a roller coaster ride instead of the entire day, or just a day during his vacation instead of the entire week at Disneyland) or in meaning/theme (e.g., not only telling about the roller coaster ride, but angling the story to show how important it is to overcome your fears). A writer who works on an informational piece may choose to write an "all about" (e.g., "All About Dogs") or be more focused (e.g., "Dalmatians") or more focused still (e.g., "Dalmatians Are Amazing Pets!"). Likewise with opinion writing, consider if the student is centered on a topic (littering) or an opinion (we should stop littering) or a complex idea (littering is not only an eyesore but also negatively impacts our environment). Look at the details she's chosen to include in her piece, and consider if the details she's chosen support her main point or focus, or if there are details that distract from it. Students who have a difficult time articulating their focus, or matching the details they've chosen to the focus, will benefit from the lessons in this chapter.

Readers usually expect that a piece of writing is about something and that the author communicates a point.

—Jennifer Serravallo

Strategies for Writing with Focus and Meaning

Strategy	Grade Levels	Genres/Text Types	Processes
4.1 Make Your Pictures and Your Words Agree	K–2	Any	Drafting, revising
4.2 Focus in Time	Late K–3	Narrative	Generating and collecting, choosing, developing
4.3 Find the Heart	2–8	Narrative	Revising
4.4 Write a Title	2–8	Any	Generating and collecting, choosing, developing
4.5 Write About a Pebble	2–8	Any	Generating and collecting, revising
4.6 Zoom In on a Moment of Importance	4–8	Personal narrative, memoir	Choosing, revising
4.7 Ask Questions to Focus	4–8	Any	Choosing, developing, revising
4.8 Find Your Passion to Focus	4–8	Informational/nonfiction, opinion/persuasive	Choosing, developing, revising
4.9 Imagine Your Audience and Consider Your Purpose	4–8	Any	Choosing, developing
4.10 Write a Poem to Try On a Focus	4–8	Narrative, informational/nonfiction, opinion/persuasive	Choosing, revising
4.11 Cut It to the Bone	4–8	Any	Choosing, revising
4.12 Underline One Line (That Says the Most)	4–8	Any	Revising
4.13 Their Topic, Your Idea	4–8	Any	Choosing, developing, drafting
4.14 Use a Search Engine to Find Connections	4–8	Informational/nonfiction, opinion/persuasive	Generating and collecting, choosing, developing
4.15 Focus on an Image	4–8	Any	Developing, revising
4.16 Find a Theme in Your Collection	4–8	Any	Developing
4.17 Craft an "Elevator Speech"	4–8	Any	Developing, revising
4.18 Craft a Thesis	4–8	Opinion/persuasive	Generating and collecting, developing, choosing
4.19 The "So What?" Rule	4–8	Any	Developing, revising
4.20 Write "Off the Page"	5–8	Any	Revising
4.21 Focus on an Issue	5–8	Any	Generating and collecting, developing, rehearsing, choosing
4.22 What Problem Are You Solving?	5–8	Opinion/persuasive	Revising
4.23 Experimental Draft to Find Focus	5–8	Any	Drafting, revising
4.24 Let Available Sources Steer Your Focus	5–8	Informational/nonfiction, opinion/persuasive	Choosing, developing, revising
4.25 Shape Your Focus with Active Verbs	5–8	Informational/nonfiction, opinion/persuasive	Developing, revising

4.1 Make Your Pictures and Your Words Agree

Who is this for?

LEVELS
K–2

GENRE / TEXT TYPE
any

PROCESSES
drafting, revising

Strategy Make sure the pictures on each page agree with the words that are on that same page. Look back at all the parts of the picture. Read the words. Make any changes so that they go together.

Lesson Language *So often in picture books, the illustrations or photographs will extend what's written in the words. The pictures and the words go together, because they are both about the same moment in time (in story) or the same topic or subtopic (information). Let's look together at a few class favorites to see how the author isn't always writing the same thing as what's in the picture, but the pictures and the words clearly agree.*

Teaching Tip For primary elementary students who may draw or sketch as a planning technique prior to writing the words on the page, you can tweak the language of this strategy to encourage them to look at their picture/plan to make sure what they write goes with what they've planned to write, according to their picture.

Prompts
- Look at all the parts of your picture.
- Now that you know what's in your picture, let's read the words.
- Do all the words agree with all the parts of your picture?
- What do you think you'll need to change? The pictures or the words? Or both?
- Make them go together.
- I agree—the pictures and words agree.
- Keep trying the other pages on your own, making sure the pictures and the words go together.

Hat Tip: *One to One: The Art of Conferring with Young Writers* (Calkins, Hartman, and White 2005)

4.2 Focus in Time

Strategy Create a timeline, including each five- to ten-minute event that was part of the story. Go back to your timeline, and star the one dot that seems to be most important. Start your draft at minute 1 and end at minute 10. Ask yourself, "Did I tell the story I wanted to tell, or do I need to add in another 'dot' from my timeline to get my story across?"

Teaching Tip Focusing a story in time is often the first way children learn to focus, because it's more concrete than focusing on theme or meaning. When students start to focus on time, don't be surprised if their stories are suddenly short! You'll often need to couple instruction about *focus* with instruction about *elaboration* (see Chapter 6 for strategies to support elaboration).

Using a Mentor Here are a few of my favorite books for showing children how an author can write page after page, while staying focused in one small amount of time: *Owl Moon* by Jane Yolen (1987), *The Paperboy* by Dav Pilkey (1996), *Roller Coaster* by Marla Frazee (2003), *The Leaving Morning* by Angela Johnson (2000), and *Whistling* by Elizabeth Partridge (2003).

Prompts
- Let's work on the timeline. Each dot is an event.
- Star the one dot that is most important.
- If you focus on just that dot, are you getting across what you hope to?
- Will that stay focused in time?
- Your plan is for a story that is focused in time, and meaning!

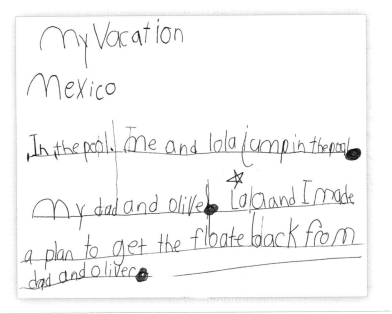

Who is this for?

LEVELS
late K–3

GENRE / TEXT TYPE
narrative

PROCESSES
generating and collecting, choosing, developing

Hat Tip: *Craft Lessons: Teaching Writing K–8, Second Edition* (Portalupi and Fletcher 2007)

4.5 Write About a Pebble

Who is this for?

LEVELS
2–8

GENRE / TEXT TYPE
any

PROCESSES
generating and collecting, revising

Hat Tip: *In the Middle, Third Edition: A Lifetime of Learning About Writing, Reading, and Adolescents* (Atwell 2014)

Strategy Don't write about a general topic or idea, write about a specific, observable experience, person, place, time, and so on. Use the language frame, "Don't write about [a mountain], write about [a pebble]" to help you explore ways to narrow the focus of your piece.

Lesson Language *Don't write about* winter, *write about* a specific winter day. *Observe the surroundings and write with detail to make readers feel they are there.*

Don't write about winter, *write about* a time that matters to a particular person by sharing a moment from one winter's day.

Don't write about winter, *zoom in on a* specific creature thriving in winter. *Try to see that creature in a new way, like a poet would, writing with description and metaphor.*

Using a Mentor Gather a collection of texts, perhaps across genres, about a common general topic that is dealt with differently. For example, *Billy Twitters and His Blue Whale Problem* (Barnett 2009), a humorous picture book about a boy who receives a whale from his parents as a consequence for not being responsible, could be compared to *Big Blue Whale,* a nonfiction book by Nicola Davies (2000), or the poem "Blue Whale" by Viraj Bhanshaly about how initial misunderstandings about a blue whale changed into an appreciation for them and a desire to protect them.

Prompts
- That is a general topic. What is something observable?
- What specific experience do you think of when you consider that topic?
- What specific person or place comes to mind?
- Write about something you could experience.
- When you focus, it helps your reader to experience what you're writing about.

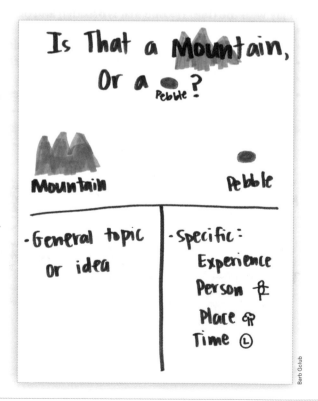

Barb Golub

4.6 Zoom In on a Moment of Importance

Strategy Think about a memory and all the events that are part of that memory. Think about what's important about that memory, or the big idea the memory leaves you with. Identify the one part of the memory that feels the most important. Write some ideas about what's important about it, and why it's important. Try to write just that one smaller part of the larger moment. Tell it bit by bit.

Lesson Language *Writing small can sometimes help you tell a big idea. For example, I could tell a story about two weeks I spent at my grandparents' house the summer when I was eight. But if I think back on all the good memories of that time, I could zoom in on just one smaller moment that shows the love between me and my grandparents. That love is the most important thing that I want to show in my piece. In this case, I probably wouldn't choose go-cart racing, although it's one thing we did and it was fun. Instead, I'd more likely choose a part of those two weeks, like the time my grandmother taught me how to make her meatballs for the first time. The story of standing beside her in the kitchen as she taught me a family recipe: I think that shows love more than the story of me in a helmet zipping around a race track. When I draft, I'll tell just that part of the larger memory bit by bit, helping my reader to experience the moment along with me.*

Teaching Tip The amount a writer will be able to reflect on the overall significance of a small moment will depend on her maturity level and experience with writing. For younger children, you may want to suggest choosing a small moment that will make a good story, rather than one imbued with a deep or heavy significance, or simply encourage them to narrow down the window of time.

Prompts

- What moment out of all of these do you want to zoom in on?
- Replay the whole story in your mind. Pick one smaller part that seems important.
- I'm going to list all the smaller moments you just mentioned to me. You tell me which you'd choose, OK?

Merridy Gnagey

Who is this for?

LEVELS
4–8

GENRES / TEXT TYPES
personal narrative, memoir

PROCESSES
choosing, revising

Hat Tip: *Small Moments: Writing with Focus, Detail, and Dialogue* (Calkins, Smith, and Rothman 2013)

Who is this for?

LEVELS

4–8

GENRE / TEXT TYPE

any

PROCESSES

choosing, developing, revising

Strategy When you realize your topic may be too big or broad, you can ask yourself questions to help focus it. You may ask, "What is it that I'm really trying to say? What am I most curious about? What do I wonder? What do I think or believe about my topic?"

Lesson Language *You may find as you write about your topic that you're trying to cover way too much. If you're writing a story, this might mean you're writing all about a two-week vacation, and you instead need to narrow down some of the time instead of telling all about it. Or that you're including too much background material on the characters and need to get the plot moving. If you're writing a nonfiction piece, you might realize you're writing a topic so broad that most authors take an entire textbook to adequately cover the material. When this happens, it's a good sign that you need to focus. Asking questions can get you to the real heart of what you're trying to write about or what aspect of the topic you're most interested in exploring in detail.*

Using a Mentor To support this lesson, you may choose to gather a variety of texts that range from broad to narrow in terms of focus. For example, you might grab a book called *The Ocean*, another called *Whales*, and still another called *Humpback Whales*. You can lead students in thinking about their topic and what narrower versions of it might be.

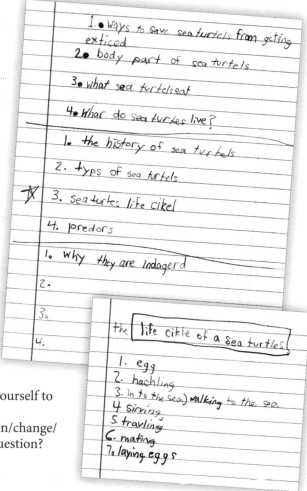

Prompts

- What are you really trying to say?
- What's most important about your topic?
- What questions can you ask yourself to help you narrow your topic?
- What are you going to work on/change/add/revise after asking that question?

Hat Tip: *Finding the Heart of Nonfiction: Teaching 7 Essential Craft Tools with Mentor Texts* (Heard 2013)

4.8 Find Your Passion to Focus

Strategy Think about your topic and the aspect of it that you're most connected to. Identify your passion and/or what you really think, feel, and believe about your topic. Write about just that part.

Lesson Language *We started writing our class piece after visiting the museum on the Upper East Side of the city and noticing that there was no garbage on the sidewalks and the snow had been carted away. Meanwhile, in the Bronx, we have lots of garbage and it's intermingled with the snow. So gross. We started wondering about why this is; we interviewed people, and we learned some information. But now I need to step back and ask myself why I really care about this. What's the part that I'm most on fire about? I think to me it's about fairness. We are in the same city, yet certain parts of town have better sanitation services. I think I want to write a letter to our mayor arguing for better sanitation in the Bronx. See how I went from a topic—garbage across the city—and narrowed down a focus? Actually, even an audience, too.*

Using a Mentor You may consider using a persuasive blogger's short piece to demonstrate how a topic can become slanted/angled/focused based on a passion. See, for example, Michael Moore's post, "10 Things They Won't Tell You about The Flint Water Tragedy: But I Will."

Prompts

- What do you really feel about your topic?
- What about this topic made you want to write about it?
- Talk about your beliefs for a couple of minutes.
- When you started, how did you feel about the topic? How are you feeling about it now?
- Of everything you've written, find the part that matters most.
- If you strayed from what you wanted to write about, how might you get back on track?

Find Your **PASSION!**

1. Think about your topic.
   → What are you most ~~connected~~ to?

2. Identify your passion.
   → What do you really ~~think, feel, believe?~~

3. Write about just that!

Barb Golub

Who is this for?

LEVELS
4–8

GENRES / TEXT TYPES
**informational/
nonfiction, opinion/
persuasive**

PROCESSES
**choosing, developing,
revising**

Hat Tip: *The Revision Toolbox: Teaching Techniques That Work* (Heard 2002)

4.9 Imagine Your Audience and Consider Your Purpose

Who is this for?

LEVELS
4–8

GENRE / TEXT TYPE
any

PROCESSES
choosing, developing

Strategy Think about your purpose for writing. Consider if you are aiming to persuade, entertain, or teach your reader. Then, think specifically about the person or people you want to read what you write. Focus your topic, or the angle about your topic.

Lesson Language *I hope you've chosen your topic because it's one that you really care about. But it's also important to think about where the writing is going to go when it's finished. Who will read it? Why would they be interested in it?*

For example, if I were going to write about dogs for someone who just received a dog, I might decide to write an informational piece that teaches my reader how to take care of a dog, what sorts of supplies to make sure they have, and maybe some simple tips about how to train the dog. If, however, I was a child trying to convince my parents that we are ready to add a dog to our family, I would probably be writing a persuasive letter. My focus wouldn't tell all about dogs, but instead would be focused on the idea that I'm responsible and I'm ready to help take care of the dog my family would adopt as a pet.

Prompts

- Who are you writing it to/for? What aspect would they be most interested in?
- What genre best fits your intention?
- Explain your purpose for writing.
- Now that you know who you're writing for, and what topic you want to write, we can think about the angle on your topic.

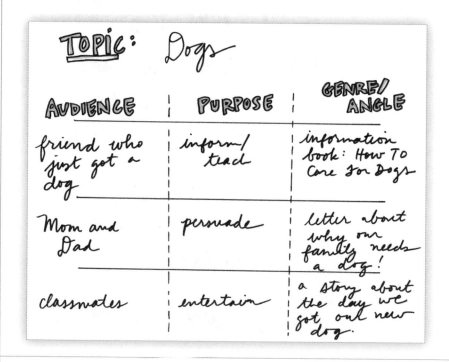

Hat Tip: *Finding the Heart of Nonfiction: Teaching 7 Essential Craft Tools with Mentor Texts* (Heard 2013)

Strategy Think about your story/nonfiction/essay topic. Consider the images, feeling, tone that the topic makes you think of. Write a poem about your topic, then reread your poem with the question, "What does it seem like the heart of my topic is, based on what I've chosen to write in my poem?"

Teaching Tip This strategy will also support students' word choices, and is similar to strategy 7.21, "Short → Long → Short," in the chapter on word choice.

Prompts

- Reread your piece. Now try to write it as a poem.
- Let's look at the poem you wrote. What are the essential details you kept?
- Consider what words you'd use when you take this multipage draft and condense it into a poem.
- Reread your poem. What does it seem like the focus of your piece is?
- Look back at your piece and cut what's not needed, and elaborate on parts connected to your focus.

Who is this for?

LEVELS
4–8

GENRES / TEXT TYPES
narrative, informational/ nonfiction, opinion/ persuasive

PROCESSES
choosing, revising

Hat Tip: *Explore Poetry* (Graves 1992)

Who is this for?

LEVELS
4–8

GENRE / TEXT TYPE
any

PROCESSES
choosing, revising

Strategy Think, or jot down, the main purpose of your writing (it could be a main idea, a main argument, or a theme). Reread your draft looking for anything you can possibly cut because it does not connect to, elaborate on, or in any way help your purpose.

Using a Mentor Cutting something you've drafted is one of the hardest things for a writer to do! Sometimes it helps to know that what gets cut might get used elsewhere. Other times, it helps to know that what you cut was weighing down the piece and with it gone, the writing is clearer, more focused, and more purposeful. You can share the following Stephen King quote, if it's appropriate for the age you teach: "Kill your darlings, kill your darlings, even when it breaks your egocentric little scribbler's heart, kill your darlings" (2000, 222).

Prompts

- Name your focus.
- What is the most important idea/theme/argument?
- What are you hoping your reader is left with?
- Let's go part by part. Tell me what stays and what goes.
- It seems like that doesn't connect to your focus. Do you think it should get cut?
- I know it's hard, but I think it needs to be cut. As you just said, it doesn't help your focus.
- Save that for another piece.

Hat Tip: *In the Middle, Third Edition: A Lifetime of Learning About Writing, Reading, and Adolescents* (Atwell 2014)

Strategy Look over your piece. Underline the one line that says the most about what you want your piece to be about. If you need to change or reword that one line, do it. Reread your whole piece with that one line in mind. Think about how you'll enhance some lines to complement the one you've chosen. Think about what lines you want to get rid of to maintain the focus on your chosen line.

Teaching Tip In persuasive writing (essays, speeches, reviews), the one line will often be the thesis statement or the claim. In poetry, there may be a line that keeps repeating, or a first or final line in the poem. In narrative writing, your writers may find that there is a concluding thought left on the page by the narrator or one of the main characters. In informational writing, the writer may be encouraged to look at the introduction or conclusion to find a sentence that states not only what the topic of the piece is, but what the author's angle on the topic, or main idea, might be.

Prompts

- What do you think your piece is really about?
- Let's look through your piece to find one line that captures that meaning.
- Now that you have your focus (with this line), let's reread.
- What do you need to cut/change/add to keep it focused?
- Talk about why that line captures your meaning.
- You found one line—that will help you with your piece's focus.

> **Underline One Line!**
>
> 1. Look over your piece.
> 2. Underline the ONE LINE that says the most (what do you want your piece to be about?).
> 3. Re-read your piece with that line in mind
> 4. What do you need to add? Take away?
>
> Barb Golub

Who is this for?

LEVELS
4–8

GENRE / TEXT TYPE
any

PROCESS
revising

Hat Tip: *Explore Poetry* (Graves 1992)

4.13 Their Topic, Your Idea

LEVELS
4–8

GENRE / TEXT TYPE
any

PROCESSES
choosing, developing,
drafting

Hat Tip: *Help! For
Writers: 210 Solutions to
the Problems Every Writer
Faces* (Clark 2011)

Strategy When you're given an assignment or need to write to a prompt, think about what your spin will be. Make a list of different angles and ideas that connect to your assignment or prompt. Choose one and do an exploratory draft.

Lesson Language *Journalists are often given story topics to cover. "Go cover the accident on Route 22," the boss might say. A good journalist tries to find the story, though, going beyond the obvious who, what, where, when, and why of the accident. Yes, those facts are important, but coming up with a way to draw the reader in and make the writing your own is also important. Perhaps the slant can be to focus on one of the people involved in the accident, and what led up to it. Another journalist might see the accident as a springboard to write about texting while driving, bringing in information about more than just that specific accident. Still another journalist might look into the commonality of accidents on that stretch of road and the legislation that's been attempted to make the road safer. Whether you're in a testing situation, or you're given an assignment by a teacher, or someday a boss, try to give it your own spin.*

Prompts

- Brainstorm some spins you could take on the topic.
- What idea connects to that?
- The obvious way to answer that would be to _____. Try to be subtle, not obvious. What might you write?
- You came up with a unique angle on that topic.

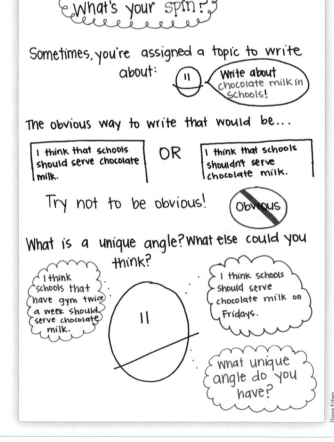

Diana Erben

Strategy Type your topic into a search engine. Explore the different angles and spins on your topic in the articles, blogs, ads, and posts that arise. After you've read, reflect. Ask yourself, "What subtopic/angle most interests me? What angle do I want to explore in my own writing?"

Lesson Language *I know that guns in America is a big topic right now, and I want to write a piece about it, but I'm not quite sure what I want my angle to be. I put "gun rights in America" into a search engine and I got a lot of possible subtopics and angles. There's a group called "Moms Demand Action for Gun Sense in America"—clearly a group that's for more gun control. Then I see some specific stories about gun violence in America and mass shootings, and I could explore any one of those specific stories. I see some links about how gun rights in America compares to that of other countries. And I also see some links that would allow me to read up on specific politician's statements and positions on gun ownership. From all of these, I think the mom angle is most interesting. I think about it being a political issue, but exploring this mom group further might help me understand the personal behind this topic, too.*

Prompts

- Search and read about your topic.
- List some of the subtopics and angles that come up that are related to your topic.
- What is surprising?
- What interests you?
- Think about what you might want your own piece to be about.
- Are there any surprises? What interests you about those surprises?

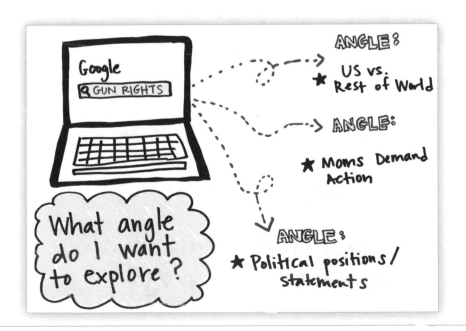

Who is this for?

LEVELS
4–8

GENRES / TEXT TYPES
informational/ nonfiction, opinion/ persuasive

PROCESSES
generating and collecting, choosing, developing

Hat Tip: *Help! For Writers: 210 Solutions to the Problems Every Writer Faces* (Clark 2011)

Who is this for?

LEVELS
4–8

GENRE / TEXT TYPE
any

PROCESSES
developing, revising

Strategy Before or after drafting, pause and ask yourself, "What is the picture I see in my mind when I think of my topic? What picture seems to symbolize my topic?" Often the visual image you are left with is what is most central to your piece. Go back to make sure that your details support your image.

Lesson Language *I just reread the story I wrote about the time I was young and I crept into my sister's room and cut off a piece of her hair while she slept. After the whole story, and all the details I included, there is one image that sort of stays with me. It's the look on my sister's face the next morning when she woke up to find her hair in the condition I'd left it. It's a look of shock and sadness. Betrayal and confusion. I'm going to reread my piece to make sure I got that tone right, at least at that part of the piece. And that I didn't make myself out to be triumphant, or the story exciting. More, that this is a story where I'm left with regret.*

Prompts

- Reread your piece, thinking about what's most important.
- Before you draft, let's see if you can focus on one image.
- When you think of your topic, what image comes up?
- If it helps to sketch that image, go ahead. It may keep you focused.
- What picture(s) symbolize your topic?
- Say, "I see . . ."

Hat Tip: *A Writer Teaches Writing* (Murray 1985)

Strategy Before you draft, look across all of the material you've collected. Think, "What idea keeps coming up again and again in the details I've collected?" Make a plan that focuses on the main idea or theme.

Teaching Tip This strategy will only be possible when the student has a collection. A notebook is a perfect place to store ideas, but it could also be that a student keeps a series of drafts or finished pieces from several months to look back on.

Teaching Tip This strategy is slated for older writers because of the cognitive demands it places on the student as a *reader*. You'll know your students are ready for this strategy when they can demonstrate the ability to synthesize and interpret in their reading. Readers who are tuned in to the main idea when reading another writer's text may be able to try this in their own writing.

Prompts

- Look back at the material you've collected.
- What patterns do you see in the details?
- What do you want your piece to be mostly about?
- What theme might focus your story?
- What main idea might focus your informational text?

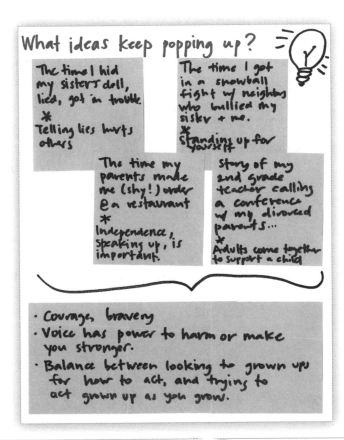

Hat Tip: *A Writer Teaches Writing* (Murray 1985)

4.17 Craft an "Elevator Speech"

Strategy Think about the draft you wrote or plan to write. If you were to pitch the central idea to someone who may be interested in publishing it, think about the three- to five-sentence gist you would share to convince her of the power of the piece. Be sure to include your central message or question as well as the most significant information that "sells" the piece.

Prompts

- What's most essential about your idea?
- Try to sell it to me.
- You included a lot of important information. Now try to say the speech in just three to five sentences.
- Pitch the idea, leave out the stuff that won't "sell" it.
- Your passion for this idea really came through in your speech!
- Now, if that's what you think is most essential, look back to your piece to see if that's communicated.

> What kid doesn't make a mistake at one point in their life, and then regret it later? This is a life-like realistic fiction story of a kid who learns about the importance of friendship and second chances. It takes place in a very relatable town that will help readers feel connected to it, with well-rounded characters they will understand like people in their own lives.

4.18 Craft a Thesis

Strategy Write a first draft of the arguments you want to make. Go back to the draft to underline possible lines, main points, or ideas that you think can be your thesis. Take them and try rewriting/rewording each several ways. Look back at your list and ask yourself, "Which is the one that feels truest to what I'm trying to say? Which do I most care to prove?"

Lesson Language *I am really concerned about the budget cuts the Board of Education is proposing in our town. They said they are going to cut the number of librarians in half, and I just can't stand by and let it happen. I decided to write a letter to the Board of Education, but I want to make sure I'm clear and I make a strong point. To get started, I listed my main points, and now I'm trying to craft my main argument statement. Watch me brainstorm a bunch of possibilities and think about which one feels truest to what I want to say.* (Proceed with demonstration, naming out five or more different possibilities, for example: librarians are crucial to schools; without librarians, schools would be less of what they are; librarians help keep the kids excited about books; and so on.)

Prompts

- Underline lines that stand out.
- Take one line that stands out.
- Let's try rewriting that line in a few ways. How else can you say it?
- Use different words. How else can you write that thesis?
- Look back across your thesis statements. Which one feels truest?
- Which one are you most interested in exploring?
- You chose one that I could tell you really care about.

Who is this for?

LEVELS
4–8

GENRE / TEXT TYPE
opinion/persuasive

PROCESSES
generating and collecting, developing, choosing

Hat Tip: *Breathing Life into Essays* (Calkins and Gillette 2006)

Who is this for?

LEVELS
4–8

GENRE / TEXT TYPE
any

PROCESSES
developing, revising

Strategy Think about your topic and what your unique spin/slant/idea about that topic is going to be. Ask yourself, "So what? What do I have to say about this that hasn't been said? What is my angle on this topic that will make my writing unique and focused?" Write a thinking entry to explore your "so what."

Teaching Tip This strategy is an important one to teach writers working in any genre. If students are writing informational texts, instead of writing all about sharks, they can be nudged to think about what it is they want to say about sharks, and then match their details/facts with their meaning. For students working on essay, the "so what" is essentially their thesis statement. For students working on poetry or narrative, the "so what" can be their theme, message, or lesson.

Prompts

• What do you think you bring to this topic?
• What hasn't been said?
• Ask yourself, "So what?"
• Say, "What I have to say about this is . . ."
• Think of a different angle or spin.

Hat Tip: *In the Middle, Third Edition: A Lifetime of Learning About Writing, Reading, and Adolescents* (Atwell 2014)

Strategy With your draft to the side, freewrite to brainstorm on a separate piece of paper. Write to think and discover about the topic(s) in your piece, the details you've chosen to include, different details you might try out that match your focus, the effects you think your piece may have on the reader, and so on. Do not rewrite the draft. Reread your "off the page" writing, and go back to your draft to consider revisions.

Teaching Tip This strategy will support students with many aspects of qualities of good writing, not only focus. The strategy can be tweaked so that students are writing about their writing—a sort of metacognition that is best reserved for more-mature writers—which will help them to find their focus. Alternatively, you can ask students to try out ways to reconsider aspects of their writing (for instance, trying out many leads), in which case it could help not only with focus, but also with elaboration or even structure.

Prompts

- Try a list.
- Write to ask and answer some questions.
- You're not rewriting your piece. You're just using this paper almost like scrap paper in math to work out the problem.
- You have a bunch of new possible directions because of what you wrote off the page.
- Ask yourself, "So what am I missing?" Now answer it on the page.
- Ask yourself, "So, what's the real problem?" Now try to write a response.

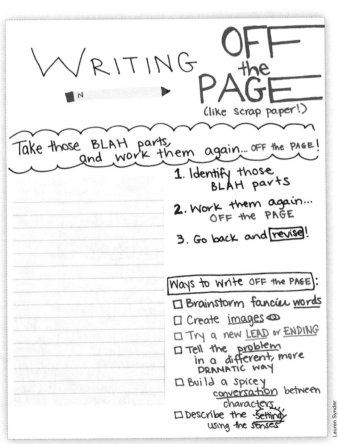

Adapted from Nancie Atwell, *In the Middle, Third Edition*

Who is this for?

LEVELS
5–8

GENRE / TEXT TYPE
any

PROCESS
revising

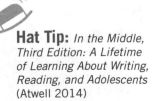

Hat Tip: *In the Middle, Third Edition: A Lifetime of Learning About Writing, Reading, and Adolescents* (Atwell 2014)

4.21 Focus on an Issue

Who is this for?

LEVELS
5–8

GENRE / TEXT TYPE
any

PROCESSES

generating and collecting, developing, rehearsing, choosing

Strategy Think of the life/social issue your piece focuses on (e.g., bullying, racism, poverty, animal rights). Think about what you have to say about that issue. Consider what details you'll include to bring the issue to life.

Teaching Tip A similar strategy, "Abstract Issues, Specific Examples" (strategy 3.32 in the chapter on generating and collecting ideas) helps a writer to get started with a social issue. Here, the emphasis is on helping a reader to focus the details of the piece connected to the issue explored.

Using a Mentor Share the very short yet powerful *Bully* by Laura Vaccaro Seeger (2013) and the video of her sharing her process for writing the story (www.youtube.com/watch?v=QU_lRytwREs). In her case, the vision and purpose for writing, and what she wanted to communicate, were very clear and central to the details and images she chose to include.

Prompts

- What issue do you want to focus on?
- What do you have to say about that issue?
- Let's think together about what details you'll include.
- How might that piece go? Let's rehearse it aloud.
- If it's a story, you'll be thinking about a theme. Say your idea in a sentence.
- If it's nonfiction, you'll be going for a main idea.
- If it's opinion, you'll want to have a thesis or argument in mind. Say it in one sentence.

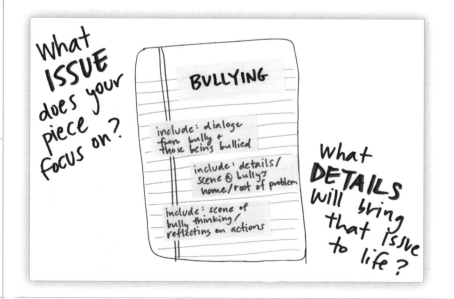

Hat Tip: *For a Better World: Reading and Writing for Social Action* (Bomer and Bomer 2001)

Strategy Think about the content of your piece. Ask yourself, "What is the one central problem that this piece is trying to solve?" The statement or question you come up with can be your focus. Reread to make sure you speak to or solve the problem with the details you've chosen to include.

Lesson Language *We're writing a class piece to the principal about the school lunches. What is the central problem we're focusing on? I think it's that the school lunches are terrible—bad taste, bad quality—and we think kids should have more nutritious and delicious choices. Let's reread to make sure all of our details try to solve that problem. The first one we listed was that the hamburgers are dry and are served on white buns instead of wheat. That speaks to the problem because "dry" shows they are tasteless, and "white bun" shows they are less nutritious than they could be.* (Continue reading through the rest of the piece, encouraging students to judge the effectiveness of the details, and to explain why/how they do or do not support the focus.)

Prompts

- What problem is your piece trying to solve?
- Try to say the problem as a statement.
- Let's read the first part of your piece. Do the details help solve the problem?
- Why did you choose to include that detail?
- What other detail(s) might you include that would help solve that problem?

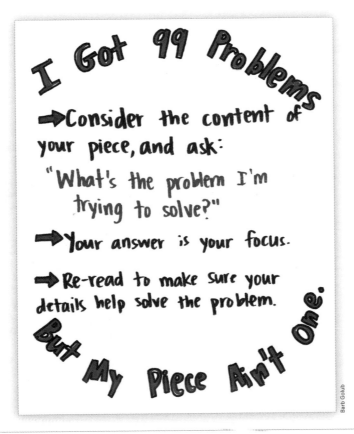

Who is this for?

LEVELS
5–8

GENRE / TEXT TYPE
opinion/persuasive

PROCESS
revising

Hat Tip: *A Writer Teaches Writing* (Murray 1985)

Barb Golub

Who is this for?

LEVELS
5–8

GENRE / TEXT TYPE
any

PROCESSES
drafting, revising

Strategy Start with a glimpse at or a hunch about the meaning you want to convey. Write fast and furious, without judgment or delay. As you write, expect that you are thinking on the page, trying to discover your central meaning through the experimental draft. Set the experimental draft aside, clarify your focus, and redraft the piece.

Teaching Tip This strategy is probably best for students who are extremely fluent writers by hand or fast typists. The idea of writing the whole thing, setting it aside, and starting over again will most likely only appeal to an experienced writer who loves revision!

Prompts
- Try to think on the page.
- Just write it, don't judge yourself.
- Ask yourself a question and then answer it.
- Explore an option.
- Look back at your experimental draft. What seems to float to the surface?
- Try redrafting now that you have a focus in mind.

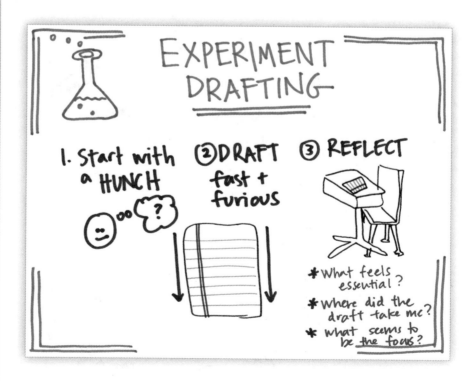

Hat Tip: *A Writer Teaches Writing* (Murray 1985)

4.24 Let Available Sources Steer Your Focus

Strategy Brainstorm ideas you're interested in researching and writing about. Investigate available sources for further study (print, online, experts available for interview, and so on). Modify the scope of the project or topic to align to something that can be studied.

Lesson Language *Let's say you're really interested in forensic science. You go to the library and find just one book on the topic. You do an Internet search and find that most of the articles available are much harder than what you'd be able to read and understand. You could choose to say, "Back to the drawing board! Let me find a completely different topic to study!" Or you could say, "What's related to the topic, or how could I spin it so that it's something I'm still interested in, perhaps related to forensics?" Maybe, for instance, you could broaden the scope of your research so that one part is about forensic science, but other parts of your project are about related careers in science. Or you could expand the scope to be about fighting crime, with other parts about the role of detectives or laws enacted to prevent crimes from happening in the first place, and then a section on forensic science. Or you could read the book about forensic science and see what other possible splinter topics are hiding within that resource.*

Prompts

- What's related to your topic that might make for an interesting study?
- Why don't you read a bit of that one resource you found to see if there is a slant on the topic you might explore?
- What if you broadened the topic? Could this idea be a part of that larger idea?
- Modify the scope of what you're writing about.

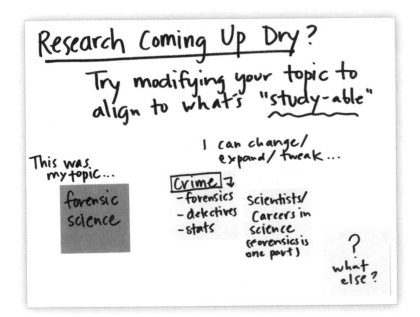

Who is this for?

LEVELS
5–8

GENRES / TEXT TYPES
informational/
nonfiction, opinion/
persuasive

PROCESSES
choosing, developing,
revising

Hat Tip: *Energize Research Reading and Writing: Fresh Strategies to Spark Interest, Develop Independence, and Meet Key Common Core Standards* (Lehman 2012)

Who is this for?

LEVELS
5–8

GENRES / TEXT TYPES
informational/
nonfiction, opinion/
persuasive

PROCESSES
developing, revising

Strategy Think of your topic. Start with "I want to find out about . . ." and then use an active verb (such as contributes, conflicts with, develops) to write a full sentence. Generate several possibilities and then choose the one that most speaks to you.

Teaching Tip Be mindful that this strategy will often cause students' topic, or the scope of what they're studying, to narrow in focus. If they intend to do research on the topic, narrowing a topic means they may be limiting the types of resources and sources they can use to find more information. Use this strategy with 4.24 "Let Available Sources Steer Your Focus" to be sure students are set up for success before plunging too far into exploring their newly narrowed topic.

Prompts
- Try an active verb like *contributes* and include your topic in a full sentence.
- Start with "I want to find out about why/how/when . . ."
- That's one! Go ahead and try a couple more so you can see which one is most interesting to you.
- What's another verb you could incorporate into a sentence about your topic?

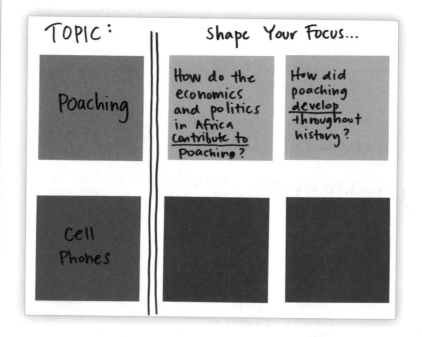

Hat Tip: *The Craft of Research* (Booth, Colomb, and Williams 2008)

Think of organization and structure as the bones of the piece, or the framing of a building. Without bones, your body is a blob. Without a frame, the building collapses.

—*Jennifer Serravallo*

Organization and Structure

◎ Why is this goal important?

One can think of organization and structure as the bones of the piece, or the framing of a building. Without bones, your body is a blob. Without a frame, the building collapses. A writer may have the ability to pick a topic and add in lots of details, but if the frame isn't there, if the piece isn't organized, the reader will become confused. Some of the lessons in this chapter help writers consider the overall structure of their piece, making sure the structure matches genre and meaning.

Another aspect of structure is the parts of the piece. To extend the building analogy, for a sturdy house, we make sure the foundation is strong, the walls are plumb, and the roof is built at the right pitch. In a piece of writing, writers need to learn how to craft strong leads, beginnings, and introductions; how to consider the length of their middle; and how to end with a sense of closure. When each part isn't strong, the overall meaning can be muddied or a reader may not feel interested enough to read on (in the case of leads) or may feel unsatisfied at the end (in the case of endings/conclusions/closure). So organization and structure is about more than just planning for the overall piece, it is also full of strategies to help writers strengthen the parts of their piece. Some of the strategies in this chapter could apply to both whole-text and part-text structure (for example, a "seesaw" structure where a writer alternates back and forth between two topics, ideas, or moments can be used to structure a whole text or only a portion of a text).

◎ How do I know if this goal is right for my student?

Student writers will not develop in lockstep stages, but what follows is a general sense of what can be expected, grade by grade, as students learn to organize and structure their narrative, informational, and/or opinion writing. This progression stands largely on the shoulders of Carl Anderson's ideas as published in *Assessing Writers* (2005), and *Writing Pathways: Performance Assessments and Learning Progressions, Grades K–8* by Lucy Calkins (2014). I hope this will give you a sense of where to begin with writers and what might be a logical next step based on what they are demonstrating they understand about organizing their writing.

Narrative Progression

	K	1	2	3	4	5	6	7	8
Sequential	X	X	X	X	X	X	X	X	X
Beginning/lead		X	X	X	X	X	X	X	X
Ending/closure		X	X	X	X	X	X	X	X
Problem–solution story structure			X	X	X	X	X	X	X
Rising action to build tension				X	X	X	X	X	X
Heart of story is more developed					X	X	X	X	X
Author shows an ability to control time						X	X	X	X
May break sequence for purpose (flashback, etc.)						X	X	X	X
Meaning/significance of story controls the organization							X	X	X

Opinion Progression

	K	1	2	3	4	5	6	7	8
Randomly lists reasons or facts to support opinion	X	X	X	X	X	X	X	X	X
Beginning		X	X	X	X	X	X	X	X
Ending/closure			X	X	X	X	X	X	X
Facts organized into categories/reasons				X	X	X	X	X	X
Beginning transition words used					X	X	X		
Reasons are parallel (of equal importance/weight) and details/facts are organized						X	X	X	X
Some sense of logic to the organization (i.e., most important info first, or info builds to a conclusion)						X	X	X	X
Sophisticated transition words showing relationship between information							X	X	X

Informational Progression

	K	1	2	3	4	5	6	7	8
Gives information in a list	X	X	X	X	X	X	X	X	X
Attempts to put related info together, some info may be overlapping		X	X	X					
Organizes same or related information together onto separate pages, or separate paragraphs		X	X	X	X	X	X	X	X
Ending/closure relates to topic		X	X	X	X	X	X	X	X
Introduction relates to topic			X	X	X	X	X	X	X
Transition words				X	X	X	X	X	X
Introduction and conclusion offer an angle to the topic					X	X	X	X	X
Logic to the organization (i.e., most compelling information first to draw in the reader)						X	X	X	X
Topics and subtopics (or organized into paragraphs or subheads within sections)						X	X	X	X
Each section/part is parallel (of equal weight, importance)						X	X	X	X

Strategies for Organizing and Structuring Writing

Strategy		Grade Levels	Genres/Text Types	Processes
5.1	Pattern Books	Emergent–1	List/pattern books	Drafting
5.2	Say Say Say, Sketch Sketch Sketch, Write Write Write	K–2	Narrative, informational/nonfiction	Rehearsing, drafting
5.3	Add a Page, Subtract a Page	K–2	Narrative, informational/nonfiction, opinion/persuasive	Revising
5.4	Move a Page to a New Place	K–2	Narrative, informational/nonfiction, opinion/persuasive	Revising
5.5	All About or One Time?	K–2	Narrative, informational/nonfiction	Rehearsing
5.6	Teaching Texts: How-Tos	K–8	Narrative procedure	Developing, drafting, revising
5.7	Organize in Sequence	K–8	Any	Developing
5.8	Uh-Oh . . . UH-OH . . . Phew	1–3	Narrative	Developing
5.9	Beef Up the Middle	1–3	Narrative	Revising
5.10	Question–Answer	1–3	Informational/nonfiction	Developing, drafting
5.11	End in the Moment	1–4	Narrative (small moment)	Drafting, revising
5.12	End with Last Words from the Character	1–8	Narrative	Drafting, revising
5.13	Start with a Table of Contents	1–8	Informational/nonfiction	Developing
5.14	Parts of a Topic: Features and Characteristics	1–8	Informational/nonfiction, opinion/persuasive	Developing
5.15	Parts of a Topic: Kinds	1–8	Informational/nonfiction, opinion/persuasive	Developing
5.16	Moving from Chunk to Chunk	1–8	Narrative, opinion/persuasive, informational/nonfiction	Revising
5.17	Line Breaks	1–8	Poetry	Revising
5.18	Start with a Plan in Mind	2–8	Any	Developing
5.19	Create Urgency	2–8	Narrative	Developing, revising
5.20	Nonfiction Leads	2–8	Informational/nonfiction	Developing, revising

Strategy		Grade Levels	Genres/Text Types	Processes
5.21	Lead by Addressing the Reader	2–8	Informational/nonfiction, opinion/persuasive	Developing, revising
5.22	Audiences for Information	2–8	Informational/nonfiction	Developing
5.23	Draw Your Layout	2–8	Informational/nonfiction	Developing
5.24	Outline, Reoutline, Outline Again	3–8	Informational/nonfiction, opinion/persuasive, narrative	Developing, revising
5.25	Lay Out Pages to See the Architecture	3–8	Any	Revising
5.26	Take Scissors to Your Draft	3–8	Any	Revising
5.27	Draw Out (Don't Summarize) to Build Suspense	3–8	Narrative	Drafting, revising
5.28	Repetition/List Structure	3–8	Any	Developing, drafting, revising
5.29	Multiscene Storyboarding	3–8	Narrative	Developing
5.30	Problem–Solution Structure for Persuasive Writing	3–8	Opinion/persuasive	Developing, drafting
5.31	Moving Quickly (or Slowly) Through Time	4–8	Narrative	Revising
5.32	Take a Piece, Rework the Genre or Structure Several Times	4–8	Any	Revising
5.33	Headings, Subheadings, Sub-Subheadings	4–8	Informational/nonfiction	Developing
5.34	Weight the Parts of Your Piece	4–8	Informational/nonfiction, poetry, opinion/persuasive	Revising
5.35	Coming Full Circle	4–8	Any	Developing, drafting, revising
5.36	Seesaw Structure	4–8	Any	Developing, drafting, revising
5.37	Conclude with the Big Idea	4–8	Any	Drafting, revising
5.38	Parallel Story	4–8	Narrative	Developing, drafting
5.39	Write the Bones, Then Go Back to Flesh It Out	4–8	Any	Drafting
5.40	Leading with Contrast	5–8	Narrative, opinion/persuasive, informational/nonfiction	Developing, drafting, revising

5.1 Pattern Books

Who is this for?

LEVELS
emergent–1

GENRE / TEXT TYPE
list/pattern books

PROCESS
drafting

Strategy When you know how to write a few sight words that can be put together to make the beginning of a sentence, you can make a pattern book. Think about what you want your pattern book to be about. Use some of the same words on each page, but change at least one. Make sure your pictures match your words.

Teaching Tip This book structure helps reinforce sight words and supports children who are almost ready to be reading level A, B, or C books. If you're teaching this strategy to the class, you can differentiate by varying the options for patterns. Some children can change the word in the middle (e.g., "The frog is green. / The leaf is green."), some children can change the last few words (e.g., "Is that a brown bear? / Is that a yellow duck?"), and still others can try a pattern that goes across two pages (e.g., "I see a dog. He says woof. / I see a duck. He says quack."). Consider creating these during interactive or shared writing before offering the idea for children to make their own. You'll also want to make sure you've introduced some high-frequency words and they are available on a word wall or chart in your classroom.

Prompts

- What words will stay the same?
- Check the word wall to help you spell those words.
- What's the pattern?
- What's going to change on this next page?
- I notice your pattern has the first few letters the same with the last one changing.
- Only one word changes on each page and the rest stay the same. That's a pattern!

Hat Tip: *Units of Study in Opinion, Information, and Narrative Writing, Grade 1* (Calkins and colleagues 2013)

Strategy Lay the pages of your book in front of you. Say one part of your story for each page. Next, sketch the pictures that will help you to remember what you said on each page. Then, go back to page 1, write the words for that page, then the next and the next. You can use the picture you sketched as a reminder of what you wanted to write.

Teaching Tip For children who are new to writing across pages, you might consider starting with two pages (beginning, end) and then work your way to three (beginning, middle, end) and then eventually four, five, or more.

Teaching Tip I once saw my colleague Alison Porcelli sing the strategy to a rug full of kindergarteners to the tune of "(Shake, Shake, Shake) Shake Your Booty" by KC and the Sunshine Band ("Say say say . . . duh duh duh duh duh duh sketch sketch sketch duh duh duh duh, Write write wriiiiite. Write write wriiiiite"). This was almost ten years ago and I haven't forgotten it yet! Seeing the students' response, she taught me that it's a great idea to make your lesson playful and fun by setting the strategy to a memorable tune.

Prompts
- Start with telling your story.
- Touch the page as you tell that part.
- You told all the parts of your story. Let's go back and start sketching.
- Remember, a sketch is a quick drawing, just to get your idea down. You can go back and work on the illustration later.
- Let's see, you've said your story. You've sketched your story. What's next?
- I see you're touching each page as you say your story—that will help you remember the order!

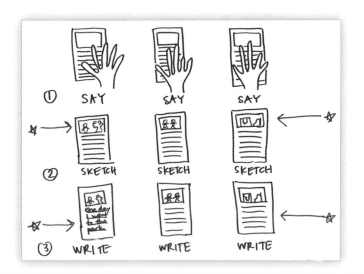

Who is this for?

LEVELS

K–2

GENRES / TEXT TYPES

narrative, informational/ nonfiction

PROCESSES

rehearsing, drafting

Hat Tip: Alison Porcelli, personal communication

5.3 Add a Page, Subtract a Page

Who is this for?

LEVELS
K–2

GENRES / TEXT TYPES
narrative, informational/ nonfiction, opinion/ persuasive

PROCESS
revising

Strategy Reread your piece. If there is a part that doesn't seem to fit, remove the page (and possibly replace it with a blank page to rewrite that part). If the piece seems like it's missing something, add a blank page in, and write what's missing.

Teaching Tip Having beginning writers write across pages helps them to understand the parts of their piece. If they are writing a story, they internalize "beginning, middle, end" with three pages. If it's a nonfiction piece, they internalize "one subtopic, another subtopic, another subtopic" as they write across pages. This strategy helps students to realize when a whole part of their piece isn't working to take it away, or when a piece of their whole is missing to add it in.

A slightly more-complex strategy, deciding when to move a page to a new place in the draft, is on the next page (strategy 5.4), "Move a Page to a New Place."

Prompts

- Is there a part that seems confusing? Could something be missing?
- What part of this story feels like it doesn't fit with the other parts?
- If you take this page out, would you write something in its place?
- I agree, that page doesn't fit with the piece you have now.
- I agree, that part is confusing.

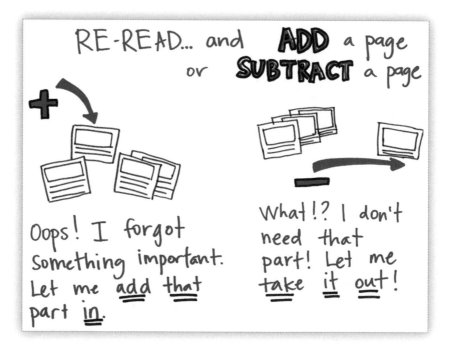

Hat Tip: *One to One: The Art of Conferring with Young Writers* (Calkins, Hartman, and White 2005)

Strategy Reread your piece. If there is a part that seems out of order, pluck the page out of your booklet. Reread the remainder of the pages thinking, "Where would this page go better?" Put it in the new spot, then read the whole piece to make sure it flows.

Teaching Tip Reordering pages in a narrative won't be necessary if a student planned based on the sequence the story occurred. However, sometimes a child will add in some details that really happened earlier in the chronology on a later page in the draft. For example, a child could write a page about getting her dog's leash and collar, then a page about being outside on the walk, then a page about how the dog always gets excited about going on the walk by barking and wagging, and then a final page about returning home. The page about being excited actually belongs before the page where they are outside.

The decision to move parts around in informational writing might be because a page fits with a subtopic that appears on another page. For example, if a child is writing about whales and has a page on where whales live, another page about plankton and what whales eat, another page about how whales are endangered, and then a page about whale migration, the child may realize that migrating goes with where they live and may choose to move that page closer to the first.

In opinion pieces, a writer might consider which arguments are the strongest, or may decide that the conclusion is a better introduction and vice versa.

Prompts

- Is there a part that seems confusing? Could it be in the wrong spot?
- What part of this story feels out of order?
- Think about where that page might go better.
- I agree, that page feels like it doesn't fit there.
- Read your whole piece now that you've moved that page.

Barb Golub

Who is this for?

LEVELS
K–2

GENRES / TEXT TYPES
narrative, informational/ nonfiction, opinion/ persuasive

PROCESS
revising

5.5 All About or One Time?

Who is this for?

LEVELS
K–2

GENRES / TEXT TYPES
**narrative,
informational/
nonfiction**

PROCESS
rehearsing

Strategy Once you have a topic in mind, you can decide what kind of piece you want to write. One option is to think about *one time* that happened and write a story that will have a beginning, middle, and end. Another option is to think *all about* your topic. In that case, your piece will be informational and you'll teach one thing, then another, then another about your topic.

Teaching Tip The larger thing you're teaching into in this lesson is a knowledge and sense of genre. One of the first things a writer needs to consider is the structure or organization of the piece. Of course, children who need support with having a clear sense of genre will also likely benefit from other lessons in the chapters on elaboration (Chapter 6) and word choice (Chapter 7) to make sure that the types of details they include and the voice of the piece also match the genre.

Prompts
• How do you want to write about your topic?
• What sorts of things do you want your reader to know?
• OK, a story. Practice how that might sound by telling the story out loud.
• OK, you want to write *all about* your topic. Plan out what you'll include on each page.

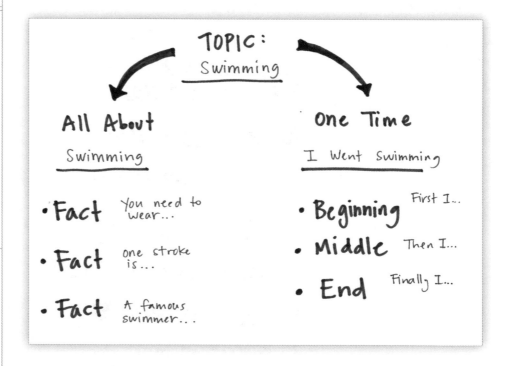

Hat Tip: *One to One:
The Art of Conferring with
Young Writers* (Calkins,
Hartman, and White 2005)

Strategy Plan to organize your piece into parts (for example: materials, introduction, steps, conclusion). Plan to use one page for each part. For the first part, think, "What do I need to include?" Then think, "How can I get my audience ready to learn how to do what I'm teaching?" For the next part, think, "What are the steps to teaching someone how to do it?" and for the last part, think, "How will I wrap it up?" Reread to make sure you didn't leave out important information.

Using a Mentor Some of my favorite mentor texts not only show the structure of a narrative procedure/how-to text, but also include a lot of voice and are about unexpected topics. See, for example, *The Beginner's Guide to Running Away from Home* (Huget 2013) where the main character explains why he's running away from home after being wronged by everyone in his family, and how he'll do it. *How to Lose All Your Friends* (Carlson 1997) is more of a what-not-to-do book, and many children catch the humor readily! *How to Read a Story* (Messner 2015a) is one of my new favorites for reading at the start of the year because it doubles as an introduction to your reading workshop and as a mentor text for organizing how-to writing.

Prompts
- What parts will your how-to book have?
- You're going to write your steps now. Let's think about what you want to include.
- Let's check to make sure you have the order of the steps right.
- Reread what you have. Did you include everything that's important?
- Do you think you teach your reader clearly?

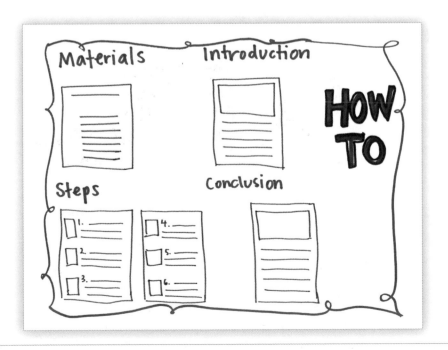

Who is this for?

LEVELS
K–8

GENRE / TEXT TYPE
narrative procedure

PROCESSES
developing, drafting, revising

Hat Tip: *Nonfiction Writing: Procedures and Reports* (Calkins and Pessah 2003)

5.7 Organize in Sequence

Who is this for?

LEVELS
K–8

GENRE / TEXT TYPE
any

PROCESS
developing

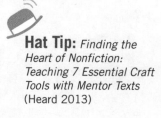

Hat Tip: *Finding the Heart of Nonfiction: Teaching 7 Essential Craft Tools with Mentor Texts* (Heard 2013)

Strategy Think about your topic. If your piece moves chronologically, it helps to first make a list of the steps or events in the order you plan to describe or explain them. Once you have the order right, then you can draft.

Teaching Tip More-sophisticated writers might plan out their sequence in their notebooks or with a graphic organizer. Less-experienced writers can rely on the paper you offer them to do this work. For example, if you want children to sequence a personal narrative into a beginning, middle, and end, you can offer them three pieces of paper with a box at the top of each for a drawing and perhaps also space below to write sentences. Teach them that each separate page represents not a separate story, but rather a part of the same story. If you want to support students' planning of procedural writing, you may consider paper that has a series of small boxes with numbered lines. Some students may want to plan out the events of a fictional story, personal narrative, or even narrative nonfiction (historical account, biography) on a timeline before beginning to draft.

Prompts

- Tell me about your topic. Is there an order you should tell it in?
- Let's start with what happens first. What happens next?
- It sounds like there are events that connect. Let's put them in order.
- Make a list in the order you want it to go in your draft.

Strategy Start your story with a clear problem. Think about how the problem gets worse. Think about how the problem gets worse still, causing your reader to root for your main character. Think about how the problem will get solved.

Teaching Tip For K–2 students who draft on separate pages in a booklet, you can write the words *uh-oh* and *UH-OH* and *phew!* on the corners of the pages to help them match their storytelling to the structure of the story. (Of course, you can have several pages of *UH-OH* in the middle—adapt the number of pages to the experience level of your writer.)

Using a Mentor Many short fiction stories in *Highlights* magazine follow this very predictable problem, problem worsens, solution structure. Consider copying a short story and cutting it into those sections and then taping the parts of the story across pages in booklets similar to the children's.

Prompts

- What problem will your character have?
- Think about how the problem might get worse.
- Make sure the way the problem is getting worse connects back to the main problem.
- Can you think of a realistic solution?
- You're really building suspense! That problem is getting worse and worse. Your poor character!

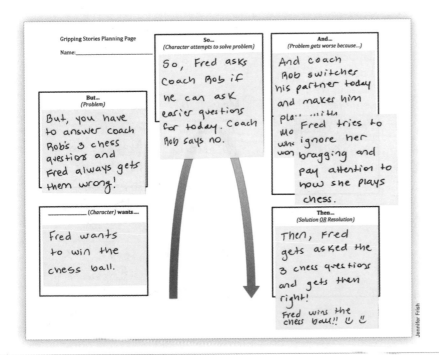

Who is this for?

LEVELS
1–3

GENRE / TEXT TYPE
narrative

PROCESS
developing

Hat Tip: *The Reading Strategies Book: Your Everything Guide to Developing Skilled Readers* (Serravallo 2015a)

Who is this for?

LEVELS

1–3

GENRE / TEXT TYPE

narrative

PROCESS

revising

Strategy Once you know how your story starts, what happens in the middle, and how your story ends, go back to the middle. Think, "What other details can I add to make this middle last longer so that there is more suspense or I help my reader get more immersed in the story?" Then, add an extra page or a flap to the bottom and reread to think about what else you'll add.

Using a Mentor If you have a leveled library in your classroom, check out some books at level F–H, such as *Frog's Lunch* by Dee Lillegard (1994). These books tend to have a one- or two-page beginning, a multiple-paged middle, and a couple pages at the end. You can hold the book on its side, grabbing the "middle" pages and say, "See how the middle isn't just one page or part? It's all of these pages together. This author added details to make the middle last longer!"

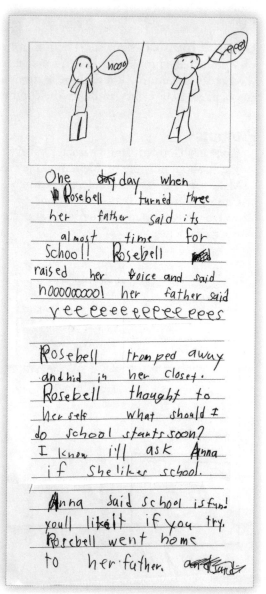

Prompts

- Show me the part that is your middle.
- What else can you add to the middle?
- Can you find a spot where you breezed by time? That might be a spot to slow down and storytell.
- You told me what happened over many minutes in just one sentence. Can you slow down and make the one sentence two?
- Think about the kinds of details you know how to add: action, dialogue, thinking, setting, character description, and so on.

Hat Tip: *Craft Lessons: Teaching Writing K–8, Second Edition* (Portalupi and Fletcher 2007)

Strategy Think of a list of questions your reader might have about your topic. Write each question on the top of a new page (or in a list in your notebook). Think about how you might answer the question in one, two, or three sentences.

Teaching Tip This structure could be used for an entire piece of writing, with a question beginning each page, almost like a heading to focus the writer on the specific subtopic that the page deals with. Alternatively, it could be a strategy for a part within a larger informational text, such as a question–answer sidebar.

Using a Mentor The If You . . . nonfiction series offers a great example of this structure type. The text is divided into categories with multiple specific questions that are used as headings. There are a plethora of topics within this series from which to choose. Steve Jenkins and Robin Page's *Creature Features: Twenty-Five Animals Explain Why They Look the Way They Do* (2014) offers questions about the features (noses, eyes, beaks) of various animals with the animals themselves giving the responses.

Prompts

- What questions do you have?
- Write that question on the top of a new page. You'll answer it below.
- What might someone wonder about your topic, that you know the answer to?
- Make sure you know the answer, or that you're willing to find it.
- It looks like you've got several very unique questions. Time to start answering them!
- These two questions—do you think the answers belong on separate pages, or are they pretty similar and therefore should be combined?

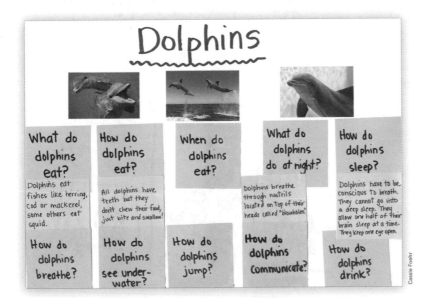

Who is this for?

LEVELS

1–3

GENRE / TEXT TYPE

informational/ nonfiction

PROCESSES

developing, drafting

Hat Tip: *Nonfiction Craft Lessons: Teaching Information Writing K–8* (Portalupi and Fletcher 2001)

5.11 **End in the Moment**

Who is this for?

LEVELS
1–4

GENRE / TEXT TYPE
narrative (small moment)

PROCESSES
drafting, revising

Strategy Think about the most important point you're making in your story, or the amount of time that passes in your story. Think about the last event that happened at that point, connected to that idea. Write a conclusion that stays in that moment.

Lesson Language *It's time for me to figure out how I want my story to end. Endings are important because they are the last thing we leave with our reader. The last thing we leave with our reader can't be off-topic, and I want to make sure I am thinking about what's most important about the story I've chosen to write. So, if my story is about riding a roller coaster for the first time, I am not going to end with the car ride home. No way! I have to end it right there, on or next to the roller coaster. If my story is about the first time I ordered ice cream for myself, without my parents doing it for me, I'm trying to show how brave I was in that moment. So I'm going to end with feelings of bravery, or my mom telling me I'm brave. I'm not going to talk about going to bed later that night.*

Prompts

- What's the most important point you're making in your story? How could you end the story, sticking to the point?
- Let's think about *where* and *when* your story takes place. Let's end the story *then* and *there*.
- You ended your story in the same place! You didn't talk about the ride home, or going to bed, or something else later that day.
- How do you think you could end it?
- Try to end it in the moment.

Hat Tip: *One to One: The Art of Conferring with Young Writers* (Calkins, Hartman, and White 2005)

Strategy Wrap up a story by staying close to the heart (the most important part) of the moment you're writing about. Instead of ending by going on to a new moment, one ending you can try is to state the final dialogue of the character(s) in the story.

Teaching Tip Look across this chapter for a number of different ways to end stories, including strategies 5.11 "End in the Moment" and 5.37 "Conclude with the Big Idea."

Using a Mentor Sanae Ishida's *Little Kunoichi: The Ninja Girl* (2015) ends with: "Oops! We're sorry Dragon-san! We missed the target. At least we added extra pizzazz to the festival" (32). *Martina, the Beautiful Cockroach: A Cuban Folktale* by Carmen Agra Deedy (2007) ends with: "Martina was too delighted to be angry. At last, she'd found her perfect match. But she had to ask, 'How did you know about the Coffee Test?' Pérez grinned. '*Well, mi amor, my love . . .*'" (30).

Prompts

- Who is the main character in your piece?
- Let's think about the last thing the character might say.
- Tell me again what the main point of your story is.
- What is the last thing you want your reader to hear from your character?

Who is this for?

LEVELS
1–8

GENRE / TEXT TYPE
narrative

PROCESSES
drafting, revising

5.13 Start with a Table of Contents

Who is this for?

LEVELS
1–8

GENRE / TEXT TYPE
informational/ nonfiction

PROCESS
developing

Strategy Think about your topic. Think about the chapters/parts/sections you could write. Make a list. Check each chapter to make sure you have a few facts to say about it. Combine chapters that are too narrow, and break down chapters that are too broad.

Teaching Tip As written, I would most likely teach this to children in grades 1–3. For upper elementary and middle school children, you can use this same technique of breaking up a topic into subtopics to plan for paragraphs, and adjust the language of the strategy (above) and the prompts (below) accordingly.

Prompts

- What chapters might you write?
- Think about how you'll break up this topic. Are there parts to it?
- List the parts.
- Let's test out this table of contents by listing facts that you plan to write in each chapter.
- Ah! If you only have one fact to say, it's not enough for a chapter.

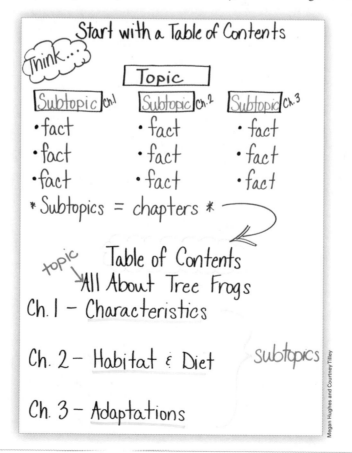

Hat Tip: *Nonfiction Writing: Procedures and Reports* (Calkins and Pessah 2003)

5.14 Parts of a Topic: Features and Characteristics

Strategy Picture your topic in your mind. Zoom in to parts of it, asking yourself, "What are the features of my topic? What are the characteristics of my topic?" Name subtopics (not facts!). Create a list of subtopics.

Lesson Language *For example, if I want to write about my dog, I can picture her in my mind. In my mind's eye, I can zoom in on her head. A fact would be "She has very floppy ears with very soft fur." But a subtopic would be "ears." If I name a subtopic, I can then go back to add many facts that expand upon my subtopic, "A bloodhound's ears are floppy. They hang so low that sometimes they drag in their water and food bowls. But they are more than just cute! A bloodhound is bred for it's great sense of smell, and the droopy ears help to waft scents up from the ground into the dog's nose." So, ears is one subtopic. Another might be about the color or appearance of the fur. Another might be about the size of the bloodhound.*

Prompts

- What's one part of your topic you think your reader would want to know about?
- That's a fact. What is a subtopic that fact might be a part of?
- It's almost like you're making a table of contents.
- Could you write a whole page about that? If not, it might be a fact rather than a subtopic.
- Think about features of your topic.

Who is this for?

LEVELS
1–8

GENRES / TEXT TYPES
informational/ nonfiction, opinion/ persuasive

PROCESS
developing

Hat Tip: *Finding the Heart of Nonfiction: Teaching 7 Essential Craft Tools with Mentor Texts* (Heard 2013)

Who is this for?

LEVELS

1–8

GENRES / TEXT TYPES

**informational/
nonfiction, opinion/
persuasive**

PROCESS

developing

Strategy Think about your topic. Break your topic into smaller parts by thinking about what kinds there are. Make a list that can serve as a table of contents.

Lesson Language *I want to write a book about dance. The first thing I'm going to try is to make a table of contents of all the kinds of dance. Will that work? Let me see. I know about ballet. That's one kind. I know about jazz, and tap, and modern. There! I've got four chapters so far. Any more kinds? Oh! Ballroom dancing. Although, there are a lot of kinds of ballroom dancing so let me cross that out and instead list separate kinds of ballroom dance: salsa, waltz, rumba, foxtrot.*

Prompts

- What's one kind of your topic you think your reader would want to know about?
- That's a fact. What is a subtopic that fact might be a part of?
- It's like we're making a table of contents. Each kind can be its own chapter!
- Could you write a whole page about that? If not, it might be a fact rather than a subtopic.

Topic: Cats
1. Bob Cart
2. Cheta
3. Loin
4. tigr

Topic: PrSin
1. Amarcin,
2. oaJtihorSiorn
3. ihuin
4. ofrcin

Topic: Dogs
1. BluD hWnD
2. Dlmashn
3. Poatl
4. Dbegul

Hat Tip: "Information Writing: Writing about Topics of Personal Expertise," in *If . . . Then . . . Curriculum: Assessment-Based Instruction, Grade 4, Units of Study in Opinion, Information, and Narrative Writing* (Calkins 2013)

Strategy Box out the parts of your draft (think "beginning, middle, end" or "first, next, then, finally" or "reason 1, reason 2, reason 3, and so on"). Read the end of one chunk and the beginning of the next chunk. Notice how you transition from one part to the next. Think, "Did I use a transition word or phrase that makes sense given the relationship between the parts?"

Teaching Tip This lesson is adaptable for first graders through eighth graders, as long as you select appropriate transition words for the grade level or developmental level of your writers. You can also adapt this strategy to work with a variety of genres, again by changing the transition words you're teaching.

Prompts
- What's the beginning of that part? End? Put a box around it.
- Underline the part that is the transition, where you move from one part to the next.
- What is the relationship between those two parts? Did you use the transition word/phrase that makes sense there?

Transitions

to compare	to contrast
likewise	despite
as well as	however
either	otherwise
similarly	even though
in the same way	rather

to show time	to give examples
before	for example
recently	such as
following	in fact
after	for instance
finally	in addition
first, next, then	specifically

Megan Hughes and Courtney Tilley

Who is this for?

LEVELS
1–8

GENRES / TEXT TYPES
narrative, opinion/ persuasive, informational/ nonfiction

PROCESS
revising

5.17 Line Breaks

Who is this for?

LEVELS
1–8

GENRE / TEXT TYPE
poetry

PROCESS
revising

Strategy Reread your poem. Try to rewrite the words with breaks for pauses. Then rewrite it a different way with different line breaks. Reread each version and listen to the sound. Decide which rhythm best matches your meaning (or, if neither does, try it another way!).

Teaching Tip One way to teach the manipulation of words across lines is to take a poem and write each word on a separate index card. Using a pocket chart, organize the words across lines one way. Do a choral reading to feel the rhythm. Reorganize the words with new line breaks. Discuss how the sound of the poem is different.

Using a Mentor Before students try this with their own poems, you may take a short poem such as William Carlos William's "Wheelbarrow" and write it on sentence strips. Cut each word apart and grab a pocket chart. Work with children to arrange and rearrange the lines, considering how the meaning shifts, the rhythm shifts, and maybe even the tone shifts, depending on where the lines break.

Prompts

- If you break it here, this is what it would sound like. If you break it here, this is what it would sound like. Which do you like better?
- Try it another way.
- You broke up the lines, now let's hear you read it aloud.
- When you read it aloud, pause at each break.
- Now that you've heard the rhythm of it with those line breaks, try it another way.

> cat lna
> restront
> be carfl
> it sometins
> has
> bonty hinters

Hat Tip: *Poetry: Powerful Thoughts in Tiny Packages* (Calkins and Parsons 2001)

Strategy Before beginning to draft, visualize the shape of what you're going to make. Create some sort of quick visual, in pictures or in words, to represent the overarching structure. As you write, check back to see where you are in your plan.

Lesson Language *When a sailor decides to take a journey, he doesn't simply push his boat into the water, hike up the sail, and then wait to see what happens. Sailors have a planned course ahead. When we write, we should aim to do the same thing, draw a sort of map for ourselves of what we intend so that as we journey through adding lots of details and words, we can stay on track.*

Teaching Tip This is going to be most helpful after students have learned a variety of ways to structure their pieces and have been introduced to a variety of graphic organizers that would help them to organize, or shape, the information into a structure.

Using a Mentor *The Whisper* by Pamela Zagarenski (2015) is a gorgeously illustrated picture book about a little girl who imagines a story in a wordless picture book. She relies on her knowledge of the structure of how stories go to help her go from beginning, to middle, to end.

Prompts
• What genre are you writing in?
• What do you know about how that genre is organized?
• Draw a picture (or graphic organizer) to represent the shape of what you'll make.
• Take a look at some of the graphic organizers I have here. Which one best matches the way your piece will go?
• You said you want to write a _____. Usually the structure will be _____.

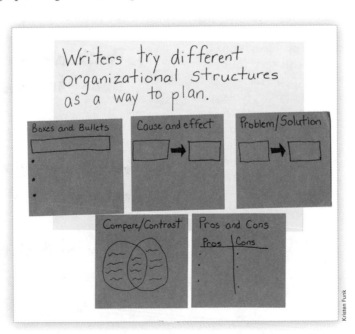

Who is this for?

LEVELS
2–8

GENRE / TEXT TYPE
any

PROCESS
developing

Hat Tip: *The Elements of Style, Fourth Edition* (Strunk and White 1999)

Who is this for?

LEVELS
2–8

GENRE / TEXT TYPE
narrative

PROCESSES
developing, revising

Strategy Think about a problem or goal your main character might have. Brainstorm ideas for obstacles the character will have to overcome the problem. Think, "Will the story end with a resolution or solution?"

Lesson Language *In a story, it helps if there is some urgency that keeps the reader wanting to read. Oftentimes, this is accomplished by giving the main character a clear problem and/or a goal. Once you've figured out the main problem or goal, build the plot around it, thinking about what will lead up to it and what will happen once it's revealed. Sometimes you'll want to make the problem get fixed—give it a solution. Other times you'll find a way to resolve the tension without actually having everything work out perfectly for the main character. Planning out this overall arc of your story before you begin helps you know where you're going!*

Using a Mentor On the first page of *Enemy Pie* by Derek Munson (2000), the reader is clued in on the main problem that will focus the story: "It should have been a perfect summer. But it wasn't." We learn on the following couple of pages about the new boy, Jeremy, who has moved in next to his best friend and soon becomes the main character's enemy #1.

Prompts
- What problem might your character have?
- That sounds like a smaller problem; it may be an obstacle. Is there a bigger problem connected to that?
- That problem is one that will keep your readers on their toes!
- You've got a problem and some obstacles. Now what do you think you'll do about the ending? Add those ideas to your story plan.

Hat Tip: *The Plot Thickens: 8 Ways to Bring Fiction to Life* (Lukeman 2002)

CREATE URGENCY!

1. Think about a problem/ goal for your character.

2. Brainstorm ideas
   ↳ what does your character need to overcome?

3. How will it end?
   Resolution?
   Solution?

Barb Golub

Strategy Think about what information or idea is the most important. Try out three different leads (see figure below) that include information that introduces your reader to the important ideas of your piece. Think about which works best to introduce your topic and also to draw your reader in to want to read more.

Teaching Tip This strategy requires that the lead types have been taught in the past, or that the student is an experienced enough writer to work off of an example as a model. For more beginning writers, consider teaching the types of leads provided in the visual below in separate lessons before asking students to try several.

Prompts
- Try out a narrative lead. Tell the beginning like a story.
- How else can you lead off this piece?
- Look back at the leads you've drafted. Which one seems to work best?

Lead Your Reader to the FACTS

[Narrative Lead: Starting off with a short story

Example: "Rodney Fox had almost run out of time. He needed to find a big fish — and he needed to find it soon."
from Shark Attack! Cathy East Dubowski (4)

[Scene-Painting Lead: descriptive

Example: "Sunlight shines through seawater into a coral reef. The reef is an underwater world of brilliant colors and strange shapes."
from Gail Gibbons, Coral Reefs (3)

[Leads that [Personalize] the topic and speak straight to the reader

Example: "Yikes! Bugs look scary close up. But you don't need to worry. Most bugs are a danger only to other insects. They are the bugs that really bug other bugs."
from Jennifer Dussling, Bugs Bugs Bugs p. 4–5

Megan Hughes and Courtney Tilley

5.21 Lead by Addressing the Reader

Who is this for?

LEVELS
2–8

GENRES / TEXT TYPES
informational/
nonfiction, opinion/
persuasive

PROCESSES
developing, revising

Hat Tip: *Finding the Heart of Nonfiction: Teaching 7 Essential Craft Tools with Mentor Texts* (Heard 2013)

Strategy Think about the focus of your piece. Revise your lead by changing from third person to second person. Try to imagine talking right to your reader, using *you* and *your.*

Lesson Language *Nonfiction writing can sometimes feel cold, distant, and sterile. When a writer simply reports fact, fact, fact, it can make a reader feel less connected to the content. One thing to try is to reconsider the lead of your piece in a different voice, from third person to second person. This will mean changing from using words like* he, she, they, it *to* you. *For example, consider the beginning of my piece right now about holidays in Central America:*

> Holidays can be a time for songs, dance, food, fun, and parades. Many holidays have religious significance in Central America because many people in that area of the world are Catholic. For example, on November 1st, All Saints' Day, Catholics believe that the spirits of the dead visit their homes. This holiday is also known as *El día de los muertos,* or the Day of the Dead. On this holiday, families gather to decorate family members' graves with flowers. They believe it's very important to honor the dead so that they may have better life on earth, free of illness and bad luck.

Now, if I wanted to play around with the voice of the piece, trying to change it to second person, I'd need to imagine what it would be like to talk directly to the reader, using you *and perhaps even asking questions to draw them in:*

> Imagine yourself in Central America on the morning of November 1st. Can you see the first rays of sunlight, peeking through your window? Time to get up! You'd go with a family member soon after rising to gather flowers, not to decorate your own home, but to honor your family members who have passed on. This holiday is not about the spookiness you may associate with Halloween in the United States. Instead, you are at the graveyard to place flowers and decorate the grave. You are honoring your deceased loved ones in the hopes of a good year ahead, free of illness and with good luck and healthy crops on your farm.

Prompts

- Play around with the voice of the piece.
- Change it to *you*—use the same information, but write it as if you're talking to someone.
- Now you have two versions! Which works better for your topic?
- Talk about the differences between these two leads you've created.

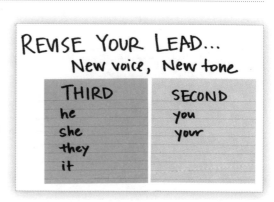

5.22 Audiences for Information

Strategy Think about what you have to say, and who you want to say it to. Consider the options for different types of information writing (each with its own structure). Choose a text type and structure that matches the audience you plan to write to.

Lesson Language *The purpose of your piece is an important thing to consider when you think about how you want to present your information. You could decide to write an all-about book, or a report. It could be a poster, or a blog post. Each structure will be organized a different way. Depending on the structure, you'll include a different amount of information and your writing will have a different feel—formal or informal, highly visual or text dense.*

Using a Mentor *Written Anything Good Lately?* (Allen and Lindaman 2006): *A* is for *autobiography*, *B* is for *book report*, *C* is for greeting *cards*, *D* is for *directions*. This alphabet book includes short informational writing pieces in a variety of text types. It would make a great read-aloud, and a wonderful addition to your classroom's writing center.

Prompts
- What's your topic?
- Who is your audience?
- Let's look to see what types of information writing might fit your topic.
- Who do you want to read your piece? What kind of text might work best?
- You think you might choose a _____. When do you usually see those? Who reads them?
- I think _____ makes a lot of sense! It matches your topic and your audience.

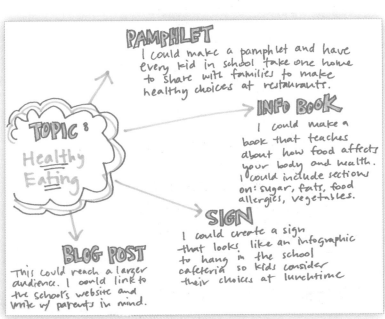

Who is this for?

LEVELS
2–8

GENRE / TEXT TYPE
informational/ nonfiction

PROCESS
developing

Hat Tip: *The Writing Thief: Using Mentor Texts to Teach the Craft of Writing* (Culham 2014)

5.23 Draw Your Layout

Who is this for?

LEVELS
2–8

GENRE / TEXT TYPE
**informational/
nonfiction**

PROCESS
developing

Strategy Once you've collected the information you plan to write about, it may help to visualize how the information will be laid out on the page. Look to some examples for ideas, then take blank paper to draw your layout. Consider how much space you need for the main text and how much space you need for features.

Teaching Tip After allowing students some time to experiment with layouts, you may find it helpful for younger students to provide premade templates in the writing center that mirror the kind of layouts they draw.

Using a Mentor Find a variety of nonfiction texts, such as interesting two-page spreads from books in your classroom library and/or feature articles from publications such as *Time for Kids*, *Ranger Rick*, or *Scholastic News*. Consider creating a bulletin board in your classroom devoted to layouts, perhaps enlisting the help of your students with labeling each example with what they notice and why the author did it.

Prompts
- Take a look at some mentor texts. Think about why the author chose the layouts.
- How do you imagine this page being laid out?
- Think about the information you want to share. What layout would work?
- You told me you had a couple of illustrations planned and some text. Show me what that would look like.
- Sketch the plan.

Hat Tip: *Nonfiction Craft Lessons: Teaching Information Writing K–8* (Portalupi and Fletcher 2001)

5.24 Outline, Reoutline, Outline Again

Strategy Take your topic and create an outline of how the piece of writing might go. Then, reimagine the piece by organizing it by a different principle, or by zooming into the topic or broadening out. Look over your outlines and choose the one that feels the closest to what you want to write.

Teaching Tip Aside from helping a writer to have a strong organizational structure before beginning, you could tweak this strategy to be a revision strategy. That is, after students draft, they could create a bare-bones outline of what they've created, then look at what they have and consider structural changes. I always tell student writers that it is so much easier for me to invest some time planning the structure before writing than having to cut apart a draft and rearrange it. That said, some writers like to draft to see what emerges and then return to the writing later to make structure changes. Other writers do a little of both.

Prompts
- You have one possible outline. Let's try another.
- You can try to narrow your focus, and outline that narrowed focus.
- Take one chapter and imagine that as the book. What will your new chapters be?
- Take a different angle on the topic to create a new outline.
- You have three versions now! Which one do you want to go with? Why?

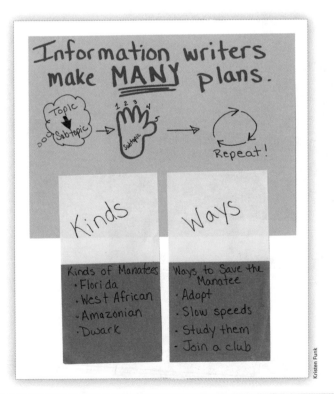

Kristen Funk

Hat Tip: "Try This! Outline, Re-Outline, Re-Outline Again" (Serravallo 2015b)

5.25 Lay Out Pages to See the Architecture

Who is this for?

LEVELS
3–8

GENRE / TEXT TYPE
any

PROCESS
revising

Strategy Take all the pages of your draft and spread them out on a table or the floor. Look across the pages for balance, structure, organization, architecture. Consider if any parts feel too long, any parts feel too short, or if anything needs to change with the layout. Make revisions as you see fit.

Teaching Tip As many upper elementary and middle school writers move to word processing for their draft, it's important to consider the option to print when implementing this strategy. It's something I need to do at least twice as I'm working on a book—I'll print out all 400 pages, lay them out, and read a hard copy. It's simply too hard to get the sense of the whole when you're scrolling on a screen through a small window.

Prompts

- Look at all the pages. What do you notice about the organization?
- Do any parts feel too long?
- Do any parts feel too short?
- Do you think anything needs to be rearranged?
- What might you revise, now that you've seen it laid out like this?

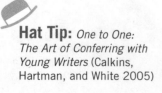

Hat Tip: *One to One: The Art of Conferring with Young Writers* (Calkins, Hartman, and White 2005)

Strategy Notice the different parts of your piece. Draw lines to separate the parts. Cut on the lines and consider rearranging. Consider places where you need to add in a new strip or page. Reread the piece with the new organization. Reorganize again as needed!

Teaching Tip You could certainly have students cut and paste on word-processing programs, but working digitally creates such finality—delete, and it's gone! For writers working on the computer, I'd advise printing out the page(s), cutting, reorganizing on a table, handwriting any additions deemed necessary, and then returning to the computer to make the desired changes. Sometimes there is no substitute for tactile manipulations!

Prompts

- Let's work together to find the parts.
- Identify the parts and draw a line.
- Cut the parts apart. What new organization will you try?
- Now that you have the parts separated, reconsider the organization.
- Reread to see what you may want to add in.

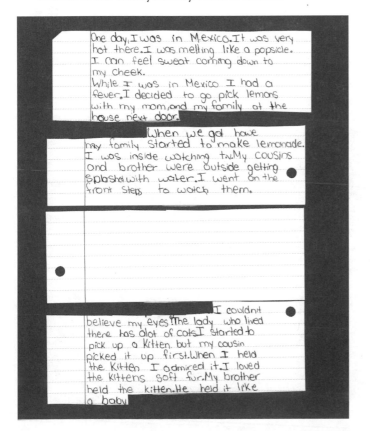

Hat Tip: *The Elements of Style, Fourth Edition* (Strunk and White 1999)

5.27 Draw Out (Don't Summarize) to Build Suspense

Who is this for?

LEVELS
3–8

GENRE / TEXT TYPE
narrative

PROCESSES
drafting, revising

Strategy Find the part in your story where your character solves his problem or gets what he wants. Box out the part of the story leading up to that moment. Try to slow down the action of that part by telling it with lots of detail. The added detail will delay the resolution and cause suspense!

Teaching Tip This lesson will work nicely with some of the lessons in the elaboration chapter that teach children about the kinds of detail to include. In other words, once children are able to identify the part that needs "slowing down" structurally, they will often benefit from support with how to slow the action down.

Using a Mentor Lester Laminack's *Snow Day* (2010) starts with the characters imagining and hoping for a snow day, with lots of detail to slow down the action and build suspense. Then, when the characters wake up to find there was no snow, there is a suspenseful rush as the family gets ready for school. Finally, a twist: We learn the narrator, the one hoping and wishing for the snow day, is the father, the teacher!

Prompts
- Where does the character get what he wants?
- Where is the problem resolved?
- Box out the part before it. Does it look like you summarized that part, or really drew it out step by step?
- Let's see if you can go slower in this part. Storytell it.

Hat Tip: *One to One: The Art of Conferring with Young Writers* (Calkins, Hartman, and White 2005)

I took the woman's hand and we walked toward the main building. I clasped my fingers tightly around hers, careful not to let go. As we walked up the stairs, the sun peered out over the top of the building. The rays hit the ocean and sparkled like diamonds in the sea. I turned around and looked out over New York harbor. How beautiful, I thought to myself. Just then, I heard the familiar sound of my papa's voice. "Anna, Anna," he screamed. He came running towards me, my mother following on his heels. He reached out and scooped me up into his arms. "Oh Anna," he said "we were so worried!"

(annotations: Tiny action; setting description; Internal thought; dialogue)

Writers draw out their story to build suspense!
1. Where is the problem resolved?
2. Re-read the part before it.
3. Storytell this part.

Think about:
Tiny Action   Setting description   Internal Thought
dialogue   Show not Tell feeling

Tiara Silvas

5.28 Repetition/List Structure

Strategy Think about what's most important in your piece. Think, "Is there a line or a part you could repeat to drive home the importance?" Consider what will be new each time you repeat it. Make a short list or series of sketches to plan out your draft.

Teaching Tip In the chapter on elaboration, you'll find repetition named as an elaboration technique in strategy 6.24, "Use a Refrain." This strategy asks students to consider a repetitive structure, which works well for some memoir, poetry, informational texts, and even speeches. This structure is a very efficient choice for children who have chosen to write about topics that are challenging to organize in another way, or when they are writing about a series of similar things. This can work across genres. In informational writing, a child may want to list all of the animals of Africa she can think of, writing about each on a new page and sharing a detail about what they look like, one about what they eat, and one about how they care for their young. In narrative, a child may want to tell a series of moments, perhaps with a repeating refrain, such as Rylant's *When I Was Young in the Mountains* (1982). In poetry, a child may choose to structure a series of stanzas each with a similar rhythm, number of lines, or repeating refrain.

Using a Mentor *If You're Not from the Prairie* (Bouchard 1993), like *When I Was Young in the Mountains* (1982) offers a repeated refrain to give a list-like feel to the overall piece.

Prompts

- What will repeat? Why?
- If that's your central idea, what phrase or structure might repeat?
- How often do you plan to repeat it?
- What will be new each time that it repeats?
- You should have a balance between what repeats and what's new.

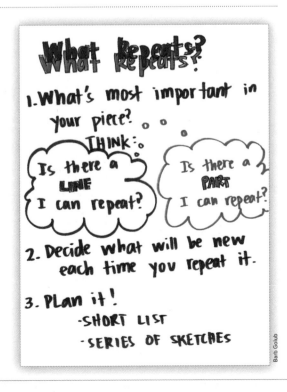

Barb Golub

Who is this for?

LEVELS
3–8

GENRE / TEXT TYPE
any

PROCESSES
developing, drafting, revising

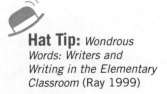

Hat Tip: *Wondrous Words: Writers and Writing in the Elementary Classroom* (Ray 1999)

Who is this for?

LEVELS
3–8

GENRE / TEXT TYPE
narrative

PROCESS
developing

Strategy Take a long strip of paper (a sentence strip works well) and create boxes. Each time there is a new setting or a new character, sketch a picture in the next box. Use your boxes to storytell, and then draft each scene on a separate piece of paper.

Teaching Tip When students are writing multiscene narratives, it's important that they don't rush through each scene so that the entire story ends up sounding like a summary. Instead, asking them to take a separate sheet of paper for each box on their storyboard helps them to see each scene as a story. You can then remind them of ways to draw out their story, bit by bit, and/or ask them to consider if this particular scene needs to be sped up to keep the narrative moving (see "Moving Quickly (or Slowly) Through Time," strategy 5.31, for more information on controlling time). Storyboarding ahead of time also helps the teacher get a quick glimpse at their plan before they draft. It's easier to resketch a picture than to rewrite an entire page.

Using a Mentor It's often helpful to storyboard a familiar read-aloud with the students so that they can envision how the storyboard relates to a story. I like using short picture books such as Lester Laminack's *Saturdays and Teacakes* (2004).

Prompts

• Is it a new setting or new character? Then it needs a new box!
• Just a quick sketch—enough to remind you about what you wanted to write.
• Now that you have your storyboard sketched, try to storytell it.
• Remember to stay on one picture to tell the entire story; don't skip over the good stuff by just telling a one-sentence summary.

Hat Tip: *Writing Fiction: Big Dreams, Tall Ambitions* (Calkins and Cruz 2006)

Strategy Clarify the problem that focuses your piece. Describe and give evidence for the problem. Name the solution you suggest. Give reasons with backup to convince your reader why your solution will work. Write an introduction and conclusion to frame the piece.

Teaching Tip If your students don't have experience with crafting introductions and conclusions, they will need other strategies in addition to this one. See other lead strategies in this chapter such as "Create Urgency," strategy 5.19, and strategy 5.21, "Lead by Addressing the Reader." See other conclusion strategies such as strategies 5.35, "Coming Full Circle," and 5.37, "Conclude with the Big Idea."

Prompts
- First, figure out what you're trying to convince your audience is the problem.
- Why is that a problem?
- Can you explain why?
- Now that you know the problem, try to explain the solution that will work.
- How can you introduce your topic?
- Conclude and wrap up.

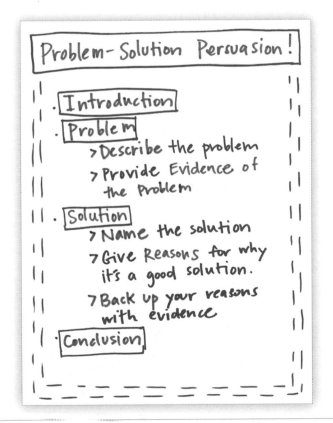

Who is this for?

LEVELS
3–8

GENRE / TEXT TYPE
opinion/persuasive

PROCESSES
developing, drafting

Hat Tip: *Inside Information: Developing Powerful Readers and Writers of Informational Text Through Project-Based Instruction* (Duke 2014)

Who is this for?

LEVELS
4–8

GENRE / TEXT TYPE
narrative

PROCESS
revising

Strategy Think about the moments in your story that are less important. Put a box around those parts. Save the in-depth description for parts that are more important to the heart of your story. Summarize what you want to get through quickly.

Teaching Tip This strategy could be used in conjunction with ones that teach children to slow down the important parts of their story (for example, "Find the Heart," strategy 4.3), and ones that help them consider the overall "parts" of their narrative (for example, "Multiscene Storyboarding," strategy 5.29).

Using a Mentor From *The Relatives Came*: "So they drank up all their pop and ate up all their crackers and traveled up all those miles until they finally pulled into our yard" (Rylant 1993). The heart of this story is really about the time the relatives spend visiting, so the traveling part is told in one sentence. However, with the list of descriptive details like "traveled up all those miles," she still communicates the amount of time that passes.

Prompts

- Find a part you want to shorten.
- Think about a part that your reader still needs to know, but isn't central to the heart of your story.
- What part do you think you need to get through more quickly?
- Try to say these four sentences in one or two.
- I agree, that part seems important to mention, but not worth spending a lot of time on.

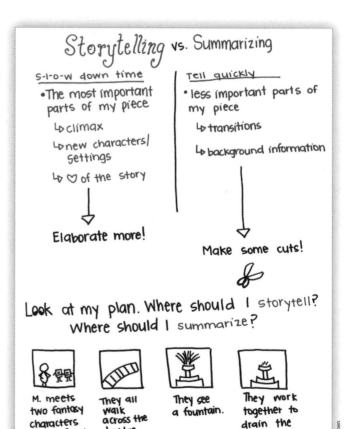

Hat Tip: *Wondrous Words: Writers and Writing in the Elementary Classroom* (Ray 1999)

Strategy Choose a piece of your writing that focuses on a topic for which you have a strong passion. Reread it. Try to reimagine it in a new genre. Draft a new piece based on the same topic, but with a new genre or structure.

Teaching Tip One of the most exciting things about revision is that you have the opportunity to completely reimagine your piece. What's more reimagined than changing the genre or the structure of the piece?

Nancie Atwell (2014) and others have said that writers often have "territories"—the topics they return to again and again. If you find yourself writing about a topic that really matters, it may be the case that that topic could work for you in other genres, too.

Take a personal narrative, and try to reimagine it as a poem, for example. You may consider the most essential words that you'd keep to communicate the message you want to send. Or take that same personal narrative and fictionalize it. Change the central problem, invent a new character or two, or write a resolution that's more what you wished had happened than what actually did. You could even take that same story and think about writing an informational text, to teach your reader about the topic.

What's interesting about this exercise is that you may find yourself surprised by the "truth" that comes out of changing the genre. Or you may find that new details or descriptions or images emerge when the genre changes, and those new bits can be reincorporated into the original piece.

Prompts

- How else could you write about this topic?
- You wrote a _____. Now let's try _____.
- What other genres might work for this topic?
- Reimagine this as a different genre, or taking on a different structure.

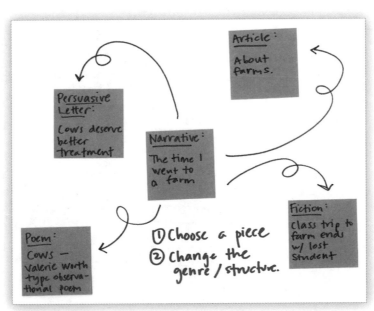

Who is this for?

LEVELS
4–8

GENRE / TEXT TYPE
any

PROCESS
revising

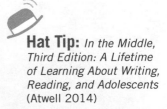

Hat Tip: *In the Middle, Third Edition: A Lifetime of Learning About Writing, Reading, and Adolescents* (Atwell 2014)

Strategy Think of your topic. Use your favorite strategy to break it down into large categories (parts, kinds, features, characteristics, etc.). Focus on one of the smaller categories as if that is the new topic. Break it down further into smaller categories (not facts!). Test out each category to make sure you have several facts to share.

Teaching Tip See strategy 7.16, "Clever Titles, Headings, and Subheadings," for ideas for ways to help kids jazz up the language in their headings. This strategy is really about understanding the way to break down information into parts and categories. Some children may want to do this out loud, and others may prefer to web or outline their ideas.

Using a Mentor Most of Bobbie Kalman's nonfiction books are set up with headings and subheadings. In *What Is a Bat?* for example, there is a section titled "On the Wing" with subheadings "A Bat's Wings" and "Up, Up, and Away!" (Kalman and Levigne 1998, 14).

Prompts

- You already have five subtopics that are a part of the larger topic. Let's take one and see if it can be broken down further.
- The parts of your subtopics can be paragraphs in your section about that subtopic.
- That's a fact. What's a subtopic that fact belongs in?
- Let's check to make sure there isn't overlap here. Are these two subtopics really different? You can check to make sure they will have different facts.

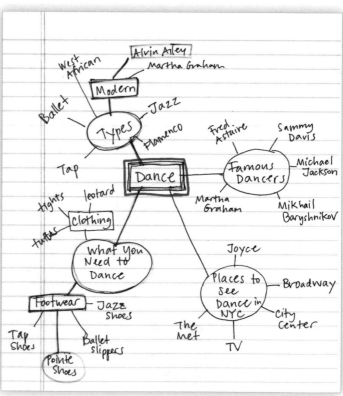

Strategy Take your draft and box out or draw horizontal lines to indicate the parts of the whole piece. Think about what your piece is mostly about (main idea or argument). Look back at each part asking yourself, "Is there too much or too little in this part?" Make decisions to cut or add based on how much weight you give each part of your piece.

Teaching Tip This strategy is similar to one that asks a reader to think about the heart of their story, or controlling time, which helps a reader consider which parts to slow down or speed through in a narrative. By thinking instead about the main argument/thesis of an opinion piece, the central meaning of a poem, or the main idea of an informational text, a writer can consider the amount of detail included in each part of a piece and how the amount of detail included lends "weight" to that part.

Prompts
- What's the most important thing about your piece? How much space did you dedicate to that?
- What part seems most important?
- What part seems least important?
- Are there any parts that you think you could speed up or abbreviate? Why?
- Go back and make some cuts to that part.
- Go back and elaborate more there, because that's the most important part.

Barb Golub

Who is this for?

LEVELS

4–8

GENRES / TEXT TYPES

informational/
nonfiction, poetry,
opinion/persuasive

PROCESS

revising

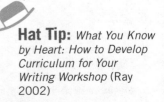

Hat Tip: *What You Know by Heart: How to Develop Curriculum for Your Writing Workshop* (Ray 2002)

5.35 Coming Full Circle

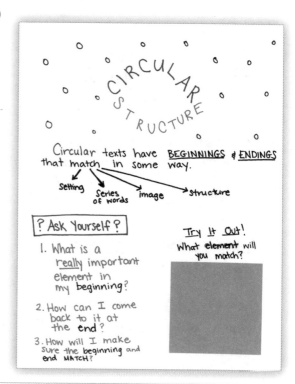

Who is this for?

LEVELS
4–8

GENRE / TEXT TYPE
any

PROCESSES
developing, drafting, revising

Hat Tip: *Wondrous Words: Writers and Writing in the Elementary Classroom* (Ray 1999); *Finding the Heart of Nonfiction: Teaching 7 Essential Craft Tools with Mentor Texts* (Heard 2013)

Strategy Reread the beginning of your piece. Identify some of the story elements—what is the setting, who are the characters and what are they saying, what is happening. Consider an ending that returns to one or more of the elements you describe at the beginning.

Teaching Tip Circular texts have beginnings and endings that match in some way, usually ending in the same place they began. It can be a literal, physical return to a setting. It could be a series of words or an image that begins and ends. Or, in the case of "Eleven" by Sandra Cisneros (2013), it could be that it begins and ends with reflection, with a scene in the middle. You can also use this structure when teaching children in other genres. An information piece may start with an announcement of the topic and the author's slant on the topic and end by reminding the reader yet again what the core of the piece was about. Likewise, opinion writing can begin with the writer stating a thesis or focus for the piece and concluding with a repetition of that thesis.

Using a Mentor

My Mama Had a Dancing Heart (Gray 1995)

The Sunsets of Miss Olivia Wiggins (Laminack 1998)

The Relatives Came (Rylant 1993)

"Poem" (Hughes 2003)

The Lotus Seed (Garland 1993)

Surprising Sharks (Davies 2005)

A Sweet Smell of Roses (Johnson 2007)

Prompts

- Name some things that are true about your beginning.
- What might you come back to at the end of your piece?
- As you come to the end of your piece, reread the beginning. If you were to end in a similar way, how might it sound?
- Now that you've tried a circular structure, does it work?

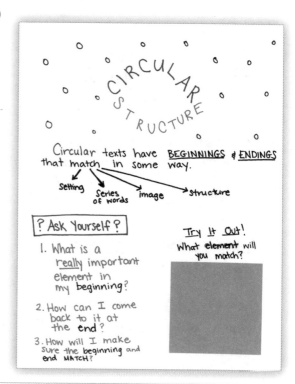

Strategy Think about what two things you want to alternate between—two settings, two ideas, two rhythms. Write one part, then the second. Repeat something from the first part, and then repeat something from the second part.

Teaching Tip The seesaw structure can be used in many genres. In informational texts, you might find a seesaw of question and answer, or as a way to compare and contrast. In narrative, you might find a back-and-forth between two settings. In poetry, you may be alternating between two voices. For any genre, it may be that the sentence structure is similar in each seesawing part, perhaps a long sentence then short, then long and then short. The structure can be used for an entire text, or for just a portion of a text, such as a paragraph.

Using a Mentor In *Tough Boris* (Fox 1994), the narrator describes the title character by saying "He was . . ." followed by "All pirates are . . ." with a new adjective like *scruffy*, *greedy*, *fearless* on each two-page spread.

The poetry collection *Joyful Noise: Poems for Two Voices* (Fleischman 1988) offers poems that alternate between two perspectives or two of the same animal.

No No Yes Yes by Leslie Patricelli (2008) is a simple picture book/board book that teaches children what to do and not to do with alternating examples, such as cutting your hair with scissors (no!) and cutting paper with scissors (yes!).

Prompts
- What's the back-and-forth going to be?
- Explain your idea for a pattern.
- On this page you ____, so if you want to do a seesaw, then on this page you could ____.
- I see that you're alternating back and forth between ____ and ____.

Who is this for?

LEVELS
4–8

GENRE / TEXT TYPE
any

PROCESSES
developing, drafting, revising

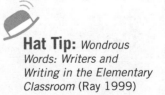

Hat Tip: *Wondrous Words: Writers and Writing in the Elementary Classroom* (Ray 1999)

See-Saw Structure

1. Decide what you'll alternate between. *(RHYTHM IDEA SETTING)*

2. Write one part, then the next. *(IDEA / SETTING)*

3. Repeat something from the 1st part then the 2nd. *(IDEA / SETTING SETTING)*

5.37 Conclude with the Big Idea

Who is this for?

LEVELS
4–8

GENRE / TEXT TYPE
any

PROCESSES
drafting, revising

Hat Tip: *The Writing Thief: Using Mentor Texts to Teach the Craft of Writing* (Culham 2014)

Strategy Reread your piece. Think about the big idea you want to leave your readers with. Write a few sentences summing up your whole piece, and making the big idea clear.

Using a Mentor *On a Beam of Light: A Story of Albert Einstein* (Berne 2013) is an example of one informational narrative text where the ending offers the reader closure and the opportunity to reflect on the big, powerful ideas about the subject of the biography.

> [Albert] asked questions never asked before. Found answers never found before. And dreamed up ideas never dreamt before. Albert's ideas helped build spaceships and satellites that travel to the moon and beyond. His thinking helped us understand our universe as no one ever had before. But still, Albert left us many big questions. Questions that scientists are working on today. Questions that one day you might answer. By wondering, thinking and imagining. (56)

Marshfield Dreams: When I Was a Kid (Fletcher 2012) ends with last lines that both wrap up the big ideas and communicate the purpose of the memoir genre:

> "Coming!" I yelled back. I sat up and brushed off the pine needles. Bits of light danced in the deep forest shadows around me. I knew I'd never forget that place. Then I stood up and stepped into my new life, whatever that might be. (183)

Prompts

- What's the big idea?
- Think about all you wrote about. Think about the one thing you want to leave your reader thinking about.
- Let's try a few sentences aloud that will sum up your big idea.
- You just told me your big idea. Now try to put that into a few sentences.
- How will you end your piece?

"You played well" she finally spoke.
"Thank you" I said pleased as I raised my hand higher. When the T.D came, he asked us our names and who won.
"White wins on board 27" I said quickly. He told us to shake hands and reset the board. After that was done, I raced to the exit of the cafeteria.
"I won, I won" I kept saying repeatedly. I raced up the stairs with all the energy I had left. Then I realized, I had been scared for no reason. Anybody can beat someone else even though they are younger or have a lower raiting.

5.38 Parallel Story

Strategy Think of the two main characters in your story. Plan out what one character's experience will be on a timeline or story mountain. Draw a second line parallel to the first. Plan out what the second character will do. Try to make the events on each timeline relate to or echo each other. Then, circle the similar events on both timelines and when you're writing, incorporate what's in a circle on the same page/part of your draft.

Teaching Tip This strategy may make the most sense to students who are reading narratives that have multiple plotlines and who are able to track the journeys of two separate characters in their books. If you have *The Reading Strategies Book: Your Everything Guide to Developing Skilled Readers*, take a look at strategy 5.25, "Double Plot Mountain," for ideas on how to teach this to readers (Serravallo 2015a).

Using a Mentor *The Paperboy* by Dav Pilkey is a text where the boy and the dog do similar, parallel things throughout the story (1996).

Prompts

- What are the main events your character will experience?
- Create the timeline for your main character.
- I see you thinking about the timeline for the second character, and you're careful to make the events align in some way.
- I can see how the events connect. What's next?

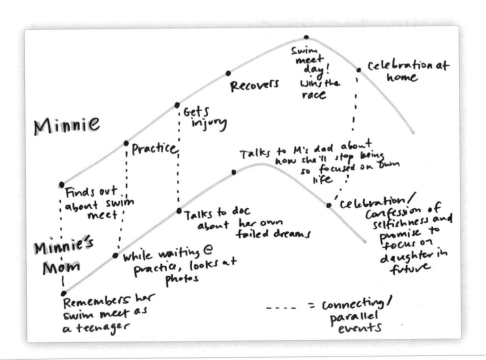

Who is this for?

LEVELS
4–8

GENRE / TEXT TYPE
narrative

PROCESSES
developing, drafting

Hat Tip: *Craft Lessons: Teaching Writing K–8, Second Edition* (Portalupi and Fletcher 2007)

Who is this for?

LEVELS
4–8

GENRE / TEXT TYPE
any

PROCESS
drafting

Strategy Try writing your draft quickly, getting just the gist of things down. Leave holes that you plan to fill in later by hitting the return button, skipping lines, or leaving the initials TK, meaning "to come." Stay in the flow of the draft and don't let anything (like the need to look up a fact or find a reference or Google an example) stop you. Once you have the shape of the draft down, go back to revisit and fill in the holes.

Teaching Tip When I began working on this book, I had a conversation with one of my editors about my process. She asked, "Are you a plodder or a dumper?" Plodders are people who write very slowly, revise and reread a lot, and won't move on until everything is in good shape. Dumpers just want to get it out as quickly as possible and can let go of things being perfect, as they know they'll return to things later. This strategy is best for a "dumper." (In case you're curious: I'm a dumper, she's a plodder. You should have seen my first draft of this book!)

Prompts
• Just get the gist down.
• Instead of getting stuck there, just put a *TK* and come back to it later.
• Try to stay in the flow.
• Just make a note to yourself of what you'll go and look up later.

Hat Tip: *A Writer Teaches Writing* (Murray 1985)

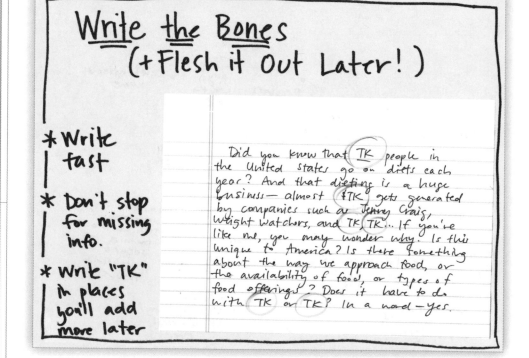

5.40 Leading with Contrast

Strategy To help your reader to see the focus of your piece, it sometimes helps to set up a contrastive example. First, show the reader what the focus is not. Then, lead into what the focus is.

Lesson Language *In the story I've been working on—the true story about a time I cut my sister's hair while she was sleeping—I decided I wasn't happy with the lead. After I thought about it, I felt like it just jumped into the story too quickly and the whole story felt too one-note. I am thinking I'll try instead starting off with something that feels like the opposite. Because I'm telling a story of something so terrible, maybe I'll lead with the setting, and I'll describe a calm, cool, quiet night: "A gentle moonlight glow spread across the wood floors in her bedroom. Not a sound could be heard except the gentle breeze blowing the curtain. And then I stepped into the room."*

Using a Mentor Take a look at Leonard Pitts Jr.'s piece, "Hey, Star Wars Toymakers, Where's Rey?" (2016), which begins with the lead: "I used to consider women pitifully weak and pathetically delicate. For this, I blame Marvel Comics." This leads into his discussion of the leading character from the latest Star Wars movie and how she is anything but weak and delicate, and his argument that children need images of strong female characters like Rey in their toys today.

Prompts
- What do you want your focus to be? Think about the opposite.
- How can you lead your reader to think one thing, and then switch it on them?
- How might you show a character's traits with contrast?

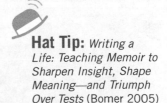

OPPOSITES ATTRACT

1. Consider the focus of your piece. Then, plan the OPPOSITE!

2. How can you draw your reader to think one thing...
   - setting
   - lead
   - character traits

3. ... then switch it on them!
   ★CREATE A CONTRAST★

Barb Golub

Who is this for?

LEVELS
5–8

GENRES / TEXT TYPES
narrative, opinion/ persuasive, informational/ nonfiction

PROCESSES
developing, drafting, revising

Hat Tip: *Writing a Life: Teaching Memoir to Sharpen Insight, Shape Meaning—and Triumph Over Tests* (Bomer 2005)

Elaboration

◎ Why is this goal important?

Elaboration is the specific information a writer uses to develop her topic. Elaboration includes but is not limited to: details, facts, anecdotes, dialogue, inner thinking, setting description, character description, statistics, reasons, information, and direct quotations from interview subjects. With strong use of purposeful detail, a piece of writing comes to life and the author's intended meaning is clear. With an absence of detail to develop the character, paint the world of the story, explain the content, or offer reasons and facts for the purpose of persuasion, the writing often falls flat or feels confusing to a reader.

Choosing this goal means you'll be helping writers to take the skeleton of the piece they have and flesh it out, adding more details to help the reader envision the story they are telling, understand the argument they are making, or comprehend the subject they are informing the reader about. However, more detail doesn't always mean better. As William Zinsser writes in *On Writing Well: The Classic Guide to Writing Nonfiction*: "Clutter is the disease of American writing. We are a society strangling in unnecessary words, circular constructions, pompous frills and meaningless jargon" (2001, 7). To say it another way, this chapter will help writers to add more details, sure. But the strategies will also help children to improve the quality of those details by teaching them to write with more precision and care. Offering a variety of elaboration strategies will also help students to vary the types of details they may include in their piece, so that their drafts don't end up sounding one-note. Overall, we should aim to not just to say to children, "Add more details," but rather, "Think about what it is you're trying to say/show/tell. Now what details would best help you do that?" (Murray 1985; Anderson 2005).

⊙ How do I know if this goal is right for my student?

Students who write with very few details, need help varying details, or need support considering purposes behind the details they include can be good candidates for this goal.

Also, students who are new to writing with a narrow, specific focus will often need help fleshing their writing out. For example, if a student has learned to take a personal narrative that was all about his summer vacation and narrow the focus down to just the roller-coaster ride at the amusement park, he may need support taking what was only a sentence in the original draft and expanding it into a full story.

A typical first step is to help students develop a *sufficient amount* of detail (Cali 2003). What's sometimes challenging for students is that they assume that their reader knows everything they know. Writers then neglect to include enough information so that the reader can also visualize what the writer is visualizing.

A next step may be to help students to vary the *types* of details they are including. For example, a student writing a narrative with simply character action can be taught to also include dialogue, inner thinking of the character, and some setting description. A student working on informational writing who is including generalized facts can be taught to add some statistics, quotes from experts, or survey results.

Once a student is comfortable with a variety of detail types, it would then be useful to help the student be sure that the details they include are *relevant* (Cali 2003). For instance, this means you will be teaching students to not only add character dialogue to their narrative, but to also ask, "What are you trying to show about your character? What dialogue can help you show that?" It means, for example, helping a child who is writing an argument essay to think about what the counterarguments might be and to include details that will help rebut those counterarguments. At this point, the goals of elaboration and focus may have some natural overlaps, and you may find yourself referencing both Chapter 4 and this one to support a child with purposeful elaboration.

Strategies for Elaborating

Strategy	Grade Levels	Genres/Text Types	Processes
6.1 Pictures Teach, Words Teach	K–2	Informational/nonfiction	Drafting, revising
6.2 Add More to Your Pictures (Then, Maybe More to Your Words!)	K–2	Any	Drafting, revising
6.3 Speech Bubbles Let Your Characters Talk	K–2	Narrative	Drafting, revising
6.4 Act It Out . . . Then Get It Down	K–3	Narrative, informational/nonfiction	Drafting, revising
6.5 "Nudge" Paper	K–8	Any	Revising
6.6 Teach with Diagrams	K–8	Informational/nonfiction	Drafting, revising
6.7 See the World like a Poet (Metaphor and Simile)	K–8	Any	Developing, drafting, revising
6.8 Flaps and Carets	K–8	Any	Revising
6.9 "What *Else* Happened?"	K–8	Narrative	Revising
6.10 Prove It	1–8	Opinion/persuasive, informational/nonfiction	Developing, drafting, revising
6.11 Take Notes from an Illustration or a Photo	1–8	Any	Developing
6.12 Cracking Open Nouns	1–8	Any	Revising
6.13 Show, Don't Tell: Using Senses to Describe Places	1–8	Narrative	Developing, drafting, revising
6.14 Show, Don't Tell: Emotions	1–8	Narrative	Revising
6.15 Let Your Readers Know Who's Talking!	1–8	Narrative	Drafting, revising
6.16 Read Mentor Texts with Two Lenses: Information, Aesthetic	2–8	Any	Developing, drafting, revising
6.17 Research from People (Interviews)	2–8	Informational/nonfiction, opinion/persuasive	Developing, revising
6.18 Keeping a Research Notebook	2–8	Informational/nonfiction	Developing
6.19 Read, Sketch, Stretch	2–8	Informational/nonfiction	Developing
6.20 External Character Description	2–8	Narrative	Developing, drafting, revising
6.21 Write the "Inside Story"	2–8	Narrative	Drafting, revising
6.22 Support Your Facts	2–8	Informational/nonfiction, opinion/persuasive	Drafting, revising
6.23 Partner Facts: Ask Yourself, "How?"	2–8	Informational/nonfiction, opinion/persuasive	Drafting, revising

Strategy	Grade Levels	Genres/Text Types	Processes
6.24 Use a Refrain	2–8	Narrative, poetry, opinion/persuasive	Drafting, revising
6.25 Cracking Open Verbs	2–8	Any	Revising
6.26 Exploring Options for Setting	3–8	Fictional narrative	Developing, revising
6.27 Picture Your Character	3–8	Narrative	Developing, drafting, revising
6.28 Tell What It's Not (to Say What It Is)	3–8	Any	Developing, drafting, revising
6.29 Be Patient, Go Slow	3–8	Narrative	Drafting, revising
6.30 Bring in the Periphery	3–8	Any	Generating and collecting, drafting
6.31 Use Empathy to Figure Out What to Add	3–8	Narrative	Developing, drafting, revising
6.32 Writing Through a Mask (Perspective and Point of View)	4–8	Any	Developing, drafting, revising
6.33 How Does Your Character Talk?	4–8	Narrative	Developing, drafting, revising
6.34 Character Dialogue and Dialect for Historical Accuracy	4–8	Narrative nonfiction, historical fiction	Developing, revising
6.35 Use Imagery to Make a Fact Come Alive	4–8	Informational/nonfiction, opinion/persuasive	Developing, revising
6.36 Get the Sound (of Some Mentors) in Your Head	4–8	Any	Drafting, revising
6.37 Be Your Own Harshest Critic	4–8	Any	Revising
6.38 Mentor Sentence	4–8	Any	Revising
6.39 Talk to Yourself	4–8	Any	Developing, drafting, revising
6.40 Character Gestures to Show Traits	4–8	Narrative	Developing, drafting, revising
6.41 Anecdotes Can Teach and Give Evidence	4–8	Informational/nonfiction, opinion/persuasive	Developing, drafting, revising
6.42 Rule of Threes	4–8	Any	Developing, drafting, revising
6.43 Lie (to Tell the Truth)	4–8	Personal narrative, memoir	Developing, drafting, revising
6.44 Weave in Symbolism	5–8	Narrative	Drafting, revising
6.45 Clue In the Reader to the Past (Flashback)	5–8	Narrative	Developing, drafting, revising

Who is this for?

LEVELS
K–2

GENRE / TEXT TYPE
**informational/
nonfiction**

PROCESSES
drafting, revising

Strategy Reread what you wrote. Look at the picture. Make sure the picture gives the same information as the words or adds on a few more details that fit with the topic.

Lesson Language *The pictures in nonfiction often teach as much as the words do. Sometimes the picture's job is to show what the words say. Other times, the pictures can add on more facts beyond what the words on the page say. When they add more facts, they still stick to the topic. I'm looking back at my page here about zebras. I wrote: "Zebras have stripes. The stripes are black and white. When they walk or run in a group, it's hard for a lion to see one. They look like one big black and white blob. That's why zebras have stripes, to protect themselves." If I look at my picture, I see that I drew one zebra with stripes. So let me think, do these go together? Should I make any changes? Well, in my words I talked about a lion and I also talked how the stripes help them when they are in a group. I feel like I want to change my picture to add in at least one more zebra so my reader can see what I mean by a lion getting confused when they are in a group. (Continue the demonstration, perhaps offering another example where the picture and words don't match at all, and you decide to get a new half page of blank paper to cover the picture box entirely and draw a picture that matches.)*

Prompts

• Do your pictures and words go together?
• What is your picture teaching? What are your words teaching?
• What change do you want to make?

PICTURES TEACH WORDS TEACH

If you don't know how to swim make sure you are with a grown-up. ✗

To go swimming you have to wear a bathing suit. ✓

Merridy Gnagey

Hat Tip: *One to One: The Art of Conferring with Young Writers* (Calkins, Hartman, and White 2005)

Strategy Look carefully at your picture. Think, "What do I have in my mind that is not yet on the page?" Add more details to your picture. Then, looking at your picture, try to add more to your words.

Teaching Tip This strategy is, in a way, the "reverse" of the "Pictures Teach, Words Teach" (6.1) strategy. You can also use this strategy in combination with any of the strategies in this chapter that teach children about particular types of details, such as dialogue (see "Speech Bubbles Let Your Characters Talk," strategy 6.3) if you're working on narrative, or evidence (see strategy 6.10, "Prove It") if you're working on opinion writing.

Prompts
- Tell me what you see in your mind. What else can you add to your picture?
- Look at your picture. What might you want to write?
- Touch your picture, tell me what you drew.
- Now that you told me about your picture, add to your words.

Who is this for?

LEVELS
K–2

GENRE / TEXT TYPE
any

PROCESSES
drafting, revising

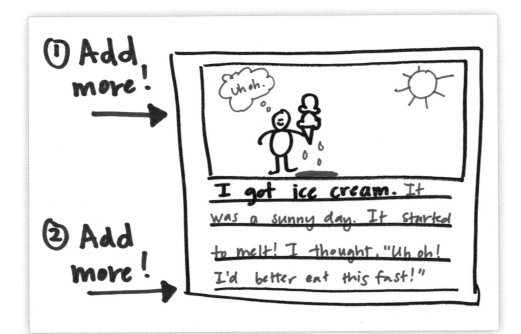

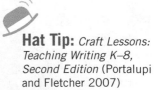

Hat Tip: *Craft Lessons: Teaching Writing K–8, Second Edition* (Portalupi and Fletcher 2007)

Who is this for?

LEVELS
K–2

GENRE / TEXT TYPE
narrative

PROCESSES
drafting, revising

Strategy Look at the scene you've drawn on your page. Think about what's happening. Then think, "What would my characters say here?" Draw a speech bubble and add their talking inside it.

Teaching Tip For some writers, the dialogue will stay in the speech bubbles on the picture. Other writers can be nudged to add what they put in their speech bubbles into the words on their page.

Using a Mentor Mo Willem's Elephant and Piggy series and Pigeon series tell the story through hilarious illustration and speech bubbles. Comic books and graphic novels would offer other examples of speech bubbles.

Prompts
- What's happening in your picture?
- Think about what your character would say.
- What would you write in the speech bubble?
- Just write the words that would come out of your character's mouth.
- Letting your readers know what the character says helps them picture your story!

Hat Tip: *Craft Lessons: Teaching Writing K–8, Second Edition* (Portalupi and Fletcher 2007)

Strategy Think about what you want to write. Act out the first part. Sit and write down what you just acted out, using as much detail as you can. Act out the next part. Write it. After you finish, you can go back and act it all out again, to make sure everything you've acted shows up on your page.

Lesson Language *I know I want to write about the time when I got soaked by a passing car as I was walking to school. So let me think how it starts. Oh, yeah! The walking by myself part. Here I go acting it out* (Act out walking, maybe looking around, maybe bending down to double-check the lacing of the shoes). *OK, let me sit and get this first part down on my page. "It was a regular day. I was putting one foot in front of the other, looking around at the changing leaves on the trees. I noticed my shoe was untied so I crouched down to tie it." Do you see how I didn't just say, "I was walking to school?" Acting it out helped me get more details down on my page!* (Continue demonstration with the next part if you feel students need a second example.)

Teaching Tip This strategy works well for narrative, but could also work for informational writing. A child can act out the things an elephant does, for instance, and then write down the information she just acted out.

Teaching Tip Students can do this independently, or with a partner.

Prompts
- Act out the first part.
- Say exactly what you did when you were acting it out.
- Get down all the details on your page.
- Think back to what you acted out. Now look at your page. Did you forget anything?

Merridy Gnagey

Who is this for?

LEVELS
K–3

GENRES / TEXT TYPES
narrative, informational/ nonfiction

PROCESSES
drafting, revising

Hat Tip: *One to One: The Art of Conferring with Young Writers* (Calkins, Hartman, and White 2005)

6.5 "Nudge" Paper

Who is this for?

LEVELS
K–8

GENRE / TEXT TYPE
any

PROCESS
revising

Hat Tip: *Explore Poetry*
(Graves 1992)

Strategy When you feel like a part of your draft (or notebook entry) needs work, but you're cautious about making the changes right on the page, take a strip of scrap paper. Try out your idea(s) on that separate page. Consider if you want to apply them to your entry or draft.

Teaching Tip In your writing center, you can keep a stack of this paper, labeled "nudge paper" or whatever clever title you come up with. You may also carry some around with you as you confer with students, gently encouraging them to try things on separate pages if they seem otherwise reluctant. Although this strategy could help children with any goal (for instance, it could support students working on organization if the paper is used to reimagine a structure by creating an outline, or trying out a new lead or ending), I chose to include it in the elaboration chapter because often what kids are testing out (but may be reluctant to add in right away) are added details or different details.

Prompts

- What do you think you want to try out on a separate page?
- That's OK if you don't want to keep it, let's just try it on this separate page.
- It's an experiment. You can decide later if you like what you've written.
- Instead of putting it here, you can just try it on this paper.

Strategy Draw a picture of what you want to teach. Think, "What are the important parts?" Draw a line to one important part. Write word(s) (or letter(s)!) to label each part. Repeat for other important parts of your picture.

Lesson Language *Because I am writing to teach people about my dog, I'm going to think, "What are the important parts?" I already drew a picture of her, and to make it a diagram, I'm going to try to add labels. Let's see. She's a bloodhound, and bloodhounds have very floppy ears. I'm going to draw a line to her floppy ears and write a label. What else? She has black spots on her back. I'm going to draw a line to that part and write "Black spots."*

Prompts

- What is this picture teaching?
- What's an important part?
- Draw a line to that part. Let's label it.
- What word do you want to write?
- What do you call that part?
- Are there other parts you want to label?

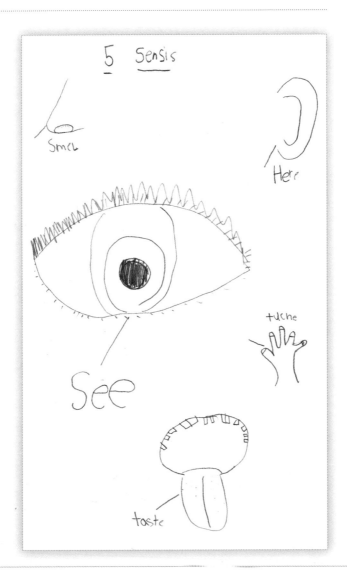

LEVELS

K–8

GENRE / TEXT TYPE

informational/ nonfiction

PROCESSES

drafting, revising

Hat Tip: *Nonfiction Craft Lessons: Teaching Information Writing K–8* (Portalupi and Fletcher 2001)

6.7 See the World like a Poet (Metaphor and Simile)

Who is this for?

LEVELS
K–8

GENRE / TEXT TYPE
any

PROCESSES
developing, drafting, revising

Hat Tip: *One to One: The Art of Conferring with Young Writers* (Calkins, Hartman, and White 2005)

Strategy Think of the features of what you want to compare. Think, "What has similar features?" Make a comparison by connecting your subject to something else like it.

Lesson Language *My daughter is a shell collector, and I brought in a few shells for us to practice with today. I'm going to show you with this conch shell how I can describe it beyond what it literally is and compare it to something else. I'm going to look at it and think about a feature: its shape. It's shaped like . . . a tornado! Or an ice-cream cone. It's spiked like a prehistoric creature. Now, I'll think about texture. It is as smooth as glass. It isn't actually an ice-cream cone or glass, but it is like it—its shape is sort of like a cone, and it feels like glass does.*

Using a Mentor Valerie Worth's *All the Small Poems and Fourteen More* (1996) is a collection of poems of everyday objects that the poet has reimagined. The poems are short, easy to read, and offer great examples of metaphor and simile. The picture book *You're Toast and Other Metaphors We Adore* by Nancy Loewen (2011) includes a collection of metaphors woven into a hybrid informational/narrative text.

Prompts

- Say just what it is, and what you see. Now think, "What's it *like*?"
- You can think about what it's like based on how it looks.
- You can think about what it's like based on what it does.
- Say, "The ____ is like a ____."
- I never would have thought of that! You're really thinking like a poet does.
- You saw that in a very original way!

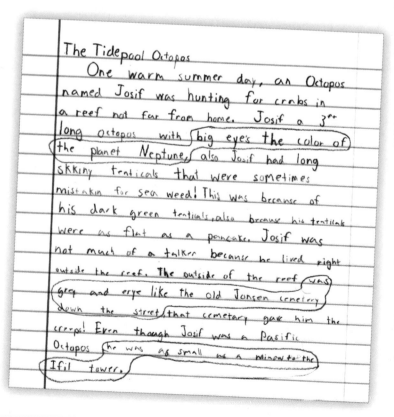

6.8 Flaps and Carets

Strategy If you know you want to add more, but you don't have the space, you can use a revision strip or flap, or a caret, to squeeze more details into your draft.

Teaching Tip Keep a variety of "revision" strips in your kindergarten, first-, or second-grade writing center. The strips can be one-quarter or one-half pages with lines, and even a "strip" with a picture box for children to tape on top of their existing picture if they want to make changes to it. Sticky notes work well for students of all ages, so be sure to have those on hand, too.

Prompts

- Where do you want to add on? Think about how much space you need.
- Add on a flap—three sentences means you'll need more room!
- Let's go ahead and try to squeeze that into the margin using a caret.
- Say aloud what you want your draft to say. Now point to where you want to make a change. How will you add it in?

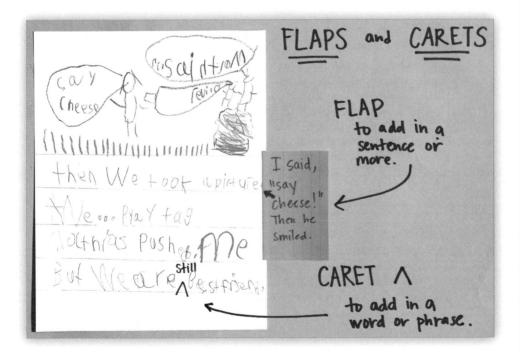

Hat Tip: *One to One: The Art of Conferring with Young Writers* (Calkins, Hartman, and White 2005)

Who is this for?

LEVELS
K–8

GENRE / TEXT TYPE
any

PROCESS
revising

6.9 "What *Else* Happened?"

Strategy Read one event in your story. Ask yourself, "What else happened? What did I leave out that I'm assuming my reader would know but really doesn't?" Go back to add details to the event in the order they happened.

Teaching Tip One way to help make this strategy concrete for K–1 students is to teach them to add more to their pictures, then go back to their pictures to jog their memory about all that happened at that part of their story. [See strategy 6.2, "Add More to Your Pictures (Then, Maybe More to Your Words!)".] Then, they can go to their words to compare if what they told themselves is also in the words.

Prompts

- Did anything else happen there?
- You said _____ and then _____. It feels like something else happened you're not telling your reader.
- Reread to check if you've got all the events down.
- Ah! You thought of something else to add that would help your reader.

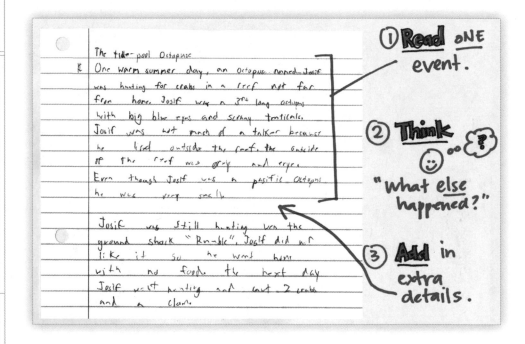

Hat Tip: *One to One: The Art of Conferring with Young Writers* (Calkins, Hartman, and White 2005)

THE WRITING STRATEGIES BOOK

Strategy Think of your idea/claim/thesis. Think, "What are my reasons for thinking that way? What details prove what I want to say?" Make a list of reasons and facts that support your point.

Teaching Tip Depending on the type of opinion writing, you will want to offer students a way to organize all of these reasons and facts into some sort of logical, easy-to-follow order. See strategies such as 5.18, 5.24, or 5.30 from Chapter 5, "Organization and Structure," for more support with this.

Teaching Tip This strategy leads children to elaborate with reasons (categories for their proof) and details (facts that elaborate on the categories). Less-experienced writers may only list reasons or facts, but not both. More-experienced writers should do both.

Prompts
- What might convince your reader?
- Think of a fact you know that proves it.
- Let's list a few reasons why.
- Now that you have reasons, can you think of some facts that back up those reasons?

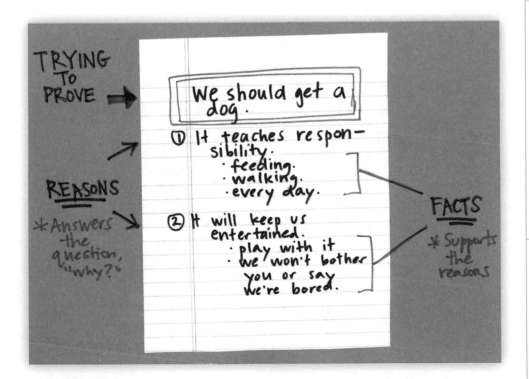

Who is this for?

LEVELS
1–8

GENRES / TEXT TYPES
opinion/persuasive, informational/ nonfiction

PROCESSES
developing, drafting, revising

Hat Tip: *Breathing Life into Essays* (Calkins and Gillette 2006)

Strategy Look closely at an illustration or photograph that can teach you about the topic you are writing about. Jot quick notes—in single words or short phrases—that capture what you're learning.

Teaching Tip This strategy is helpful for students doing research who need to add more facts/information to their piece. Some younger students will appreciate the strategy if they've chosen a topic for which there are no books or materials that they can read and understand. All students will appreciate learning ways to get information from rich photographs, illustrations, or diagrams.

Prompts
• Look closely at the photo, part by part.
• What do you see?
• What's a fact that you know from looking at that photograph?
• Jot down what you're learning. You can use it later in your draft!

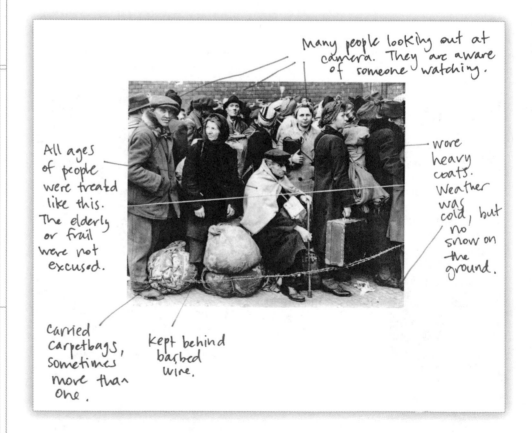

Many people looking out at camera. They are aware of someone watching.

All ages of people were treated like this. The elderly or frail were not excused.

wore heavy coats. Weather was cold, but no snow on the ground.

Carried carpetbags, sometimes more than one.

kept behind barbed wire.

Hat Tip: *Craft Lessons: Teaching Writing K–8, Second Edition* (Portalupi and Fletcher 2007)

Strategy Return to your draft looking for places that may need more description or detail. Underline single nouns or noun phrases that seem to summarize rather than describe. On a sticky note or in your notebook, try to take the single word or phrase and turn it into a long descriptive phrase.

Lesson Language *I found one spot in my draft where I used a phrase that needs more description—a lot. What is "a lot"? Listen to how it sounds now: There is a lot you can see when you look at the night sky. Well, if I think about what you can see, and am specific and make a list instead, maybe I could write something like: "When you look at the night sky, you can see a moon's craters, stars twinkling in all different sizes, and if you're lucky, maybe even a sailing meteor." Which one will better help the reader to imagine what I imagined?*

Using a Mentor "Description begins in the writer's imagination, but should finish in the reader's" (King 2000, 174).

Prompts
- Underline your nouns.
- Which of those nouns seem to give a quick summary, rather than describe?
- Take that one word and turn it into a descriptive phrase.
- By making that revision, you've added in much more detail!

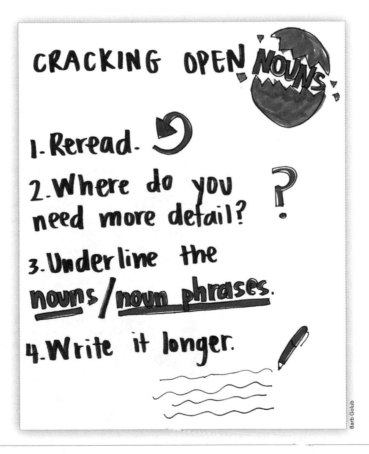

CRACKING OPEN NOUNS

1. Reread.
2. Where do you need more detail?
3. Underline the nouns/noun phrases.
4. Write it longer.

Barb Golub

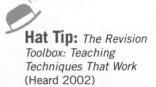

Hat Tip: *The Revision Toolbox: Teaching Techniques That Work* (Heard 2002)

6.13 Show, Don't Tell: Using Senses to Describe Places

Who is this for?

LEVELS
1–8

GENRE / TEXT TYPE
narrative

PROCESSES
developing, drafting, revising

Hat Tip: *Writing a Life: Teaching Memoir to Sharpen Insight, Shape Meaning—and Triumph Over Tests* (Bomer 2005)

Strategy Imagine where your story is taking place. Think "What do I hear, see, smell, taste, feel?" Add in as many sensory details as you can. Go back and reread, deciding which to keep and which to cut.

Lesson Language *A mistake that writers sometimes make is that we assume our reader knows what's in our mind. The truth is, what we imagine is clearest to us, and one of our jobs as writers is to help make it clear to our readers, too. Including details about how we experience the topic with each of our senses can help readers feel almost like they are there with us.*

Using a Mentor There are so many examples of descriptive setting. One of my favorite evocative descriptions is throughout the book *Come On, Rain!* by Karen Hesse (1999), the story of a little girl in a hot, hot city wanting it to rain. The author describes the sounds of trucks rolling past and thunder, the feel of "drooping" people and plants, the smell of "hot tar and garbage," and the images of "heat waves off tar patches." *If You're Not from the Prairie* (Bouchard 1993) is a nonnarrative picture book that elaborates each detail about the setting of the prairie (wind, sky, sun, and more) with sensory details across several lines.

Prompts
- Use your senses.
- Slow down and describe. What do you see? Hear? Feel?
- Add in more details about what you'd experience if you were there.
- *(Nonverbally cue child to add details by touching your eye, your ears, your nose.)*
- You just added two more sense details! Now I feel like I'm right there!

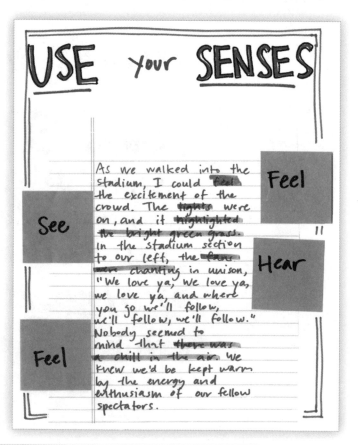

Strategy Find a feeling word in your draft. Ask yourself, "What does it look like when I have that emotion?" Use a phrase to describe, or show, the feeling, rather than telling the reader by using the feeling word.

Teaching Tip This lesson helps students to understand how to use this process with feeling words (*sad, mad, happy*). You could also refer to the lesson "Cracking Open Verbs" (strategy 6.25) or "Cracking Open Nouns" (strategy 6.12) to help children be more precise and/or descriptive when using words like *went* or *nice*.

Using a Mentor Take a look at the character Trixie from Mo Willem's *Knuffle Bunny* (2004). When she gets frustrated that her dad can't understand her, the author doesn't say *frustrated*—he says she "went boneless." She "bawled." And she started exclaiming using the almost-words "Aggle flaggle klabble!"

Prompts
- Name the emotion. Describe what it looks like when someone feels that way.
- Can you find feeling words in your writing?
- Let's think about that feeling. What does it look like?
- Use more than one word to really show that feeling.

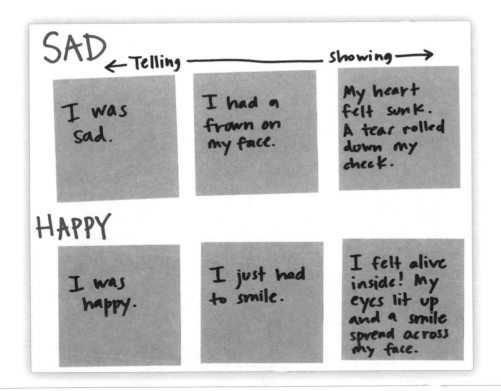

Who is this for?

LEVELS
1–8

GENRE / TEXT TYPE
narrative

PROCESS
revising

Hat Tip: *The Craft of Revision* (Calkins and Bleichman 2003)

Who is this for?

LEVELS
1–8

GENRE / TEXT TYPE
narrative

PROCESSES
drafting, revising

Strategy Make your character(s) talk. When you write the dialogue, make sure it is clear who said it (and maybe how they said it or what they were doing when they said it). You can add the tag before the dialogue, in the middle of the dialogue, or after the dialogue. Just make sure it's clear who's talking!

Teaching Tip Adapt this strategy for the age and experience of your writers. For some, just adding dialogue that is direct speech versus summarized speech (e.g., "'Get downstairs,' my mom said" versus "My mom told me to get downstairs") will be a big change. For more-experienced writers, teaching them to add not just what was said but how it was said or the actions associated with the dialogue ("'Get downstairs,' my mom shouted, leaning against the banister."). For the record, I don't think "said is dead" or that we should be teaching children to go through their drafts replacing *said* with a more specific action. For more on this topic, I recommend a *Washington Post* opinion piece by Alexandra Petri (2015).

Using a Mentor The following dialogue exchange between Cotton and Charlie from *Boys of Blur* by N. D. Wilson (2015) shows various placement of the dialogue tag and an occasional inclusion of actions associated with the dialogue. In one instance, the author used *ask* instead of *said*, but *said* is still the most often used (as you'll find in most books):

> "Well?" Cotton asked. Charlie nodded, staring at the collapsed and rotten shacks.
> Cotton picked up the snake by the tail and stood, grinning.
> "Wanna hold it?"
> "Cotton," Charlie said, and he took a step back.
> Cotton laughed and jiggled the snake. "Dead. See?" (Wilson 2015, 15)

Prompts
- What did your character say? Who said it?
- I see dialogue on the page. See if you can find it, too.
- Dialogue is when your character talks. Did you add any dialogue here?
- Write who said it.
- Add, "Said _____."

Hat Tip: *The Elements of Style, Fourth Edition* (Strunk and White 1999)

Strategy Read a mentor text first to get the information. Return to the text, this time focusing on images, interesting words the author used, and/or figurative language. Name what the author did and then try it in your own writing.

Using a Mentor Georgia Heard quotes William Zinsser in saying that the texts that a writer (or teacher of writing) chooses need to do more than just simply give information (2013). The writing from ideal mentor texts must feel alive, have warmth, and have humanity. Compare, for example, the tone and craft of the following two texts, both about animals.

From *Exploding Ants: Amazing Facts About How Animals Adapt*:

Sharing a nest with a newly hatched cuckoo bird can be a deadly proposition. Cuckoo young aren't big on sharing. In fact, they make certain they won't have to share food or space by throwing their nest mates out of the nest. Cuckoos are nest stealers, or *brood parasites*. (Settel 1999, 10)

From *Amazing Salamanders*:

Salamanders are amphibians, like frogs and toads. Most begin their life in water, then grow into air-breathing adults. Many salamanders go through incredible changes as they grow and become adults. (Shanahan 2010, 6)

Both texts serve a purpose to teach the reader facts about animals. The second one feels straightforward and direct, but the first one appeals to the reader and uses surprising language (e.g., "deadly proposition").

Prompts
- What are some of the interesting language choices the author used?
- How did the author use details here?
- What did the author include? Why do you think the author did that?

What did you learn?	What did you notice that will help your writing? (Images, Words, Language, Craft)...
• cuckoo birds don't like to share • cuckoo birds throw "nestmates" (siblings) out of the nest.	• strong language to draw the reader in ("deadly proposition") • specific vocab with definition ("nest stealers or brood parasites.") • personification (sort of) → "Cuckoo birds aren't big on sharing."

Who is this for?

LEVELS
2–8

GENRE / TEXT TYPE
any

PROCESSES
developing, drafting, revising

Hat Tip: *Finding the Heart of Nonfiction: Teaching 7 Essential Craft Tools with Mentor Texts* (Heard 2013)

Who is this for?

LEVELS

2–8

GENRES / TEXT TYPES

informational/
nonfiction, opinion/
persuasive

PROCESSES

developing, revising

Hat Tip: *A Writer
Teaches Writing* (Murray
1985)

Strategy Think about the people who have knowledge of your topic. Create an interview to get information from them. Ask open-ended questions that will get your interviewee to talk, sharing details that you can add to your piece.

Lesson Language *As you craft your questions, be sure to ask questions that get the interview subject talking beyond a yes-or-no answer and take into account the types of information the person would know about. When you interview, take notes on their responses and also on the gestures, expressions, or behavior of the person being interviewed.*

Teaching Tip For a different spin on interviewing, see "Interview to Dig for and Uncover Topics" (strategy 3.9 in the chapter on generating and collecting ideas).

Prompts

- Think about the people you'll interview, and what they might know.
- Think about what they'd be able to tell you. Craft a question to get that information from them.
- Check your question—can it be answered with "yes" or "no"?
- Rewrite that question so it doesn't seem like you are expecting a certain answer.
- That question will get your interviewee to talk a lot! It's very open-ended.

Barb Golub

Strategy Think about the subtopics for which you'll want to collect information. Write each of your subtopics as a heading on a notebook or booklet page. As you find new information for your topic, think, "What page in my notebook should this go on? Which subtopic does it provide details for?"

Lesson Language *I just found this interesting fact: Ballerinas really wear out their shoes. Many go through as many as 2–3 pairs per week! I'm going to look across the pages of my booklet to see where this would best fit. Would it belong in the section called "Types of Ballet Positions?" No, that's not about the positions. Would it go in the section called "Famous Ballets?" No. "What Ballerinas Wear?" Well, I do talk about pointe shoes in this section, so it might be cool to add this fact about how many pairs of pointe shoes the average ballerina needs. I'll keep the fact here.*

Prompts
- Let's put a heading on the top of each page of your notebook.
- What are the categories of information you're looking for?
- You found a fact that fits with your topic.
- Where might you put that information?
- What category does that information belong to?

Who is this for?

LEVELS
2–8

GENRE / TEXT TYPE
**informational/
nonfiction**

PROCESS
developing

What Ballerinas Wear

Pointe shoes have a hard toe so ballerinas can stand on their toes.

Most ballerinas wear out 2–3 pairs of pointe shoes per week.

Many of hours of practice are spent in soft slipper shoes

Types of Ballet Positions

First position is when heels are together, toes are apart.

There are arm positions that go with 5 foot positions.

Positions have french and English names.

Hat Tip: *Crafting Nonfiction, Intermediate* (Hoyt 2012)

Strategy Read to learn some information about the topic you'll be writing about. Stop and make sure you understand what you read. Sketch a picture or diagram to show the information you learned. Add labels and captions to your notes using your own words.

Teaching Tip One common problem with teaching children to add more information about their research topic is that they tend to copy the information straight from the book. Do they understand what they copy? Who knows, but probably not. Instead, having them convert the words they read into pictures and labeling and captioning with their own words ensures that they note only what they comprehend. When they convert these notes to a draft, their writing will sound like it's in their own voice. This is also a great strategy to use with younger students who may be able to write sketch notes more fluently than notes in sentences.

Prompts

- What's the important information you learned from this page?
- Now check to make sure you understand it.
- Sounds like you understand what you read! What sketch will you draw?
- Draw a sketch quickly to hold onto that information.
- Now label.
- Can you add a caption or sentence to explain what you've drawn?
- I see you're using your own words. That shows you understand it.

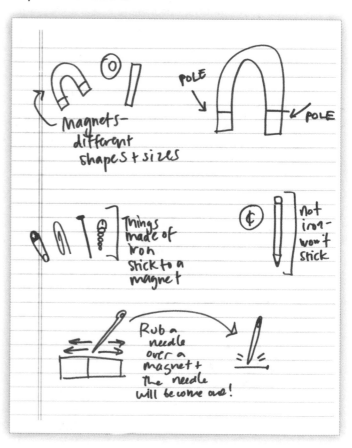

Strategy Visualize the character you're creating. Describe your character with details that show what he or she is like and how he or she is unique from the other characters in your story.

Using a Mentor The Newbery Honor book *Inside Out and Back Again* (Lai 2011) is inspired by the author's experience fleeing Vietnam after the fall of Saigon and immigrating to Alabama. On page 142, Lai offers us vivid descriptions of external character traits from both the main character and the characters she meets in the new, foreign land.

Prompts
- Describe your character. What do you see?
- Which of those descriptive details will be important to share with your reader?
- What makes your character stand out?
- Let's see where you can weave those details into your draft.

Barb Golub

Who is this for?

LEVELS
2–8

GENRE / TEXT TYPE
narrative

PROCESSES
developing, drafting, revising

Hat Tip: *The Writing Thief: Using Mentor Texts to Teach the Craft of Writing* (Culham 2014)

6.21 Write the "Inside Story"

Strategy Think about the reactions characters have to events and include their feelings. Imagine what might be going on in their minds as the events are happening and include their thoughts.

Lesson Language *When you write, try to say what people can see (actions) and hear (dialogue and setting details). Make sure you're also writing the inside story—how your characters are feeling inside their hearts and what they are thinking inside their heads.*

Using a Mentor Holly Goldberg Sloan's *Counting by 7's*, told from the perspective of the main character, is rich with examples of internal thinking and feeling. Here's just one selection: "My teeth start to chatter. I want to shut my eyes and make everything stop. I no longer care if my heart pounds in my chest or if my lungs move. Who are they even moving for?" (Sloan 2014, 110).

Prompts
- What's going on in your character's mind?
- Write what your character does, then what your character thinks.
- Think about a character's reaction: thoughts or feelings.
- By including what the character thinks, you've let me know more about them inside!

Mary Ellen Wallauer

Hat Tip: *Writing a Life: Teaching Memoir to Sharpen Insight, Shape Meaning—and Triumph Over Tests* (Bomer 2005)

Strategy Look over your draft for facts that could use some more explaining. Underline them. Ask yourself what kind of follow-up might help to explain your fact: "Should I use an example? An analogy? A story?" Add in more sentences to help your reader really learn and understand what you're teaching!

Lesson Language *Here's one sentence I found from my book that could use a little more: "The moon has craters." If my reader doesn't already know what a crater is, that sentence doesn't really help teach it to them. Let me think of some ways I could add more to better support that fact. I could add a definition: "A crater is a bowl-shaped dent in the surface of the moon." Or I could add a story, "A long time ago, a meteor flew through the air and landed on the surface of the moon. When it hit, boom! A big dent was left in its place."*

Teaching Tip This is a strategy that can be divided into a sequence of four or more lessons: one for adding stories, one for adding definitions, one for adding examples, maybe even one for adding analogies.

Teaching Tip This lesson would pair nicely with strategy 7.2 ("Write with Authority: Domain-Specific Vocabulary") in the word choice chapter. Once children use specific words of an expert, it helps if they go a step further to teach their reader what they mean!

Prompts
- Can you find a fact that needs more detail?
- Underline that sentence. Think about what kind of extra information you want to add.
- Add another sentence that explains that fact.
- What part of that fact needs more detail?

Hat Tip: *Nonfiction Craft Lessons: Teaching Information Writing K–8* (Portalupi and Fletcher 2001)

> ## Support Your Facts
>
> When a fact could use some more explaining... ask yourself what would help.
>
> ———————
>
> • Should I use a <u>definition</u>?
>   A lizard is a reptile. A reptile is a cold-blooded vertebrate, which lays eggs, breathes with lungs, and has dry, scaly skin.
> • An <u>example</u>?
>   Geoge Washington was a founding father of the U.S. He was the first president.
> • A <u>story</u>?
>   Women fought in the American Revolution. Deborah Sampson disguised herself as a man to fight. She fought even after being wounded. She fell ill and was discovered to be a woman.

Megan Hughes and Courtney Tilley

LEVELS

2–8

GENRES / TEXT TYPES

**informational/
nonfiction, opinion/
persuasive**

PROCESSES

drafting, revising

Strategy Be sure that your reader clearly understands by explaining not only *what* but also *how*. Reread your draft looking for places that you've left a fact unsupported. Picture what you know about that fact. Ask yourself, "How?" Then write another sentence to partner with the first one to give more information.

Using a Mentor Take a look at some well-written nonfiction, such as any of Nicola Davies' books. Consider this example sentence from *What's Eating You: Parasites—The Inside Story*: "The most basic approach to host-hitching is to hang around and hope that one will pass by. This is what ticks do" (Davies 2009, 16). She then continues, as if answering the question, "How?": "These little bloodsucking relatives of spiders stay on their hosts only long enough to get a meal. They climb into grass and bushes, and when they smell an animal close by, they wave their legs to grab a ride" (Davies 2009, 16).

Prompts

- What's a fact you wrote that you think could use more detail?
- Reread the fact. Now ask yourself, "How?"
- You explained the "what." Now explain the "how."
- Can you imagine it? Explain how. Break it down step by step.

> ## What's the HOW?
>
> 1. Think, "What's a fact that can use more detail?"
>
> 2. Re-read the fact. Ask the HOW?
>
> 3. Take that HOW, and:
>   Think it
>   Plan it
>   Write it

Hat Tip: *Nonfiction Craft Lessons: Teaching Information Writing K–8* (Portalupi and Fletcher 2001)

Barb Galub

Strategy Reread your writing looking for a line (or lines) that may work as a repeated refrain. Read your piece trying out that line in multiple places. Each time you do, allow the line to be like a sentence starter that helps you add more. Think about if the repeated line emphasizes a meaning.

Using a Mentor Note the repeated refrain, "Koala Lou, I do love you." in *Koala Lou* by Mem Fox (1988). You might tell children that if Mem Fox wanted to repeat that line, she'd have to think up new reasons for bringing the refrain back in. It first appears in the beginning when her mom says it and then later throughout the middle when Koala Lou is remembering and hoping that she'd say it again, in bed at night, in preparations for the Olympics, and many times after that. *Julius, Baby of the World* by Kevin Henkes (1995) is another example: "They kissed his wet pink nose. They admired his small black eyes. And they stroked his sweet white fur. 'Julius is the baby of the world,' chimed Lily's parents" (2). For a nonnarrative example for upper elementary or middle school students, consider the "I Have a Dream" speech by Martin Luther King.

Prompts

- Would it work if this line repeated? Let's try it.
- Where would you repeat that line?
- When you repeat that line, what's the meaning you communicate?
- Now that you repeated it, what will you add on?

USE A REFRAIN

1. Re-read and look for a line / lines that can repeat

2. Try that line again in many places.

3. Does that refrain make your piece better?

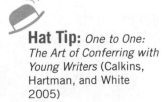

Hat Tip: *One to One: The Art of Conferring with Young Writers* (Calkins, Hartman, and White 2005)

Who is this for?

LEVELS
2–8

GENRE / TEXT TYPE
any

PROCESS
revising

Hat Tip: *The Revision Toolbox: Teaching Techniques That Work* (Heard 2002)

Strategy Return to your draft looking for a dull verb. Reread around it and think, "Exactly how did the character do it?" Replace the dull verb with a verb or phrase that describes or explains.

Lesson Language *I went back to my draft and found this rather blah, dull sentence: "She went over to the teacher's desk." The word* went *is one I'm going to underline because I feel like it doesn't really give the reader the clear picture I see in my mind. What do I really mean by* went? *Consider if I wrote it like this: "As she moved toward the teacher's desk, her feet dragged along the floor as if someone had a hold of her ankles." That would show she is going to the teacher's desk reluctantly. But if I wrote it like this: "She jumped out of her seat and practically skipped to the teacher's desk," I'm showing there that she's eager, excited. I need to really think about what I mean to write, because* went *just isn't clear!*

Using a Mentor Read any single page of *Older Than the Stars* (Fox 2010) and you'll find a collection of carefully chosen verbs. On just one page I found: *shone, died, exploded, forced, melt, searing.* Use this to talk to writers about what the writer *could have* written instead of these, and how the verbs she chose aid a reader's visualization.

Prompts

- Find some verbs that feel vague.
- Ask yourself, "Exactly *how* did it happen?"
- Let's brainstorm a list of other verbs that might work there.
- You can use a whole phrase instead of the word.
- You may find you need to rewrite the whole sentence, not just swap out that one word.

> **Invigorating Verbs!**
>
> Writers try to <u>precisely</u> <u>describe</u> how a character does something.
>
> 1.) Look for a dull sentence. **BLAH**
>   She <u>went</u> over to the teacher's desk.
>
> 2.) Exactly how did s/he do it? Brainstorm!
>   *skipped   ran   shot straight towards   meandered   ambled*
>
> 3.) Rewrite the whole sentence.
>   She <u>jumped out of her seat</u> and <u>skipped</u> to the front of the teacher's desk.
>
> **Help me spice this up!**
>
> Josh walked to the park. There were clouds in the sky blocking the sun. He went to the swings and sat down. He kicked his feet against the ground and began to swing.

Diana Erben

Strategy Place your characters in a setting. Write a scene exploring how they act in that place. Repeat once or twice more with new settings. Look back at your entries and ask yourself, "Does the setting matter? Does it change the way the characters act?" Choose the setting that makes the most sense for your story.

Using a Mentor *Crow Call* by Lois Lowry (2009) gives the reader a sense of the time, locale, and weather. *Fireflies* by Julie Brinkloe (1986) provides explicit setting details that also set a tone.

Prompts

- Think of a setting that would make sense for your characters.
- Where do you think this story should take place?
- Let's start by listing a few possibilities for settings out loud.
- Reread your scene. Does the setting matter?
- How does the setting change the way your characters act/interact?

SETTING MATTERS

1. Place your characters in a setting.

2. Write a scene. How do your characters act in that place?

3. Repeat (change the settings)

4. Choose the setting that makes the most sense for your story.

> She crept through the deep dark woods, always glancing over a shoulder. Her eyes wide, she wondered who or what was watching...

> At home, she locked all the doors and windows and settled into her favorite chair. Her cat jumped into her lap, and she laughed at him.

Barb Golub

Who is this for?

LEVELS
3–8

GENRE / TEXT TYPE
fictional narrative

PROCESSES
developing, revising

Hat Tip: *What You Know by Heart: How to Develop Curriculum for Your Writing Workshop* (Ray 2002)

6.27 Picture Your Character

LEVELS
3–8

GENRE / TEXT TYPE
narrative

PROCESSES
developing, drafting, revising

Strategy Find a photograph of a person (in a magazine, a book, or online) that matches the character in your story. Keep the photo with you and look at it as you plan your character and draft your story. Look back at the photo to anchor you to keeping the character consistent.

Teaching Tip This strategy works well when children are creating fictional narrative, to maintain a focus of reality in their writing. It would also work well when writing memoir or personal narrative—they could bring in photographs of the real people in their stories from their collections at home!

Using a Mentor There are wonderful author interviews on Scholastic's website. Take one from Karen Hesse, for example. She speaks about the research she did to get ready to write her dustbowl novel in verse *Out of the Dust* (1997). Although she doesn't speak of looking at actual photographs, she does write about using the names of real people and reading about them in newspapers, before creating her fictional characters (Hesse, "Karen Hesse Interview Transcript").

Prompts

- Looking at the photo, think about how you'd describe your character. How can you add that to your story?
- Looking at the photo, think about how your character talks. Add some dialogue to show it.
- Looking at the photo, think about how your character acts. Where will you add that in?

Hat Tip: *What You Know by Heart: How to Develop Curriculum for Your Writing Workshop* (Ray 2002)

Strategy Find a place where you mention a concept, idea, or person without much description or detail. Think about what you most want to highlight about it. Think of something that is quite opposite. In a sentence, contrast the two.

Prompts

- What's most important about that concept/idea/person?
- What do you want to highlight?
- Now, think of something that seems quite opposite.
- How can you write a sentence to contrast the two?
- That sentence highlights what you told me is most important/significant about your concept/idea/person.

Concept/ Idea Person	Highlight?	Opposite?	Sentence...
Play time	creativity	worksheets.	Unlike sitting at desks filling out blanks on a worksheet, play lets children be creative.
home	charming, stone, historic	Apple store	Unlike the glass and steel Apple store at the mall, my house has warmth and charm from the stone exterior to the cozy fireplace.

Who is this for?

LEVELS
3–8

GENRE / TEXT TYPE
any

PROCESSES
developing, drafting, revising

Hat Tip: *The Big Book of Details: 46 Moves for Teaching Writers to Elaborate* (Linder 2016)

Who is this for?

LEVELS
3–8

GENRE / TEXT TYPE
narrative

PROCESSES
drafting, revising

Strategy Be careful not to jump too quickly from one idea to the next. Go slow, playing back the memory in your mind as you write. Try to get down all the details you can.

Teaching Tip The advice to writers, when at their desk writing, to slow down a memory can help to get more detail into the writing. It also helps if the writer is "slower" as she goes about life: slowing down your eye to notice all of what's around you; slowing down your heart to really feel as you live in a moment; slowing down your mind to let yourself pay attention to your thoughts. Living life in a way that allows you to capture more will also help you when you're back at your desk. Use this lesson in combination with strategy 5.31 to help writers consider when to keep many details, and when to move more quickly through time.

Using a Mentor Using Marla Frazee's *The Roller Coaster* (2003), you can give kids a contrastive example. You can point out that she mentions the lining up, the buckling in, the ringing of the starting bell, the release of the brake, the first jerk of the train, and so on. Instead, she could have just said, "The ride started." To make this strategy into one for revision, challenge children to go back to their drafts to see where they have a single sentence where the action could be slowed down to include multiple steps or sentences. Use this lesson in combination with strategy 5.31 to help writers consider when to keep many details, and when to move more quickly through time.

Prompts

- It seems like this part jumps through time. Go back and slow down.
- Really replay the memory.
- Try to get in all the details you can. What else can you add?
- I see, in this part, you went slow and included all the details you remember. This will help your reader to picture it, too!

Too Fast!

We went to the zoo. We saw a lot and then we left.

Slow + Detailed!

We went to the zoo on our class field trip. We paid our admission and each got a stamp on our hand as our ticket. I got a zebra. Then we went to the first exhibit. I got to see monkeys! They were hanging all over the place.

Your Turn...

I got up and then went to school.

Hat Tip: *After "The End": Teaching and Learning Creative Revision* (Lane 1993)

Strategy Write rapidly, deliberately trying to bring in the periphery (what's on the edges) of what you're writing about. Write details about what is literally there, observable, happening, and also details about connections and ideas you have that feel tangential, yet related, to the focus or center of topic. Don't worry about naming which is which.

Teaching Tip When children finish this exercise, their writing will likely feel unfocused and possibly flooded with details that aren't too helpful. That's OK. This is really an exercise to try to get lots more to work with; a next step will be to weed through what they have to find the gems!

Prompts
- Try not to stop your pencil.
- You're writing a lot about what you observe. Now try to let in some peripheral details.
- Now jump to what that's making you think.
- Now add in what that makes you feel, or what connections you can make to it.

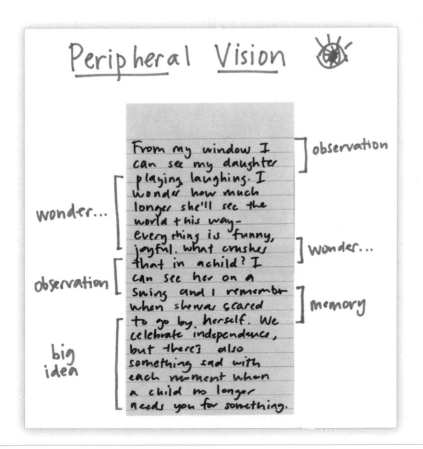

Who is this for?

LEVELS
3–8

GENRE / TEXT TYPE
any

PROCESSES
generating and collecting, drafting

Hat Tip: *Explore Poetry* (Graves 1992)

Strategy As you write, try to climb "inside the skin" of the person or people you are writing about, whether they are real or fictional, similar to you or unlike you. Think, "How would I feel in this situation? What would I think? How would I react? What would I say?" Add in details that help your reader experience their character as you do.

Prompts

- Imagine what she's going through. If you were in her shoes, what would you think?
- What would you be feeling if this was happening to you?
- Can you imagine this? Close your eyes and put yourself there.
- What can you add to help your reader feel what your character is feeling?

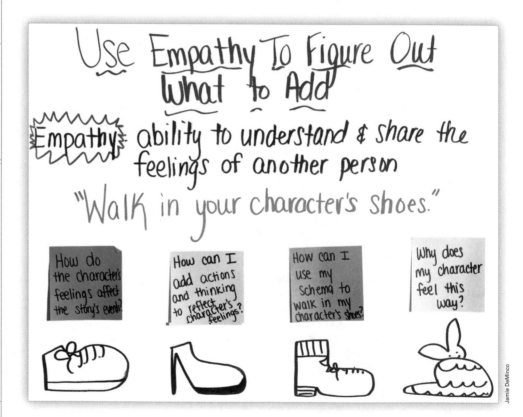

Hat Tip: *A Writer Teaches Writing* (Murray 1985)

Strategy Think about someone or something who could study the thing you're writing about. Put a "mask" on to see it through their eyes. Add details that person or thing would see, notice, feel, or comment on. Try writing your piece more than one way to see which way gets at the meaning you want!

Using a Mentor A great example is the poem "Song of the Dolphin" by Georgia Heard (1997) which is clearly told through the "mask" or perspective of the dolphin, and the point of view is first person. You could also explore some fractured fairy tales, such as Scieszka's *The True Story of the Three Little Pigs* (1996) to explore how stories told from the perspective of different characters (i.e., the wolf versus the pigs or a narrator) change the details that are included.

Prompts
- Who is telling this story?
- Think about what details to include because you're writing from that perspective.
- Because of that perspective, what can you see/feel/notice?
- Jot down some relevant information your narrator would know because it's being told from that point of view.

> MASK
> Wear A 👓 To Write With
>
> PERSPECTIVE
>
> 1. Who or what could view your subject?
>
> 2. Put on a mask & SEE IT THROUGH THEIR EYES.
>
> 3. Add the details you see/notice/feel from this PERSPECTIVE.
>
> 4. Try it more than once!

Barb Golub

6.33 How Does Your Character Talk?

Who is this for?

LEVELS
4–8

GENRE / TEXT TYPE
narrative

PROCESSES
developing, drafting, revising

Hat Tip: *Breathing In, Breathing Out: Keeping a Writer's Notebook* (Fletcher 1996)

Strategy Think of the characters you create as being real people. Think about the details of how they talk (voice, cadence, slang, dialect, accents). Plan for or revise for details in the dialogue to help make your character unique.

Lesson Language *Each of the characters in your story should have a distinct voice. So clear, so different, that a reader may be able to tell who said what even without the dialogue tags. You can think about different aspects of your character's speech to develop this. One aspect is the speaker's cadence. Think about if your character would talk in short, simple sentences or long, run-on sentences. Another aspect is slang. Think about what expressions your character might use, or a word or phrase they use in common situations. You could also consider any accent or dialect your character might have and include some words spelled phonetically to reflect how they talk.*

Teaching Tip Note that this could be broken up to be several different lessons—one on cadence, one on slang, one on dialect, and so on.

Using a Mentor

One example of note is the Judy Moody series. Point out to children that Judy always says, "Rare!" when she likes something. It's something the author created for just that character, and it isn't something we've seen in other books or even heard in our lives, most likely (McDonald 2007).

Prompts

- Think about how your character will speak.
- Look back at the dialogue you've written.
- What changes might you make to the dialogue so that the character's voice is distinct and clear?

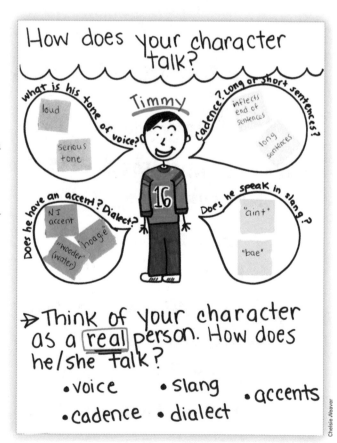

6.34 Character Dialogue and Dialect for Historical Accuracy

Strategy Read other narratives that take place in the time period you're writing about. Note the vocabulary and/or manner of speaking of the characters in the text. When creating dialogue in your piece, try to incorporate the same speech patterns and vocabulary to give your characters authenticity.

Using a Mentor Be sure to choose a mentor text with dialogue and where the dialogue clearly gives away the time period. For example, notice this selection from *Going to School in 1876* by Loeper:

"I ain't afraid of her," Tommy says.

"She's just a weak old lady," Billy adds.

"She's no bigger than a post rail," says Bart. "Why, she ain't got the muscle to harm anyone!"

The boys laugh together.

"What are you boys carrying on about?" a stern voice demands. It is Miss Parsons, the new teacher. "Get to your seats and behave yourselves," she shouts, rapping them on their heads with a stick. "I won't tolerate any nonsense. And if I catch you at any, I'll whale the daylight out of you!" (1984, 69)

A writer studying this passage may notice words like *ain't* as well as the comparison to a *post rail* or the teacher's threat to *whale the daylight* out of the children who misbehave.

Prompts

- What's the time period you're writing about?
- Let's look at some examples of other stories written in that time period.
- Now that you've seen some other examples, what are some of the words the characters use that are unique to that time period?
- Now try to apply some of that vocabulary and/or way of speaking to your draft.

Who is this for?

LEVELS
4–8

GENRES / TEXT TYPES
narrative nonfiction, historical fiction

PROCESSES
developing, revising

Hat Tip: *Finding the Heart of Nonfiction: Teaching 7 Essential Craft Tools with Mentor Texts* (Heard 2013)

Handwritten student draft:

12/12

While Pheobe Whites ma, was out harvesting out in the garden, Pheobe was talking to her pa and dog cornelious, in the kitchen about how she was bored all day long.

"Pa, I have nothing to do, ma do the things I love to do like, running around. I can't even be a kid like everyother kid!" Pheobe moaned.

"Well then, wanna go on out' huntin with your old pa?" Pa suggested.

"Ha, that would be a dream come true but ma would never ever agree to that.

"Only one way to know" Pa confidently said.

"Oh than lets see what happens" Pheobe rudly said.

So they went out to the garden where ma was out harvesting.

"Good marrow ma! Pa and I were just wondering if I could go on out' huntin with pa. We just wanted to see if you were ok with it." Pheobe sweetly asked.

"No Pheobe, you are never going to die because of something you are not supposed to do, us woman should not hunt because people dont know what us woman can do, they understimate us, and you prayth not going, on out hunting with pa." Ma fiercly said.

"ok mah mah" Pheobe angrily said. Then Pheobe looked out the window.

"Pa, Pa, I see 'em the indians, there coming!"

"I ma go shoot, em, I have to do it" Pa said.

Strategy Write a fact about your topic. Make the fact come alive by creating a scene. Try to write using imagery, giving the topic actions (perhaps even personifying it), and/or metaphors. Reread to make sure your facts are still true.

Lesson Language *I've done some research on my topic, rockhopper penguins. Let me first reread the facts I've collected:*

- *Rockhoppers are small crested penguins.*
- *They are good at jumping and climbing on steep cliffs.*
- *They jump feetfirst into water, instead of headfirst.*
- *They "surf" waves and bump into rocks as they land.*

As I look at an image of the penguin and think about the facts, I could make the penguin come more alive by comparing it to a rock and roll star. Their feathers stick up like a Mohawk! I also look at their actions and can think about how I'd describe them. Maybe I'd use words like fearless *or* daredevils *to describe them with all the jumping and banging into rocks. I'd also want to be sure to paint a picture of a scene with all of the actions. Let me try to weave some of this together:*

> Look up, up there on the cliff, and you'll see him. In black and white like most penguins, looking as if he's dressed for the opera. But the bright red eyes and black spiked feathers seeming almost like a Mohawk let you know this one's different. He's bolder, braver, perhaps more of a daredevil. Just then, he jumps feet first into the icy cold water! Once he emerges, he finds his way to the top of a big wave. Is he surfing? Just as you realize he is, he crashes with a "boom!" into some of the rocks on the shore. He rebounds, and then is up on his feet, to finally show off the move that gave him his name: The rockhopper penguin hops from rock to rock and up the steep cliff, ready for more.

Prompts

- Think about that fact. Can you imagine that taking place in a scene?
- Describe what a realistic scene might be.
- You can try to personify a bit, as long as you don't steer too far from fact/nonfiction.

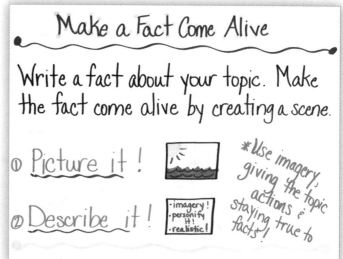

Hat Tip: *Finding the Heart of Nonfiction: Teaching 7 Essential Craft Tools with Mentor Texts* (Heard 2013)

Strategy Decide the kind of piece you're trying to write. In addition to genre, think about the sound or tone of the writing. Find a mentor or two who writes just like what and how you want to write. Read their writing once or twice to get the feel and sound of it in your mind. Draft your piece.

Teaching Tip Often we ask students to read mentor texts and name what they see the author doing, and then try to emulate that thing in their own writing. But sometimes, it's enough to get the cadence and quality of the writing in your mind and without even having to name it, you'll be able to write like it. Read Martin Luther King's "I Have a Dream" speech, then try to write one of your own. I dare you not to include a repeating refrain!

Prompts
- What type of piece are you trying to write? Be specific.
- Who writes like that?
- Name an author who writes like how you want to write.
- Name a piece that you've read that sounds like how you want your piece to sound.
- Read it twice, then draft.

Who is this for?

LEVELS
4–8

GENRE / TEXT TYPE
any

PROCESSES
drafting, revising

Hat Tip: *What You Know by Heart: How to Develop Curriculum for Your Writing Workshop* (Ray 2002)

Who is this for?

Strategy Add a margin to your writing with a strip of paper or sticky note down the side. Read line by line, annotating your thoughts and reactions to the details and words you've chosen. Try to be critical, as if the writing isn't your own. Go back and consider what changes you'd make to your details based on your critique.

Teaching Tip Being critical of your own writing is an important stance to teach writers. Sometimes writers will need to put their work away for a while, and take it back out to see it again with "fresh eyes" to have the necessary distance to be able to do this work successfully.

Prompts
- What would you say about this part, if it wasn't your own work?
- Say one thing you think is working about this part and one thing you think could be better.
- What ideas do you have about this part?
- React to your word choice.
- What else does this part need?

Hat Tip: *Explore Poetry* (Graves 1992)

Strategy Find a sentence in a text that you admire for its power, cadence, or rhythm. Find a sentence in your own writing that you'd like to try revising. Tap out the beat of the mentor sentence or identify the types of words used in the order they are used. Try to revise your sentence with your ideas and words, but the mentor sentence's rhythm and syntax.

Lesson Language *I found a sentence in our read-aloud,* The Tale of Despereaux *(DiCamillo 2003), that packs such a punch it leaves me wishing I could write like this. I'm going to read it trying to identify the rhythm and parts.*

> Mig did not wave back; instead, she stood and watched, open-mouthed, as the perfect, beautiful family passed by her (132–33).

The first part is a character and an action, then a semicolon, which means the next part could be its own sentence. It gives us two actions, a describing word (open-mouthed), then as *and the actions of other characters. I think what I like about this sentence is that Kate DiCamillo just layers on more and more details to help form my mental picture. So now, let me take my sentence: "Jake was watching all the other swimmers and thinking he'd never win the race." If I rewrite my sentence to model it after Kate's, I might try: "Jake did not jump in the water yet; instead, he stood and thought, worried, as the probable champions walked before him." Do you see how that revision makes my writing have a different cadence, but also provides more details that help describe and help build my reader's mental image?*

Prompts

- What do you love about that sentence?
- Name the parts of that sentence.
- Let's tap out the beat of that sentence.
- Try rewriting your sentence to have that same beat.

Who is this for?

LEVELS
4–8

GENRE / TEXT TYPE
any

PROCESS
revising

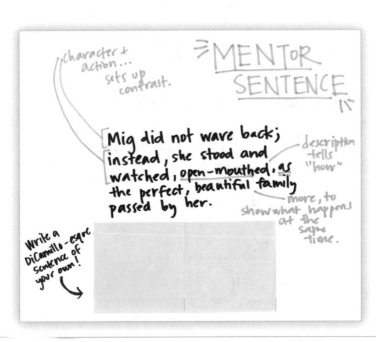

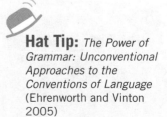

Hat Tip: *The Power of Grammar: Unconventional Approaches to the Conventions of Language* (Ehrenworth and Vinton 2005)

Who is this for?

LEVELS
4–8

GENRE / TEXT TYPE
any

PROCESSES
developing, drafting, revising

Strategy Speak aloud what you want to say. Pay attention not only to what you say, but the voice you use. As you listen, think about how you might translate what you're speaking into writing. After you feel comfortable with the sound of the language aloud, turn to the page and try to capture that same sound in writing.

Teaching Tip This strategy can help students get more details down (talking is often more fluent for children than writing, and talk can be a rehearsal for what goes on the page). It also can help support students with voice and the way they want their writing to sound, therefore impacting the quality of the details they write.

Prompts
- What do you want to write? Say it out loud.
- Speak it first, and then try to get it down.
- When you speak, really listen to yourself.
- Maybe say it once more before writing it.
- What you wrote down here really captures the sound of your voice.

Capture Your *Voice*

❋ Speak aloud what you want to say.

❋ Pay attention not only to what you say, but the voice in which you say it.

❋ Hear the way you may write.

❋ After you feel comfortable with the sound of the language aloud, turn to the page and try to capture that same sound in writing.

Wendy Koler

Hat Tip: *A Writer Teaches Writing* (Murray 1985)

Strategy Find a scene in your story where you want to give the reader clues about the kind of person your character is or how your character is feeling. Visualize the gestures and actions your character might have that would show the trait or feeling. Weave in mentions of gestures, movements, and facial expressions occasionally throughout the scene.

Using a Mentor The title character in the novel *Oggie Cooder* by Sarah Weeks (2008) has some interesting quirks that help you infer he's an odd character, and he does things that set you up to be ready to laugh along with him and his story. Here are a few details from the opening chapter:

> *"Prrrrr-ip! Prrrrr-ip!"* Oggie fluttered his tongue against the roof of his mouth. He always made that sound when he was excited about something. (3)
>
> Oggie crumpled the letter into a ball and threw it across the room, missing the wastebasket he'd been aiming for by a good foot and a half. (7)

Prompts
- Imagine your character. What would she do here?
- You wrote what the character said. Describe how you picture his face in that part.
- Can you add a gesture to go with that dialogue?
- Look across what you have so far and think about where you could add in a clue about how your character is moving or what expressions he is making.

If I want to show my character is...	Gestures, movements, facial expressions...
Sneaky	• looking left to right quickly • hiding under a hat • slow, careful
Generous, selfless	• leans in to listen + show she cares • smiling, nodding along while others share • shows a look of concern in her eyes.

Who is this for?

LEVELS
4–8

GENRE / TEXT TYPE
narrative

PROCESSES
developing, drafting, revising

Hat Tip: *Craft Lessons: Teaching Writing K–8, Second Edition* (Portalupi and Fletcher 2007)

6.41 Anecdotes Can Teach and Give Evidence

Who is this for?

LEVELS
4–8

GENRES / TEXT TYPES
informational/
nonfiction, opinion/
persuasive

PROCESSES
developing, drafting,
revising

Hat Tip: *Breathing Life into Essays* (Calkins and Gillette 2006)

Strategy Think of the fact you're trying to teach, or the point you're trying to make. Think, "Do I have a short story that can demonstrate this point?" Write a summary that includes just the information that supports your point, not every detail from the story.

Teaching Tip See the lesson "Angled Summaries" in *The Reading Strategies Book* (Serravallo 2015a) for students who could use some more support with what it means to not tell the entire story but to just "angle" their information toward a particular point or idea. Some children will need to write a longer story/scene and then go back and cut out everything but the details that are true support for their fact or point.

Using a Mentor For an opinion example, take a look at *If You Ever Want to Bring an Alligator to School, Don't!* by Elise Parsley (2015). In this story, the narrator states a reason for why you shouldn't ("It'll be trouble!") and then elaborates with a story about what happens if you do.

Prompts

• Find one point that you think needs elaborating.
• What story can you think of that can add more detail to that point?
• Let's think about what information to include from your story.
• You have a story in mind that will work! Now let's just make sure you tell the information that will support your point.

Add an ANECDOTE* to Teach + Give Evidence

Point: Too much homework can interfere with important family time.

Anecdote: The other night, I had homework in every subject. Instead of having dinner with my family, I took a plate to my room and ate while I worked. I could hear my family laughing and talking about their days. This is time I'll never get back.

*A quick, abbreviated story. Like a summary.

THE WRITING STRATEGIES BOOK

6.42 Rule of Threes

Strategy Find a place in your writing where you want to give examples, explain, or add humor. Think about making a list of three things within one sentence that makes your example build, repeat, give chronology, or add a twist.

Teaching Tip Once you're aware of the rule of threes, you'll likely find them everywhere. Consider these commonplace examples:

- "Life, liberty, and the pursuit of happiness" (American Declaration of Independence)
- "Government of the people, by the people, for the people" (Gettysburg Address)
- "Friends, Romans, Countrymen" (Shakespeare, *Julius Caesar*)
- "Blood, sweat, and tears"—a common phrase attributed to Winston Churchill's 1940 wartime speech, but which has been reused often, including as the name of a popular rock band
- "Location, location, location"—a turn of phrase used by realtors to emphasize what makes properties most desirable/valuable
- "Shake, Rattle and Roll"—blues song recorded by many including Bill Haley & His Comets

Prompts

- You've got one example. List two more.
- With each item in the list, can you build or give more information?
- What are three related things that you can list?
- You can end with a twist. Set your reader up with two that are similar, and the third and final that surprises them.

3 { RULE OF THREES } 3

Sisters can be _____, _____, and _____.

When I'm at school, I think _____, I want _____, and I wonder _____.

Enough is enough! You need to stop _____, _____, and _____!

3   3

Who is this for?

LEVELS
4–8

GENRE / TEXT TYPE
any

PROCESSES
developing, drafting, revising

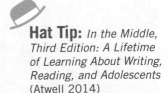

Hat Tip: *In the Middle, Third Edition: A Lifetime of Learning About Writing, Reading, and Adolescents* (Atwell 2014)

6.43 Lie (to Tell the Truth)

Who is this for?

LEVELS
4–8

GENRES / TEXT TYPES
personal narrative, memoir

PROCESSES
developing, drafting, revising

Hat Tip: *Writing a Life: Teaching Memoir to Sharpen Insight, Shape Meaning—and Triumph Over Tests* (Bomer 2005)

Strategy Think about the truth that you are trying to tell in the personal story you've chosen to write. Think about what details you'll exaggerate and which ones you'll diminish to make that truth shine through. Invent some "facts" that help to make the story more believable, even if those facts didn't really happen.

Lesson Language *I'm working on a story that I remember from my childhood. I think I remember it, but I could be confusing some details with my family's retelling of the story. The story is the time I went up to my dad's rototiller and put my hand right on it when he wasn't looking. I got a terrible burn and had to sleep with my hand in a bowl of ice for weeks afterward. That's the gist of the story, anyway, but I know when I storytell it I need to do things like describe the setting and include dialogue. Things I don't exactly remember. For example, when I describe the day it happened, I think I'll describe it as a warm spring day because it just feels right for a story about starting a garden. I'll probably include dialogue like "Jennifer! What did you do!?" from my dad, which is probably what he said even if it wasn't truthfully exactly what he said. It makes sense with the story. Maybe I'll exaggerate the details of what the burn looked like on my hand, or what the cold ice felt like because I want to make that part more dramatic—even though truthfully I don't remember the sensations of either.*

Prompts

- What is the thing you want your reader to know about this (character/setting/moment)?
- If you could exaggerate details to let your reader know about that, what might you exaggerate?
- That's the truth of the moment. What details help make that clear?
- Even if it didn't exactly happen like that, what could help make the story's purpose clearer to the reader?

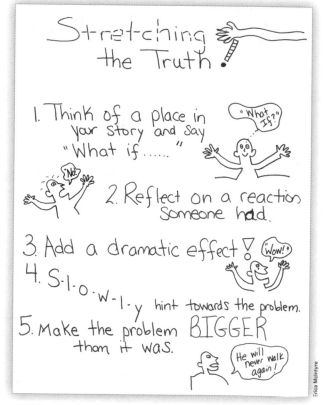

6.44 Weave in Symbolism

Strategy Think about an abstract idea or issue that is in your story. Choose a symbol (a concrete object, an animal, a setting, and so on) that can represent that issue. Reread your draft, thinking about how you'll use the symbol throughout your piece while hinting at its symbolic meaning.

Using a Mentor Consider pulling together a set of texts that all use a similar symbol, or sample texts that use a variety of symbols. For example, the picture books *Bully* (Seeger 2013) and *The Other Side* (Woodson 2001) both use the image of a fence to symbolize division at one point in the story, but unity once the fence line is crossed. You could discuss with children the purpose for the illustrator's use of the color red in *Journey* by Aaron Becker (2013), which may help them to consider their uses of color in their own stories. Every story in *Every Living Thing* by Cynthia Rylant (1988) centers around a different animal. You could discuss the symbolic significance of each animal and help children to consider the decision to include the animals they do in their own pieces.

Prompts
- What abstract idea is central to your story?
- What object might represent that?
- Think about the qualities each animal/object/setting has. What connects best to your writing?
- Find a place where you can weave in some details about this symbol.

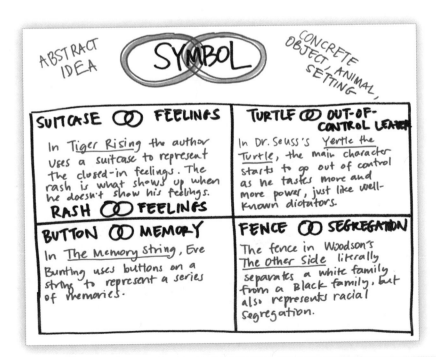

Who is this for?

LEVELS
5–8

GENRE / TEXT TYPE
narrative

PROCESSES
drafting, revising

Hat Tip: *Writing Fiction: A Guide to Narrative Craft, Ninth Edition* (Burroway and Stuckey-French 2014)

6.45 Clue In the Reader to the Past (Flashback)

Who is this for?

LEVELS
5–8

GENRE / TEXT TYPE
narrative

PROCESSES
developing, drafting, revising

Strategy Think about your story. Ask yourself, "Is there something from the character's past that I want the reader to know?" Write a scene or moment of internal thinking that will be included as a memory. Decide where in the current story it makes sense to include it.

Teaching Tip One additional lesson that writers may need is help with how to transition from the present scene to the flashback and from the flashback back to the present scene. See strategy 5.16, "Moving from Chunk to Chunk," for some examples.

Using a Mentor Many of the novels that you are choosing for read-aloud for upper elementary and middle school readers will likely have examples of flashback. For example, *Stone Fox* by John Reynolds Gardiner (1980), *The Tiger Rising* (2001) or *Because of Winn Dixie* (2000) by Kate DiCamillo, or *Sarah, Plain and Tall* by Patricia MacLachlan (1985). Help your children identify these scenes within scenes, and help them to consider the function they serve to teach us about characters and why the author may have chosen to include them.

Prompts

- What's the information about your character you think your reader ought to know?
- When/where would it make the most sense to include it?
- Let's rehearse out loud what that flashback might sound like.
- How will you alert your reader that this is a flashback?

Hat Tip: *After "The End": Teaching and Learning Creative Revision* (Lane 1993)

Chapter 3

December 18 1773

Dear diary, today has been terrible, why can't anyone else realize how the King is only trying to do us good. They were throwing 342 BOXES OF TEA IN THE HARBOR! Those sons of liberty are slowly destroying our colonies bit by bit. We kindly take away most taxes, but in return, we don't get kindness, instead THEY BOYCOTT ALL BRITISH GOODS! They should be ashamed of themselves, our fine companies are going out of business because of their selfishness. I am OUTRAGED!

I don't even want to remember what happened 2 years ago.
Twas January 3 1771
Me and my son were walking around Boston for some fresh air and my son started to walk over to one of his friends. I had never seen this family before so I thought that they must just moved here. I went to get a closer look, and I almost screamed ^(as loud as loud as a goat) of fury and frestration after I heard what I thought I just did. His friends were PATRIOTS and they were insulting a group of redcoats, the ones that King George sent over, the man that we were going to stay loyal to. I snatched him by the arm, and I scowled at him all the way home...

In my opinion all the kings people should do what is right, we must make all colonists pay for the damage that they took part in. If we are paying the taxes that are required of us, the other colonists should be willing to help as well.

Goal
7

Word Choice

◎ Why is this goal important?

Making careful decisions about word choice is not just for the dictionary-loving, thesaurus-clutching writers among us. The words we choose have the power to communicate tone, clarify an intended meaning (or not), and give writing voice. Without carefully considering word choice, writing can end up vague, or flat, or as William Zinsser puts it, "If the nails are weak, your house will collapse. If your verbs are weak and your syntax is rickety, your sentences will fall apart" (2001, 19).

For some writers, word choice isn't something they need to give deliberate attention to. Their writing just comes out sounding full of voice and rich with clarity and specificity. For others, using the strategies in this chapter as exercises to practice revision or careful consideration of their writing on the word level will help elevate their writing or help it to be filled with more style. After all, when you think of a novel that just stayed with you, or a speech you can't get out of your mind, oftentimes it isn't the whole thing you remember as much as a few lines, or words used in surprising ways. Focusing on word choice as a goal will help your students' writing to be memorable as well.

Many of the strategies in this chapter lean on a student's understanding of grammar and how language works. Specifically, there are strategies about making your verbs more surprising, nouns more precise, or eliminating adverbs and adjectives where they are unnecessary. Although understanding parts of speech is not a prerequisite to using these strategies, clueing children in to how sentences are structured and the "jobs" that words have within a sentence will help them to make wiser choices when it comes to word-level revisions. You can find support for developing grammar knowledge in the ninth chapter.

A warning, though, about all of the strategies in this chapter: As children attempt word revisions based on the sound of their language, playing with words, or swapping out words for ones they deem to be "better," be sure to encourage them to come back to the question, "What is it I'm trying to say?" to inform their revisions. Just like the time you teach exclamation points and every sentence ends with one! or three!!!, expect that less-experienced writers may litter their piece with sound words, hyperbole, or fancy verbs when sometimes, simple language is best. When they make changes, encourage them to consider the effects the changes have had: Do they help to set the mood or feeling of the piece? Does it help your reader feel like they are there? Does it build tension? Do they clarify? Make the reader laugh?

◎ How do I know if this goal is right for my student?

Students who are ready to consider word choice are those whose writing is organized and detailed, but who could use work communicating their meaning by being more specific or precise, by varying the words they use, or considering the tone or voice implications of their work.

This student learned one strategy for reconsidering her word choice and then changed just about every noun! Over time, she'll learn a variety of strategies she can employ to make her words more precise, and she will also learn restraint: when every verb is "surprising" and every noun is "precise," the writing can start to feel cluttered or stuffy or inauthentic. She's a perfect candidate for this goal.

Running to the Other Side

3,000 coach-parent crowd
The crowd is screaming like the pope has arrived. 1000 watt bulbs The lights are flashing from all directions. Even when I try to close my eyes, the fluorescent white light shines through, keeping me aware of my surroundings.

Coachella
Taylor Swift concert
Sounds like a concert, huh? Oh, uh, uh. This is far from the place where you get to be in the same vicinity as your idol.

'You're at a track meet-' STOP! I tell myself, 'concentrate, go back to the concert, go back to the concert' I'm with my friends Paige& Julia dancing to our favorite song, Billboard hit/spotify tune clapping our hands to the fast beat and -" POP - CHK" I'm shot back into the place I'm trying to get myself out of. The gun shoots, air soft blanks and each of the girls spring off the track like a gazelle running my mother from a cheetah. for my brother when he is trying to sneak marshmallows They have faces that say determination and they elbow one another to get to the inside of the track. orange rubber track

One park slope girl
One girl starts to fall behind as she begins to hunch her back as a multi-colored chunky substance ejects from her mouth. 'Well she's out of the race,' I think to myself. But no, she wipes her mouth with her uniform spandex, Nike uniform and begins to catch up. The girls shove

Strategies for Considering Word Choice

Strategy		Grade Levels	Genres/Text Types	Processes
7.1	Onomatopoeia: Sound Effects	K–8	Any	Drafting, revising
7.2	Write with Authority: Domain-Specific Vocabulary	1–8	Informational/nonfiction, opinion/persuasive	Developing, drafting, revising
7.3	Precise Nouns	1–8	Any	Revising
7.4	Personify to Bring Objects to Life	1–8	Any	Developing, drafting, revising
7.5	Verbs That Match the Meaning	2–8	Any	Revising
7.6	Shades of Meaning	2–8	Any	Drafting, revising
7.7	Alphabox	2–8	Informational/nonfiction	Developing, drafting, revising
7.8	Sneaky Sounds: Alliteration, Consonance, and Assonance	3–8	Any	Developing, drafting, revising
7.9	Rhythm	3–8	Any	Developing, drafting, revising
7.10	Read Aloud to Find "Clunks"	3–8	Any	Drafting, revising
7.11	Words That Match the Audience	3–8	Any	Developing, drafting, revising
7.12	Revisit the Language Gems in Your Notebook	3–8	Any	Generating and collecting, revising
7.13	Make Your Own Word	3–8	Any	Developing, drafting, revising
7.14	Leave Only the Essential Words	3–8	Any	Revising
7.15	Rhyme Time	3–8	Any	Developing, drafting, revising
7.16	Clever Titles, Headings, and Subheadings	3–8	Informational/nonfiction	Revising
7.17	Hyperbole	3–8	Any	Developing, drafting, revising

Strategy		Grade Levels	Genres/Text Types	Processes
7.18	Vary Words to Eliminate Repetition	3–8	Any	Drafting, revising
7.19	Watch Your Tone	4–8	Any	Drafting, revising
7.20	Choose Your Pronouns	4–8	Any	Drafting, revising
7.21	Short → Long → Short	4–8	Any	Revising
7.22	Gut Check Each Word	4–8	Any	Revising
7.23	Not "So" "Very" "Nice"	4–8	Any	Revising
7.24	Know When to Keep an Adverb	4–8	Any	Revising
7.25	Work for More-Precise Language (by Taking Out Adjectives and Adverbs)	4–8	Any	Revising
7.26	Rewrite a Line (Again and Again and Again)	4–8	Any	Revising
7.27	Surprising Verbs	4–8	Any	Revising
7.28	Surprising Nouns	4–8	Any	Revising
7.29	Name Your Characters and Places	4–8	Fiction	Developing, drafting, revising
7.30	Specific, Definite, Concrete: Allow Your Words to Call Up Pictures	5–8	Any	Revising
7.31	Omit Needless Words	6–8	Any	Revising

Who is this for?

LEVELS
K–8

GENRE / TEXT TYPE
any

PROCESSES
drafting, revising

Strategy Imagine yourself in your story (or book, or poem). Listen to what you hear. Add in sound words so your reader can hear what you hear in your imagination.

Using a Mentor Brian Floca's *Locomotive* (2013) is a breathtakingly illustrated and lyrically written picture book that utilizes onomatopoeia to bring the reader on a journey along the tracks with an 1800s steam train. The reader feels transported with every "clang-clang," "hisssssss," "spit!," and "huff huff huff" the writer includes. Other favorites for this strategy are Donald Crews' *Shortcut* (1996) and Eloise Greenfield's *Honey I Love* (1995).

Prompts
- What do you hear?
- How would you write that sound word?
- Write the sound word so your reader can hear it, too.
- Think about whether a sound word would help here.

Merridy Gnagey

Hat Tip: *One to One: The Art of Conferring with Young Writers* (Calkins, Hartman, and White 2005)

Strategy As you're researching your topic, keep a list of the words other authors with authority use to teach about the topic. As you write your piece, be sure to use the domain-specific words so you sound authoritative as well.

Teaching Tip This strategy language could easily be tweaked to be a revision lesson by asking students to go back to their draft and underline words that aren't as specific to the topic as they could be. They could then return to their primary sources (if they did research) to learn what words should be there instead. Glossaries may be especially helpful places to look. Or you can teach them to think, "What would an expert call this?" and replace their general language with language that's more precise.

Prompts
- What word would an expert use?
- Let's check back to some of the words you came across when you were reading about your topic.
- Think about what you're teaching here. What word(s) would an expert use?
- What would an expert call that?
- Use the words of an expert.

If you're writing about ___ then you can sound like ___ by using –,–,–

If you're writing about **weather** then you could sound like a **meteorologist** by using	If you're writing about **dinosaurs** then you could sound like a **paleontologist** by using	If you're writing about the **Revolution** then you could sound like a **historian** by using
• prediction	• petrified	• independence
• forecast	• fossils	• allies
• measure	• dig	• patriots

Megan Hughes and Courtney Tilley

<blockquote>
Who is this for?

LEVELS
1–8

GENRES / TEXT TYPES
informational/ nonfiction, opinion/ persuasive

PROCESSES
developing, drafting, revising
</blockquote>

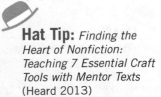

Hat Tip: *Finding the Heart of Nonfiction: Teaching 7 Essential Craft Tools with Mentor Texts* (Heard 2013)

7.3 Precise Nouns

Who is this for?

LEVELS
1–8

GENRE / TEXT TYPE
any

PROCESS
revising

Strategy Return to your draft, underlining nouns. Look back at the nouns thinking, "Can I get any more specific?" Replace the broad, nonspecific nouns with more concrete, precise words instead.

Using a Mentor Lois Lowry's *Crow Call* (2009) tells the story of a young girl learning to reconnect with her father after he's been gone for years in the war. To communicate the time (the fall, post–World War II) and places (Pennsylvania farmlands, diner, Kronenberg's department store), she chooses her nouns and phrases carefully: *November, stranger who is my father, wool shirt, crow call, plaid hunting shirts, duck decoys, rolled-back cuffs, pigtails, cherry pie, black coffee, hunter,* and so on.

Prompts

- Can you get more specific?
- Use a concrete word.
- That word really tells precisely what you mean. That revision will be helpful to your readers!
- Think of some words you can write instead of that one.
- Underline your nouns.
- This noun seems broad/vague. What do you really mean?

Hat Tip: *Finding the Heart of Nonfiction: Teaching 7 Essential Craft Tools with Mentor Texts* (Heard 2013)

Strategy Brainstorm some facts about your topic. Use language (both verbs and adjectives) often associated with people to describe an object or an object associated with a fact.

Teaching Tip Although the examples on this page center around nonfiction writing, this strategy is easily adaptable to any genre. Imagine, for example, a student who is writing a personal narrative and wants to use personification to describe the trees in the setting: "The leaves on the trees waved at me, telling me it was time to go inside and be safe, before the storm came." Words like *waving* and *telling* are human characteristics that, when used in this scene, help to make something (the tree) seem almost like a character.

Using a Mentor In Dianna Aston's *A Butterfly Is Patient* (2011), the butterfly is described as having characteristics typical to a person: patient, creative, helpful. In *Mike Mulligan and His Steam Shovel* by Virginia Lee Burton (1939), the steam shovel is named (Mary Ann); the narrator refers to her as *she* and even talks to her.

Prompts
- What is one action associated with that object?
- What's a word that's similar to the verb you used but is typically associated with people?
- What does it remind you of that people do?
- Think of some words that you'd use if a human did those things.

Who is this for?

LEVELS
1–8

GENRE / TEXT TYPE
any

PROCESSES
developing, drafting, revising

PERSONIFICATION

The train turned into the tunnel.
The headlights lit the path ahead.
Doors open.
Passengers out.
Ready for more.

The subway train slithered through the tunnel.
Its eyes glaring, lighting the path ahead.
Ssss. It hisses to a stop.
Mouth open passengers escape
Now ready for its next victims.

7.5 Verbs That Match the Meaning

Strategy Find all the action verbs in your piece. Focus on any that you think aren't as clear, precise, or exact as they could be. List several options for what might replace that word (use a thesaurus if you need it!). Choose the word that best matches your meaning.

Teaching Tip For this strategy to work, children will need to understand what an action verb is, so identification of verbs is a first step in this strategy. Many teachers weave in some instruction during other balanced literacy components such as word study, read-aloud, and/or shared reading. You could also plan to teach direct minilessons to the class or small groups for those who do not understand parts of speech.

Using a Mentor Novels told in verse, such as Applegate's *The One and Only Ivan* (2012), may offer some of the best opportunities to show students the power of a powerful verb. Consider this passage: "Mack groans. He stumbles to his feet and hobbles off toward his office" (154). What images do you get of the kind of person Mack is, and what the author wants us to think about him? Groaning, stumbling, hobbling are all verbs that help us to create visualizations and inferences.

Prompts

- Find all the verbs in your piece. Which ones need revision?
- What are you trying to say in this sentence?
- Let's list some other options for verbs that would mean something similar.
- As you look at your choices, which do you think is most exact?
- Choose the one that matches your meaning.
- That verb you chose is so much more precise. It really helps me picture what you're talking about.

Who is this for?

LEVELS
2–8

GENRE / TEXT TYPE
any

PROCESS
revising

Hat Tip: *Explore Poetry* (Graves 1992)

From Perch to Pond Rat

Perched   Surveying my surroundings
I stood on the edge of the weathered diving board, looking around. The sun shone burst
                                                                                      flipping
brightly in my eyes, and the faint sound of cicadas buzzing and the splash of fish jumping in and
            occupied   leap
out of the water filled my ears. The pond was so smooth it was glass, I could jump off the diving
                                              glance
board, onto it and walk. I took one last look of the rolling, vivid green, Vermont hills, one last
                                     catapulted
sniff of the humid summer air, and dove in.

Kick! Kick! Keyhole, breathe! Kick! Kick! Keyhole, breathe! Through my foggy,
                                   eye
condensated goggles, I finally spot the murky rope ahead marking the end of Camp Betsey Cox's
              stream   cease   soar
pond. Pearly bubbles shoot out of my nose as I stop my butterfly stroke and float to the surface.

Yes! I think, exhilarated, *I did it! I passed my swim level!*

… … … … … … … … … …

I go to Camp Betsey Cox Sleepaway Camp for Girls, in Pittsford, Vermont. Camp BC for
                                              attending
short! It's basically my second home. I've been going since I was seven years old, and my Mom

went there, too. My goal since I started was to pass my swim level, Perch. Well, I'm guessing

you figured out that I achieved it.
                emerge
As I climb out of the pond and onto the dock, I hear the words I've been waiting to hear

for so long:
                                                                  announced
"Everyone, Violet passed Perch!" Rachel, one of the swim counselors yelled, her British

accent cutting through the air like a bird crowing in the wind. Everyone cheered heartily, as I

smiled, embarrassed but pleased with all the attention. The water danced, lapping against the

7.6 Shades of Meaning

Strategy Notice a word in your current draft that isn't quite right, or is too vague. List synonyms and ask yourself, "Which of these words is most correct for what I mean to say in this sentence?"

Teaching Tip Many teachers I know use hardware store paint chips to communicate that some words' synonyms have varying degrees of intensity. The lighter color means "a little bit" and the darker color means "a lot." For example, you might write the word *sad* on a lighter shade of the purple paint chip and *despondent* or *forlorn* on a darker shade. These variations of word choice can often impact the tone the author is using and can have subtle, but significant, variations on meaning. Although some children will have synonyms in their own vocabularies, many students will benefit from a resource such as a thesaurus, the ability to access a thesaurus online, and/or a vocabulary resource wall in the classroom. Read-aloud time, or other times when you have shared texts, would offer a great opportunity to incorporate a routine for introducing and teaching these words.

Using a Mentor *The Right Word: Roget and His Thesaurus* by Jen Bryant (2014) is a biography of Peter Mark Roget that will help a reader appreciate the importance of careful word choice and a wonderful tool: the thesaurus.

Prompts
- You wrote _____. Do you really mean that?
- You wrote _____. Check the shades of meaning chart to see if there is a more precise word you could consider.
- Consider some other options for that word.
- You came up with three other options for that one word.
- I agree—that's much more precise!

Shades of Meaning - Feelings

Sad Unhappy	Nervous Uneasy	Happy Glad
Gloomy Sorrowful	Jumpy	Joyful Jovial
Forlorn Depressed Desolate	Overwhelmed Panicky Anxious	Exultant Exuberant Ecstatic

Who is this for?

LEVELS
2–8

GENRE / TEXT TYPE
any

PROCESSES
drafting, revising

Hat Tip: *Word Wise and Content Rich, Grades 7–12: Five Essential Steps to Teaching Academic Vocabulary* (Fisher and Frey 2008)

7.7 Alphabox

Who is this for?

LEVELS
2–8

GENRE / TEXT TYPE
informational/ nonfiction

PROCESSES
developing, drafting, revising

Hat Tip: *Revisit, Reflect, Retell: Time-Tested Strategies for Teaching Reading Comprehension* (Hoyt 1999)

Strategy As you think about your topic and/or read to learn about your topic, add words to an alphabox page (see bottom of page for an example). When you draft, reread the words to jog your memory about the facts you know about the topic. Use the specific words an expert would use to sound knowledgeable about the topic.

Teaching Tip This strategy could be broken up into a series of strategies that you introduce to students across the process: one strategy for collecting words, or generating words from their memories, when they are "prewriting" (developing ideas); another strategy for when they are drafting, as a way to jog their memory to write sentences; and a third time to think, "What else can I add?" and/or to look through their draft to make sure they're using precise words that an expert would use as they revise.

Prompts
- What words do you know that fit with this topic?
- Add some words to the alphabox that go with your topic.
- Look back at your words. Which will you use in a sentence?
- Think about a fact that goes with that word.
- Look back to see that you used the word an expert would use!

Alphabox Topic: Ballet

A Arabesque	B Ballet Baryshnikov Barre	C Choreography	D Développé
E	F French Fondu First position	G	H
I	J Jeté	K	L
M	N	O	P plié Pointe Pas Pirouette
Q	R Relevé Russian	S Second position	T tutu turn out
U	V	W working leg	X, Y, Z

7.8 Sneaky Sounds: Alliteration, Consonance, and Assonance

Strategy Pinpoint a word whose sound you want to repeat because doing so would highlight the meaning, or highlight a sound in the word that connects to the tone or feeling of the piece. Brainstorm other words that have the same sound and also match the meaning of what you're trying to write. Revise the words to have a repeated sound.

Teaching Tip *Alliteration* is when a sound repeats in the first stressed syllable. *Assonance* is the repetition of vowel sounds. *Consonance* is the repetition of consonant sounds. You may need to teach these as three separate strategies depending on the experience of the writer you're teaching.

Using a Mentor Most children will be familiar with the giant in *Jack and the Beanstalk* yelling "Fe Fi Fo Fum!" For the older set, Edgar Allen Poe's "The Raven" has various repeated sounds: "And the silken sad uncertain rustling of each purple curtain." The /s/ sound at the beginning of each stressed syllable in the words *silken, sad, uncertain, rustling,* and the /ur/ sound in *uncertain, purple,* and *curtain* offer a double example (1845).

Prompts
- Try alliteration. Use words that all start with the same first letter or sound for this line/sentence.
- What's the sound you want to repeat?
- Brainstorm some other words that have the same sounds, but match the meaning of this part.

Who is this for?

LEVELS
3–8

GENRE / TEXT TYPE
any

PROCESSES
developing, drafting, revising

1. FIND a word with a sound you want to repeat. Think about meaning + tone when choosing.

   * Snake
   * SSSS....

2. BRAINSTORM other words w/ the same sound.

   - Slither · storm
   - slide · sneaky
   - slink · sinister
   - sashay · smile

3. REVISE to include the repeated sounds.

   Through the storm, the snake slithered with a sinister smile.

Hat Tip: *Explore Poetry* (Graves 1992)

7.9 Rhythm

Who is this for?

LEVELS
3–8

GENRE / TEXT TYPE
any

PROCESSES
developing, drafting, revising

Strategy Tap out or clap out a rhythm you want to use in your piece. Clap or tap again, matching syllables and words to the rhythm of your clap. Change the words or order of the words to match the rhythm you're trying to keep.

Teaching Tip This strategy can be used together with others that help students accomplish rhythm: "Mentor Sentence" (strategy 6.38) in the previous chapter, as well as "Considering Sentence Length" in the chapter on grammar (strategy 9.31).

Using a Mentor The story *The Rain Stomper* (Boswell 2008) echoes the sounds of a thunderstorm and big-band parade by using many sound techniques, including rhythm ("BOOM walla BOOM, walla walla BOOM!"). *Hoops* by Robert Burleigh (2001) echoes the rhythm of the basketball with the choice of words and line breaks ("Hoops. / The game. / Feel it.") (1). Many successful speeches can be studied for their rhythm accomplished by the varying length of sentences as well as their word choice. Check out the NPR interview from 2004 with Obama speechwriter Favreau and other experts (Shapiro 2014).

Prompts
- Clap out the rhythm.
- Say the words as you clap.
- What words can you use that match that beat?
- Try new words that have the same meaning.

We've Got the Beat

1. Clap out the rhythm.

2. Say the words as you clap.

3. Try out words that match that beat.

4. Try out new words!

Barb Golub

Hat Tip: *Seeing the Blue Between: Advice and Inspiration for Young Poets* (Janeczko 2006)

Strategy Read your piece aloud, listening to yourself as you read it. As you listen, think, "Does this sound like my natural voice?" Any time you come to a place that seems to "clunk," circle the word or phrase. Go back to choose new words that feel more true to you.

Teaching Tip The issue of using words that are true to you relates to the issue of writing with voice. As Ralph Fletcher explains in *Live Writing: Breathing Life into Your Words*, "When I think about voice in writing, all I mean is the sense of the author's personality that comes through the words on the paper. Writing with voice sounds honest and authentic" (1999, 33).

Prompts
- Read it aloud. Listen.
- This part sounds like you. But something seems to "clunk" in this last part. Read it again to see if you hear it, too.
- You found a spot that doesn't feel right. Brainstorm what other words you might use there instead.
- Try some other words.
- Now that you have some other words, reread it to see which you'll choose.

Hat Tip: *In Pictures and in Words: Teaching the Qualities of Good Writing Through Illustration Study* (Ray 2010)

Who is this for?

LEVELS
3–8

GENRE / TEXT TYPE
any

PROCESSES
developing, drafting, revising

Strategy Think about the audience you expect to read your piece. Think about what words and phrases will help them understand what you are trying to say. Think about what words and phrases they will connect with. Reread your piece, making decisions about words to cut, keep, or change.

Teaching Tip This strategy has a number of practical applications. Here are just a few examples:

- Imagine a student who is writing an informational text for a younger child, or for a person with limited experience about the topic the student is writing about. That writer would need to carefully choose words that could be understood and/or decide to define words that might be new to the reader.
- Writers who speak another language, or speak nonstandard English, might decide to include words and phrases that will connect to their intended "insider" audience.
- A fifth grader who is writing an application for middle school acceptance will decide to choose words that sound appropriately academic and sophisticated.
- Helping students to articulate their intended meaning and intended audience is an important first step of being able to practice this strategy.

Prompts

- Who do you expect to read this piece?
- Think about the language that would be appropriate for that audience.
- What kind of language would that audience expect in a piece about ___?
- Let's recheck your draft, thinking about your word choice.

Hat Tip: *The Skin That We Speak: Thoughts on Language and Culture in the Classroom* (Delpit 2002)

> **Who's Your Audience?**
>
> 1. Who will read your piece?
> 2. What language will they need?
> 3. Try those words and phrases out.
> 4. Re-read and decide what to cut, keep, change.

Barb Golub

Strategy Return to your notebook. Look for words or lines you've collected. Think about what you're writing now. Think, "What might fit? Where would it fit?"

Lesson Language *You've learned how important it is to live your life like a writer, collecting bits and scraps of stuff you might use later. Some of you have come upon a person who offers a particular pearl of wisdom, or someone who says something in an original way. Others of you have visited a new place and when there, you were struck by the beauty and you took time to describe it in your notebook in a way that feels original. Some of you might not have known why you've collected what you did, or what future purpose the bits might have. That's what today is about! When you're in the midst of writing a story or a poem, or crafting a speech and in need of a metaphor, you may find that returning to these gems that you've collected enhances the piece you're working on. And keep in mind in the future that it's important to be alert to language and to collect it—words you love in books you read, words you overhear in conversation on the subway or in TV shows, words or ways of saying things that you find yourself saying or thinking—even if you're not sure where it might go.*

Prompts

- Let's look back at what you've collected. How might you use what you have?
- I notice you collected a lot of ___. I think they could fit in your writing!
- Think about where that might fit.
- How might you incorporate that detail into your writing?

 Find the GEMS

1. Re-read through your notebook.

2. Find the GEMS!
   - WORDS you've collected
   - LINES you've collected

3. Look at your current writing.
   - Where might those GEMS fit?

Who is this for?

LEVELS
3–8

GENRE / TEXT TYPE
any

PROCESSES
generating and collecting, revising

Hat Tip: *Breathing In, Breathing Out: Keeping a Writer's Notebook* (Fletcher 1996)

Who is this for?

LEVELS
3–8

GENRE / TEXT TYPE
any

PROCESSES
developing, drafting, revising

Hat Tip: *Wondrous Words: Writers and Writing in the Elementary Classroom* (Ray 1999)

Strategy When you can't find the just-right word, you can make your own. Combine words that exist or parts of words that exist that communicate what you're trying to say (but for which no word currently exists!).

Using a Mentor

In *Maniac Magee*, Spinelli (1990) writes: "That's why his front steps were the only *un-sat-on* front steps in town" (17).

In *Nocturne*, Yolen (1997) writes: "in the wraparound *blacksurround* velvet night."

Robo-Sauce (Rubin 2015) offers a recipe involving "gluten-free kookamonga flakes" and "baroney balls (scrubbed)."

Douglas Florian, in his poem "The Cobra" (2001), uses the made-up word "Octobra" instead of "October" to rhyme with cobra.

See also *Jabberwocky* (Carroll 1871).

Prompts
- What are you trying to say?
- What are some words that almost—but not quite—mean what you're trying to say?
- Could you combine parts of those words?
- Play with the language a bit and see what you get.
- If you changed a part of that word, what would you change?
- I see you took the beginning of the word ___ and the end of the word ___. Even though you made it up, I'd think this word means something like ___. Is that what you meant?

CAN'T FIND THE WORD?

MAKE ONE UP!

1. What are you trying to say?
2. Which words sort of already say that?
3. Combine some parts.
4. Try it, re-read it, revise it (try it again)!

Strategy Return to a piece that is written in sentences. Cut out all words but the most essential (most likely nouns and verbs) that can paint a picture in your reader's mind. If the verbs and nouns that are left are less than clear, consider revising them to be more precise and/or surprising.

Teaching Tip This is a helpful exercise to help children turn prose into poetry. It's also helpful for children to consider their word choices and to be sure that the words they've chosen communicate clear ideas and visual images.

Using a Mentor *Eight Days Gone* by Linda McReynolds (2012) is a rhyming picture book about *Apollo 11* and the first moon landing. Consider the setting established with these four lines, only seven words:

Desolation.
Silent. Dark.
Tranquil sea.
Barren. Stark.

Share this or a similar example with children and discuss how powerful and clear each word must be when the writer has so few!

Prompts
- Which words seem most important?
- Let's find the nouns and verbs. Eliminate the rest to see what you're left with.
- Look at the words—are there any you'd like to revise?
- That word is very precise. I can really picture it!

Who is this for?

LEVELS
3–8

GENRE / TEXT TYPE
any

PROCESS
revising

Hat Tip: *The Writing Thief: Using Mentor Texts to Teach the Craft of Writing* (Culham 2014)

The Spot

Inside the swamp we sit and play, full of fresh and rotton decay. You can come and play with us to! (watch your step it may swallow you!) There is lots of critters, lots of bones because they never find there way home. For this is our hang out, this is the spot! Please join us, you'll love it a lot! So, have you made up your mind? yes, on the sheet you circled decline.

circle:
agree
or
decline?

①
green. gross.
acid. decay.
The swamp is were we like to play.

bubbly. bones.
sticky. rotten.
The air bubbles feel like slimy cotton.

7.15 Rhyme Time

Who is this for?

LEVELS
3–8

GENRE / TEXT TYPE
any

PROCESSES
developing, drafting, revising

Strategy Choose the part of your piece where you want to rhyme—at the ends of lines or sentences, or in the middle of lines or sentences? Generate a list of words that rhyme that could fit in either the sentences or lines. You may need to change the order of the words in your sentence, not just the one word, to make the new rhyming word fit. If you can't make rhyming words work with the original words in your lines, you may need to find syllables or change the order of the words in the original line.

Lesson Language *I am writing a piece about boats, and I want to use rhyme. What I have now is: "The boats are gliding on the water / they leave trails behind them / Pushed by the wind." No rhyme at all! If I generate a list of words that might rhyme, maybe I should try to rhyme with* wind *because that's an important part of the sailboat. Let's see,* skinned. Thinned. Pinned. *Hm. I'm not getting anywhere with that. Let me try a syllable for* wind—gust. *Rhyming words:* Trust. Rust. Dust. Fussed. Must. *Let me work with that: "Boats are gliding on the water / Pushed by a wind gust / Sails up to catch the force / Something something is a must." Or, "In something something I will trust." Or, "Bright and shiny, without rust."*

Teaching Tip Rhymezone.com offers a rhyming dictionary/thesaurus tool that can help children generate rhyming words, phrases that contain a rhyming word, and words that almost rhyme.

Using a Mentor Douglas Florian's poems about insects (*Insectlopedia*) (1998) and amphibians (*Lizards, Frogs, and Polliwogs*) (2001) offer endless examples of clever use of rhyme while maintaining meaning.

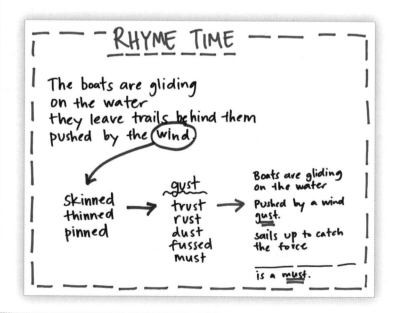

7.16 Clever Titles, Headings, and Subheadings

Strategy Take a careful look at the title of your piece or a section. Ask yourself, "Does my title simply label, or does it also grab my reader's attention and intrigue them?" When you want to jazz up your language, think about using words that will surprise your reader, make your reader laugh, or be fun for your reader to say aloud.

Teaching Tip See "Headings, Subheadings, Sub-Subheadings" (strategy 5.33 in the chapter on organization and structure) for advice about how to help writers organize their information into sections, then come back to this lesson to help them fine-tune their language choices. See "Write a Title" (strategy 4.4 in the chapter on focus and meaning) for language to explain to children how reconsidering the language of their title may help them reconsider the focus of their section or piece.

Using a Mentor Authors Bobbie Kalman and Heather Levigne are clever with titles, headings, and subheadings. Consider these from their book *What Is a Primate?* (1999):

surprise: "What's that Smell?" (a section on scent glands and how prosimians mark their territories) (26)

humor: "Look, Mom—Five Hands!" (a section about how monkeys use their front and back "hands" as well as their prehensile tail) (25)

alliteration: "Different Diets" (a section about omnivores versus folivores) (23).

Prompts

- What is this section about? What other ways can you title it?
- Think about some of the other wordplay techniques you've learned about (alliteration, rhyme, etc.). What else could a title be?
- The title doesn't have to just label what the section is literally about.
- You chose some words for this title that are surprising and funny! It adds more personality to your writing.

Who is this for?

LEVELS
3–8

GENRE / TEXT TYPE
informational/
nonfiction

PROCESS
revising

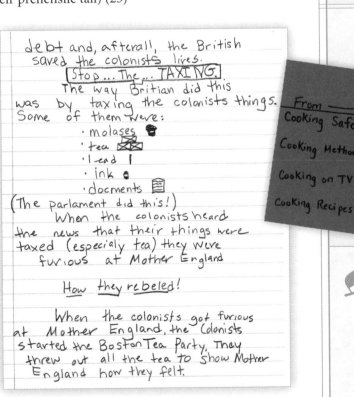

Hat Tip: *Nonfiction Craft Lessons: Teaching Information Writing K–8* (Portalupi and Fletcher 2001)

7.17 Hyperbole

Who is this for?

LEVELS
3–8

GENRE / TEXT TYPE
any

PROCESSES
developing, drafting, revising

Strategy Find a place where you want to emphasize or dramatize a point, or where you want to inject some humor. Think about what words you'd change to deliberately exaggerate.

Teaching Tip Share with students some examples of common hyperbole in our language, and work with them to imagine some new expressions: When someone is cold, they might say they are "freezing," when someone is hungry, they might say they are "starving." When a joke is so funny you can't stop laughing, you might say you're "dying of laughter." When you eat something delicious, you might remark that it's the "best thing you've ever had in your whole life."

Using a Mentor *It Figures! Fun Figures of Speech* by Marvin Terban (1993) includes examples of six different types of figures of speech, one of which is hyperbole. With explanations and lots of examples, it could make a nice addition to your writing center, or excerpts could be used during lessons or conferences.

Prompts
- What's the place you want to emphasize?
- How might you exaggerate that?
- Maybe use words like *most* or *best* or *worst*.
- Reread it. Do you think your reader will understand it's not meant to be taken literally?
- What effect do you think the hyperbole has on your writing?

Hyperbole (Figurative)	Literal
This backpack weighs a ton!	It's heavy
I'm starving! I could eat a horse.	I'm hungry; I could eat a big meal.
These shoes take a million years to put on.	The shoes are complicated to put on and will take a long time.
I nearly died laughing!	It was funny and I laughed a lot.
I tried a thousand times but in the end I couldn't do it.	I tried a lot.

Hat Tip: *Pyrotechnics on the Page: Playful Craft That Sparks Writing* (Fletcher 2010)

7.18 Vary Words to Eliminate Repetition

Strategy If you find you've used the same word again and again in your draft, circle every instance where it occurs. Generate a list of synonyms. Choose where you'll use each of the synonyms to create variety and balance across your piece.

Teaching Tip Keep a couple of good thesauri and/or some tablets with access to thesaurus.com in your writing center to aid your students with generating the synonyms needed for this strategy.

Prompts

- Circle all the places where you see the same word.
- What synonyms do you know for that word?
- The synonym could be a word or a phrase.
- If you can't think of another word, can you think of a phrase that could mean the same thing?

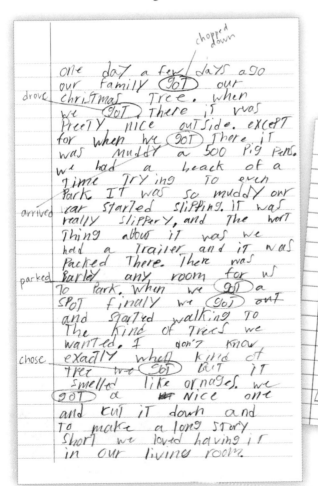

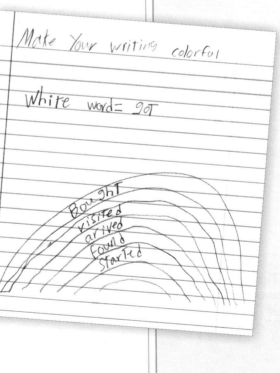

7.19 Watch Your Tone

Who is this for?

LEVELS
4–8

GENRE / TEXT TYPE
any

PROCESSES
drafting, revising

Strategy Think about your topic and the feeling you want to communicate. Read through a part of your draft, underlining words that you think contribute to the tone, and circling words that you think might change or detract from the tone. Revise words as needed.

Teaching Tip Tone is communicated in part by word choice, but also by cadence, which relates to sentence length, and by the types of details the writer chooses to include.

Using a Mentor Choose several pieces from one author that show different tones—for example, three op-ed pieces from the same author, or three speeches from Barack Obama that offer different tones reflected in word choice. Consider his 2016 State of the Union speech, which communicates a tone of hope because of words and phrases like *promise, next frontier, we did,* and *we saw opportunity*:

> America has been through big changes before. We made change work for us, always extending America's promise outward, to the next frontier, to more and more people. And because we did—because we saw opportunity where others saw only peril—we emerged stronger and better than before. (Obama 2016b)

Compare that with his January 5, 2016, speech about gun violence that strikes a tone of urgency and also impatience and frustration:

> I'm not looking to score some points. I think we can disagree without impugning other people's motives or without being disagreeable. We don't need to be talking past one another. But we do have to feel a sense of urgency about it. In Dr. King's words, we need to feel the "fierce urgency of now." Because people are dying. And the constant excuses for inaction no longer do, no longer suffice. (Obama 2016a)

Prompts

- What tone are you trying to communicate?
- How do you want your reader to feel after reading this piece?
- Circle words that don't help communicate that tone.
- Underline words that connect with your tone.
- Try writing that sentence with different words that will get your tone across.

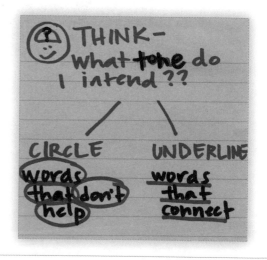

Hat Tip: *In Pictures and in Words: Teaching the Qualities of Good Writing Through Illustration Study* (Ray 2010)

Strategy Read through part of your draft, underlining the pronouns you chose. Change the pronouns to switch from one point of view (first, second, or third person) to a different point of view. Consider the effect the change had on your tone and the voice of your writing. Decide which to keep for the entire draft.

Teaching Tip Writing informational and persuasive pieces from different points of view can have an impact on the relationship of the reader to the writer, and even the tone of the writing. For example, first person (*I, we, us*) is typically reserved for autobiographical writing, although using it in informational writing can tone down the authority, or make the tone more informal (consider, for example, the effect starting with "I think" or "I believe" instead of simply writing the fact) or uniting the audience with the writer ("Can't we all agree that . . ."). Using second person (*you, your, yours*) can set up some distance between the writer and the audience, or can create an authoritative tone ("As you consider ____, be sure you're thinking about . . .") or can have a friendlier tone ("If you want to have the best hamburger you've ever had, you have to try . . ."). For a look at revising leads by considering pronoun choice, see strategy 5.21, "Lead by Addressing the Reader" in the chapter on organization and structure).

Prompts
- What is the point of view of your piece now?
- What effect do you think that point of view has?
- If you were to change to a different point of view, what might you try?
- Now that you've made the change, reflect on the effect it has on you as a reader.
- Consider which point of view is more true to your intentions for this piece.

Who is this for?

LEVELS
4–8

GENRE / TEXT TYPE
any

PROCESSES
drafting, revising

Hat Tip: *Strategic Writing Conferences: Smart Conversations That Move Young Writers Forward* (Anderson 2008)

1. This anamill is strong and vishas it has erange and white stripe its meen at night it eats deet. it's a tiger

2. you're in the jungel waking around then you see a big black shadow and you look up and see a big stript tiger!

Who is this for?

LEVELS

4–8

GENRE / TEXT TYPE

any

PROCESS

revising

Strategy Choose a poem you've written. Rewrite it as prose, using full, descriptive sentences. Look back at the prose to find the poem hidden inside—choose the best descriptive moments and the words that communicate the images and messages you want to focus on.

Teaching Tip The idea behind this strategy is that by forcing yourself to use fewer words, in going from long-form writing (a whole essay, a report, a story) to a poem, you will have to make choices about which words matter most when trying to communicate your idea. Then, when students revise their work to be long-form writing, again, they will keep the most essential elements. It's possible, too, that through forcing yourself to write short, you may refocus or refine or redefine your meaning, which would also have an impact on word choice. See strategy 4.10 for more information on a similar strategy to support students with their focus.

Using a Mentor Novels written in verse may be a nice go-to to help writers imagine how they could shift between narrative and poetry. See, for example, *Love That Dog* (Creech 2001), *Home of the Brave* or *The One and Only Ivan* (Applegate 2007, 2012), or James Howe's *Addie on the Inside* (2012).

Prompts

- Look through the prose to see what words are most important.
- As you look at your prose, let's go through and underline the lines you'll keep as you convert this back into a poem.
- What words and phrases from this prose best match your meaning?
- Take that one line from your poem, and turn it into a paragraph of prose.
- Take that paragraph, and write just one line from it.

Hat Tip: *Explore Poetry* (Graves 1992)

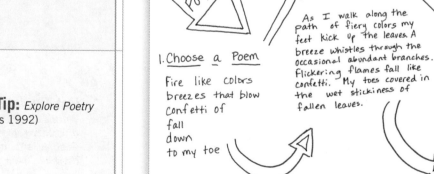

THE WRITING STRATEGIES BOOK

Strategy Go back through your piece. Read the piece aloud. Check word by word, asking yourself, "Is this exactly the right word? Do I need this word? Would another word be better here?" Make changes as necessary.

Teaching Tip This may be best for poetry, as reading longer pieces word by word may be tedious. Students who want to try this with informational texts, persuasive writing, or narratives may want to select an excerpt (such as a scene with dialogue between two characters, or just the introductory paragraph).

Using a Mentor

Mark Twain, *The Wit and Wisdom of Mark Twain* (1999): "The difference between the right word and the almost right word is the difference between lightning and a lightning bug."

William Zinsser, *On Writing Well: The Classic Guide to Writing Nonfiction* (2001): "Examine every word you put on paper. You'll find a surprising number that don't serve any purpose" (13).

Prompts
- Read a sentence, word by word, aloud. Did anything not ring true?
- Which words feel like they don't exactly say what you want to say?
- Think about what word might work better in this spot.
- Which words felt right?

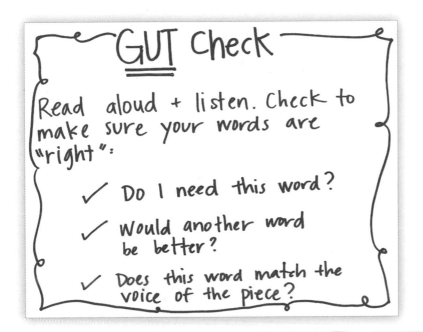

Who is this for?

LEVELS

4–8

GENRE / TEXT TYPE

any

PROCESS

revising

Hat Tip: *In the Middle, Third Edition: A Lifetime of Learning About Writing, Reading, and Adolescents* (Atwell 2014)

LEVELS
4–8

GENRE / TEXT TYPE
any

PROCESS
revising

Strategy Look for places in your draft where you use a vague word such as *nice* or a qualifying word such as *so* or *very*. Aim to choose words that say exactly what you mean. Cross out vague words and replace with clear ones.

Teaching Tip Consider creating a bulletin board in your classroom where students can post examples of ways they've moved from vague to precise wording in their writing.

Prompts
- Where do you see *nice, so*, or *very*? Let's underline.
- Reread the sentence. Can you replace one word with another that is more precise.
- You wrote _____. What other word might fit where the word _____ is?
- _____ is a much clearer word than _____! I can really picture what you mean now.

Instead of . . .	Be Clearer
Nice house	What exactly do you mean to say about the house? Was it *beautiful, elegant, comfortable, simple*?
He was **so** smart.	Eliminate *so* and use a precise word, such as *intelligent, brilliant, genius, clever.*
She was **very** kind.	Eliminate *very* and use a precise word, such as *thoughtful, helpful, generous, compassionate.*

Hat Tip: *The Elements of Style, Fourth Edition* (Strunk and White 1999)

Strategy Go back through your draft, highlighting your adverbs (words that describe verbs). Think about each one carefully to decide if you should eliminate it, eliminate the adverb and change the verb, or keep it. An adverb worth keeping usually has at least one of these two qualities:

- It supplies necessary information.
- It helps your reader visualize something that they wouldn't be able to without it.

Teaching Tip Take a look at the next strategy, "Work for More-Precise Language (by Taking Out Adjectives and Adverbs)," as a complement to this one. Writers eliminate adverbs because they are often overused. When precise nouns and verbs are used, adverbs may not be necessary. This strategy, when offered in conjunction with the following one, will help writers carefully consider when to keep and when to cut.

Prompts

- Let's start by finding the adverbs.
- Is that an adverb? It is if it describes a verb.
- Read the sentence with it. Now read the sentence without it. Do you think it's essential?
- Explain why you want to keep it.
- How does keeping it change what you picture?

Who is this for?

LEVELS
4–8

GENRE / TEXT TYPE
any

PROCESS
revising

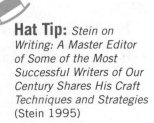

Hat Tip: *Stein on Writing: A Master Editor of Some of the Most Successful Writers of Our Century Shares His Craft Techniques and Strategies* (Stein 1995)

7.25 Work for More-Precise Language (by Taking Out Adjectives and Adverbs)

Strategy Look back through your draft to see where you can tighten your language by eliminating words. Highlight all the adjectives and adverbs. Reread and ask yourself:

- What adjectives can I remove by making the noun more precise?
- What adverbs can I remove by making the verb more precise?

Lesson Language *Adjectives and adverbs often clutter your writing, slowing down the pace and maybe even boring your reader. Although it may seem like a good idea to add more description, you can often accomplish this by simply changing the nouns and verbs instead of adding extra words. Here are two examples, one where the adverb feels redundant and can simply be cut. The second is an example of changing the verb to something more precise.*

- *Instead of "She really, truly cared for him"* → *"She cared for him."*
- *Instead of "She slowly, carefully, walked down the stairs"* → *"She tiptoed down the stairs."*

Using a Mentor

I believe the road to hell is paved with adverbs, and I will shout it from the rooftops. To put it another way, they're like dandelions. If you have one on your lawn, it looks pretty and unique. If you fail to root it out, however, you find five the next day . . . fifty the day after that . . . and then, my brothers and sisters, your lawn is totally, completely, and profligately covered with dandelions. By then you see them for the weeds they really are, but by then it's—GASP!!—too late. (King 2000, 125)

Most writers sow adjectives almost unconsciously into the soil of their prose to make it more lush and pretty, and the sentences become longer and longer as they fill up with stately elms and frisky kittens and hard-bitten detectives and sleepy lagoons. (Zinsser 2001, 70–71)

Prompts

- First, identify the types of words you have in this sentence.
- Where do you see adjectives? Try to rewrite this sentence without the adjective. Change the noun you chose.
- Where in your sentence do you see the verb, the action word? The word before it describes the verb. If you take the adverb out, how might you change the verb?

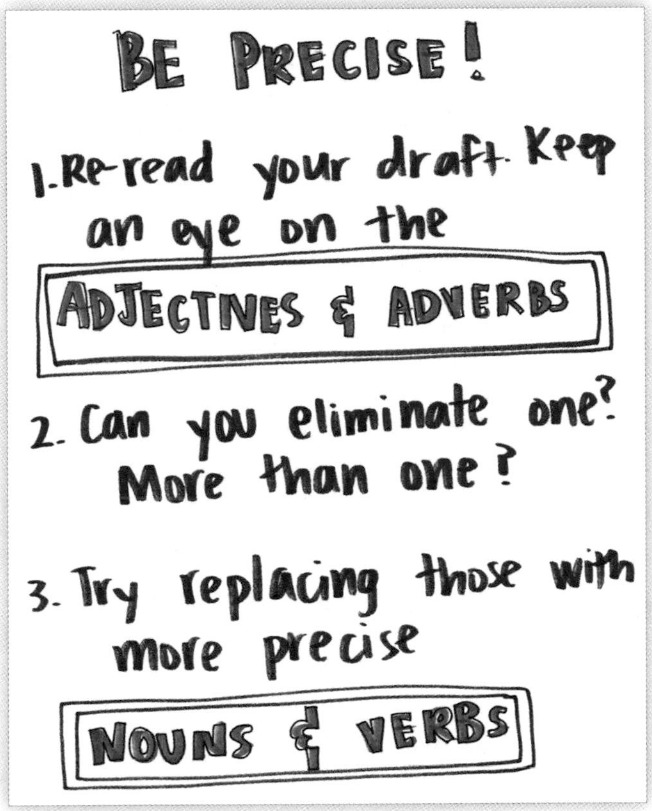

BE PRECISE!

1. Re-read your draft. Keep an eye on the

ADJECTIVES & ADVERBS

2. Can you eliminate one? More than one?

3. Try replacing those with more precise

NOUNS & VERBS

Image credit: Barb Golub

7.26 Rewrite a Line (Again and Again and Again)

Who is this for?

LEVELS
4–8

GENRE / TEXT TYPE
any

PROCESS
revising

Strategy Find a sentence or line in your piece that seems very important, but that doesn't feel quite right. Try using different words to say the same idea. Try to rearrange the order of the words in your one sentence/line. Reflect on all the "drafts" of that line you have. Ask yourself, "Which one feels the most right?"

Prompts

- Try changing the order of the words.
- Say it again, this time changing something else.
- Don't say a new idea, keep the idea but change the words or order of the words you're using to say it.
- Try saying it aloud before writing it on paper.

Re-write a Line...

The house where I grew up was a special place.

My house holds many memories.

Sometimes it feels like my house had a hand in raising me; It was more than a home, it was like a parent.

... Then ask, "Which feels the most right?"

Hat Tip: *What You Know by Heart: How to Develop Curriculum for Your Writing Workshop* (Ray 2002)

Strategy Return to your draft, underlining the verbs. Go back to places that are particularly important. Think, "What can I compare this to? What verbs would I choose to show that comparison?" List different verbs that would make a comparison clear.

Teaching Tip When strong, surprising verbs are used, a writer can often cut needless adverbs without sacrificing description. This strategy is a step beyond "Verbs That Match the Meaning" (strategy 7.5), which asks children to identify verbs and be more *precise*. Here, we're going for the unexpected use of language that will communicate something figuratively/metaphorically.

Using a Mentor

The Whales by Cynthia Rylant (1996): "In the blackness of the Black Sea, the whales are *thinking* today." (italics added)

Maniac Magee by Jerry Spinelli (1990): "especially when he got a load of the kid *drowning* in his clothes" (85, italics added).

Prompts

- Find your verbs.
- If you see a place where you have an adverb, it might help you find a place where there is a verb you may consider revising.
- Think figuratively. What is this *like*? What verb would match that?
- What can you compare your subject to? What words do you typically see connected to that other subject? Try them out here.

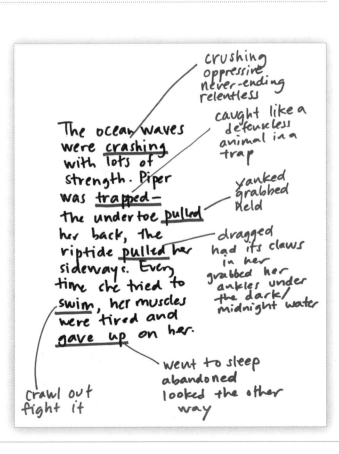

Who is this for?

LEVELS
4–8

GENRE / TEXT TYPE
any

PROCESS
revising

Hat Tip: *Finding the Heart of Nonfiction: Teaching 7 Essential Craft Tools with Mentor Texts* (Heard 2013)

7.28 Surprising Nouns

Who is this for?

LEVELS
4–8

GENRE / TEXT TYPE
any

PROCESS
revising

Strategy Look closely at each noun in your piece. Ask yourself if there is another word that might also work in that spot. Generate a list of a few options. Look over your list to see if any of the new noun choices match the meaning and are also perhaps surprising.

Teaching Tip This strategy may be an entry point into helping students to write with puns, though not all surprising nouns will also be puns and not all puns are made from double-meaning nouns.

Using a Mentor *Stick and Stone* (Ferry 2015) is a funny story about kindness and friendship, told in single words or two-word phrases. What makes this book particularly clever is the double meanings of many of the nouns (and other types of words!). For example, in the beginning of the story, Ferry establishes that stick and stone are both alone and lonely and in need of a friend. Then comes a single page with only "A zero." and a picture of stone by himself. He is both shaped like a zero and feeling like nothing.

Prompts

- Let's start by finding the nouns.
- What other nouns might have more than one meaning?
- Look over the list of nouns you've thought up. Which one might work best?
- You tried it! I see that noun is surprising because it means more than one thing.

SURPRISE !
(YOURSELF WITH MORE NOUNS)

1. Re-read your piece, and find the ~~nouns~~
2. Ask, "Is there ~~another word~~ that can also work here?"
3. Generate a ~~list~~ of a few options.
4. Look over your list. Do any of those ~~new nouns~~ match the meaning?

Barb Golub

Hat Tip: *Pyrotechnics on the Page: Playful Craft That Sparks Writing* (Fletcher 2010)

7.29 Name Your Characters and Places

Strategy Think about the places and characters in your story. Think about the kind of people they are and what name their parents might have given them. For places, think about the mood or feeling you want to get across and choose a name that fits.

Teaching Tip Colleen Cruz (coauthor of Units of Study books on fiction and author of the novel *Border Crossing*) suggests keeping a baby-naming book or two in your writing center as a reference for students who are trying to think up names. She says that when you think of a character's name, it's helpful to think of the kind of parents the character would have had and what the parents would have named the character. To help with naming places, maybe having an atlas handy in your writing center will help, too!

Using a Mentor Consider the story *What Jamie Saw* by Carolyn Coman (2012). The author chose the name Stark, New Hampshire. What does *stark* make you think of? Bleak, cold, hopeless, and wintery. In this case, the name chosen communicates mood and tone. Think about Jerry Spinelli's (1990) choices of Maniac Magee in the novel by the same title, or Penn, the pacifist, in *Crash* (1996), as a nod to the famous Quaker William Penn. Or share the title characters of Sara Pennypacker's (2015) picture book, *Meet the Dullards*, about a family who needs to branch out of the gray, mundane, and boring (dull!) and experience a little liveliness in their lives.

Prompts

- What's the mood you want to create? What could you call the town where the story takes place?
- Think about what you know about the character's parents. What name might they have given him?
- Generate a list of names that fit the character's personality.
- Underline the names (of people, places). Let's carefully consider if they're just right.

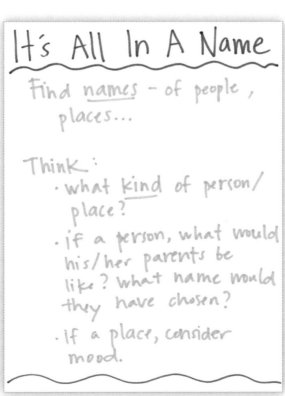

It's All In A Name

Find names – of people, places...

Think :
- what kind of person/place?
- if a person, what would his/her parents be like? what name would they have chosen?
- if a place, consider mood.

Hat Tip: *Experiment with Fiction* (Graves 1989)

7.30 Specific, Definite, Concrete: Allow Your Words to Call Up Pictures

Who is this for?

LEVELS
5–8

GENRE / TEXT TYPE
any

PROCESS
revising

Strategy Reread your draft, looking for a place where you used language that was vague, general, or abstract. Ask yourself, "What is it I'm trying to say here? What image do I want my reader to have?" Try rewriting the sentence with specific, concrete language.

Using a Mentor You could rewrite a poem that uses very specific language to help the reader create a mental image, and then read the vague version first, asking your students to sketch it, and then read the real version second, asking them to sketch a new picture. Show both versions and study the differences between the vague language and specific language and the effects it had on their images.

Prompts
- Why do you think that word is vague?
- What did you really mean when you wrote _____?
- Say, "What I'm really trying to say is . . ."
- I agree, that part is a bit general and vague. Let's think of specific, concrete ways that will help your reader picture what you're describing.
- Try rewording that part so it's clearer in your reader's mind.
- Say it another way so that your reader can picture it.

> Writers use clear and
> Specific vocabulary to
> paint a picture for their
> reader. ☺
>
> Writers
> 1. Re-read their draft 👓 👀
> 2. Ask themselves "What am
>   I trying to say here?"
> 3. Think about all the vocabulary
>   we know. ☺ glossary
> 4. Try rewording. ✎🗒

> After the Seven
> Years War, Great Britain
> sent soldiers to protect
> ~~them.~~ the Colonists England said the
> colonists needed to
> ~~pay them back.~~ pay back their debt. ~~They~~ Parliament
> began imposing taxes.
> The colonists were angry
> about the taxes and
> decided to ~~stop buying~~ boycott British
> goods.

Hat Tip: *The Elements of Style, Fourth Edition* (Strunk and White 1999)

Tiana Silvas

7.31 Omit Needless Words

Strategy Look through your draft for places where you used several words to say something that only needs a few words. (Check the table below for some common offenders.) Cross out the words that aren't needed.

Teaching Tip For many students, the key to making this strategy click will be to engage them in repeated models and shared practice. Help the students to identify their own worst offenders. For example, I know that I tend to use lots of parenthetical expressions. If I was forced to go back into my writing to find all the places I did that, then I could look critically to see if there is a way to eliminate the parenthetical to write a more direct sentence. A good friend of mine tends to use hesitating language, "If it would be OK I would like to . . ." and "There are times when I would want to . . ." and she knows to always go back through her writing to look for places where she can eliminate the qualifiers and just state what she wants to say more directly.

Prompts
- Do you see any phrases you can replace with a single word?
- I found a phrase. Let me underline that for you. Let's think how you can say this with more brevity.
- See this part? Try to use fewer words.
- Yes! That can be said in a shorter way.
- Check the chart to see if you have any of those common phrases.

Instead of . . .	Use . . .
He is a man who	He
The reason why is that	Because
In spite of the fact that	Though/although
Who is a ____ Example: Her sister, who is a doctor at . . .	(delete the phrase) Example: Her sister, a doctor at . . .
Which is/was ____ Example: Times Square, which is an area in . . .	(delete the phrase) Example: Times Square, an area in . . .

Who is this for?

LEVELS
6–8

GENRE / TEXT TYPE
any

PROCESS
revising

Hat Tip: *The Elements of Style, Fourth Edition* (Strunk and White 1999)

Conventions

Spelling and Letter Formation

◎ Why is this goal important?

We teach students to consider purpose and audience as they write, so it stands to reason that someday someone will be reading their work. Learning how words are spelled and spelling conventionally so that others can comprehend what has been written are important to making what we have to say clear to our readers.

When students first arrive at school, they will naturally use invented spelling, writing the best they can based on the sounds they hear in words. These early spellings are ripe opportunities for emergent writers to practice letter-sound correspondence and are an empowering way for them to get their thoughts and ideas down on the page (Routman 2005; Graves 1983; Calkins 1994; Snowball and Bolton 1999). Encouraging invented spelling is not sending the message "spelling doesn't matter," but rather, "you are a writer!"—even if the spelling isn't completely correct yet, as young writers are still learning many of the confusing and contradictory rules of written English.

As beginning writers read more, see more words they can recognize in print, and generally develop more awareness of conventional spellings, they will start to realize that some of the words they write don't look right. Because they care about what they are writing, they are motivated to work on their spelling so they can write with more accuracy on the first go and edit their pieces for spelling accuracy as well. At this point, they will start relying not only on their ear—writing the sounds they hear in the words they want to write—but also on spelling rules and remembering how words are spelled from seeing them in print (Graves 1983). As students progress through the grades, they will learn more spelling rules and patterns, and they will also memorize exceptions. Daily reading and interaction with language will expose them to and equip them with a larger vocabulary of words they can spell conventionally. This will help them feel more comfortable applying and generalizing spelling rules (spelling by analogy), and will help fine-tune their sense of "it doesn't look right" when they write a word.

◎ How do I know if this goal is right for my student?

It's important to work from the assumption that children are doing their very best to spell the words they write, at every age and stage. Spelling errors very rarely mean that children are being careless, rather that they are learning and doing the best they can to write as they learn. When composing any piece of writing, keep in mind all of the things that a writer needs to be aware of (the focus of the piece, structure, the types of details, letting your natural voice come through, making sure the punctuation is correct, and on and on). Oftentimes, young writers' papers will be filled with invented or approximated spellings because they are not perfect spellers yet. (A claim, by the way, many adults make about themselves! Thank goodness for spell-check.)

To learn more about your students' spelling understandings, I recommend doing a spelling assessment, such as the spelling inventory that is included in *Words Their Way: Word Study for Phonics, Vocabulary, and Spelling Instruction, Sixth Edition* (Bear et al. 2015); using the assessment as described in Don Graves' *Writing: Teachers and Children at Work* (1983, 184–94); or leaning on the work of Snowball and Bolton in *Spelling K–8: Planning and Teaching* (1999) to create your own assessment. When you know a student's spelling stage, you can tailor your word study program to support students with the specific spelling features they are working to learn—inflected endings, medial vowels, initial blends, and so on (Snowball and Bolton 1999). The strategies in this chapter are no supplement for a strong word study program, which should complement every teacher's writing program. Instead, the strategies in this chapter offer students some advice for getting words down on the page (as best they can), proofreading their own work to find spelling errors, self-correcting errors, using resources to help them spell, as well as a few commonly used spelling rules.

Although the spelling inventory, or simply looking at student writing samples and noticing the frequency and types of spelling errors, may indicate a child who is a prime candidate for support in this area, be mindful not to introduce too-complex spelling strategies too soon. Instead, consider the developmental stage children are in as writers and teach them something that will feel like a slight nudge forward but won't shut down their creativity and ability to write fluidly. For example, teaching students to focus on spelling while they are just starting to get words on the page may cause students to be self-conscious about their approximations, drastically reduce their writing volume as they may become paralyzed with the fear of being wrong, or cause them to play it safe and only write down words they are sure they know how to spell. Also, we don't want students to spend all their time going in search of words to fix rather than focusing on making meaning. As in other chapters, I've tagged strategies according to grade levels, but as always, assessing your students' readiness for strategies is far better than just going by the grade level. Just because a child is in kindergarten doesn't mean he is ready for every strategy marked *K*, and across the kindergarten year, the student will likely benefit from different ones.

Strategies for Spelling and Forming Letters

Strategy		Grade Levels	Genres/Text Types	Processes
8.1	Long or Short Word?	Emergent–K	Any	Drafting, editing
8.2	Talk like a Turtle	Emergent–1	Any	Drafting, editing
8.3	Consult the Alphabet Chart	K–1	Any	Drafting, revising, editing
8.4	Write, Reread, Write, Reread, Repeat	K–1	Any	Drafting
8.5	When's It Big? When's It Small?	K–2	Any	Editing
8.6	Penmanship Counts!	K–2	Any	Editing
8.7	Write Word Wall Words in a Snap!	K–2	Any	Drafting, editing
8.8	Vowel Charts for the Middles of Words	K–3	Any	Drafting, editing
8.9	Spell as Best You Can—on the First Go	K–3	Any	Generating and collecting, developing, drafting
8.10	Use Your Resources to Spell	K–8	Any	Generating and collecting, developing, drafting, editing
8.11	Part-by-Part Spelling	1–3	Any	Generating and collecting, developing, drafting, editing
8.12	Chin Drops	1–3	Any	Generating and collecting, developing, drafting, editing
8.13	Visualize the Word and Have a Go	1–8	Any	Generating and collecting, developing, drafting, editing
8.14	Use Words You Know to Spell Unknown Words	1–8	Any	Generating and collecting, developing, drafting, editing
8.15	Read Your Writing Backward (and Catch Spelling Mistakes!)	2–8	Any	Editing
8.16	Circle and Spell	2–8	Any	Generating and collecting, developing, drafting, editing
8.17	Making It Plural (Consonants Plus -s or -es)	2–8	Any	Generating and collecting, developing, drafting, editing
8.18	Turn to Spell-Check	3–8	Any	Editing
8.19	Check for Homophones	3–8	Any	Editing
8.20	Apostrophes for Contractions	3–8	Any	Editing
8.21	To Apostrophe or Not to Apostrophe? (Possessives)	3–8	Any	Editing
8.22	Making It Plural (While Changing the Base Word)	4–8	Any	Editing

8.1 Long or Short Word?

Who is this for?

LEVELS
emergent–K

GENRE / TEXT TYPE
any

PROCESSES
drafting, editing

Strategy Say the word. Is the word long or short? If it's long, put a lot of letters in it, even if you don't know exactly which ones to put. If it's short, don't use too many letters.

Lesson Language *I'm writing a book about things we do in the computer lab. Can you help me think about whether the word I need to write is long or short? Here is a picture of our class in the computer lab. I want to label the computer so people can tell what it is. Let's all say the word* computer *and decide if it's a long word, because we hear a lot of sounds, or if it's a short word. Say the word with me.* Computers. *Yes, that does sound long doesn't it? Then I want to write* desk *to show where the teacher's computer is. Say it with me.* Desk. *Yeah, that one does sound short, doesn't it? How about if I label this* screen. *Say the word with me.* Screen. *Yup, another short one!*

Teaching Tip The goal in this strategy is not that students use the correct letters, but that they start to learn to represent sounds they hear with letters and develop awareness about the correlation between the number of sounds they hear and the number of sounds represented by letters as they write.

Prompts
• Say the word.
• Do you hear a few sounds or a lot of sounds?
• Think about if the word is long or short.
• Write down letters to show how long the word is.

Strategy When you don't know how to write a word, you can say it s-l-o-w-l-y, like how a turtle might talk. Listen for each sound as you say it. Write down the sounds you hear. When you have it all down on your page, say it again like a turtle, this time running your finger under the letters you wrote down. If you realize you're missing any sounds, fix it!

Teaching Tip A more sophisticated version of this could be to first say the word to hear the sounds, then check it visually to see if it looks right. This will be helpful for students who are reading and are likely to have seen the word in print.

Prompts
- Say it slowly.
- Try to hear each sound.
- What do you hear? Write down the letter that makes that sound.
- Run your finger under the word you wrote, as you say it again, slowly. Are you missing any sounds?

Cassie Foehr

Who is this for?

LEVELS
emergent–1

GENRE / TEXT TYPE
any

PROCESSES
drafting, editing

Hat Tip: *One to One: The Art of Conferring with Young Writers* (Calkins, Hartman, and White 2005)

LEVELS
K–1

GENRE / TEXT TYPE
any

PROCESSES
drafting, revising, editing

Strategy Say the word you want to write. Listen for the first sound. If you know what letter makes that sound, write it. If not, check the alphabet chart. Say the word again, listening for the next sound; repeat the steps until you have written all the sounds you hear.

Lesson Language *Let's try this with the word* monkey *in our story about our class trip to the zoo. First, I'm going to say the word slowly. Say the word with me,* m-o-n-k-e-y. *OK, so the first sound I hear is /m/. What letter makes that sound? Not sure? Let's check our alphabet chart. As I look on the chart, I'm looking for a picture of a word that starts like /m/ just like /m/—monkey. Is it koala? No. Is it leaf? No. Is it mouse? Yes! Mouse. Mouse* starts just like monkey. Monkey *and* mouse *both start with the letter* M. *So I'm going to write an M on my page. Now let me say the word again and I'm going to ask you what sound you hear so I can add it to my label. Will you help me?*

Teaching Tip A word of caution: For very young writers, it's important that the writing of words is balanced with creating meaning on the page, often through illustration (see strategies in Chapter 1, "Composing with Pictures"). It is important to help all young writers in your community feel confident by valuing their approximations. For some, this will mean waiting on introducing an alphabet chart or advancing the expectation that they will write words, until after you're sure they have a good sense of letter-sound correspondence from a letter-sound identification assessment.

Prompts
• Say the word slowly.
• What sound do you hear?
• What letter makes that sound?
• Check the alphabet chart.
• Find a picture of something on the chart that has the same sound.

Hat Tip: *One to One: The Art of Conferring with Young Writers* (Calkins, Hartman, and White 2005)

Write, Reread, Write, Reread, Repeat

Strategy Write down the first word in your sentence. Reread what you have so far. Write the next word. Back up to the beginning of the sentence, reading both words. Continue as you finish the whole sentence.

Teaching Tip This process is slow but necessary for young writers who expend so much energy hearing sounds in the words and getting those letters to represent the sounds down on paper. Rereading all they've written after each new word will ensure that they hold on to the meaning of what they want to write. Don't be concerned if the sentence changes slightly as they keep going. It may be that they've forgotten exactly what they wanted to write, or that they are doing revision on the go! This process would be great to model during interactive writing and/or shared writing lessons.

Teaching Tip As children progress from writing single-word labels to writing multiword sentences, they will need to place spaces between their words. See strategies 9.1, "Make Lines for What You Want to Write" and 9.2, "Finger Space" in the next chapter for ways to support students with word spacing.

Prompts
• You got your word down! Now reread.
• You went back to the beginning to read all you've written so far.
• What's the next word?
• Back up and reread to remind yourself of the next word you planned to write.

Merridy Gnagey

Who is this for?

LEVELS
K–1

GENRE / TEXT TYPE
any

PROCESS
drafting

Hat Tip: *One to One: The Art of Conferring with Young Writers* (Calkins, Hartman, and White 2005)

Who is this for?

LEVELS
K–2

GENRE / TEXT TYPE
any

PROCESS
editing

Strategy Check through each word—beginning to end. Make sure a capital letter starts a sentence, the word *I*, and a name of a specific person or place. Make sure all the other letters are lowercase.

Teaching Tip You could break this strategy up into a series of strategies, helping students edit for different instances of capitalization. For example, they could search for the periods in their draft, and then check the first letter of the next word to make sure it's a capital letter.

Teaching Tip It will be helpful for each student to have an alphabet chart or strip with uppercase and lowercase letters taped to their desk as a reference. Using the same picture cues as your phonics/word study program and/or handwriting program will help encourage transfer.

Prompts

• Should that be a capital or lowercase letter?
• It's at the beginning of a sentence. What kind of letter should you use?
• You have a capital letter here. Does it belong here?
• Is that a capital or lowercase letter?
• Is it a specific place?
• Make sure the rest of the word is lowercase!

Penmanship Counts!

Strategy Reread your draft, paying close attention to how you wrote your letters. Any time you find a letter that is difficult to read, stop and fix it. You can erase and rewrite, cross out and write above, or add a flap on top of your writing.

Lesson Language *You worked so hard on your writing so that you can share it with your friends and your family. Now, it's important to make sure that they'll actually be able to read it! We don't want our readers to need secret decoder rings to figure out what we we're trying to say. That's why we try to write our letters in a way that any reader can recognize them. So they can read and enjoy our stories like we meant for them to!*

Teaching Tip Although this strategy is indicated as appropriate for kindergarten, be sure that teaching it won't get in the way of a developing writer's ability to get words down on the page. This would be appropriate once a child is able to write clear letters and has the energy to go back and fix up some. When a child is new to writing letters, going back to make every one better may cause the child to think, "This is hard work! If I have to fix all my letters I'll just write less so there is less to work on." You also don't want children to get so overly focused on forming letters that they lose the flow of what they are trying to write. So, this strategy will be right for some kindergarten writers, but would seriously impede others.

Prompts
- Can you find anything your reader might find hard to read?
- I'm having a hard time with this word. What are you trying to write?
- You found one on your own! Now let's check the alphabet chart to remember how to write those letters so someone else can read it.
- All the words you fixed means your reader will be able to read and enjoy your story!

Who is this for?

LEVELS
K–2

GENRE / TEXT TYPE
any

PROCESS
editing

Samantha Pestridge

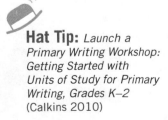

Hat Tip: *Launch a Primary Writing Workshop: Getting Started with Units of Study for Primary Writing, Grades K–2* (Calkins 2010)

Write Word Wall Words in a Snap!

Who is this for?

LEVELS
K–2

GENRE / TEXT TYPE
any

PROCESSES
drafting, editing

Strategy Say the word you want to write. Think, "Have I seen that word on the word wall?" If yes, check the wall to find it, then write it down. As you write it, say the letters aloud, trying to commit the word to memory.

Teaching Tip Word walls can be a helpful resource to students—*if* they are used correctly. If you put up fifty or more words before the students arrive in your classroom, the wall will probably just be wallpaper. Instead, if you involve students in adding a few carefully chosen words each week, during a lesson such as shared reading or interactive or shared writing, then your wall will be used more often. I generally recommend no more than twenty-five words on the wall at any one time. This means that as students learn the words, they become "retired" to a Rolodex on the shelf nearby or on library pockets that are stapled to the bottom of the bulletin board beneath each letter. Alphabetizing your word wall and teaching children to look for the letter first and then the word will help your students use it quickly and with ease. As you teach throughout the day, find opportunities to encourage children to reference the word wall. For example, during a shared writing lesson you might say, "Wait! We know how to spell that. Everybody, check the word wall and tell me how to spell that word."

Prompts
- Check the word wall!
- You knew _____ was on the word wall! Where would you find it?
- Think about where you'd find that word.
- Now that you found it, write it in a snap.
- Say the letters of the word. Try to remember it for next time!

Hat Tip: *One to One: The Art of Conferring with Young Writers* (Calkins, Hartman, and White 2005)

Strategy Say the word slowly. Record what you hear at the beginning. Say it again, now listening for the middle of the word. Check your vowel chart to see which letter most often makes that sound. Write down a letter from the vowel chart for the middle of your word.

Teaching Tip This lesson can be adapted for a variety of levels. Ideally, the vowels on the vowel chart match what you've taught students during word study. For example, kindergarteners may only know the short vowel sound each vowel can make, but beginning first graders may know short and long vowel sounds and maybe even different vowel combinations (*oo, ou, oa,* etc.). To make the chart usable, make sure you've taught what's on it!

Prompts
- Say the word slowly. What do you hear?
- You got the beginning down, now let's try to hear the middle.
- What letter or letters make that sound?
- Now that you have the beginning and middle down, say the word again to listen for the ending.

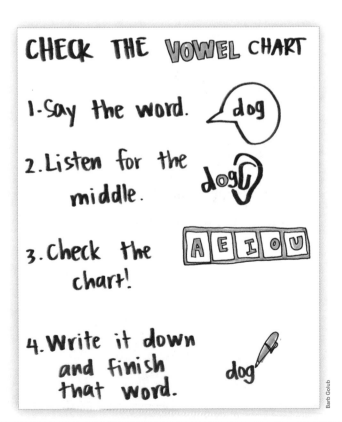

Barb Golub

Who is this for?

LEVELS
K–3

GENRE / TEXT TYPE
any

PROCESSES
drafting, editing

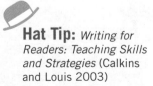

Hat Tip: *Writing for Readers: Teaching Skills and Strategies* (Calkins and Louis 2003)

Who is this for?

LEVELS
K–3

GENRE / TEXT TYPE
any

PROCESSES
generating and collecting, developing, drafting

Strategy When drafting or writing in a notebook, try to spell as best as you can so that you aren't piling up your work for editing time. Pause and think, "Do I know how to spell this word?" If you do, write it. If you're not sure, write it as best you can.

Teaching Tip There's a fine line between putting so much emphasis on correct, conventional spelling that it interferes with a child's flow and ability to get the words down, and sending a message that "spelling doesn't matter." This lesson is an attempt to tell kids, "Yes, spelling does matter. Do your best. Pay attention. But if you don't know it, just keep going." The decision to teach this strategy should be made with consideration of the child's development. Likely, they are working hard to write words with the best spelling they can. But if a child is writing fast and confidently, making errors (perhaps repeatedly, such as *liek* for *like*) then she would benefit from being told to pause and think about the word before writing it.

Prompts
- You know that word!
- Unsure? Spell it as best you can and keep going.
- I can see you're hearing the sounds and writing that word as best you can.
- You know that's not spelled right? You could just put a circle around it so you can come back to it later.

Do you know it?

YES
Write it down.

NO
Do your best and keep going!

Merridy Gnagey

Hat Tip: *Spelling K–8: Planning and Teaching* (Snowball and Bolton 1999)

Strategy When trying to spell a word (or editing to correct the spelling of a word), stop and ask yourself, "Have I seen that word written somewhere else before?" Check the chart, book, or tool where that word may appear.

Teaching Tip Many teachers in grades K–2 find it helpful to have a word wall in their classroom with high-frequency words. By the time children are in third grade and up through middle school, a more common practice is to offer students a personalized dictionary or word wall with commonly misspelled words (*through*, *because*, *their/they're/there*, *to/two/too*) and quick definitions for identification purposes. This strategy also encourages children to use the print-rich environment of your classroom, which may include anchor charts, shared reading texts, and more. Many teachers have students keep word study notebooks where students practice sorting and writing words that align to the features they are studying and/or have a spelling book that children can be encouraged to check. Teachers of upper elementary and middle school students may choose to have a writing reference center that includes dictionaries and thesauri. However, with all of these resources, be careful to keep an eye on how they are being used. Some students will become so stymied by correct spelling that they are afraid to approximate and end up spending all their time looking up words and not enough time generating writing. Or, students will write only using words that are on the word wall, which then means they lose any sense of voice or choice in their writing. So, when teaching this strategy also be sure to lend advice about *when* and *how often* to use it and to send the message that glancing at a tool should be quick and not interrupt the flow of writing.

Prompts

- Do you think you can find that word in the room somewhere?
- Where do you remember seeing that word?
- We had that word in our story yesterday! Go see if you can find it.
- I think that's a word wall word.
- Could you find that word in a _____ (*name source such as word wall, dictionary, or storybook*)?

STOP and ASK...
"Have I seen that word written somewhere else before?"
1. word wall
2. word study notebook
3. in a book I have read before
4. in a personal dictionary

THINK...
"I should look around the room!"

Betsy Hubbard

Hat Tip: *Writing for Readers: Teaching Skills and Strategies* (Calkins and Louis 2003)

8.11 Part-by-Part Spelling

Hat Tip: *Spelling K–8: Planning and Teaching* (Snowball and Bolton 1999)

Strategy Say the word you want to write. Clap the syllables. Listen to the first syllable. Think about what group of letters spell that first part. Say the word again, part by part. Write down the letters for the next syllable. Continue until the whole word is written.

Teaching Tip This lesson can be modified to include onset and rime, or single letters and familiar words inside of larger words (for example, *panda* is *p* and *and* is *a*). Teaching children to go through the word in parts, rather than letter by letter, is more efficient and can help them recognize one syllable as a group of letters.

Prompts
- Say the word, part by part.
- Clap the syllables.
- What letters will spell that first part?
- Write that part down.
- What's the next syllable you hear?

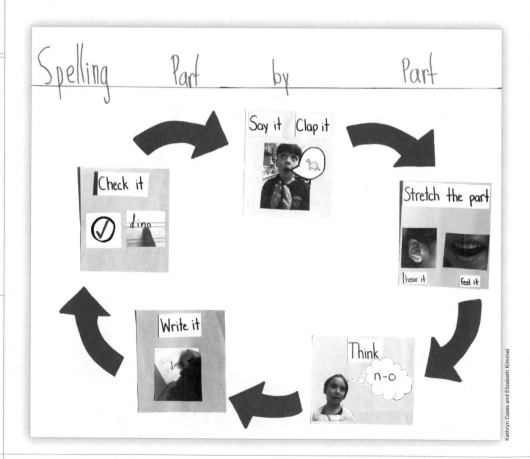

Kathryn Cazes and Elizabeth Kimmel

Strategy Put a flat hand under your chin, palm down, and say the word you're trying to spell aloud. Each time your chin drops is a new syllable. Go back and say the first syllable. Write the syllable, making sure there is at least one vowel or *y* in the syllable. Say the word again, listening for the next syllable. Spell that syllable.

Teaching Tip There is a very small set of words in the English language for which this strategy does not work: Words that have spelling patterns similar to *chasm* and *rhythm* as well as a few obscure words only SCRABBLE players would know about. For the elementary set, this is a pretty trustworthy strategy to teach! Here is a video to share with students to introduce and practice this method: www .youtube.com/watch?v=TvcgVRULaWw.

Prompts
- Put your hand under your chin. Say the word.
- Say the word slower, notice when your chin drops.
- Go back and say it again. Say the first syllable. Now write it.
- Remember, there needs to be a vowel in each syllable.

To count the number of syllables in a word, place your hand under your chin and say the word NORMALLY

butterfly

Feel the number of times your chin "bumps" your hand.
Count your Chin bumps on your fingers

but   ter   fly   = 3 syllables

Cassie Foehr

Who is this for?

LEVELS
1–3

GENRE / TEXT TYPE
any

PROCESSES
generating and collecting, developing, drafting, editing

Who is this for?

LEVELS
1–8

GENRE / TEXT TYPE
any

PROCESSES
generating and collecting, developing, drafting, editing

Strategy When trying to spell a word, try to visualize where you've seen it written and how you've seen it written before. It may help to close your eyes. Then, in a margin or on a piece of scrap paper, write how you think it's spelled. Try it a second or maybe even third way. Look back at what you've written and ask yourself, "Which of these tries looks right to me?"

Prompts
- Check off the parts that look right to you.
- Write the word as you think you've seen it before.
- Which parts look right? Which part looks off?
- Do you think there are some letters missing?
- What part of that word is tricky for you?
- The part you're trying to spell is also in the word _____. Does that help?

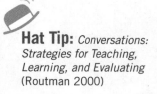

Hat Tip: *Conversations: Strategies for Teaching, Learning, and Evaluating* (Routman 2000)

Strategy Say the word you're trying to spell. Hear the sounds. Think, "What word do I know how to spell that sounds like that word?" Try spelling the word with the same spelling pattern as the word you know.

Teaching Tip Just as we teach children as they read to read by analogy, we can teach them to write by analogy. During shared writing, you can voice over your thinking: "Well, I know how to spell *it* so *bit* must be *it* with a *b* at the beginning! *b-i-t*!" We all know, however, that one of the things that makes English tricky is that there are multiple ways to spell the same sound. Therefore, I recommend that you use this strategy in conjunction with "Visualize the Word and Have a Go" (strategy 8.13). This strategy will be most powerful when students are engaged in a word study program (such as the program in *Words Their Way* by Bear et al. [2015]), that will teach children to sort and recognize different spelling patterns and make generalizations about spelling rules.

Prompts

• What word do you know that sounds like that word?
• Can you think of a word that rhymes?
• Well, you know how to spell ____. So let's think about how you might spell ____.
• ____ is on the word wall! The word you're trying to spell is very close to that one.
• You know another word that starts like that. Use that word to help you spell.

Who is this for?

LEVELS
1–8

GENRE / TEXT TYPE
any

PROCESSES
generating and collecting, developing, drafting, editing

Hat Tip: *Spelling K–8: Planning and Teaching* (Snowball and Bolton 1999)

8.15 Read Your Writing Backward (and Catch Spelling Mistakes!)

Strategy When you read your writing, your brain will often autocorrect any spelling errors you may have made so that you don't notice them. To catch them, you can try to read your writing from the last word, back to the first. Point crisply under each word as you read it out loud. As you go, think, "Does that look right?"

Teaching Tip This strategy will not work for homophones! Be sure to caution children to read any homophones in the context of the whole sentence and to check the meaning of the word against how it is used in the sentence (see strategy 8.19, "Check for Homophones," for more advice).

Prompts
- Start at the end.
- Read word by word, pointing as you go.
- Did that word look right?
- You caught a misspelling! Isn't it helpful to read from the end?
- That word is a homophone. You'll have to read it in the context of the sentence to see if you have the right one.

Samantha Pestridge

8.16 Circle and Spell

Strategy As you're writing, if you realize you don't know how to spell a word, just write it as best you can and circle it to return to it later. Make a list of circled words on a separate page. Ask your partner or teacher for the spellings for those words, or search out a trusted source to find the correct spellings. Return to your draft to make changes.

Teaching Tip The first step in helping children to be stronger spellers is to help them to acknowledge or "catch" when they've spelled a word incorrectly. Some children who are stymied by spelling perfectionism may be told to circle as they go, identifying words they plan to go back to correct later. Others may have to give concerted effort to finding the words that don't look right and circling them on a completed draft so that they can devote all of their cognitive energies to getting their ideas down first. You can decide how the child finds the correct spellings of the words based on how much work it was to identify them in the first place. For children who are working very hard on the identification stage alone, I often provide them with correct spellings on their separate page and ask them to transfer the correct spellings back on their draft. (Of course, too many of these words in a draft make the process of spell-checking tedious, so be mindful of how many words you're asking children to work on with each piece of writing.) Seeing their incorrect spellings on a separate page also helps me look for patterns that can inform future word study lessons.

Prompts

- Just circle it if you don't think it's spelled correctly, and keep going.
- Let's look back over your draft. Which words don't look right? Circle them.
- Now that you've circled the words you'd like to find the correct spellings for, what strategy will you try?
- That's it—just circle it and keep going. You can come back to it later.

Who is this for?

LEVELS
2–8

GENRE / TEXT TYPE
any

PROCESSES
generating and collecting, developing, drafting, editing

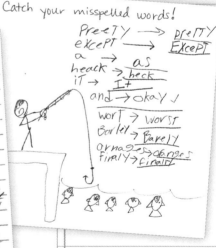

Hat Tip: *Writing: Teachers and Children at Work* (Graves 1983)

Making It Plural (Consonants Plus *-s* or *-es*)

Who is this for?

LEVELS

2–8

GENRE / TEXT TYPE

any

PROCESSES

generating and collecting, developing, drafting, editing

Hat Tip: *Catching Up on Conventions: Grammar Lessons for Middle School Writers* (Francois and Zonana 2009)

Strategy Read/say the word aloud and count the syllables. Check the ending of the word. Think about whether it needs an *-s* or *-es* to make it plural.

Lesson Language *When you mean "more than one" of a noun, you may need to add an -s to the end of the word. But for words that end with sh, ch, x, and z, you need to add -es. Another way you'll know to add -es instead of -s is if you can't say the word aloud without an extra syllable when it's plural (e.g.,* foxes*). Never add an apostrophe to make a noun plural.*

Teaching Tip It wouldn't be English without a list of exceptions! Exceptions to this rule are words for which the singular and plural are the same such as *deer, salmon,* and *fish.* There are also a class of nouns referred to as "uncountable" that refer to certain words, such as *water, knowledge, beauty, grass, art, nature, health.* And there is still another class of nouns that seem plural because they end in *-s,* but are in fact singular, such as *news, mathematics, measles.*

Using a Mentor *Happy Endings: A Story About Suffixes* includes many suffixes including *-s* and *-es* woven into a fun narrative (Pulver 2011).

Prompts

- Check the ending of the word.
- What letter ends the word? So what should you do?
- Say the word aloud. Is there an extra syllable when it's plural?
- I see you checking the rule to figure out whether to put an *-s* or an *-es*!

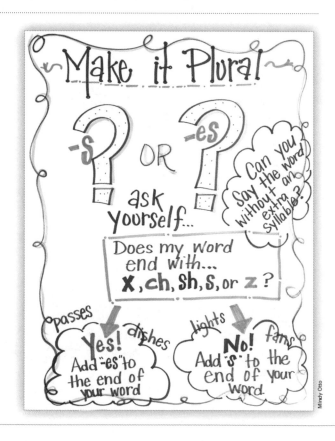

Strategy Identify the words on your page that don't look right. Type the words into a computer document. Find and click on the spell-check button. Click through the options the computer gives you, considering which one looks right. Make the change on your page.

Teaching Tip Consider having a writing center where a laptop computer or two, some dictionaries, and some other writing references are available to your students.

Prompts

- Circle the words you think you've misspelled.
- What words don't look right?
- Type the words into a Word document. If they are underlined, they are misspelled!
- Be sure to check all the options the computer provides. Does one of them look right?

Who is this for?

LEVELS
3–8

GENRE / TEXT TYPE
any

PROCESS
editing

Who is this for?

LEVELS
3–8

GENRE / TEXT TYPE
any

PROCESS
editing

Strategy Be on the lookout for commonly confused homophones (see figure below). Reread the sentence, and put the definition of the word you chose in its place. Think, "Is my sentence correct?" If not, replace it with the correct word!

Lesson Language Homo *means* same *and* phone *means* sound. *There are some words in English that sound the same, but are spelled differently. These are tricky and require a little thought to get right! The best advice is to think about the meaning of each of the words and to check and double-check your work to make sure you chose the right one for the meaning you intended in the sentence.*

Teaching Tip Depending on the age and experience of your writers, and the prevalence of their confusions with these words, you may want to break up this strategy into four separate lessons, taking each set of homophones in isolation.

Using a Mentor Read aloud *Dear Deer: A Book of Homophones* (Barretta 2007) to help children picture the different meanings of same-sounding, differently spelled words. For this strategy to be helpful, students will need to learn about homophones prior to learning this strategy. This could happen during read-aloud.

Prompts
• Did you mean ____ spelled ____? That means ____.
• There are three different spellings of ____ and they all have different meanings. Let's make sure you have the one you mean to have.
• Think, "Is my sentence correct?"
• Check to make sure you have the word you meant.

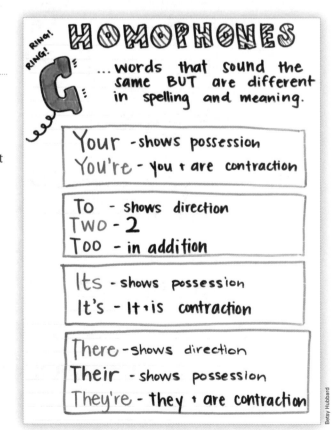

Hat Tip: *Catching Up on Conventions: Grammar Lessons for Middle School Writers* (Francois and Zonana 2009)

Strategy Slow down when you read the contraction and ask yourself, "What two words is this one word replacing?" Notice which letter or letters are missing from the second word, and place the apostrophe in their places.

Lesson Language *Apostrophes are used for contractions. A contraction is when you combine two words into one. The apostrophe punctuation mark takes the place of the dropped letters. It's important to put the apostrophe in the correct place to spell the contraction correctly. Let's look at an example. In this sentence: "It's a beautiful day so they're going out to play," It's replaces* It is. *The apostrophe goes where the* i *in* is *would go.* They're *replaces* they are. *What letter is missing? The* a *in* are. *Therefore, the apostrophe goes where the* a *would go.*

Prompts
- What two words is this word replacing?
- What letter(s) are missing?
- Where does the apostrophe go?
- Let's write out both words, and the contraction to figure it out.

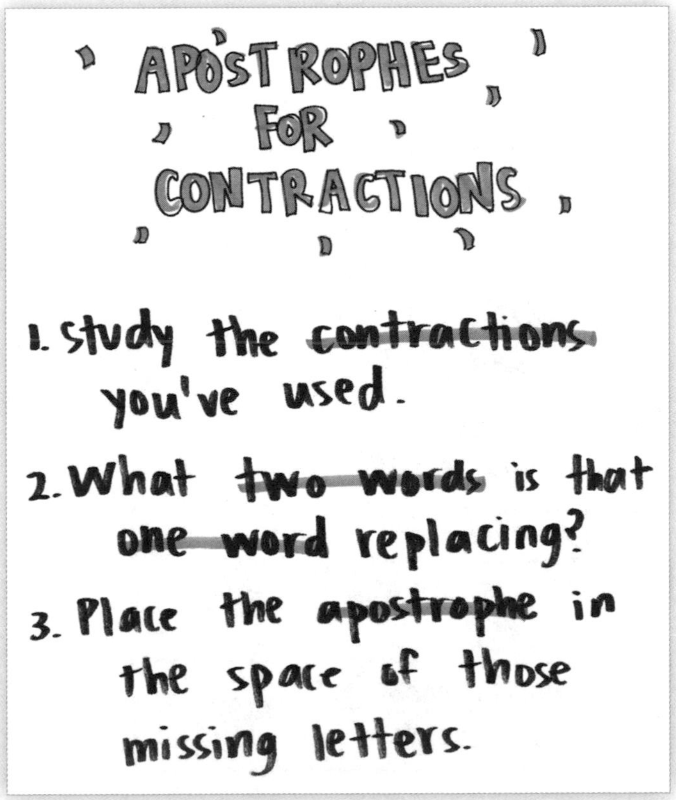

APO'ST ROPHES FOR CONTRACTIONS

1. Study the contractions you've used.
2. What two words is that one word replacing?
3. Place the apostrophe in the space of those missing letters.

Barb Golub

Who is this for?

LEVELS
3–8

GENRE / TEXT TYPE
any

PROCESS
editing

Hat Tip: *Catching Up on Conventions: Grammar Lessons for Middle School Writers* (Francois and Zonana 2009)

8.21 To Apostrophe or Not to Apostrophe? (Possessives)

Who is this for?

LEVELS
3–8

GENRE / TEXT TYPE
any

PROCESS
editing

Strategy Look through your draft for words that end with *s*. Reread the sentence to find out if the *s* is to create a plural or to show possession (or neither). If you mean to show a possessive and it's a noun, make sure there is an apostrophe. If the word is a possessive pronoun, make sure there is no apostrophe. Check the chart and check your *s*'s.

Using a Mentor Note that you may find different "rules" around apostrophes in different publisher's style guides—the rule in this strategy follows Strunk and White's *Elements of Style* (1999). In Heinemann's style guide, for example, proper names ending in *s* have no *s* after the apostrophe (i.e., *James'* rather than *James's*). Check the mentor texts you plan to use if you want to have students search for examples in published books. You may find different publishing guidelines are evident.

Prompts
• Let's find words that end in *s*.
• Reread the sentence. Can you find any words that end in *s*?
• Is there something that belongs to someone or something?
• Does that need an apostrophe?
• How do you know that needs an apostrophe?
• Think about the rule. Check the chart if you need to.
• *(Nonverbal: point to the chart.)*

Hat Tip: *The Elements of Style, Fourth Edition* (Strunk and White 1999)

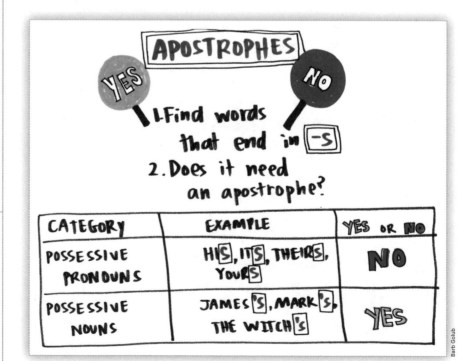

Strategy When you mean "more than one," you usually need to change the ending of the noun to make it plural. Words that end in *y, o, f,* or *v* require special attention. Check the rules chart and double-check how you pluralized those words. (But never add an apostrophe!)

Teaching Tip To introduce this strategy, you may consider doing an inquiry where children collect words that end with an *s* from their independent reading books, then sort them into categories. They may be able to generalize the rules that are similar to the ones in the chart on this page. When children discover it (rather than just being told the rule), they will often better remember it!

Using a Mentor *Happy Endings: A Story About Suffixes* (Pulver 2011) includes many suffixes including *-s* and *-es* woven into a fun narrative.

Prompts
- Do you mean "more than one" here?
- Check the chart to see how you'll add an ending to show it's plural.
- No apostrophes for plurals!
- Your word ends in ____. Do you remember the rule for how to make the word plural?

Word Ending	Example	What to Do?
Consonant + *y*	Party	Change the *y* to an *i* and add *-es*
Vowel + *y*	Key	Keep the *y* and add *-s*
F, fe, if and sounds like /f/ when plural	Chief/chiefs	Add only *-s*
F, fe, if and sounds like /v/ when plural	Wife/wives	Change the *f* to a *v* and add *-es*

Goal 9

Conventions

Grammar and Punctuation

◎ Why is this goal important?

Think about how grammar was taught to you. I can remember standing at the blackboard diagramming sentences under Mrs. Marvullo's watchful eyes in fifth grade. Daily oral language exercises copied into a notebook. Countless workbook pages to drill home The Rules.

But ask any writer, and she will tell you that grammar and punctuation are often about decision making and taking charge of one's own writing: bending or breaking rules in the name of craft. Writers know the difference between sentences and fragments, but they don't always view fragments as "wrong" and may choose to use one to create an effect. They know how to craft a complete sentence and how to edit to fix a run-on, but once in a while a run-on may be just what's called for, given the tone of the piece. They choose a dash in some places, a comma in others. They start a sentence with *and* or *but*.

To complicate things further, language is not static. New words enter the lexicon all the time. The way we use words is reinvented. Punctuation usage changes, too.

Choosing to take on some of the strategies in this chapter as a part of your individual, small-group, and/or whole-class teaching means that you're choosing to *teach* how authors make decisions around grammar and punctuation, not just *assign* that students do it correctly. It's the decision to *describe* how language is used and the choices authors make, not simply to *prescribe* them. After all, as Angelillo (2002) reminds us, "Writers use punctuation to shape the way readers read their text. The system of little symbols we know as punctuation is full of meaning, nuance, and intricacy. It helps writing make sense to readers; it allows us to control the pace and volume and rhythm of the words. Used wisely, it is an invaluable writing tool" (8).

Grammar and punctuation can be a loaded, potentially controversial topic to take on. As we teach certain guidelines around academic uses of language, we need to be sensitive to students' home language, when the home language doesn't always match the expected form of English used in the classroom (Delpit 2002; Francois and Zonana 2009). Still, as Francois and Zonana remind us: "It is rare to find a person living in the United States who speaks a language that precisely mirrors all of the rules of Standard Written English" (2009, 58).

The lessons in this chapter offer wonderful opportunities to use inquiry as a method of teaching: for example, sending children into the books they love in search of all the semicolons they can find, and with guidance from their teacher, developing a working set of guidelines about the ways that authors use them.

◎ How do I know if this goal is right for my student?

All students will benefit from paying some attention to their grammar and punctuation choices. Editing should be a part of every writer's process, and you may find that you have some editing goals for your class at various points across the year. As Stephen King says, "To write is human, to edit is divine" (2000, 13).

However, don't think of this chapter as just about editing to "fix" mistakes. Think of the strategies in this chapter as invitations to play and as entry points into considering craft, cadence, and tone (Ehrenworth and Vinton 2005).

Therefore, you may choose this goal for those students who can use support making their writing more readable, their sentences clearer, or their tone more precise for the intended audience. On the other hand, these strategies might be offered to a student who is ready to challenge conventions and play with language to discover the impact it has on his writing, and on his reader.

Strategies for Supporting Grammar and Punctuation

Strategy		Grade Levels	Genres/Text Types	Processes
9.1	Make Lines for What You Want to Write	K–1	Any	Planning
9.2	Finger Space	K–1	Any	Drafting
9.3	Read with Your Finger	K–2	Any	Revising, editing
9.4	Repeated Rereadings to Check a Checklist	K–8	Any	Editing
9.5	Does It Sound like a Book?	1–8	Any	Revising
9.6	Ellipses	1–8	Any	Drafting, revising
9.7	To *And* or Not to *And*?	2–5	Narrative, opinion/persuasive, informational/nonfiction	Editing
9.8	Guess What! Complete Sentences	2–8	Narrative, opinion/persuasive, informational/nonfiction	Editing
9.9	Don't Overdo It!	2–8	Any	Editing
9.10	Colons	2–8	Any	Drafting, editing
9.11	Punctuating (and Paragraphing) Speech	3–8	Narrative	Drafting, editing
9.12	Pause for Periods	3–8	Narrative, opinion/persuasive, informational/nonfiction	Editing
9.13	Voice Comma	3–8	Any	Revising, editing
9.14	Group Words for Comprehension: Commas	3–8	Any	Revising, editing
9.15	Say It with Feeling!	3–8	Any	Revising, editing
9.16	Paragraph Starters	4–8	Narrative, opinion/persuasive, informational/nonfiction	Drafting, editing
9.17	Read Your Draft Aloud, and *Listen*	4–8	Any	Editing
9.18	Match the Number of the Subject to the Number of the Verb	4–8	Any	Editing

Strategy	Grade Levels	Genres/Text Types	Processes
9.19 Knowing When You Need a New Paragraph	4–8	Narrative, opinion/persuasive, informational/nonfiction	Editing
9.20 Negative + Negative = Positive	4–8	Any	Generating and collecting, drafting, editing
9.21 Irregular Verbs and Subject–Verb Agreement	4–8	Any	Generating and collecting, drafting, editing
9.22 Eliminating Repetition with Sentence Combining	4–8	Narrative, opinion/persuasive, informational/nonfiction	Revising
9.23 Revising Run-On Sentences	4–8	Narrative, opinion/persuasive, informational/nonfiction	Revising, editing
9.24 Creating Complex Sentences	4–8	Narrative, opinion/persuasive, informational/nonfiction	Revising, editing
9.25 Creating Compound Sentences	4–8	Narrative, opinion/persuasive, informational/nonfiction	Revising, editing
9.26 Dashes	4–8	Any	Revising, editing
9.27 Play with Pauses	4–8	Any	Revising
9.28 *I* or *Me*? *Us* or *We*? *They* or *Them*?	4–8	Any	Editing
9.29 Parenthetic Expressions	5–8	Any	Generating and collecting, drafting, editing
9.30 Verb Tense Consistency Within a Sentence	5–8	Any	Editing
9.31 Considering Sentence Length	5–8	Narrative, opinion/persuasive, informational/nonfiction	Revising, editing
9.32 Semicolons	5–8	Any	Revising, editing
9.33 Accentuate the Positive (Tightening Up Sentences)	6–8	Narrative, opinion/persuasive, informational/nonfiction	Revising, editing
9.34 Rephrase for Clarity	6–8	Any	Revising, editing
9.35 When Did the Action Happen? (Simple, Continuous, and Perfect Tenses)	6–8	Any	Generating and collecting, drafting, editing

Who is this for?

LEVELS
K–1

GENRE / TEXT TYPE
any

PROCESS
planning

Strategy Say the sentence you want to write. Count how many words the sentence has. Draw lines on your paper, one for each word you plan to write. Go back to the beginning and write the sentence, word by word, with one word on each line. Remember to reread what you have as you go!

Teaching Tip This strategy is a great one to model during interactive and shared writing and also would be helpful to use in connection with the strategies "Write, Reread, Write, Reread, Repeat" (strategy 8.4) and "Read with Your Finger" (strategy 9.3). This helps to reinforce children's concept of word and their ability to one-to-one match and helps to ensure proper spacing between words. It's important that you wean students off of this strategy once they demonstrate an understanding of spacing between words.

Teaching Tip It is possible that as a young child is attempting to get words on the page, by the time she says the sentence, counts the words, draws the lines, and goes back to the first line, the sentence has changed (or she's forgotten it!). This is completely normal and expected. At this point, the child should think, "What do I want to write now?" and recompose the sentence.

Prompts

- Say your sentence aloud.
- How many words do you hear? Let's count them.
- Write that number of lines on your page. Leave space between each word!
- Let's go back to the start and begin writing the words. What did you want to write first?
- You said the sentence, counted the words, and made lines on your paper to hold the space!

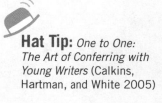

Hat Tip: *One to One: The Art of Conferring with Young Writers* (Calkins, Hartman, and White 2005)

9.2 Finger Space

Strategy Say what you want to write. Spell the word as best you can. Put down a finger to hold a space. Say the next word. Spell it as best you can. Put down a finger to hold a space. Continue!

Teaching Tip You can get creative with this strategy and its implementation by offering students special spacing tools: a Popsicle stick with a little "Space Bot" astronaut glued to the end, a small sticker placed on the fingernail of the spacing finger as a reminder, or even small cubes or stickers to lay or affix to the paper after each word. You may find a simple finger is best—the writer always has it with him!

Prompts
- You finished the word! Now what will you do?
- Put down a finger before you write the next word.
- Don't forget to leave a space.
- How can you leave a space?
- Use your finger.

Kathryn Cazes and Elizabeth Kimmel

Who is this for?

LEVELS
K–1

GENRE / TEXT TYPE
any

PROCESS
drafting

Hat Tip: *Writing for Readers: Teaching Skills and Strategies* (Calkins and Louis 2003)

9.3 Read with Your Finger

LEVELS
K–2

GENRE / TEXT TYPE
any

PROCESSES
revising, editing

Strategy Point under each word you've written. Listen to see if the writing sounds right. As you read each word, notice if you missed any words or added any words. Go back and make the change you need to make so your writing makes sense and sounds right.

Teaching Tip This strategy is a helpful complement to reading strategies that help students at levels A, B, and C read with one-to-one matching.

Teaching Tip If students find they are often leaving out words and need a way to insert them, you may need to teach them to use a caret, add an asterisk where the word should be, and write the word with an asterisk in a margin or to use a revision strip to add on. See strategy 6.8, "Flaps and Carets," for more advice on how to help students use these tools.

Prompts

- You read ___. It says ____. What's missing?
- Did you write it down how you just read it to me?
- Think about if you added in any words you don't need.
- Think about if you're missing any words you need.
- Does it match?

Read with your finger

Then I up the ladder. 😐 Uh-oh.

Then I climbed up the ladder. 😃 Yay!

Merridy Gnagey

Strategy Read the first item on your editing checklist. Read through your draft, making any changes you notice you need with that first item in mind. Read the second item on your checklist; read and edit your draft. Read the final item on the checklist; read and edit your draft.

Teaching Tip A few words about checklists. First, just because it's on a checklist doesn't automatically mean a child can do it or should be expected to do it. The best checklists are simply reminders of things that have already been taught *and learned.* That means that not only has the teacher mentioned it in a lesson and demonstrated how to edit for that particular convention, but students have shown that they are able to at least approximate editing for it, too. This may mean they can do it sometimes (catching three of the five errors in their piece) or that they are using but confusing (overapplying the "rule" such as putting periods more often than is necessary, breaking up longer compound sentences into simple sentences).

Prompts

- What are you going to keep in mind for this first draft?
- Check your checklist. What will you read for first?
- You already read for _____ and _____. What will you be thinking about as you read this one?
- Read for _____.
- Edit with _____ from your checklist in mind.
- You really paid attention to _____ from your checklist. I see you caught a few things to edit!

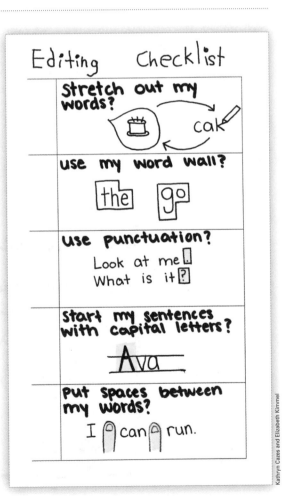

Kathryn Cazes and Elizabeth Kimmel

Hat Tip: *Units of Study in Opinion, Narrative and Informational Writing* (Calkins and colleagues 2013)

Who is this for?

LEVELS
1–8

GENRE / TEXT TYPE
any

PROCESS
revising

Strategy As you reread your draft, be on the lookout for words, phrases, or ways of saying things that you hear in everyday speech but that you don't often read in a book. In most cases, you'll want your published writing to sound like a published book (though you may have a reason for choosing otherwise!).

Teaching Tip It's important that we honor the way people in our students' lives speak. Saying to students, "That doesn't sound right" or "The way you wrote that is wrong" can communicate, perhaps unintentionally, that something is flawed with the way their parents or other members of their home community speak (Delpit 2006). Instead, you can try to change your language slightly so that you communicate that it's important for them to be aware of book language and that it may not always be the same as the spoken language they are accustomed to hearing. As a writer, they then have a choice of what they want to use.

Using a Mentor In Matt De La Peña's multiple award-winning picture book *Last Stop on Market Street*, the author uses nonstandard English to bring out the voice of the grandmother and grandson who are main characters in the book (2015). This is juxtaposed with a standard English voice of the narrator. It would make an interesting study in purposeful choice in "breaking rules" for craft.

Prompts
- Let's think about how it would sound if we saw it in a book.
- Is that book language?
- Let's try to write it another way, and think about which is book language that might be how someone speaks to a friend.
- Can you explain why you wrote it that way?

Hat Tip: *Catching Up on Conventions: Grammar Lessons for Middle School Writers* (Francois and Zonana 2009)

Strategy When you want your reader to pause with a feeling of suspense, draw out an idea or time, or show speechlessness, you can use three periods in a row: the ellipsis.

Teaching Tip This punctuation mark, like the exclamation point, is one that will likely be overused when it's first learned. You've been warned!

Using a Mentor

Dog Heaven: "They turn around and around in the cloud . . . until it feels just right, and then they curl up and sleep" (Rylant 1995). The ellipsis communicates time passing.

Shortcut: "We looked . . . We listened . . . We decided to take the shortcut home" (Crews 1996, 1–2). These ellipses seem to build suspense in the beginning of the story and also communicate some pausing of the character's actions.

The Whisper: "He promised . . ." (Zagarenski 2015). The ellipsis communicates a trailing off of thoughts.

Prompts

- Where do you want to add suspense?
- Describe the kind of pause you want there.
- What punctuation mark matches your meaning?
- If you want to draw out time, you could use an ellipsis.

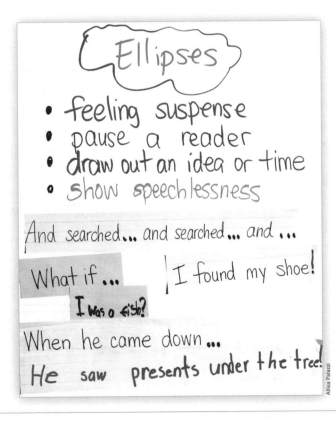

Ellipses
- feeling suspense
- pause a reader
- draw out an idea or time
- show speechlessness

And searched... and searched... and ...

What if ...   I found my shoe!
      I was a fish?

When he came down ...
He saw presents under the tree!

Allisa Palazzi

Who is this for?

LEVELS
1–8

GENRE / TEXT TYPE
any

PROCESSES
drafting, revising

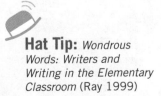

Hat Tip: *Wondrous Words: Writers and Writing in the Elementary Classroom* (Ray 1999)

Strategy Find a place where you've used *and* several times in one sentence. Reread the entire sentence and think, "Which of these ideas/details (what's before the *and* and what's after the *and*) need to stay connected?" Keep the *and* where they are related. Delete the *and* where they are not, and put a period in its place.

Teaching Tip Have you ever noticed that young children seem to understand how to punctuate a complete sentence, but as they get older they suddenly have a piece full of run-ons? As children move from writing a string of very simple sentences (We went to the park. We went on the swings. I ate ice cream.), they reach a "syntactic threshold" and start trying out longer, more-complex sentences—before they know how to punctuate them correctly (Strong 1999). This strategy can be used in conjunction with others about run-ons (9.23), sentence combining (9.22), and creating complex and compound sentences (9.24, 9.25) in this chapter.

Prompts
- Find the *and*s.
- Wow, you're right. You've got four in that one sentence. Let's think about which ones you'll want to keep.
- Does the information before the *and* relate to the information after?
- So that seems like a place where you'll delete the *and* and replace it with a period.

Hat Tip: *Strategic Writing Conferences: Finished Projects* (Anderson 2009)

Strategy Give yourself the cue, "Guess what!" Read the sentence you have on the page. If it makes sense in response to "Guess what!" then it's a complete sentence. If it doesn't seem to make sense, then rephrase it so it does. Write it, reread it, and make sure it makes sense.

Teaching Tip This will help children to write simple, declarative sentences. See other lessons in this chapter to help students write compound and complex sentences, such as strategies 9.22, 9.24, and 9.25.

Prompts

- Say, "Guess what!" then read your sentence.
- Does your sentence make sense as an answer to "Guess what?"
- Try to rephrase it so it makes sense.
- Reread it now that you've reworded the sentence.
- What's the cue?

Who is this for?

LEVELS
2–8

GENRES / TEXT TYPES
narrative, opinion/persuasive, informational/nonfiction

PROCESS
editing

Hat Tip: *Infusing Grammar into the Writer's Workshop: A Guide for K–6 Teachers* (Benjamin and Golub 2015)

Who is this for?

LEVELS
2–8

GENRE / TEXT TYPE
any

PROCESS
editing

Strategy Search your draft for places where you used the same technique over and over again. Think about the purpose of that technique, and consider what to keep and what to change.

Teaching Tip When children learn a new punctuation technique—such as adding exclamation points to the end of a sentence or the power of the ellipses to add suspense from page to page—many will overdo it. This lesson is about helping children remember the purposes behind the punctuation or craft technique to inform purposeful revision and to exercise restraint.

Prompts
- I'm noticing a pattern with your punctuation choices here.
- What do you see that you've used over and over again?
- Think about what you remember about when and why authors use that.
- Do you want to keep it in all the places you've used it?
- Which ones will you revise?

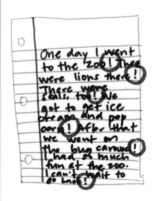

Hat Tip: *Practical Punctuation: Lessons on Rule Making and Rule Breaking in Elementary Writing* (Feigelson 2008)

Strategy When you want to surprise your reader with a reveal of information, set up the first part of your sentence, followed by a colon, followed by the surprise. You can also use the colon to set up a list.

Using a Mentor *Punctuation Celebration* by Elsa Knight Bruno (2012) offers advice about all sorts of punctuation marks—what they are used for, how they help the reader—all embedded within poems that offer examples. Here are a few other select sentences from other genres:

Stellaluna (Cannon 1993): "Except for one thing: Stellaluna still liked to sleep hanging by her feet."

Tiny Creatures: The World of Microbes (Davies 2014): "Microbes can eat anything: plants, animals (alive or dead), even oil and rocks."

Prompts
- What surprise do you have for your reader?
- Where do you hear a beat as you read your piece out loud?
- What's the purpose of the pause?

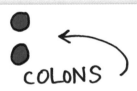

Who is this for?

LEVELS
2–8

GENRE / TEXT TYPE
any

PROCESSES
drafting, editing

Hat Tip: *Strategic Writing Conferences: Finished Projects* (Anderson 2009)

Conventions: Grammar

9.11 Punctuating (and Paragraphing) Speech

Who is this for?

LEVELS
3–8

GENRE / TEXT TYPE
narrative

PROCESSES
drafting, editing

Strategy Help your reader follow the dialogue in your piece by starting a new paragraph each time someone new speaks. Put open and closed quotes around what is being said and a comma to separate the dialogue and the dialogue tag. Capital letters begin each quotation.

Teaching Tip For writers who are new to the conventions of punctuating dialogue, you may choose to break this one strategy into a series of strategies, starting first with just quotation marks, then commas to separate dialogue and tags, and finally paragraphing for each new speaker.

Prompts
• What's being said by the character? Put dialogue marks around it.
• Make sure there is a comma separating the dialogue and the tag.
• Is that a new speaker? Then it gets a new paragraph.

New Paragraphs for Each New Speaker	Quotes Around What Is Being Said	Commas to Separate the Dialogue and the Tags
"Are we going to the mall?" she asked her mother. She looked up with a hopeful smile. "Yes, let's go!" her mother replied, grabbing her coat and purse.	"Let's have a party!"	"Probably," she said, "Although I don't know where to start." He began, "She promises you that she is the best candidate." "The zoo is by the mountain," she said.

Hat Tip: *A Fresh Approach to Teaching Punctuation: Helping Young Writers Use Conventions with Precision and Purpose* (Angelillo 2002)

Strategy Read your writing and listen for the pauses. At each pause, put a period. Then, read back each sentence (up to a period). Check to make sure it has a subject (a "who or what the sentence is about") and a predicate ("what about it or what it does").

Teaching Tip Admittedly, it's not this simple. This strategy will help children punctuate simple, declarative sentences. We all know that authors occasionally use run-ons or fragments intentionally and for effect. We have read examples of compound, complex, and other types of sentences. To top it all off, here's where it really gets frustrating: As children get older and read more and more varying sentence types, the sounds of them will get into their heads and they will approximate them as they write. The child who *used to know* how to put periods at the end of a sentence will suddenly appear unable to. You will shake your head in frustration! But rest assured that this is a sign of a writer developing more sophistication, one who is ready to learn about more-complicated sentences and the punctuation needed to write them correctly. Still, this lesson would be helpful to many writers before a lesson on, say, parentheticals (strategy 9.29) or sentence combining (strategy 9.22).

Prompts

• You put a period here. Let's look back to make sure there is a subject and a predicate.
• What is the part that is the "who or what the sentence is about"?
• What is the part that shows "what about it"?
• Is this sentence complete?
• Check to make sure it's complete. I'll watch you think aloud as you do it.

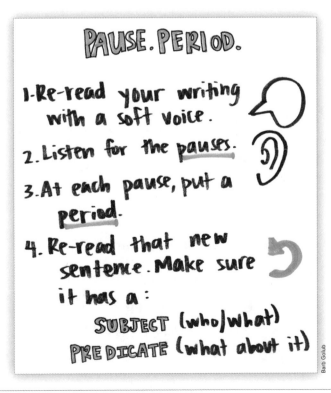

Who is this for?

LEVELS
3–8

GENRES / TEXT TYPES
narrative, opinion/ persuasive, informational/ nonfiction

PROCESS
editing

Hat Tip: *Infusing Grammar into the Writer's Workshop: A Guide for K–6 Teachers* (Benjamin and Golub 2015)

9.13 Voice Comma

Who is this for?

LEVELS
3–8

GENRE / TEXT TYPE
any

PROCESSES
revising, editing

Strategy Within a sentence, listen for a dip and a rise in intonation as you read your piece aloud. The place between the dip and rise is where a comma can go. Place one there if it helps break up the longer sentence into clearer-meaning chunks. Finally, read it back, making sure you've grouped the words to show the correct meaning.

Using a Mentor *Eats, Shoots & Leaves: Why, Commas Really Do Make a Difference!* by Lynne Truss (2006) offers examples of the same sentence, punctuated two different ways, to show two different meanings. You could show the students the sentence with no comma, then ask them to read it aloud, noticing where their voice dips and rises. Then, show the two versions in the book to show the different meanings communicated by the comma placement.

Prompts
- Listen for a dip.
- Listen for a rise.
- Where might the comma go?
- Did you hear the dip and then the rise? That's where the comma goes.
- OK, put the comma there and read it back to see if it sounds right.
- You grouped these words together before the comma. Does that make sense?

> **Watch Me Dip (Dip)**
> **Watch Me Rise-Rise :**
>
> - Re-read your piece aloud.
> - Listen for the dips, and the rises.
> - Place a comma in between!
> - Re-read your piece. Make sure you've grouped the words in a way that makes sense.

Barb Golub

Hat Tip: *Infusing Grammar into the Writer's Workshop: A Guide for K–6 Teachers* (Benjamin and Golub 2015)

Strategy Find a long sentence that may need some internal punctuation to break up all the information. Reread it. Find a group of words that go together. Use a comma to separate that group from the rest of the sentence.

Lesson Language *I found this long sentence in my piece. I'm sure it needs some commas. Think with me about where it would make sense to add commas so that I'm grouping words together that go together based on meaning: "When I looked up I saw my grandfather standing above me with tools in his hands the ones we'd use to fix the fence." It seems like the end of the sentence "the ones we'd use to fix the fence" is a group of words that make sense together because they say more about "tools." So I am going to put a comma after the word* hands. *The beginning of the sentence "when I looked up" is one of those phrases that starts off a sentence to tell the reader* when. *I think a comma after that phrase would be helpful, and everything in that phrase goes together. Let me read it back to make sure it sounds right.*

Teaching Tip This strategy is handy in that it may alleviate the need for you to teach all comma rules, which some estimate to be as many as eighteen, because this strategy will help children to be more attuned to meaning making when considering comma placement (Benjamin and Golub 2015).

Using a Mentor Send your students on an inquiry of comma usage, and they'll come back with varied and multiple findings! You may want to pull sentences from texts that explicitly show that when a comma is placed, it creates groups of words that work together.

Prompts
- This looks like a long sentence. Let's think about what sorts of punctuation might help break it up a bit for the reader.
- What words go together in a group?
- Check that the group of words makes sense together.
- I agree, it makes sense when you put a comma there.
- Separate that group of words from the rest with a comma.

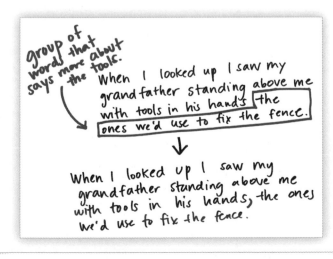

Who is this for?

LEVELS
3–8

GENRE / TEXT TYPE
any

PROCESSES
revising, editing

Hat Tip: *Infusing Grammar into the Writer's Workshop: A Guide for K–6 Teachers* (Benjamin and Golub 2015)

9.15 Say It with Feeling!

Who is this for?

LEVELS
3–8

GENRE / TEXT TYPE
any

PROCESSES
revising, editing

Strategy Think about the feeling (tone) you are trying to convey in your draft. Think about what types of punctuation can shape the rhythm of your words to help communicate that feeling. Try out some revisions to your sentences and keep the one that best matches the feeling.

Using a Mentor The Caldecott Honor book *Yo! Yes?* By Chris Raschka (1993) is a great example of how feeling and meaning are communicated through ending punctuation. The story is told with just a few words, and by using varying punctuation, the words take on different meanings across the pages.

Prompts
- What feeling do you want this sentence to show?
- What punctuation might work here?
- What made you choose a _____ to end this sentence?
- Let's try it two different ways to see which one matches the meaning you intend.
- How else could you punctuate that?
- What rhythm would help communicate that feeling?

Punctuation/ Sentence Structure	Effects	Examples*
Exclamation point (!)	• Excitement, surprise, happiness	"THE TRAIN! THE TRAIN!"
Ellipsis (…)	• Builds tension, suspense • Thoughts trailing off	We looked . . . We listened . . . We decided to take the shortcut home.
Short sentences	• Frenetic • Moves time quickly • Summarizes	We shouted. We sang.

*Examples from Donald Crew's *Shortcut* (1996).

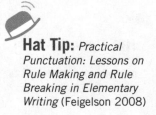

Hat Tip: *Practical Punctuation: Lessons on Rule Making and Rule Breaking in Elementary Writing* (Feigelson 2008)

Strategy Look at the beginning of each new paragraph. Make sure it's clear what the paragraph will be about. Try starting it with a sentence that sets the topic of the paragraph, establishes the direction the paragraph will take, or explains a transition from the last paragraph to this new one.

Using a Mentor An interesting inquiry would be to examine first sentences of paragraphs in the genre you're studying as a class, or that the student is studying independently, and have your students develop their sense of "rules" for when to start new paragraphs and how those paragraphs may begin.

Prompts
- Read just the first sentence. Is it clear what this paragraph will be about?
- Do you think you need a transition from this paragraph to this one? What would it be?
- Check the beginning of this paragraph again.
- What would make this paragraph clearer?

Who is this for?

LEVELS
4–8

GENRES / TEXT TYPES
narrative, opinion/persuasive, informational/ nonfiction

PROCESSES
drafting, editing

How will you start your PARAGRAPH?

Transition (time)	Sets up the Topic/Subtopic	Connects (idea to idea)
Later that day...	The first thing to understand...	As a result...
By morning...	For example...	Also important...
What happened next would have scared anyone...	Another kind...	Despite ——, ...
		In addition to...

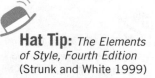

Hat Tip: *The Elements of Style, Fourth Edition* (Strunk and White 1999)

Who is this for?

LEVELS
4–8

GENRE / TEXT TYPE
any

PROCESS
editing

Strategy Read your draft aloud. Listen for how it sounds. Are the pauses in the right places? Are the sentences the length that you want them to be? Make changes to the punctuation and then read it aloud again. Make sure it sounds how you want it to sound.

Teaching Tip This strategy could be adapted for many different grammar and punctuation purposes. Reading one's writing aloud is crucial to hearing the rhythm you communicate, the tone you set. You'll likely read your own writing for the purpose of seeking revision opportunities at a different pace than you'd read another author's writing to seek information, or get lost in a story. You'll want to model the pace and the thinking aloud that accompanies this strategy.

Using a Mentor *Team Moon: How 400,000 People Landed Apollo 11 on the Moon* (Thimmesh 2006) offers a master class in varying sentence structure. Read aloud, this picture book is almost poetic with a mix of short and long sentences:

> Bales scoured his guidance and navigation data.
>
> Searching. Sifting. Sorting.
>
> Flight Director Kranz plucked details from a flood of incoming information.
>
> Juggling. Judging. (19)

Prompts

- Read aloud.
- Listen as you read.
- How did that sound to you? Is there anything you think you might change?
- Can you say what didn't sound right to you? What else might you try?
- Based on how you read it, what punctuation do you think you need?
- You read it like this (*reread aloud to the student*) but based on the way you punctuated it, it would actually sound more like this (*reread reflecting sentence length and punctuation*). What changes might you make?

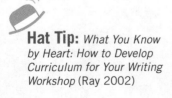

Hat Tip: *What You Know by Heart: How to Develop Curriculum for Your Writing Workshop* (Ray 2002)

Strategy Scan your writing for places where the subject and the verb in the sentence don't agree. Identify if the subject is singular or plural. Make the verb match it.

Prompts

- Find the subject. Now find the verb.
- Is the subject singular or plural?
- Is the verb singular or plural?
- Do the subject and the verb match/agree?
- Try to take out the words in between the subject and the verb. Read what's left.
- Does it sound right?

Sample Subjects	Singular or Plural Verb?	Examples
Each Either Everyone Everybody Nobody Someone	Singular verb	Everyone thinks he . . . Each of the members is . . .
None (meaning "no one" or "not one")	Singular	None of us is perfect.
None (suggesting a group)	Plural	None are so imperfect as those who . . .
Compound subject joining two nouns with *and*	Plural (almost always)	The man and woman are . . .
Singular subject, connected to other nouns using: With As well as In addition to Except Together with No less than	Singular	Her skirt as well as her shoes was covered with sparkles.

Who is this for?

LEVELS
4–8

GENRE / TEXT TYPE
any

PROCESS
editing

Hat Tip: *The Elements of Style, Fourth Edition* (Strunk and White 1999)

9.19 Knowing When You Need a New Paragraph

Who is this for?

LEVELS
4–8

GENRES / TEXT TYPES
narrative, opinion/
persuasive,
informational/
nonfiction

PROCESS
editing

Strategy Long blocks of text often need to be broken up into parts, called paragraphs. Look for places with long blocks of text. Think about where it would be logical to give your reader a pause. Break the block into new paragraph(s), being mindful of how you transition from one to another.

Teaching Tip Teach this strategy in conjunction with strategy 9.16, "Paragraph Starters," to ensure that the paragraphs still flow nicely, one to the next.

Prompts

- What is the text that you think needs to be broken into new paragraphs?
- Look for a possible paragraph break. What are you thinking?
- It makes sense to break it there, I agree. That's a new subtopic.
- Yes! You identified where a new speaker begins talking. That's a new paragraph.

When Should I Make a New PARAGRAPH?

¶ a new character comes along

¶ a new event happens

¶ the setting changes

¶ a new person is speaking

¶ time moves forward (or backward)

¶ the "camera" moves

Betsy Hubbard

Hat Tip: *The Elements of Style, Fourth Edition* (Strunk and White 1999)

Strategy Be on the lookout for sentences where you use two "negative" words (*don't, no, not, none*). Say to yourself, "Two negatives cancel each other out. Is that what I meant?" Make any change you may need to match your meaning.

Teaching Tip Using double negatives is part of many students' everyday speech. Teaching them to use only one negative in a sentence is not to teach them "right" grammar versus "wrong" grammar, but simply to clarify the difference between everyday and academic language. In other words, in teaching this lesson my aim is not to correct or change students' speech, but rather to make them aware of Standard English as it usually appears in books so they can make choices about their intended meanings.

Prompts

• Let's look closely at this sentence. Which word or words are "negative"?
• Check the chart to see which words are negative and which are positive.
• Those two negatives cancel each other out.
• You have two negatives here. Did you mean for that to happen? Remember, two negatives mean a positive.

Negative —	Positive +
Nothing, nowhere, no, none, never, nobody, don't, can't, didn't	Anything, anywhere, any, ever, anybody, do, can, did.

He didn't do nothing. → He didn't do anything.

Don't go nowhere. → Don't go anywhere.

Look out for 2 negatives in the same sentence. Two in the same sentence cancel each other out...

9.21 Irregular Verbs and Subject–Verb Agreement

Who is this for?

LEVELS
4–8

GENRE / TEXT TYPE
any

PROCESSES
generating and collecting, drafting, editing

Strategy Check the places where you've used the verbs to be (*am/are/is*), to do (*do/does*), and to have (*have/has*). Find the subject of the sentence. Make sure the subject and the verb agree.

Prompts
- What's the subject?
- What form of the verb do you need?
- Is the subject single (one) or plural (more than one)?
- Make sure the subject and the verb agree.

Tense	Subject	To Be	To Do	To Have
Present Tense	I	Am	Do	Have
	You, we, they, students	Are	Do	Have
	She, he, it, Lucy	Is	Does	Has
Past Tense	I	Was	Did	Had
	You, we, they, students	Were	Did	Had
	She, he, it, Lucy	Was	Did	Had

Hat Tip: *Catching Up on Conventions: Grammar Lessons for Middle School Writers* (Francois and Zonana 2009)

Strategy Find a spot in your draft where you see yourself repeating the same words over and over in separate sentences. Underline the unique parts of each sentence, parts you'll try to keep. Combine the sentences to create one new sentence. Reread what you wrote to make sure it makes sense. Add in comma(s) if needed.

Teaching Tip I recommend we all keep this wise quote in mind from Jeff Anderson and Deborah Dean:

> Although at first glance it may look like an exercise in creating long sentences from short ones, sentence combining is really about building relationships among ideas and showing them in clear and interesting ways. Sentence combining shows young writers options . . . [It] isn't about saying long sentences are better than short sentences, and it isn't about trying to make sentences convoluted. [It] is about playing with ideas and shaping them into effective syntactical patterns that make sense for individual writing situations. (2014, 5)

Prompts
- Do you notice any repetition?
- Look for the same words repeated.
- How might you combine those sentences?
- Think about how the info in those sentences goes together.
- Now that you've combined them, what punctuation do you need?

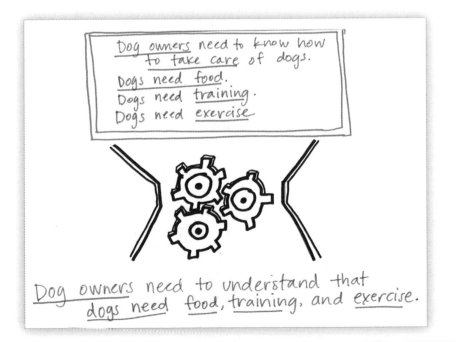

Who is this for?

LEVELS
4–8

GENRES / TEXT TYPES
narrative, opinion/ persuasive, informational/ nonfiction

PROCESS
revising

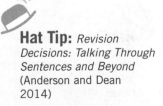

Hat Tip: *Revision Decisions: Talking Through Sentences and Beyond* (Anderson and Dean 2014)

Who is this for?

LEVELS

4–8

GENRES / TEXT TYPES

narrative, opinion/
persuasive,
informational/
nonfiction

PROCESSES

revising, editing

Hat Tip: *Infusing Grammar into the Writer's Workshop: A Guide for K–6 Teachers* (Benjamin and Golub 2015)

Strategy Identify a run-on (a sentence that has more than one subject and more than one predicate). Try to break up the run-on into more than one sentence. Read it aloud. Try joining the two sentences with a conjunction. Read it aloud. Decide which version sounds the way you want it to.

Lesson Language *In a run-on sentence, you will find two or more independent clauses (i.e., complete sentences) that are joined without appropriate punctuation or conjunction. One example is, "It is dark out and getting late when are the children coming home?" In this example, It is one subject and is dark out is the "what about it." And then we also have getting late as another "so what." Then, the children is a subject/what and coming home is another "so what." In this case, I need to think about what I want to do to make the sentences complete and clear. I think I will try separating them. "It is getting dark out. It is getting late. When are the children coming home?" Those three short sentences seem to bring a bit of drama and tension, which I like. Let me try keeping them combined but changing the connecting words (conjunctions). "It is getting late and dark and I'm wondering when the children are coming home." I think I like the first way better.*

Using a Mentor You may want to offer students examples from authors who use purposeful run-ons for effect. *All the Water in the World* by George Ella Lyons (2011) has language that flows like water. In the Joey Pigza series, Jack Gantos often uses run-ons when Joey starts to go out of control, to echo that mood.

Prompts

- Yes! You found a sentence that has two subjects and two predicates.
- Identify each independent clause.
- Will you join them with a conjunction?
- Do you want to make separate sentences or keep the two clauses together?

On The Run?

1. Identify a run-on sentence.
   - More than 1 subject
   - More than 1 predicate

2. Try to break it up into more than 1 sentence.

3. Join those 2 sentences with a conjunction? Maybe try:

For
And
Nor
But
Or
Yet
So

Barb Golub

Strategy When you want to add more information into a sentence, you may add a dependent clause before or after the independent clause with a word such as *although*, *as*, *because*, *if*, or *since*. The dependent clause can't be a sentence on its own; it needs the independent clause to make sense. Reread what you've written to make sure the entire sentence makes sense together.

Using a Mentor

Stuart Little (White 1945): "**Because he was so small**, Stuart was often hard to find around the house."

The Wonderful Wizard of Oz (Baum 1900): "The Scarecrow and the Tin Woodman stood up in a corner and kept quiet all night, **although of course they could not sleep**" (101).

Prompts

• What's the additional information you'd like to add to this sentence?
• Which word will work: *although*, *as*, *because*, *if*, or *since*?
• Reread the whole thing to make sure it all makes sense together.
• Will you end that clause before or after the main clause?
• That additional clause adds more information, and it makes sense.

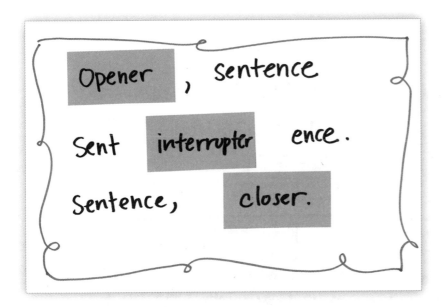

Who is this for?

LEVELS
4–8

GENRES / TEXT TYPES
narrative, opinion/ persuasive, informational/ nonfiction

PROCESSES
revising, editing

Hat Tip: *Mechanically Inclined: Building Grammar, Usage, and Style into Writer's Workshop* (Anderson 2005)

9.25 Creating Compound Sentences

Who is this for?

LEVELS
4–8

GENRES / TEXT TYPES
narrative, opinion/persuasive, informational/nonfiction

PROCESSES
revising, editing

Strategy Find two sentences that talk about the same topic. Think about the relationship between those sentences. Choose a connector word and try combining the sentences into one. Reread and decide if you like the combined way or original way better.

Lesson Language *Here's one spot in my draft where I have two sentences that I think go well together. I wrote: "A dog is something that can keep you company. A dog can cheer you up." What's the relationship between those two sentences? They both have to do with something that is positive about owning a dog, so I think they are related. I'm adding more information on. I'll try using* and *to combine those sentences: "A dog can keep you company and cheer you up." Here's another spot: "I would love to have a dog. My mom won't let me have a dog." What's the relationship between those two sentences? The second sentence gives more information that feels in contrast to the first. I'll combine them with* however: *"I would like to have a dog, however my mom won't let me." The new sentence I made seems clearer and more to the point.*

Prompts
- What's the relationship between those two sentences?
- Which two sentences go together?
- Which "connector" word will you use?
- OK, try that word and see if it makes sense based on how those two sentences fit together.

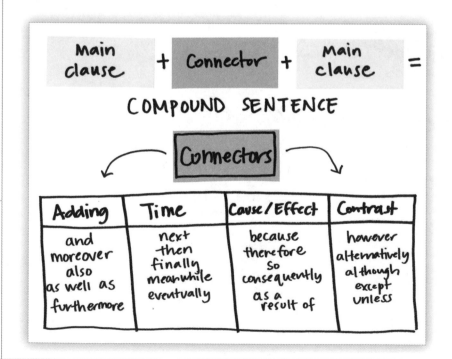

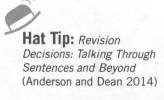

Hat Tip: *Revision Decisions: Talking Through Sentences and Beyond* (Anderson and Dean 2014)

Strategy As you're writing, notice where you want to leave a beat or pause to get your reader ready for extra, important information. Consider if a comma will do, or if you'd like to suggest a slightly longer pause to your reader by using a dash. A sentence can have one dash, or two.

Lesson Language *I found a few examples of sentences with dashes. Let's look at them together to see if we can figure how the author is using them, and if the way the author uses them might work in your piece as well.*

Example 1—The Grudge Keeper *(Rockliff 2014):* "When mischievous Sylvester Quincy snagged the schoolmaster's toupee, the schoolmaster took terrible offense—straight to Cornelius" *(3).*

Example 2—Chicken Sunday *(Polacco 1998):* "And after I'm dead, on Chicken Sundays, I want you to boil up some chicken—bones, gravy, and all—and pour it over my grave" *(32).*

Example 3—Missing May *(Rylant 1992):* "Ob was an artist—I could tell the minute I saw them—though artist isn't the word I could have used back then, so young" *(6).*

(Get ideas from the students about what they're noticing, then name for them the pattern you see.) *What I notice is that it seems like the author is giving us a little bit of extra commentary with the last two. Almost the same way we use parentheses we could use dashes. But the first example seems to be somewhat similar to a colon. A sort of "Get ready for what's coming next!"*

Prompts
- Do you see a place where you'd like to add a longer pause?
- Does this sentence need one or two dashes? How do you know?
- Yes, that information seems like something that would be in parentheses. You could use dashes there. What do you think?
- What part of this sentence feels like extra information?

> **This- is- Important**
> 1. Re-read your piece.
> 2. Think, "where do I want to get my reader ready for something important?"
> 3. If a comma won't do ▭
>   ADD A DASH!*
>
> *1-2 per sentence.

Barb Golub

Who is this for?

LEVELS
4–8

GENRE / TEXT TYPE
any

PROCESSES
revising, editing

Hat Tip: *Practical Punctuation: Lessons on Rule Making and Rule Breaking in Elementary Writing* (Feigelson 2008)

Who is this for?

LEVELS
4–8

GENRE / TEXT TYPE
any

PROCESS
revising

Strategy Find a sentence that, when you read it, there is a moment where you want to give an extra, perhaps dramatic, pause. Try structuring the sentence with four types of midsentence punctuation that could create that pause: a colon, a dash, a comma, and ellipses. You'll likely need to reorder or otherwise change the wording for it to work. Consider how the different punctuation choices affect the reading of the sentence. Copy your final version onto your draft.

Lesson Language *I found a sentence in my draft that I'd like to play with a bit. Let me read it to you:* "The next time I get asked to go on a roller coaster I will definitely tell the person that I am not interested!" *This sentence matches my meaning, but I wonder if I play with punctuation a bit, can I get a different effect? Can I make it more dramatic by adding a pause? Let me try some ellipses:* "If someone asks me to ride a roller coaster . . . I will tell them 'no thanks!'" *Let me try a colon:* "Here's what I'll say the next time someone asks me to ride a roller coaster: 'No thanks!'" *That last version seems to really emphasize the ending, which I kind of like. And there's suspense . . . what will she say? I think that's the version I'll keep.*

Prompts
- This story has a lot of drama. Is there anywhere you'd want to create a dramatic pause with punctuation?
- Where do you want to have a pause?
- Try rewriting it with different midsentence punctuation.
- Do you want to use a colon, a dash, a comma, or an ellipsis?
- How does that changed punctuation affect the meaning?

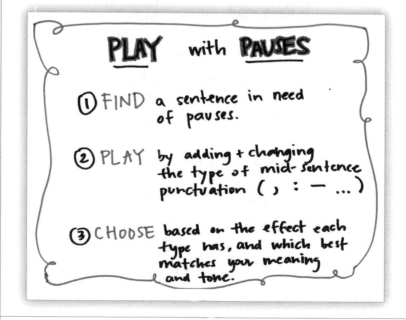

Hat Tip: *Practical Punctuation: Lessons on Rule Making and Rule Breaking in Elementary Writing* (Feigelson 2008)

Strategy Find a sentence where you used a pronoun that you want to check. Think, "Is the pronoun the one doing the action in the sentence?" If so, it's the subject. If not, it's the object. Check the chart to make sure you have the right pronoun.

Lesson Language *I want to make sure I picked the right pronouns in my writing. Let's look at this sentence: "I hit the ball." Who hit the ball? I did. I is the subject so it's correct that I use the subject pronoun (I) not the object pronoun (me). Here's another: "Nancy gave the gift to . . ."—is it me or I? Well, who is the subject of the sentence? Nancy. So I can't use a subject verb here. I need to use the object verb, so that means me is correct here.*

Using a Mentor The poem "Me" by Elizabeth Swados (2002) could help children remember which form of the pronoun to use.

Prompts
- What's the subject of the sentence?
- Which pronoun should you use?
- Read it back to see if it sounds right.
- Will you use a subject pronoun? Remember, that's when a pronoun is the subject of the sentence.

Who is this for?

LEVELS
4–8

GENRE / TEXT TYPE
any

PROCESS
editing

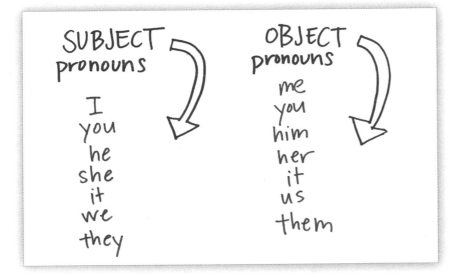

9.29 Parenthetic Expressions

Who is this for?

LEVELS
5–8

GENRE / TEXT TYPE
any

PROCESSES
generating and collecting, drafting, editing

Strategy Notice if there is a part of your sentence that seems like an aside to the reader, or one that offers an extra bit of information. Put a comma before that part of the sentence and another after that part of the sentence. Reread it with a drop in your voice at the beginning of the comma and a rise at the end. Ask yourself, "Does that sound right?"

Teaching Tip The same parenthetical expressions can be punctuated with . . . you guessed it: parentheses. Also, dashes.

Using a Mentor (parentheticals in bold)

Tiny Creatures: The World of Microbes (Davies 2014): "Then, inside you, **where they are warm and well fed**, they split and split and split until just a few germs have turned into thousands, then millions."

How to Look for a Lost Dog (Martin 2016): "Uncle Weldon, **who was sitting at the Formica kitchen table with me**, looked at my father from under his eyelashes and said, 'I could go, if you want'" (12).

Prompts

• Underline the information that feels like an aside.
• What's the part that gives the reader extra information?
• What part of the sentence feels like it's in parentheses?
• You identified the part that's a parenthetical. Where do the parentheses go?
• Let's check to make sure it sounds right. Read it back with the parentheses.

My room

You cannot describe my
room in one word or
name, it is somewhat like
a pigpen (or evenly the same.)

I can barly find my
clusterd bed, my messy
artwork hangs overhead.

"You need a specialist!"
my mom screames.

"I wish!" I yell back,
"That is a dream!""

Well I oughta go,
(before my room swallows
me.) Never come in, you
don't want to see.

Hat Tip: *The Elements of Style, Fourth Edition* (Strunk and White 1999)

Strategy Go through your draft, underlining all the verbs. For each verb, ask yourself, "Is this happening now (present), did it happen earlier (past), or is it about to happen (future)?" Check to make sure the verbs within a sentence show the same time.

Teaching Tip There is an exception to this rule! There are certain sentence constructions where you are communicating about different times within the same sentence. For instance, in the sentence "When Mary gets here, everyone will laugh at her," *gets* is present and *will laugh* is future. This makes sense with the sentence as the first and second parts of the sentence communicate different times. Depending on the writers you teach, you may want to offer the rule and the exceptions to the rule. For less-experienced writers and/or English language learners, it may be helpful to have a list of verbs conjugated in present, past, and future tense to provide them with examples. Be sure to use both regular (e.g., *walk/walked*) and irregular (e.g., *stand/stood*, *go/went*) verbs.

Prompts
- When did it happen?
- Check the other verbs in that sentence.
- Let's identify the tense of each verb.
- Is it happening now? Or in the past?
- I see you caught two different tenses in the same sentence. Which one will you change? Why?

Who is this for?

LEVELS
5–8

GENRE / TEXT TYPE
any

PROCESS
editing

Mixed Tenses	Tense Consistency
During the lesson, Marco **stood** up then **dives** into the water. (past/present)	During the lesson, Marco **stood** up then **dove** into the water. (past/past) *Or* During the lesson, Marco **stands** up then **dives** into the water. (present/present)
The tiny bird **sits** on the ground and **cried** out for its mother. (present/past)	The tiny bird **sits** on the ground and **cries** out for its mother. (present/present) *Or* The tiny bird **sat** on the ground and **cried** out for its mother. (past/past)

Hat Tip: *Catching Up on Conventions: Grammar Lessons for Middle School Writers* (Francois and Zonana 2009)

Who is this for?

Strategy Read your writing aloud, listening to the rhythm and pace. Every period means a pause. Ask yourself, "Does the pace of the writing match the feeling/mood/ tone?" Consider combining sentences to make longer ones or breaking up longer sentences to make shorter ones to achieve the pace you are after.

Using a Mentor Turn to any well-written picture book, short story, speech, or novel and you're bound to find examples of the author varying sentence length purposefully and with intention. Ask your students to consider the purpose or effect the pacing and rhythm has on the meaning of the piece. Anything by Hemmingway or Gary Paulsen would be perfect choices to study short sentence masters. Jack Gantos' Joey Pigza series offers examples of purposeful run-ons during moments when Joey feels out of control.

Prompts

- What do you think about your pacing?
- What do you notice about the rhythm of the piece?
- I'm hearing lots of long sentences. Think about how that affects the mood.
- I'm hearing lots of short sentences, are you?
- Think about the pace.

Short Sentences	Long Sentences
• To hook a reader at the beginning of a piece • To deliver a "bang" • To emphasize a point • To move the action along quickly • In the midst of dialogue • In narration, to capture the feeling of a thought process as being choppy or staccato	• To hook a reader at the beginning of a piece • Stream-of-consciousness effect • To capture a viewpoint, such as an obsessive character whose mind wanders • To communicate a slower, gentler pace

Hat Tip: *A Dash of Style: The Art and Mastery of Punctuation* (Lukeman 2007)

Strategy Find two sentences that feel related in an important way. Consider which feels more "right"—a semicolon or a period? Join them with a semicolon instead of separating them with a period.

Lesson Language *The semicolon is a punctuation mark that can be used instead of a period. But not always. The test to know whether it's appropriate or not is to ask yourself if the sentences feel related. If so, the semicolon actually brings them closer together, meaning-wise. Let's take an example:*

We are related, actually. We are sisters.

I could rewrite those two sentences with a semicolon in between, like this:

We are related, actually; we are sisters.

In that example, the meaning of the two sentences is enhanced by choosing to join the sentences with a semicolon instead of separate with a period.

Using a Mentor

Ruby's Wish (Bridges 2002): "Alas, bad luck to be born a girl; worse luck to be born into this house where only boys are cared for."

My Rotten Redheaded Older Brother (Polacco 1998b): "The one thing that my bubbie didn't seem to know was how perfectly awful my brother really was! Mind you, he was always nice whenever she was around us; but as soon as she'd leave, he would do something terrible to me and laugh."

Prompts
- Are these two sentences related?
- Yes, instead of the period you can put a semicolon.
- Read it back with the semicolon to see if you agree that that's the right punctuation to use there.
- It's your call actually, period or semicolon?
- Yes, I think those sentences are related.

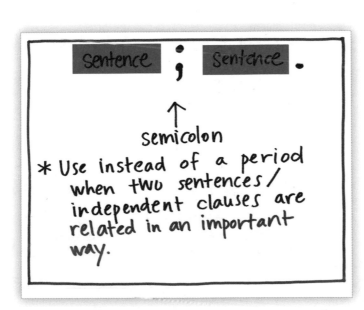

Who is this for?

LEVELS
6–8

GENRES / TEXT TYPES
**narrative, opinion/
persuasive,
informational/
nonfiction**

PROCESSES
revising, editing

Strategy Scan your draft for the word *not* in a sentence. Read the sentence. Ask, "Can I change this sentence so that I state *what is* rather than *what's not*?" Try rewriting the sentence in its positive form to see if the meaning is clearer, more direct, and tighter.

Using a Mentor In *On Writing Well: The Classic Guide to Writing Nonfiction,* Zinsser (2001, 12) writes: "Writing is hard work. A clear sentence is no accident. Very few sentences come out right the first time, or even the third time. Remember this in moments of despair. If you find that writing is hard, it's because it *is* hard."

Prompts
• Find *not*.
• Now that you found it, let's try to rephrase it without using the word *not*.
• Change it to be a positive sentence.
• Look at the change. Does it seem clearer or tighter to you?
• Look at that! By changing the wording and eliminating *not*, you've said exactly what you meant to say.

Hat Tip: *The Elements of Style, Fourth Edition* (Strunk and White 1999)

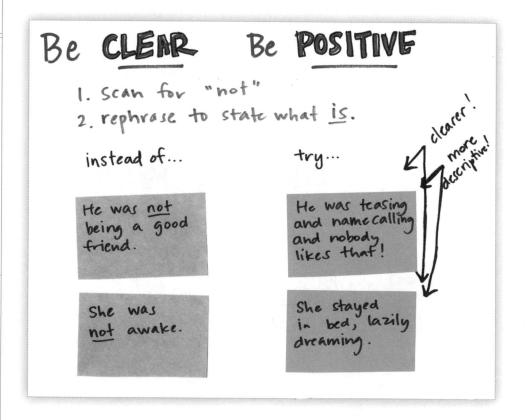

Strategy Reread a sentence that feels clunky. Ask yourself, "Are the related words together? Are unrelated words separated?" Try rephrasing the sentence, changing the order of phrases. Look back to see which is tightest and clearest.

Prompts
- What words are related in this sentence?
- Which words need to stay together?
- Let's try it a few ways.
- You tried three ways. Let's see which one is clearest.

Who is this for?

LEVELS
6–8

GENRE / TEXT TYPE
any

PROCESSES
revising, editing

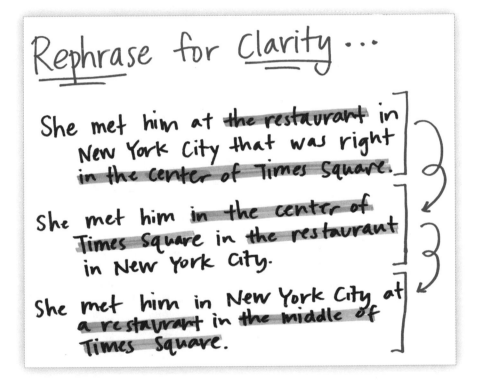

Rephrase for Clarity...

She met him at the restaurant in
New York City that was right
in the center of Times Square.

She met him in the center of
Times Square in the restaurant
in New York City.

She met him in New York City at
a restaurant in the middle of
Times Square.

Hat Tip: *The Elements of Style, Fourth Edition* (Strunk and White 1999)

9.35 When Did the Action Happen?
(Simple, Continuous, and Perfect Tenses)

Strategy Think about when the action in your sentence is taking place. Choose the right form of the verb to show that action.

Teaching Tip This lesson is helpful to use in conjunction with those on subject-verb agreement (such as strategies 9.18 and 9.21) and on verb tense consistency (such as strategy 9.30).

Prompts
- When did the action happen?
- Reread your sentence to see what tense you think it's in.
- Should you use simple, continuous, or perfect tense?
- This verb is in _____ tense. Is that the tense you want your sentence to be in?
- Is it happening now? Is it continuing to happen?

	Present	Past
Simple	I dance on Thursdays.	I danced on Thursdays.
Continuous	I am dancing right now.	I was dancing until the music stopped.
Perfect	I have danced on Thursday afternoons since kindergarten. (It began in kindergarten and is still happening.)	I had danced on Thursday afternoons until my parents ran out of money for lessons. (It began in the past, but it's now over.)

Hat Tip: *Catching Up on Conventions: Grammar Lessons for Middle School Writers* (Francois and Zonana 2009)

Decide to teach by *describing* how language is used and the choices authors make, not simply by *prescribing* them.

—*Jennifer Serravallo*

Collaborating with Writing Partners and Clubs

◎ Why is this goal important?

Writing can feel very lonely. There you are, in your head, thinking your thoughts. There you are, by yourself, getting the words down on the page. Working through the hard parts. So much problem solving, checking, and rechecking. A constant test of stamina, will, endurance.

But it doesn't have to be that way.

Writing partners and clubs can offer us so much—motivation and accountability, critical feedback in times of need, opportunities to get "unstuck" when we can't figure out on our own what's next, more ideas for our topics, practice teaching or storytelling as oral rehearsal, a critical reader when we need it most, an expert to compensate for our own weak spots (Cruz 2004).

While we are endeavoring to create independent writers—writers who can work alone, who can set deadlines and meet them, who can come up with their own ideas for pieces and read back their writing to make revisions—the truth is that even the most independent, professional, published writers often lean on outside support occasionally—and throughout the writing process. This book would be a fraction of what it is without the critical moments I spent talking through ideas and questions and getting invaluable feedback from my editors, Zoë and Katie. In addition, I am part of a writing group with other authors who are working on professional books for teachers, and I've brought excerpts and outlines and problems and questions to our group and relied on them for support, critique, and encouragement.

The decision to establish partners and clubs in your classroom is best when used regularly, flexibly, and across the process. In many classrooms I've visited, partners are used mostly to edit each other's work, but that use is limiting and even potentially problematic. Nancie Atwell (2014) has found that with her middle schoolers, partners tended to *add* errors and misspellings during peer editing, and she consequently decided to have partners support each other more with focus, style, and content and leave the copyediting to the teacher. The strategies in this chapter will support students with all aspects of the writing process—from generating ideas, to testing them out before writing, to reviewing their drafts for opportunities for revision.

◎ How do I know if this goal is right for my student?

I hope that you offer your students opportunities to meet together in partnerships or small groups (clubs) at various points throughout the writing process. If you do, it's likely they will need some support. You can offer the strategies in this chapter as whole-class lessons to get the collaborative work going, or you can use them to teach a pair or group once they have already started working together.

Strategies for Collaborating with Partners and Clubs

Strategy		Grade Levels	Genres/Text Types	Processes
10.1	Use a Partner to Hear More Sounds in Words	K–1	Any	Editing
10.2	Using Partners to Make Writing More Readable	K–2	Any	Revising, editing
10.3	Storytelling from Sketches	K–3	Narrative	Rehearsing, developing
10.4	Talk Around the Idea, Then Write	K–8	Any	Rehearsing, generating and collecting, developing, drafting
10.5	Make Promises (You Can Keep)	K–8	Any	Any
10.6	Partner Inquisition (to Get Your Thinking Going)	1–8	Any	Revising
10.7	Tell Me: Does It Make Sense?	1–8	Any	Revising
10.8	Partner Space	2–8	Any	Any
10.9	Help Wanted/Help Offered	2–8	Any	Any
10.10	PQP (Praise, Question, Polish)	2–8	Any	Developing, drafting, revising, editing
10.11	Tell Me: Does It Match My Intention?	3–8	Any	Revising
10.12	Interrupt Your Partner	3–8	Narrative	Rehearsing, developing
10.13	Dig for Fictional Details with a Partner	3–8	Narrative	Developing, drafting, revising
10.14	Form a Club	4–8	Any	Any
10.15	Storytelling to Figure Out Point of View and Perspective	4–8	Narrative	Developing, revising
10.16	Tell Me: How Does It Affect You?	4–8	Any	Revising
10.17	Code the Text	4–8	Any	Revising
10.18	Written Response	4–8	Any	Developing, drafting, revising, editing
10.19	Changes and Choices	5–8	Any	Revising

The truth is that even professional, published writers lean on outside support occasionally, and throughout the writing process.

—*Jennifer Serravallo*

10.1 Use a Partner to Hear More Sounds in Words

Who is this for?

LEVELS
K–1

GENRE / TEXT TYPE
any

PROCESS
editing

Strategy Work with a partner to find the words in your piece you think might be spelled wrong. Circle them. Go back to a word and say it slowly, together. Work together to hear all the sounds and write the letters that show those sounds.

Teaching Tip By practicing with a partner, children will often internalize the prompts as they say them. Then, when they are back at their seats for independent writing time, they may be able to coach themselves through the same strategy work!

Prompts
• Work with your partner to find the words that might need some fixing.
• You found so many words! Now work together to fix them.
• Tell your partner what sounds you heard.
• Ask your partner, "Did we catch all the sounds?"
• Both of you can point under the word as you read it back slowly.

Writing Partners

1- Read together

2- Circle incorrect words

It was my bthday!
I cud not wat
to eat the ck Mom
mad me a chklit
ck with vnla ising.

3- Stretch together

4- Write it
cake

Kathryn Cazes and Elizabeth Kimmel

Hat Tip: *Writing for Readers: Teaching Skills and Strategies* (Calkins and Louis 2003)

Strategy Ask your partner to read your piece aloud, sliding a finger under each word as she reads it. Listen for a spot when her reading doesn't match what you meant, or when she gets stuck or confused. Work together to make the writing more readable.

Teaching Tip Partners could use a checklist together, to focus themselves on a few conventions that they have learned. Alternatively, they could do this strategy without a checklist, just looking for when something doesn't seem right. It could be that they are looking for capitalization, spelling, punctuation, or even penmanship. The overarching goal is to make the writing readable to others.

Prompts
- Ask, "What doesn't match?"
- Tell your partner if there is anything that you mean to be different than how he is reading it.
- Is there anything that your partner read that didn't match what you meant?
- Ah! There's a spot your partner couldn't read. What did you mean to write there?
- You just helped your partner! You helped her identify a mistake.
- Now you can work together to make the change.

Who is this for?

LEVELS
K–2

GENRE / TEXT TYPE
any

PROCESSES
revising, editing

Hat Tip: *Writing for Readers: Teaching Skills and Strategies* (Calkins and Louis 2003)

Who is this for?

LEVELS
K–3

GENRE / TEXT TYPE
narrative

PROCESSES
rehearsing,
developing

Strategy Think of a story from a shared experience. Work with a partner or group to draw sketches on a strip of paper or a series of sticky notes. Point to the first picture, tell the story. Try to stay on the picture for several sentences. Point to the next picture, continue with the story. When you've told it once, go back to see if you can tell it again, but with more detail.

Teaching Tip Dedicating time for storytelling in your classroom is a great way to support your young writers. Whole-class storytelling from a shared experience (a fire drill, an author's visit, finding the teacher's lost glasses) is a great first step. Once children are comfortable telling and retelling stories (adding in more information and details to help the listener picture the story with each subsequent retell), you can transition children to do this same work in partners or clubs. Storytelling for storytelling's sake helps develop oral language skills and listening skills. Coupling it with writing the story they tell (during whole-class or small-group shared or interactive writing or during independent writing time) helps support elaborated writing.

Prompts

- Point to the picture.
- Tell what's happening.
- You said what you see in one sentence. Let's try to stay on the picture and say a couple of sentences.
- Check the chart to see what kinds of details you can add.
- Go back and storytell it again, this time with more detail.
- Each time you told the story, it got more specific. I can really picture it now.

Hat Tip: *Oral Mentor Texts: A Powerful Tool for Teaching Reading, Writing, Speaking, and Listening* (Dierking and Jones 2014)

Strategy Tell your partner about the idea you have for a writing project. Spend some time having a conversation about the idea. You can imagine what form the idea might take and what kinds of details to include. You might also ask questions about the idea. Then, keep your conversation in mind as you go back to your desk to write.

Teaching Tip Talk as a rehearsal tool is important for every age level, not just the youngest writers in your school. Truthfully, many adult writers use talk to get ready to write, myself included. Often I'll give a workshop several times to clarify my ideas, try out language, or play with anecdotes before what I have to say becomes a blog post or a book chapter.

Prompts
- What are you wondering about the topic?
- Ask your partner some questions about the topic.
- What is important about the topic?
- Can you add anything to what your partner is already thinking about the topic?

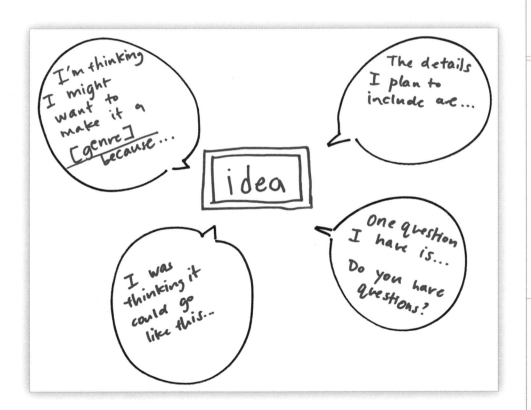

Who is this for?

LEVELS
K–8

GENRE / TEXT TYPE
any

PROCESSES
rehearsing, generating and collecting, developing, drafting

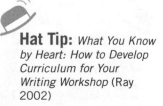

Hat Tip: *What You Know by Heart: How to Develop Curriculum for Your Writing Workshop* (Ray 2002)

10.5 Make Promises (You Can Keep)

Who is this for?

LEVELS
K–8

GENRE / TEXT TYPE
any

PROCESS
any

Strategy Talk with your partner about your goals (for the writing period, for the week, and/or for writing work to take place at home, and so on). Discuss together how you might get that work done. Write the goal, and make the promise . . . then check in with your partner soon.

Teaching Tip Reflect on your own life and goals you've set out to accomplish. Now think about how successful you've been and whether or not you made your goals public ahead of time. I know that when I share my goals with my partner, my friends, my colleagues, my editor, I am more likely to get things done. The built-in accountability, the opportunity to celebrate together, the lifeline of support in case something does not go according to plan—these are invaluable.

Using a Mentor As Stephen King says in *On Writing: A Memoir of the Craft* (2000, 74): "Writing is a lonely job. Having someone who believes in you makes a lot of difference. They don't have to makes speeches. Just believing is usually enough."

Prompts

- Tell your partner specifically what you plan to accomplish.
- OK, now that you've named it, it's time to make a plan for how it'll get done.
- What do you think you'll do to celebrate together when it happens?
- Can you help your partner troubleshoot those possible obstacles?

Hat Tip: *Independent Writing: One Teacher—Thirty-Two Needs, Topics, and Plans* (Cruz 2004)

Strategy Read your piece aloud to your partner (or have your partner read it silently). Ask your partner to ask questions that challenge what you've written. Welcome the challenge! Try to answer openly and honestly, taking notes when you get new ideas for ways to revise your piece.

Lesson Language *Sometimes when you've finished writing a piece, it's hard to step back and make changes. You wrote it, after all, so it says what you wanted it to say. A partner can be a great help to challenge and critique what you have on the page. Sometimes the most helpful challenge is not for them to tell you what to do or change, but rather for them to ask a probing question to get you, the writer, to figure out the change yourself!*

Teaching Tip This lesson can be modified depending on the sophistication of the writers you teach. The sample questions in the figure below may be best for grade 3 and above, but you could simplify the questions so even the youngest writers could benefit from this strategy.

Prompts

- What could you ask your partner?
- What are you curious about?
- Think about changes you'd make. Can you turn a possible change into a question?

Kathryn Cazes and Elizabeth Kimmel

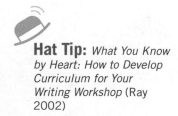

Hat Tip: *What You Know by Heart: How to Develop Curriculum for Your Writing Workshop* (Ray 2002)

LEVELS

1–8

GENRE / TEXT TYPE

any

PROCESS

revising

Strategy Read your piece aloud to your partner. Ask your partner to retell what he heard. Listen to see if the way the partner retold the piece matches how you wanted it to read. Make changes to clarify your piece.

Teaching Tip This strategy depends on a partner having good listening comprehension and retelling skills. This is a strategy that helps both members in the partnership—one gets help with her writing, the other gets help with her retelling.

Prompts
- Listen carefully as your partner reads. Be thinking, "How would I retell this?"
- Say back the big important events/ideas/thoughts from your partner's piece.
- What changes do you think you'd make based on how your partner retold the piece?
- What did you hear in the retelling that matched your meaning?
- What did you hear that didn't match your meaning?

What You Know by Heart: How to Develop Curriculum for Your Writing Workshop (Ray 2002)

10.8 Partner Space

Strategy If you feel like you need support from another writer, first think or jot down what specific help you need. Then, tap your partner's shoulder and move to the partner space in the room. When there, work quickly and with purpose so as not to waste a minute of your writing time.

Lesson Language *There are times when I am writing when I simply cannot write another word without talking to another writer. Sometimes it's about overcoming some self-doubt and I need a cheerleader. Other times, I'm about to make a big decision about structure and I don't want to go full steam and end up having to delete it all later, so I want to check on my thoughts before progressing. Other times, I'm just flat-out stuck and I need someone to help me. Still other times, I need to talk it out before I can get to the writing. Because this is something that truly, honestly happens to me, I'm guessing it may happen to some of you, too. I want to honor that need for you to buddy up to overcome a writing hurdle. So, I'm creating a space in our classroom called "Partner Space" where you can go and spend a few minutes with a friend during the writing time to get rebooted.*

Teaching Tip You'll want to set up clear expectations for what can and cannot take place in the space you designate for partnerships: it is space for a quick writing conference with a peer before jumping back into writing, not a space to check out, get distracted, or otherwise avoid writing. You may consider having a simple sign-up sheet where the partners record their name, the date, and what they did (if the students are upper elementary or middle school and can write quickly), or setting some time limit for how long they can be there. You'll also want to be sure that the student who needs the help isn't pulling his partner from a moment of high engagement and messing up her writing. I usually offer kids the option to indicate "Give me a minute" with a hand gesture and/or to politely decline the invitation to work with their partner that day.

Prompts
- How will you use your partner time?
- Sounds like it's time to get some ideas from your partner.
- Visit the partner space with your partner to see if that helps.

Who is this for?

LEVELS
2–8

GENRE / TEXT TYPE
any

PROCESS
any

Hat Tip: *A Quick Guide to Reaching Struggling Writers, K–5* (Cruz 2008)

LEVELS

2–8

GENRE / TEXT TYPE

any

PROCESS

any

Strategy Think about the strengths you have as a writer. Post an offer to help others under "help offered" on the board. Think about help you could use from others. Post your request for support under "help wanted." Use partner time to meet with people other than your typical partner to get the help you need or to offer your help to others.

Teaching Tip Partnership time doesn't always need to be time for students to meet with their assigned, formal partnership or writing group. Occasionally, it could be helpful to open up the classroom to allow people to work together in mixed-ability groupings. Without structure, though, this time could just mean that the "stronger" member of the partnership does all the work. Instead, getting children to think about how they all have something to offer the writing community, and how they all have needs that can be answered by others within it, helps to strengthen not only the children's writing but your classroom community as well.

Prompts

- How might you help your classmates?
- Check out the "help wanted/offered" board. Who might be able to support you with that goal?
- What can you offer your peers?
- Think about what you feel really confident about.

Hat Tip: *Independent Writing: One Teacher— Thirty-Two Needs, Topics, and Plans* (Cruz 2004)

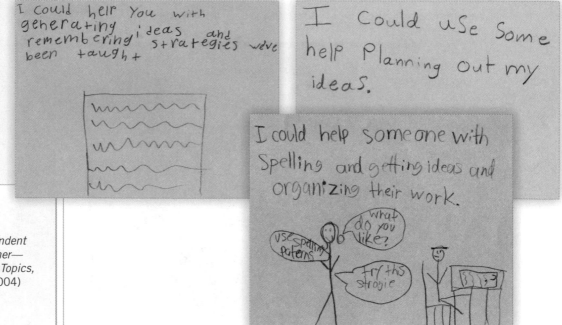

Strategy Read the writer's paper, considering how you'll give feedback in three areas. Choose one thing to *praise*, one thing to *question*, and one thing to suggest for *polishing*.

Lesson Language *Think of these as discussion starters, not stoppers. Try to use the questions to help you read the piece with a few lenses in mind. When giving feedback, try to elaborate on why you responded how you did—in the praising, questioning, and polishing. Aim to be as specific as you can. For example, instead of saying, "That part was great," name specifically what was so great, such as, "The way you started the story right in the scene helped me envision it and get in the mood of the story." Engage the writer in a conversation to help the writer consider what revisions and edits might help the piece.*

Prompts

- Name one thing you can praise about the writing.
- What is a question you're left wondering after reading the piece?
- Ask your question.
- Name something that needs to be polished.

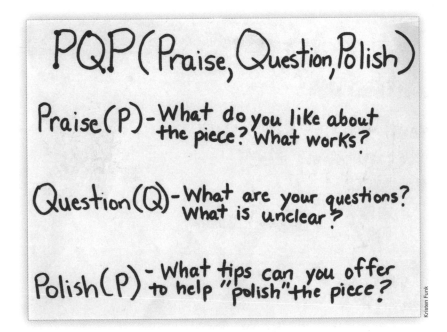

PQP (Praise, Question, Polish)

Praise (P) - What do you like about the piece? What works?

Question (Q) - What are your questions? What is unclear?

Polish (P) - What tips can you offer to help "polish" the piece?

Kristen Funk

Hat Tip: "The PQP Method of Responding to Writing" (Lyons 1981)

Who is this for?

LEVELS
3–8

GENRE / TEXT TYPE
any

PROCESS
revising

Strategy Tell your partner what you think is most important about your piece (a theme, a main idea, a feeling, a focus). Read your draft, pausing often. Ask your partner to think, "Do these details I just read fit with my focus? Is there anything I should change, delete, or add to be clearer?"

Teaching Tip This strategy will help children to make careful choices about their details and word choice as they connect to their focus/meaning. Rereading with this critical lens is often so challenging for young writers (or sometimes even adult writers!) that it often helps to have another set of eyes and ears.

Prompts
- Tell your partner what your focus is.
- Think about what details match the focus.
- You think something is fuzzy in that last part? Can you try to explain it to your partner?
- How did that sound? Focused?
- Explain how you think the part she just read matches her stated focus.
- Say, "From what you just read, it sounds like your focus is . . ."

Hat Tip: *Explore Poetry* (Graves 1992)

> **"Does It Match My Intention?"**
>
> 1. Tell your partner the most important thing about your piece:
>
>   THEME   MAIN IDEA   FEELING   FOCUS
>
> 2. Read your draft. Pause often. Ask:
>
>   "DO THESE DETAILS I READ FIT WITH MY FOCUS? WHAT MIGHT I CHANGE? ADD? DELETE?"

Barb Golub

10.12 Interrupt Your Partner

Strategy Listen to your partner as she tells her story. As soon as you notice your partner is skipping important information, gently interrupt with a prompt for more information. Your partner will then rewind and storytell the same part, but include the information you asked for.

Teaching Tip Students may need some visual anchor from which to launch their story, such as a storyboard with quick sketches to represent each part. See strategy 10.3, "Storytelling from Sketches," for an example. As you sit beside partnerships, try to coach/prompt the listening partner, not the one sharing the writing. Use the prompts below to get the child to prompt his partner.

Prompts
- Stop your partner. What types of details do you want?
- Use this prompt to get more information.
- It sounds like your partner just told you a lot of action. What other details can you prompt for?
- *(Nonverbally prompt the child to jump in and coach by using gestures or nodding your head.)*

Who is this for?

LEVELS
3–8

GENRE / TEXT TYPE
narrative

PROCESSES
rehearsing,
developing

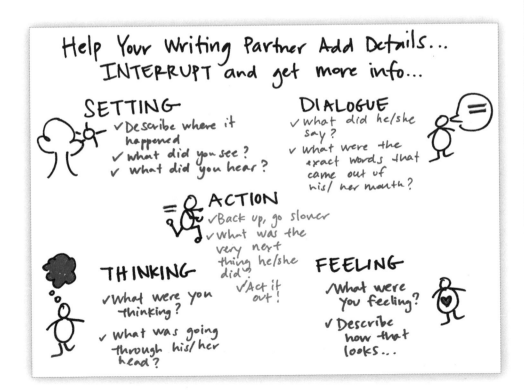

Help Your Writing Partner Add Details...
INTERRUPT and get more info...

SETTING
✓ Describe where it happened
✓ what did you see?
✓ what did you hear?

DIALOGUE
✓ what did he/she say?
✓ what were the exact words that came out of his/her mouth?

ACTION
✓ Back up, go slower
✓ what was the very next thing he/she did?
✓ Act it out!

THINKING
✓ What were you thinking?
✓ what was going through his/her head?

FEELING
✓ What were you feeling?
✓ Describe how that looks...

Who is this for?

LEVELS
3–8

GENRE / TEXT TYPE
narrative

PROCESSES
developing, drafting, revising

Strategy Come up with a premise for your fictional piece. Jot it in a sentence or two. Next, list about a dozen specific details: about the setting, characters, plot, or some other aspect of your story idea. Now, meet with a partner and have your partner ask you several questions to generate more specific details from the first details you listed.

Prompts

• Ask your partner, "Why is your character _____?"
• Ask your partner to tell you more about the _____.
• What are you wondering? Make up a question to ask.
• It's OK if you haven't thought it up yet—that's why your partner is here, to prompt you to imagine it now.
• Stick with _____, and ask a few more questions.

Dig Deeper For Fictional Details

*List a premise for your fictional piece.

Character / Setting / Plot Details

Have your partner ask you several questions to get more specific details...

Jamie DeMinco

Hat Tip: *After "The End": Teaching and Learning Creative Revision* (Lane 1993)

Strategy Find a group of other writers whose support and advice you respect. Decide on how often you'll meet and the rules of your club. Figure out what sorts of support you can use from your teacher to keep your club productive.

Teaching Tip Some students will do best staying in partnerships for the year, but others may like to form clubs. These clubs can form because they represent a balance of different strengths (one is good at helping the other writers flesh out ideas before writing, someone else is a great editor, someone else is a great coach to keep people motivated and on track) or they could form around a common interest (for example, students want to study how to write graphic novels and they plan to study mentor texts and come up with a course of study on their own).

Prompts
- It will help to plan out some protocols.
- How will your time together go?
- What will you study together? How will you study it?
- How can I help you make this time productive?
- I see you've got a clear set of goals that you want to work on for this time.
- Think about your individual areas of expertise and what you can each offer.

The Write Time Club
Club Rules:

1. Listen.
2. Be ready to share writing.
3. Give a compliment before a suggestion.
4. Have fun!

Who is this for?

LEVELS
4–8

GENRE / TEXT TYPE
any

PROCESS
any

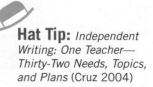

Hat Tip: *Independent Writing: One Teacher—Thirty-Two Needs, Topics, and Plans* (Cruz 2004)

10.15 Storytelling to Figure Out Point of View and Perspective

LEVELS
4–8

GENRE / TEXT TYPE
narrative

PROCESSES
developing, revising

Strategy Work with your partner to storytell aloud. Tell your story once, and have your partner listen. Then, try to tell your story from a different perspective (perhaps from the point of view of another character in the story, or from a narrator if it was first person). Ask your partner to give you feedback on how the two (or more) versions of the stories changed the meaning or changed the feeling/tone of the story.

Prompts
- Think about whose perspective the story is being told from.
- What is another perspective you could try?
- Think about the voice you'd use to tell the story from that perspective.
- Because you're working from that perspective, what details should you include? What should you leave out?
- Ask your partner, "How did the two stories differ?"
- Ask your partner, "Which story did you prefer? Why?"

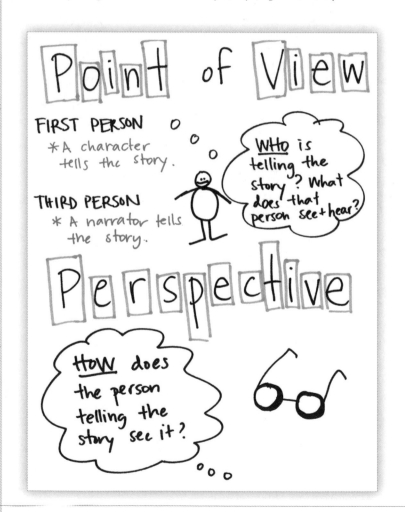

Hat Tip: *What You Know by Heart: How to Develop Curriculum for Your Writing Workshop* (Ray 2002)

Strategy Without introduction, read your piece to your partner or club members. At the end, have a conversation about how the piece affected them as readers/listeners. You can talk about the feelings evoked or the understandings gained. Consider how your partner/group's feedback aligns to your intentions as the writer of the piece.

Teaching Tip Feedback about mood, emotion, and message are helpful for a reader before a piece goes out into the world. More than just "That's a great piece!," this strategy is really about pushing partners and club members to articulate what they got from it, so that the writer can match that feedback up with her meaning to inform revisions.

Prompts

- Tell the writer how the piece made you feel.
- Tell the writer what you think the message of the piece is.
- Tell the writer what you think the purpose of his piece is based on what you heard.
- (*To the writer*) What do you think you'll change? Keep?
- (*To the writer*) Does that feedback help? Explain how.

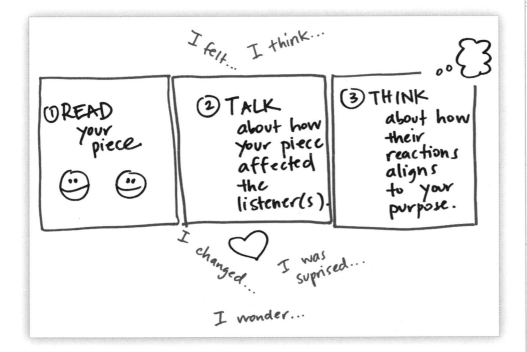

Hat Tip: *Explore Poetry* (Graves 1992)

10.17 Code the Text

Who is this for?

LEVELS
4–8

GENRE / TEXT TYPE
any

PROCESS
revising

Strategy Read through your partner's draft. Code the text with symbols showing places where you are responding as a reader (check the figure below for examples). After 5–10 minutes of reading, get together with your partner to discuss your reactions. The writer of the piece should then consider whether his intentions match the reader's response.

Lesson Language *Our writing is meant to be read, and therefore we should care about readers' responses. When you are working toward publication, it is crucial that you get feedback from some readers to find out if your intended meanings are coming across clearly and if there are any loose ends that need tying up. That said, don't feel the need to change everything based on a single reader's feedback. Use that person's reactions and responses as information and gather more from other sources if needed! You may find you get feedback from two different people, then go to a third person for advice on ways to revise. Or you may get feedback from one reader and then approach a second with more-specific questions or things to read for.*

Prompts

- Jot a code in the margin to capture your thinking.
- Don't read too much before stopping to consider your reaction. Just a few lines, then stop.
- Read in chunks, so you don't miss anything.
- Check the figure below for ideas of ways to code and respond.

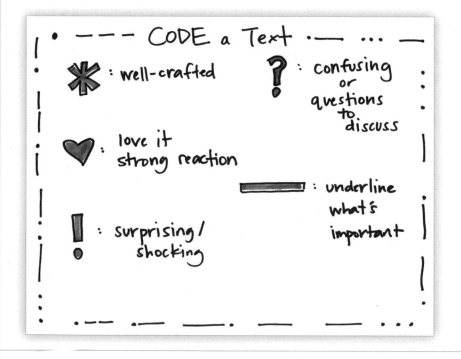

Hat Tip: *Micro Lessons in Writing: Big Ideas for Revising* (Vopat 2007b)

Strategy Prior to conversation about a writing piece, read your peer's piece and reflect on paper. You might jot bullet points and questions for discussion, or write complete thoughts meant for the writer to read and reflect on. Share your feedback.

Prompts

- Now that you've read your partner's piece, take a moment to reflect on paper.
- Your reflections could be questions or comments.
- Be sensitive to how you phrase things. How would you want to hear it if you were the writer?
- Jot down some suggestions.
- What you write could simply be topics for conversation starting!

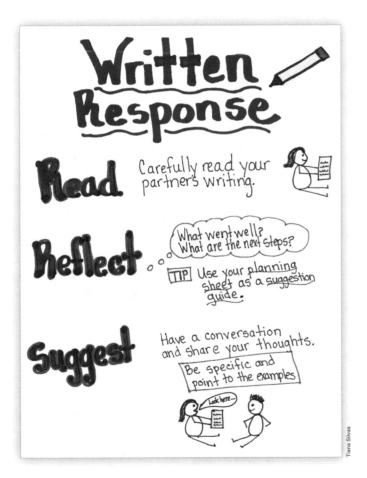

Who is this for?

LEVELS

4–8

GENRE / TEXT TYPE

any

PROCESSES

developing, drafting, revising, editing

Hat Tip: *Micro Lessons in Writing: Big Ideas for Revising* (Vopat 2007b)

10.19 Changes and Choices

Who is this for?

LEVELS
5–8

GENRE / TEXT TYPE
any

PROCESS
revising

Strategy Prepare the multiple drafts you have with notes for how you'd want feedback, or what questions you have. Give your partner or club members time to look across the pages and make a list of their questions and noticings about the *changes* you've made and the *choices* that led you to make those changes. Get together to discuss and reflect on your process and possible future revisions.

Teaching Tip You will likely need to divide this lesson into two (or more) sessions, teaching children first how to reflect on different iterations of their work. They may, for example, highlight an area (say, the lead) where they've made several changes, and be ready to discuss why they made the changes. They may prepare for their club or partner's feedback by jotting a list of questions about their different versions, "Do you like X better or Y? Why? What does it do for you as a reader?" If writers come with five-page scrolls rewritten three ways and no focus or direction, the time may not be well spent and/or the work will be messy.

Using a Mentor

Interviewer: How much rewriting do you do?

Hemingway: It depends. I rewrote the ending of *Farewell to Arms*, the last page of it, 39 times before I was satisfied.

Interviewer: Was there some technical problem there? What was it that had stumped you?

Hemingway: Getting the words right. (Hemingway 1958)

Prompts

- Explain to your club members why you made the changes you did.
- Do you have a question in mind about the different versions your club members might help you to answer?
- How can they help you? Think about what feedback you'd like.
- Show me how you've prepared to show your partner these different versions.

Hat Tip: *In the Middle, Third Edition: A Lifetime of Learning About Writing, Reading, and Adolescents* (Atwell 2014)

> ### CH-CH-CH-CHANGES (AND CHOICES)
>
> 1. Share several iterations of your work with your partner or club.
> 2. Give them time to ponder your changes and choices. They'll come up with questions and noticings.
> 3. Get together. Reflect together. Revise together.

Barb Golub

When students know their
work will be published,
it helps them to envision
an end to the writing
process and an audience
for their piece.

—Jennifer Serravallo

Appendix: Publishing and Celebrating Writing

Symbol Key

Cost

$ costs nothing or next to nothing

$ $ spend a little or ask for a small donation from parents

$ $ $ requires considerable supplies

Planning Time

⊘ so easy to plan, you could decide to do it in the morning and pull it off an hour later

⊘⊘ takes minimal planning, such as a note home to invite parents

⊘⊘⊘ takes more planning, like a trip to the store, or arranging a field trip

School Time

▦ quick, less than a typical writing period

▦▦ about as long as a typical writing period

▦▦▦ a half day or longer

Although some writers in your class may want to submit their work to be published online in blogs or in print in children's magazines, for most of your students, *publication* will mean adding a cover and some color to illustrations, writing an about the author blurb, and sharing it with parents and/or friends. For many writers, publication helps motivate them to do their best work. When students know their work will be published, it helps them to envision an end to the writing process and an audience for their piece. Therefore, it's often helpful to set aside times of year when you'll be able to celebrate student "publication."

What follows are some ways to bring the celebration of student writing to your classroom. You may use some of these celebration ideas at the conclusion of a whole-class writing unit, and other times you may choose to highlight individual writers who may have taken on independent projects and are ready to publish in the midst of a regular class unit. Some of these ideas won't cost a dollar; others may require fund-raising or the help of some generous donations ($—less expensive; $ $ $—more expensive). Some take next to no preparation; others will take careful planning (⊘—less planning; ⊘⊘⊘—more planning). Some can be done in a few spare minutes; others take a chunk of school time (▦—short celebration; ▦▦▦—longer celebration). Some include inviting visitors into your classroom; others send your authors out into the world. You'll likely choose different types of celebrations across the year to match different purposes.

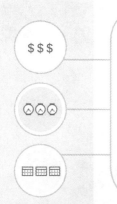

Author's Day

Every few months, turn your classroom into a bookstore that welcomes an author for readings of excerpts and book signings. You can involve your students in creating marketing materials (emails, posters, postcards) to invite family members and school community members. Each author's day can feature a couple of authors from your classroom, and students can take turns signing up to be featured when they feel like their piece is ready to be shared (Vopat 2007c).

About the Author

Work with your soon-to-be-published writers to create about the author pages that entice a would-be reader to pick up the book and read more. Study a few such pages from class favorites. Consider supporting younger writers with template pages that have a spot for a profile picture or illustration and lines to write some facts about the author. You may want to have a parent volunteer who is handy with the camera come in to school to take official author "headshots" that students can use for occasions such as these. Students can come to school dressed up for the occasion. Alternatively, you can ask parents to donate a bunch of wallet-sized school pictures to be used for this purpose.

Time in the Author's Chair

Consider creating a special, prestigious place where the celebrating writer gets to sit to share his work. It could be a director's chair, a stool, or an old chair salvaged from a secondhand store that your students help you to paint and decorate. When a student is ready to share a published work, she can sign up for time in the chair.

Reader's Theater

Help readers adapt a portion of their writing into a script to be shared in a theatrical reading. Some students may want to be narrators, others may want to take on character roles, and still others may want to direct or offer their support with sound effects. This works best when a small troupe of "actors" and minimal props are used; it's important that this doesn't turn into a three-week project taking away from the time a writer might begin work on the next project.

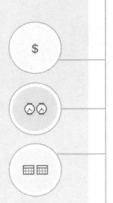

Gallery Walk

Transform your classroom into a gallery with each piece of student work featured on a spot on the wall or each piece on a desk. Visitors circulate reading pieces while offering compliments and comments on note cards or sticky notes. Teaching students to give specific compliments (e.g., "You really cracked open the verbs to help me visualize!" versus "Nice writing!") helps students to read like writers and notice craft, and their compliments offer you insight into the sorts of craft techniques they can notice and name. You may also want to give a "cheat sheet" to your visiting guests (parents, administrators) telling them what students have worked on in the unit and the sorts of things to be looking for and complimenting. Students can put their work out as is, or they can create a brief plaque with a title and short description of the work or interesting facts about its creation. Turn this into a fund-raiser by offering copies of student writing for a fee, displayed on the plaque. Champagne optional.

Illustrator-Author Match-Ups

Discuss with children that authors are often matched up with illustrators by their publishing houses. In fact, in many cases, authors never meet or have a chance to speak with the illustrator who is responsible for the cover or interior artwork. Shuffle the work in your classroom so each student gets another author's work. Ask the student to read the work carefully, thinking about an image that seems to capture the work. Have the "illustrator" create a cover for their peer's piece. Get together in groups to celebrate the writing and unveil the cover art, discussing what part of the work inspired the design (Vopat 2007c).

Powerful Lines

Ask students to reread their work to find one strong example of powerful language that stands alone. Give each student a sentence strip on which to write the powerful line and to decorate how they wish. Fill the classroom with these sentence strips that will serve as mentor sentences for future units. (Note: This suggestion would be a great pairing for a class that has been spending a lot of time working with lessons from the word choice, elaboration, or grammar chapters.)

Symphony Share

Have students sit in a circle with their published pieces in hand. Ask them to locate a sentence or two, or even a single word, that they find to be powerful. Perhaps the sentence is a demonstration of a particular craft technique, or it is an example of language that they carefully considered. The rule of the share is that you can speak when there is quiet. Without calling on anyone, have students share out the line or word they found. The result sounds like a symphony, with different voices joining in to fill quiet spaces.

"Audiobook" or Podcast Using QR Codes

Have students record themselves reading their work to create an audio podcast. Link the audio recordings to QR codes. When visitors come to the classroom, ask them to bring their cell phone and a set of headphones to walk around the room scanning the QR code to listen to the author reading the piece as they look at it in front of them. Send home all the QR codes and students will have their own minilibrary of audiobooks to listen to at home!

Create a Portfolio

Celebrate a year's work in writing by asking students to curate a portfolio. Looking back across their pieces, they can reflect on which piece may have challenged them the most, which they are most proud of, which piece feels like a start to something bigger. They can write short reflections to attach to each piece and pass the work along to their soon-to-be teacher, or bring the work home to share with family (C. Anderson 2005).

Poetry Slam/Coffeehouse

Help students get in the mood that best fits their piece. For free-verse poetry, introduce them to the beatnik vibe by creating a poetry café. Hand out berets, serve warm beverages, allow students to read into a microphone, and congratulate the writer with snaps instead of claps.

Send Your Writing Out in the World

Think about the genre the students wrote and who the most appropriate audience is for that piece. If the work is a letter, for example, make sure it goes to its intended receiver! Teach students how to address envelopes and where to put the stamp, and then go on a class trip to a mailbox near the school (Taylor 2008).

Allow Your Writing to Bring Joy to Others

Visit a nursing home or hospital and have students share their writing out in the world. Residents and patients get to hear great stories, poems, or other writing, and students have a chance for their writing to have an audience outside of the walls of the school.

Toast!

Add sparkling cider and cookies for an instant celebratory feel. Instead of reading their writing, students can make a short speech—a toast—to their piece. They might thank the writing for what it taught them, or cajole the writing for the hard times it gave them. After the speeches, students can circulate around the room and read the work that's placed out on tables (Cruz 2003).

Create a Class Book

Work together to create a class book. Books can be more formally bound, or simply photocopied and stapled. Once everyone gets a copy, students can read each other's writing and then spend some time in a circle share where they ask questions or give compliments to other class authors.

Cross-Grade Buddy Reading

Many older-grade students have younger-grade buddies who they meet to read to throughout the school year. This pairing can also be great for a publishing celebration. After the students read their pieces, they can take questions about their process, their decisions, or what they learned the most. This is also a fun idea when multiple grades are working on the same genre. Younger students can see what their work will look like in years to come, and older students can reflect on how they used to write when they were younger and appreciate all they've learned since then.

Letter (or Tweet) to the Author

Celebrate your work by honoring mentor authors you studied during the process of writing your piece. Write a letter to the author sharing how they inspired you, and include a copy of the student's work. For a twenty-first-century version, you can also take a photo of the student work and tweet it along with thanks to the author. Many will write back!

"Ask Me About" Necklaces

Have students create a necklace or button to wear home and out in the world announcing their recent success and hard work. Their wearable can announce the genre ("Ask Me About How to Write a Poem!") or about their piece specifically ("Ask Me to Tell You the Story of My First Roller Coaster Ride!") (Zimmerman 2013).

Weeblys, Wikis, and Blogs

Create a class Web page that allows student work to be posted and viewed once the URL is shared. Turn on the ability to leave comments to allow readers to share their thoughts about student pieces.

Celebrate the Journey

Help others see how much work went into the finished pieces by unveiling the process. Students can share the journey they went on to create their piece by selecting and annotating notebook work and/or earlier drafts alongside their finished piece. They may choose to ask readers to write to them with guiding questions such as, "What do you notice changed the most?" or "What revision seems to have made the biggest difference?"

Chalkabration

Take the writing celebration outdoors, and fill the boring gray sidewalks and black asphalt with colorful student words. Students can use multicolored chalk to write down best lines from stories, fun facts from informational texts, calls to action from persuasive writing, or entire poems. Passersby, other students, and visitors to the school will be able to enjoy the writing until the rain comes to wash it away (Ayers and Overman 2013).

Small-Group Shares

Set up four author chairs in the four corners of the room. Divide your class into four groups, one for each corner. Kids in each group take turns sitting in one of the four author's chairs while the others listen in. This can be an in-class celebration only, or you can invite other students from the school or families.

Skype

Connect with other students anywhere around the globe, and invite them into your classroom to enjoy your celebration. Connect virtually with a mentor author who inspired the work, another class who has worked on another similar writing project, or an elected official who needs to hear your persuasive pieces (Ayers and Overman 2013).

Speed Share

Create two concentric circles of chairs. Arrange students so they are sitting in a chair facing a partner. Partners will have a couple minutes each to share a favorite part or best line from their piece. When the bell rings, the outer circle rotates clockwise and each student has a new partner to share again. After the circle has gone all the way around, students can write compliments to each other, sharing their favorite parts or commending the efforts that went into creating the piece.

Slumber Party

Invite students to wear their pajamas to school, bring in a flashlight and sleeping bag from home, and transform your classroom into a slumber party. Turn off the lights and allow students to read their pieces by flashlight.

Fancy Publishing

Use a company like Student Treasures (www.studenttreasures.com) or Scribblitt (http://scribblitt.com) to turn students' books into bound hardcovers, just like the published pieces from your classroom and school library (Ray and Cleveland 2004).

Library Ribbon Cutting

Create a section of the library in your town, school, or classroom for student-published books. Add the students' books and invite family and community members for a ribbon cutting. Authors can then read from the new additions.

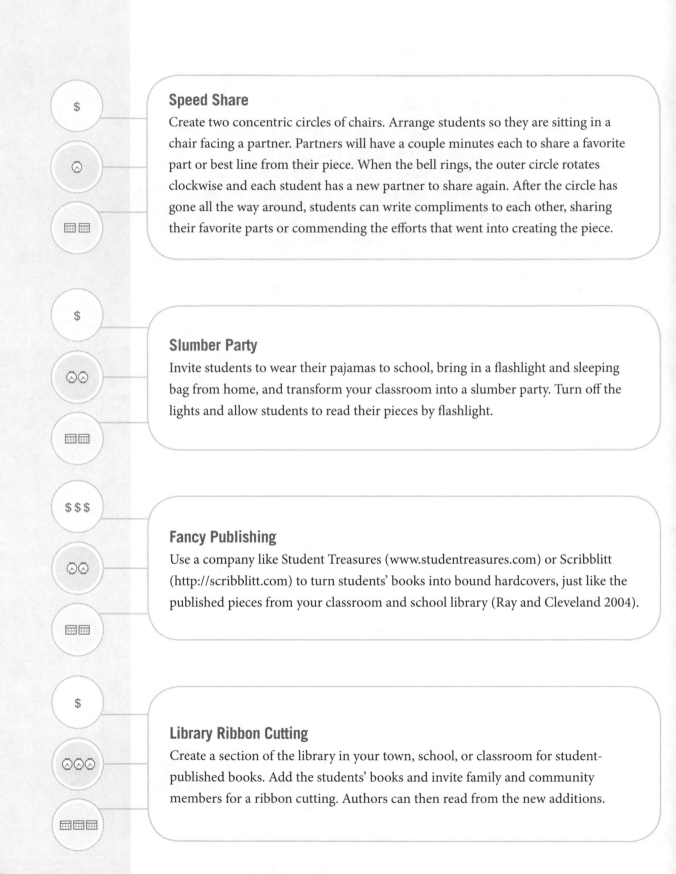

Campfire

Create a campfire using colored paper, tissue paper, and upturned flashlights. Have students sit around the "campfire" (maybe with s'mores!) and enjoy storytime (Ayers and Overman 2013).

$$

Popcorn and a Movie

Record students in your class reading their entire piece or excerpts of it. Create an iMovie from all the clips. Host a screening for your class and maybe invite visitors. Serve popcorn and drinks, of course (Moore 2013)!

$$

T-shirt Publishing

Print a student's cover artwork on the front of a T-shirt and their writing on the back. During a publishing celebration, students and other invited guests circulate around the room and read off each other's shirts. You could do a permanent T-shirt printing, or simply pin the work to a T-shirt for a temporary and less expensive option.

$$$

Connect with the Art Teacher

The possibilities for connecting art and writing are endless! Bring a story to life by creating a sculpture with the setting or a key scene. Create beautiful prints or collages to go alongside each student's poem, and put the class' work together for an anthology. Create illustrations in the style of the illustrator who most frequently works with the mentor author you studied. The list goes on and on!

$

Bulletin Board

Instead of just hanging the student writing in the hallway after school, have students get involved in the bulletin board displays. You can have a class discussion about what it is students want to showcase. For example, perhaps they want to invite commentary from the other kids in the school, and they'll decide to hang a basket with sticky notes and pens so friends can comment and leave sticky notes with their thoughts on the published pieces (Ayers and Overman 2013).

Placemats

Lay out a multipage piece of student writing on large construction paper. Have students decorate and embellish the border, and then send it through the laminating machine. Once laminated, these pieces can delight the family's dining table and be read and reread along with the morning cereal boxes and daily newspaper.

Mentor Author Inspiration

Share a page of student writing side by side with a page of a mentor author who inspired some of the craft in the student's writing. Students can invite readers to notice the craft techniques they tried out and ask for feedback on how their work seems inspired by the mentor author (Ayers and Overman 2013).

Family Writing Workshop

Families join the classroom and students act as teachers, putting their parents through the writing process they just went through. Students can give small-group lessons and use their own writing as a model or mentor text (Ayers and Overman 2013).

$

Give a Gift

What parent, grandparent, or sibling wouldn't appreciate a piece of kid writing as a gift? After students finish their piece, they can prepare their work to be gifted. Bring wrapping paper, ribbons, and bows into the classroom and allow students to wrap their writing like the present it is (Ayers and Overman 2013).

$ $

Bookbinding

Invite a crafty community member into your classroom to lead an art workshop, or go online to find directions for how to make various books for a very polished look. One idea, an accordion book, would be easy and fun to make (Bonney 2013).

$ $

Bibliography

Allen, Susan, and Jane Lindaman. 2006. *Written Anything Good Lately?* Minneapolis, MN: Millbrook Press.

Anderson, Carl. 2000. *How's It Going? A Practical Guide to Conferring with Student Writers.* Portsmouth, NH: Heinemann.

———. 2005. *Assessing Writers.* Portsmouth, NH: Heinemann.

———. 2008. *Strategic Writing Conferences: Smart Conversations That Move Young Writers Forward.* Portsmouth, NH: Heinemann.

———. 2009. *Strategic Writing Conferences: Finished Projects.* Portsmouth, NH: Heinemann.

Anderson, Jeff. 2005. *Mechanically Inclined: Building Grammar, Usage, and Style into Writer's Workshop.* Portland, ME: Stenhouse.

Anderson, Jeff, and Deborah Dean. 2014. *Revisions Decisions: Talking Through Sentences and Beyond.* Portland, ME: Stenhouse.

Angelillo, Janet. 2002. *A Fresh Approach to Teaching Punctuation: Helping Young Writers Use Conventions with Precision and Purpose.* New York: Scholastic.

Applegate, Katherine. 2007. *Home of the Brave.* New York: Square Fish.

———. 2012. *The One and Only Ivan.* New York: HarperCollins Children's Books.

Aston, Dianna. 2011. *A Butterfly Is Patient.* San Francisco: Chronicle Books.

Atwell, Nancie. 2014. *In the Middle, Third Edition: A Lifetime of Learning About Writing, Reading, and Adolescents.* Portsmouth, NH: Heinemann.

Ayers, Ruth, and Christi Overman. 2013. *Celebrating Writers: From Possibilities Through Publication.* Portland, ME: Stenhouse.

Barker, Clive. 1993. *The Thief of Always.* New York: Harper Collins.

Barnett, Mac. 2009. *Billy Twitters and His Blue Whale Problem.* New York: Hyperion Books.

Barretta, Gene. 2007. *Dear Deer: A Book of Homophones.* New York: Henry Holt and Company.

Baum, L. Frank. 1900. *The Wonderful Wizard of Oz.* Chicago, IL: George M. Hill Company.

Bear, Donald R., Marcia Invernizzi, Shane Templeton, and Francine Johnston. 2015. *Words Their Way: Word Study for Phonics, Vocabulary, and Spelling Instruction.* 6th ed. London: Pearson.

Becker, Aaron. 2013. *Journey.* Cambridge, MA: Candlewick Press.

Becker, Bonny. 2008. *A Visitor for Bear.* Cambridge, MA: Candlewick Press.

Benjamin, Amy, and Barbara Golub. 2015. *Infusing Grammar into the Writer's Workshop: A Guide for K–6 Teachers.* New York: Routledge.

Berne, Jennifer. 2013. *On a Beam of Light: A Story of Albert Einstein*. San Francisco: Chronicle Books.

Bhanshaly, Viraj. "Blue Whale." www.poemhunter.com/poem/blue-whale. Last accessed May 7, 2016.

Bomer, Katherine. 2005. *Writing a Life: Teaching Memoir to Sharpen Insight, Shape Meaning—and Triumph Over Tests*. Portsmouth, NH: Heinemann.

———. 2016. *The Journey Is Everything: Teaching Essays That Students Want to Write for People Who Want to Read Them*. Portsmouth, NH: Heinemann.

Bomer, Randy. 1995. *Time for Meaning: Crafting Literate Lives in Middle & High School*. Portsmouth, NH: Heinemann.

Bomer, Randy, and Katherine Bomer. 2001. *For a Better World: Reading and Writing for Social Action*. Don Mills, ON: Pearson Education Canada.

Bonney, Grace. 2013. "Bookbinding 101: Accordion Book." www.designsponge .com/2013/03/bookbinding-101-accordion-book.html. Last accessed September 8, 2016.

Booth, Wayne C., Gregory G. Colomb, and Joseph Williams. 2008. *The Craft of Research*. 3rd ed. Chicago: University of Chicago Press.

Boswell, Addie. 2008. *The Rain Stomper*. Tarrytown, NY: Marshall Cavendish.

Bouchard, David. 1993. *If You're Not from the Prairie*. Vancouver, BC: Raincoast Books.

Bridges, Shirin Yim. 2002. *Ruby's Wish*. San Francisco: Chronicle Books.

Brinkloe, Julie. 1986. *Fireflies*. New York: Aladdin Paperbacks.

Brooks, Gwendolyn. 1999. "We Real Cool." In *Selected Poems*. New York: Harper Perennial Modern Classics.

Bruno, Elsa Knight. 2012. *Punctuation Celebration*. New York: Henry Holt and Company.

Bryant, Jen. 2014. *The Right Word: Roget and His Thesaurus*. Grand Rapids, MI: Eerdmans Books for Young Readers.

Burleigh, Robert. 2001. *Hoops*. Orlando, FL: Voyager Books.

Burroway, Janet, and Elizabeth Stuckey-French. 2014. *Writing Fiction: A Guide to Narrative Craft*. 9th ed. London: Pearson.

Burton, Virginia Lee. 1939. *Mike Mulligan and His Steam Shovel*. New York: Houghton Mifflin.

Cali, Kathleen. 2013. "Support and Elaboration." www.learnnc.org/lp/editions /few/685. Last accessed May 7, 2016.

Calkins, Lucy. 1994. *The Art of Teaching Writing*. Portsmouth, NH: Heinemann.

———. 2010. *Launch a Primary Writing Workshop: Getting Started with Units of Study for Primary Writing, Grades K–2*. Portsmouth, NH: Heinemann.

————. 2013. *If . . . Then . . . Curriculum: Assessment-Based Instruction.* In *Units of Study in Opinion, Information, and Narrative Writing, Grade 4* by Lucy Calkins and colleagues.

————. 2014. *Writing Pathways: Performance Assessments and Learning Progressions, Grades K–8.* Portsmouth, NH: Heinemann.

Calkins, Lucy, and Pat Bleichman. 2003. *The Craft of Revision.* In *Units of Study for Primary Writing: A Yearlong Curriculum* by Lucy Calkins and colleagues. Portsmouth, NH: Heinemann.

Calkins, Lucy and colleagues. 2006. *Units of Study for Teaching Writing, Grades 3–5.* Portsmouth, NH: Heinemann.

————. 2013. *Units of Study in Opinion, Information, and Narrative Writing, Grade 1.* Portsmouth, NH: Heinemann.

Calkins, Lucy, and Colleen M. Cruz. 2006. *Writing Fiction: Big Dreams, Tall Ambitions.* In *Units of Study for Teaching Writing, Grades 3–5* by Lucy Calkins and colleagues. Portsmouth, NH: Heinemann.

Calkins, Lucy, and Cory Gillette. 2006. *Breathing Life Into Essays.* In *Units of Study for Teaching Writing, Grades 3–5* by Lucy Calkins and colleagues. Portsmouth, NH: Heinemann.

Calkins, Lucy, Amanda Hartman, and Zoë White. 2005. *One to One: The Art of Conferring with Young Writers.* Portsmouth, NH: Heinemann.

Calkins, Lucy, and Ted Kesler. 2006. *Raising the Quality of Narrative Writing.* In *Units of Study for Teaching Writing, Grades 3–5* by Lucy Calkins and colleagues. Portsmouth, NH: Heinemann.

Calkins, Lucy, and Natalie Louis. 2003. *Writing for Readers: Teaching Skills and Strategies.* In *Units of Study for Primary Writing: A Yearlong Curriculum* by Lucy Calkins and colleagues. Portsmouth, NH: Heinemann.

Calkins, Lucy, and Marjorie Martinelli. 2006. *Launching the Writing Workshop.* In *Units of Study for Teaching Writing, Grades 3–5* by Lucy Calkins and colleagues. Portsmouth, NH: Heinemann.

Calkins, Lucy, and Stephanie Parsons. 2003. *Poetry: Powerful Thoughts in Tiny Packages.* In *Units of Study for Primary Writing: A Yearlong Curriculum* by Lucy Calkins and colleagues. Portsmouth, NH: Heinemann.

Calkins, Lucy, and Laurie Pessah. 2003. *Nonfiction Writing: Procedures and Reports.* In *Units of Study for Primary Writing: A Yearlong Curriculum* by Lucy Calkins and colleagues. Portsmouth, NH: Heinemann.

Calkins, Lucy, Abby Oxenhorn Smith, and Rachel Rothman. 2013. *Small Moments: Writing with Focus, Detail, and Dialogue.* In *Units of Study for Primary Writing: A Yearlong Curriculum* by Lucy Calkins and colleagues. Portsmouth, NH: Heinemann.

Cannon, Janell. 1993. *Stellaluna*. Orlando, FL: Harcourt.

Carlson, Nancy. 1997. *How to Lose All Your Friends*. New York: Penguin Books.

Carroll, Lewis. 1871. "Jabberwocky." In *Through the Looking-Glass, and What Alice Found There*. London: Macmillan.

Cisneros, Sandra. 2013. *Eleven*. St. Louis, MO: Booksource.

Clark, Brian. 2012. "10 Steps to Becoming a Better Writer." www.copyblogger.com /become-a-better-writer/. Last accessed September 8, 2016.

Clark, Roy Peter. 2011. *Help! for Writers: 210 Solutions to the Problems Every Writer Faces*. New York: Little, Brown and Company.

Clay, Marie M. 2000. *Concepts About Print: What Have Children Learned About the Way We Print Language?* Portsmouth, NH: Heinemann.

Collins, Kathleen, and Matt Glover. 2015. *I Am Reading: Nurturing Young Children's Meaning Making and Joyful Engagement with Any Book*. Portsmouth, NH: Heinemann.

Coman, Carolyn. 2012. *What Jamie Saw*. South Hampton, NH: Namelos.

Creech, Sharon. 2001. *Love That Dog*. New York: HarperCollins Children's Books.

Crews, Donald. 1996. *Shortcut*. New York: Greenwillow Books.

Cronin, Doreen. 2000. *Click, Clack, Moo: Cows That Type*. Jacksonville, IL: Perma-Bound Books.

Cruz, Maria Colleen. 2003. *Border Crossing*. Houston, TX: Arte Publico Press.

Cruz, M. Colleen. 2004. *Independent Writing: One Teacher—Thirty-Two Needs, Topics, and Plans*. Portsmouth, NH: Heinemann.

———. 2008. *A Quick Guide to Reaching Struggling Writers, K–5*. Portsmouth, NH: Heinemann.

Culham, Ruth. 2003. *6+1 Traits of Writing: The Complete Guide, Grades 3 and Up*. New York: Scholastic.

———. 2005. *6+1 Traits of Writing: The Complete Guide for the Primary Grades*. New York: Scholastic.

———. 2014. *The Writing Thief: Using Mentor Texts to Teach the Craft of Writing*. Newark, DE: International Reading Association.

———. Traits Writing Program. New York: Scholastic.

Dahl, Roald. 2007. *Charlie and the Chocolate Factory*. London: Puffin Books.

———. 2007. *The Twits*. London: Puffin Books.

———. 2007. *The Witches*. London: Puffin Books.

———. 2016. *James and the Giant Peach*. London: Puffin Books.

———. 2016. *Matilda*. London: Puffin Books.

Davies, Nicola. 2000. *Big Blue Whale*. Cambridge, MA: Candlewick Press.

———. 2005. *Surprising Sharks: Read and Wonder*. Cambridge, MA: Candlewick Press.

———. 2009. *What's Eating You? Parasites—The Inside Story*. Reprint ed. Cambridge, MA: Candlewick Press.

———. 2014. *Tiny Creatures: The World of Microbes*. Cambridge, MA: Candlewick Press.

De La Peña, Matt. 2015. *Last Stop on Market Street*. New York: G.P. Putnam's Sons Books for Young Readers.

Deedy, Carmen Agra. 2007. *Martina, the Beautiful Cockroach: A Cuban Folktale*. Atlanta, GA: Peachtree.

Delpit, Lisa. 2002. *The Skin That We Speak: Thoughts on Language and Culture in the Classroom*. New York: New Press.

———. 2006. *Other People's Children: Cultural Conflict in the Classroom*. New York: New Press.

DiCamillo, Kate. 2000. *Because of Winn-Dixie*. Cambridge, MA: Candlewick Press.

———. 2001. *The Tiger Rising*. Cambridge, MA: Candlewick Press.

———. 2003. *The Tale of Despereaux*. Cambridge, MA: Candlewick Press.

Dierking, Connie, and Sherra Jones. 2014. *Oral Mentor Texts: A Powerful Tool for Teaching Reading, Writing, Speaking, and Listening*. Portsmouth, NH: Heinemann.

Dorfman, Lynne R., and Rose Cappelli. 2007. *Mentor Texts: Teaching Writing Through Children's Literature, K–6*. Portland, ME: Stenhouse.

———. 2009. *Nonfiction Mentor Texts: Teaching Informational Writing Through Children's Literature, K–8*. Portland, ME: Stenhouse.

Dubowski, Cathy East. 2009. *Shark Attack!* London: Dorling Kindersley.

Duke, Nell. 2014. *Inside Information: Developing Powerful Readers and Writers of Information Text Through Project-Based Instruction*. New York: Scholastic.

Dussling, Jennifer. 1998. *Bugs Bugs Bugs!* 1st American ed. New York: DK Publishing.

Ehrenworth, Mary, and Vicki Vinton. 2005. *The Power of Grammar: Unconventional Approaches to the Conventions of Language*. Portsmouth, NH: Heinemann.

Engle, Margarita. 2015. *Drum Dream Girl: How One Girl's Courage Changed Music*. New York: HMH Books for Young Readers.

Feigelson, Dan. 2008. *Practical Punctuation: Lessons on Rule Making and Rule Breaking in Elementary Writing*. Portsmouth, NH: Heinemann.

Ferry, Beth. 2015. *Stick and Stone*. New York: Houghton Mifflin Harcourt.

Fig, Joe. 2009. *Inside the Painter's Studio*. New York: Princeton Architectural Press.

Fisher, Douglas, and Nancy Frey. 2008. *Word Wise and Content Rich, Grades 7–12: Five Essential Steps to Teaching Academic Vocabulary*. Portsmouth, NH: Heinemann.

Fleischman, Paul. 1988. *Joyful Noise: Poems for Two Voices*. New York: HarperTrophy.

Fletcher, Ralph. 1993. *What a Writer Needs*. Portsmouth, NH: Heinemann.

———. 1996. *Breathing In, Breathing Out: Keeping a Writer's Notebook*. Portsmouth, NH: Heinemann.

———. 1999. *Live Writing: Breathing Life into Your Words*. New York: Avon Books.

———. 2003. *A Writer's Notebook: Unlocking the Writer Within You*. Reissue ed. New York: HarperCollins.

———. 2010. *Pyrotechnics on the Page: Playful Craft That Sparks Writing*. Portland, ME: Stenhouse.

———. 2012. *Marshfield Dreams: When I Was a Kid*. Reprint ed. New York: Square Fish.

Fletcher, Ralph, and JoAnn Portalupi. Craft Lessons series. Portland, ME: Stenhouse

———. 2007. *Craft Lessons: Teaching Writing K–8*. 2nd ed. Portland, ME: Stenhouse.

Floca, Brian. 2013. *Locomotive*. New York: Atheneum Books for Young Readers.

Florian, Douglas. 1998. *Insectlopedia*. Orlando, FL: Harcourt.

———. 2001. "The Cobra." In *Lizards, Frogs, and Polliwogs*. San Diego, CA: Harcourt Books.

Fox, Karen C. 2010. *Older Than the Stars*. Watertown, MA: Charlesbridge.

Fox, Mem. 1988. *Koala Lou*. Chicago: Houghton Mifflin Harcourt.

———. 1989. *Wilfrid Gordon McDonald Partridge*. Madison, WI: Demco Media.

———. 1998. *Tough Boris*. Orlando, FL: Voyager Books.

Francois, Chantal, and Elisa Zonana. 2009. *Catching Up on Conventions: Grammar Lessons for Middle School Writers*. Portsmouth, NH: Heinemann.

Frazee, Marla. 2003. *Roller Coaster*. San Diego, CA: Harcourt Books.

Gantos, Jack. 2002–2014. Joey Pigza series. New York: Macmillan.

Gardiner, John Reynolds. 1980. *Stone Fox*. New York: HarperCollins Children's Books.

Garland, Sherry. 1993. *The Lotus Seed*. Orlando, FL: Harcourt Brace & Company.

Gibbons, Gail. 2010. *Coral Reefs*. Reprint ed. New York: Holiday House.

Glover, Matt. 2009. *Engaging Young Writers, Preschool–Grade 1*. Portsmouth, NH: Heinemann.

Graham, Steve, Debra McKeown, Sharlene Kiuhara, and Karen R. Harris. 2012. "Meta-Analysis of Writing Instruction for Students in Elementary Grades." *Journal of Educational Psychology* 104 (4): 896.

Graves, Donald H. 1983. *Writing: Teachers and Children at Work*. Portsmouth, NH: Heinemann.

———. 1989. *Experiment with Fiction*. Portsmouth, NH: Heinemann.

———. 1992. *Explore Poetry*. Portsmouth, NH: Heinemann.

Graves, Donald H., and Penny Kittle. 2005. *Inside Writing: How to Teach the Details of Craft*. Portsmouth, NH: Heinemann.

Gray, Libba Moore. 1995. *My Mama Had a Dancing Heart*. New York: Orchard Books.

Greenfield, Eloise. 1992. *Koya Delaney and the Good Girls Blues*. New York: Scholastic.

———. 1995. *Honey I Love*. New York: HarperFestival.

Greenfield, Eloise, and Lessie Jones Little. 1979. *Childtimes: A Three-Generation Memoir*. New York: HarperCollins Children's Books.

Hattie, John. 2009. *Visible Learning. A Synthesis of Over 800 Meta-Analyses Relating to Achievement*. New York: Routledge.

Heard, Georgia. 1997. "Song of the Dolphin." In *Creatures of Earth, Sea, and Sky*. Honesdale, PA: Boyds Mills Press.

———. 1999. *Awakening the Heart: Exploring Poetry in Elementary and Middle School*. Portsmouth, NH: Heinemann.

———. 2002. *The Revision Toolbox: Teaching Techniques That Work*. Portsmouth, NH: Heinemann.

———. 2013. *Finding the Heart of Nonfiction: Teaching 7 Essential Craft Tools with Mentor Texts*. Portsmouth, NH: Heinemann.

———. 2016. *Heart Maps: Helping Students Create and Craft Authentic Writing*. Portsmouth, NH: Heinemann.

Hemingway, Ernest. 1958. "The Art of Fiction No. 21." The Paris Review. Spring, No. 18. New York: The Paris Review.

Henkes, Kevin. 1995. *Julius, Baby of the World*. Reprint ed. New York: Greenwillow Books.

Hesse, Karen. 1997. *Out of the Dust*. New York: Scholastic.

———. 1999. *Come On, Rain!* New York: Scholastic.

———. "Karen Hesse Interview Transcript." www.scholastic.com/teachers/article/karen-hesse-interview-transcript. Last accessed May 7, 2016.

Hjemboe, Karen. 2000. *Laundry Day*. New York: Bebop Books.

Howe, James. 2012. *Addie on the Inside*. New York: Atheneum Books for Young Readers.

Hoyt, Linda. 1999. *Revisit, Reflect, Retell: Time-Tested Strategies for Teaching Reading Comprehension*. Portsmouth, NH: Heinemann.

———. 2012. *Crafting Nonfiction, Intermediate*. Portsmouth, NH: Heinemann.

Huget, Jennifer. 2013. *The Beginner's Guide to Running Away from Home*. New York: Schwartz & Wade Books.

Hughes, Langston. 2003. "Poem." In *The Collected Works of Langston Hughes, Volume 11: Works for Children and Young Adults: Poetry, Fiction, and Other Writing*. Columbia, MO: University of Missouri Press.

If You . . . series. New York: Scholastic.

Ishida, Sanae. 2015. *Little Kunoichi: The Ninja Girl*. Seattle, WA: Little Bigfoot.

Janeczko, Paul B. 2006. *Seeing the Blue Between: Advice and Inspiration for Young Poets*. Reprint ed. Cambridge, MA: Candlewick Press.

Jenkins, Steve, and Robin Page. 2014. *Creature Features: Twenty-Five Animals Explain Why They Look the Way They Do*. New York: Houghton Mifflin Harcourt.

Johnson, Angela. 2000. *The Leaving Morning*. Boston, MA: Houghton Muffin.

———. 2007. *A Sweet Smell of Roses*. New York: Aladdin Paperbacks.

Kalman, Bobbie, and Heather Levigne. 1998. *What Is a Bat?* St. Catharines, ON: Crabtree Publishing.

———. 1999. *What Is a Primate?* St. Katharines, ON: Crabtree Publishing.

KC and the Sunshine Band. "(Shake, Shake, Shake) Shake Your Booty." *Part 3*. TK Records. Recorded 1976.

King, Martin Luther, Jr. August 1963. "I Have a Dream." www.archives.gov/press /exhibits/dream-speech.pdf. Last accessed May 7, 2016.

King, Stephen. 2000. *On Writing: A Memoir of the Craft*. New York: Scribner.

Lai, Thanhha. 2011. *Inside Out and Back Again*. New York: HarperCollins.

Laminack, Lester L. 1998. *The Sunsets of Miss Olivia Wiggins*. Atlanta, GA: Peachtree.

———. 2004. *Saturdays and Teacakes*. Atlanta, GA: Peachtree.

———. 2010. *Snow Day*. Atlanta, GA: Peachtree.

Lamott, Anne. 1994. *Bird by Bird: Some Instructions on Writing and Life*. New York: Pantheon Books.

Lane, Barry. 1993. *After "The End": Teaching and Learning Creative Revision*. Portsmouth, NH: Heinemann.

Lehman, Christopher. 2011. *A Quick Guide to Reviving Disengaged Writers, 5–8*. Portsmouth, NH: Heinemann.

———. 2012. *Energize Research Reading and Writing: Fresh Strategies to Spark Interest, Develop Independence, and Meet Key Common Core Standards*. Portsmouth, NH: Heinemann.

Lillegard, Dee. 1994. *Frog's Lunch*. New York: Scholastic.

Linder, Rozlyn. 2016. *Big Book of Details: 46 Moves for Teaching Writers to Elaborate*. Portsmouth, NH: Heinemann.

Loeper, John J. 1984. *Going to School in 1876*. New York: Atheneum Books for Young Readers.

Loewen, Nancy. 2011. *You're Toast and Other Metaphors We Adore*. Mankato, MN: Picture Window Books.

Lowry, Louis. 2009. *Crow Call*. New York: Scholastic.

Lukeman, Noah. 2002. *The Plot Thickens: 8 Ways to Bring Fiction to Life*. New York: St. Martin's Press.

———. 2007. *A Dash of Style: The Art and Mastery of Punctuation*. New York: W.W. Norton & Company.

Lyon, George Ella. 1993. "Where I'm From." www.georgeellalyon.com/where.html. Last accessed May 7, 2016.

Lyons, Bill. 1981. "The PQP Method of Responding to Writing." *The English Journal* 70 (3): 42–43.

———. 2011. *All the Water in the World*. New York: Atheneum Books for Young Readers.

MacLachlan, Patricia. 1985. *Sarah, Plain and Tall*. New York: HarperCollins Children's Books.

———. 1994. *Skylark*. New York: HarperCollins Children's Books.

Macmillan Childrens. "Laura Vaccaro talks about her picture book *Bully*." www .youtube.com/watch?v=QU_lRytwREs. Last accessed June 3, 2016.

Martin, Ann M. 2016. *How to Look for a Lost Dog*. London, United Kingdom: Usborne Publishing.

Martinelli, Marjorie, and Kristine Mraz. 2012. *Smarter Charts, K–2: Optimizing an Instructional Staple to Create Independent Readers and Writers*. Portsmouth, NH: Heinemann.

———. 2014. *Smarter Charts for Math, Science & Social Studies: Making Learning Visible in the Content Areas, K–2*. Portsmouth, NH: Heinemann.

———. Digital Campus Course. Portsmouth, NH: Heinemann.

———. 2016. "chartchums: Smarter Charts from Majorie Martinelli & Kristine Mraz." https://chartchums.wordpress.com. Last accessed May 7, 2016.

Mayer, Kelly. January. 2007. "Research in Review: Emerging Knowledge About Emergent Writing." *Young Children* 62 (1): 34–40.

Mayo Clinic Staff. 2014. "Organic Foods: Are They Safer? More Nutritious?" www .mayoclinic.org/healthy-lifestyle/nutrition-and-healthy-eating/in-depth /organic-food/art-20043880. Last accessed November 17, 2016.

McCarrier, Andrea, Gay Su Pinnell, and Irene Fountas. 1999. *Interactive Writing: How Language & Literacy Come Together, K–2*. Portsmouth, NH: Heinemann.

McDonald, Megan. 2007. *The Judy Moody Totally Awesome Collection: Books 1–6*. Box ed. Cambridge, MA: Candlewick Press.

McReynolds, Linda. 2012. *Eight Days Gone*. Watertown, MA: Charlesbridge.

Messner, Kate. 2011. *Over and Under the Snow*. San Francisco: Chronicle Books.

———. 2015a. *How to Read a Story*. San Francisco: Chronicle Books.

———. 2015b. NCTE Workshop. November 21, Minneapolis, MN.

———. 2015c. *Up in the Garden and Down in the Dirt*. San Francisco: Chronicle Books.

Moore, Beth. 2013. "It's That Time of Year: Publishing Parties." https://twowritingteach-ers.wordpress.com/2013/09/24/pubparties/. Last accessed September 8, 2016.

Moore, Elizabeth. 2013. "Pump Up the Volume." https://twowritingteachers.wordpress.com/2013/10/19/pump-up-the-volume. Last accessed May 7, 2016.

Moore, Michael. "10 Things They Won't Tell You about The Flint Water Tragedy: But I Will." http://michaelmoore.com/10FactsOnFlint. Last accessed May 7, 2016.

Munson, Derek. 2000. *Enemy Pie*. San Francisco: Chronicle Books.

Murray, Don. 1985. *A Writer Teaches Writing*. 2nd sub ed. Chicago: Houghton Mifflin Harcourt.

———. 2009. *The Essential Don Murray: Lessons from America's Greatest Writing Teacher*. Portsmouth, NH: Boynton/Cook Publishers.

Noble, Trinka Hakes. 2004. *The Scarlet Stockings Spy*. Ann Arbor, MI: Sleeping Bear Press.

Obama, Barack. 2016a. "Remarks by the President on Common-Sense Gun Safety Reform." https://obamawhitehouse.archives.gov/the-press-office/2016/01/05/remarks-president-common-sense-gun-safety-reform. Last accessed January 23, 2017.

———. 2016b. "Remarks of President Barack Obama—State of the Union Address as Delivered." https://obamawhitehouse.archives.gov/the-press-office/2016/01/12/remarks-president-barack-obama-%E2%80%93-prepared-delivery-state-union-address. Last accessed January 23, 2017.

Orme, Helen. 2006. *Polar Bears in Danger*. New York: Bearport Publishing.

Parsley, Elise. 2015. *If You Ever Want to Bring an Alligator to School, Don't!* New York: Little, Brown and Company.

Partridge, Elizabeth. 2003. *Whistling*. New York: Greenwillow Books.

Patricelli, Leslie. 2008. *No No Yes Yes*. Cambridge, MA: Candlewick Press.

Paulsen, Gary. 1987. *Hatchet*. New York: Simon Pulse.

Pennypacker, Sara. 2015. *Meet the Dullards*. New York: Balzer + Bray.

Petri, Alexandra. December 2015. "'Said' is not dead. Save boring words!" *Washington Post*. www.washingtonpost.com/blogs/compost/wp/2015/12/03/said-is-not-dead-save-boring-words/. Last accessed May 7, 2016.

Pilkey, Dav. 1996. *The Paperboy*. New York: Orchard Books.

Pink, Daniel. 2011. *Drive: The Surprising Truth About What Motivates Us*. New York: Riverhead Books.

Pitts, Leonard Jr. January. 2016. "Hey, Star Wars Toymakers, Where's Rey?" www.miamiherald.com/opinion/op-ed/article56732473.html. Last accessed May 7, 2016.

Poe, Edgar Allen. 1845. "The Raven." *The New York Evening Mirror.* January 29.

Polacco, Patricia. 1998. *Chicken Sunday.* New York: Philomel Books.

———. 1998. *My Rotten Redheaded Older Brother.* New York: Aladdin Paperbacks.

———. 1998. *Thank You, Mr. Falker.* New York: Philomel Books.

Portalupi, JoAnn, and Ralph Fletcher. 2001. *Nonfiction Craft Lessons: Teaching Information Writing K–8.* Portland, ME: Stenhouse.

Pulver, Robin. 2011. *Happy Endings: A Story About Suffixes.* New York: Holiday House.

Raschka, Chris. 1993 *Yo! Yes?* New York: Orchard Books.

Ray, Katie Wood. 1999. *Wondrous Words: Writers and Writing in the Elementary Classroom.* Urbana, IL: National Council of Teachers of English.

———. 2002. *What You Know by Heart: How to Develop Curriculum for Your Writing Workshop.* Portsmouth, NH: Heinemann.

———. 2010. *In Pictures and in Words: Teaching the Qualities of Good Writing Through Illustration Study.* Portsmouth, NH: Heinemann.

Ray, Katie Wood, and Matt Glover. 2008. *Already Ready: Nurturing Writers in Preschool and Kindergarten.* Portsmouth, NH: Heinemann.

Ray, Katie Wood, and Lisa Cleveland. 2004. *About the Authors.* Portsmouth, NH: Heinemann.

Reynolds, Peter H. 2004. *Ish.* Cambridge, MA: Candlewick Press.

Roberts, Kate, and Maggie Beattie Roberts. 2016. *DIY Literacy: Teaching Tools for Differentiation, Rigor, and Independence.* Portsmouth, NH: Heinemann.

Rockliff, Mara. 2014. *The Grudge Keeper.* Atlanta, GA: Peachtree.

Routman, Regie. 2000. *Conversations: Strategies for Teaching, Learning, and Evaluating.* Portsmouth, NH: Heinemann.

———. 2005. *Writing Essentials: Raising Expectations and Results While Simplifying Teaching.* Portsmouth, NH: Heinemann.

Rubin, Adam. 2015. *Robo-Sauce.* New York: Dial Books for Young Readers.

Rylant, Cynthia. 1982. *When I Was Young in the Mountains.* New York: Puffin Books.

———. 1988. *Every Living Thing.* New York: Aladdin Paperbacks.

———. 1992. *Missing May.* New York: Orchard Books.

———. 1993. *The Relatives Came.* New York: Aladdin Paperbacks.

———. 1995. *Dog Heaven.* New York: The Blue Sky Press.

———. 1996. *The Whales.* New York: The Blue Sky Press.

Schotter, Roni. 1999. *Nothing Ever Happens On 90th Street.* New York: Orchard Books.

Scieszka, Jon. 1996. *The True Story of the Three Little Pigs.* New York: Puffin Books.

Seeger, Laura Vaccaro. 2013. *Bully.* New York: Roaring Book Press.

Serravallo, Jennifer. 2010. *Teaching Reading in Small Groups.* Portsmouth, NH: Heinemann.

———. 2012. *Independent Reading Assessment: Fiction*. New York: Scholastic.

———. 2013a. *Independent Reading Assessment: Nonfiction*. New York: Scholastic.

———. 2013b. *The Literacy Teacher's Playbook, Grades K–2*. Portsmouth, NH: Heinemann.

———. 2014. *The Literacy Teacher's Playbook, Grades 3–6*. Portsmouth, NH: Heinemann.

———. 2015a. *The Reading Strategies Book: Your Everything Guide to Developing Skilled Readers*. Portsmouth, NH: Heinemann.

———. 2015b. "Try This! Outline, Re-Outline, Re-Outline Again." www .sharingournotebooks.amylv.com/p/outline-re-outline-re-outline-again -by.html. Last accessed October 3, 2016.

Settel, Joanne. 1999. *Exploding Ants: Amazing Facts About How Animals Adapt*. New York: Atheneum Books for Young Readers.

Shanahan, Kerrie. 2010. *Amazing Salamanders*. South Yarra, VIC. Victoria Eleanor Curtain.

Shapiro, Ari. June. 2014. "Speechwriters Deliberately Use Rhythm To Help Make Their Point." www.npr.org/2014/06/19/323510652/speechwriters-deliberately -use-rhythm-to-help-make-their-point. Last accessed May 7, 2016.

Sloan, Holly Goldberg. *Counting by 7s*. Reprint ed. New York: Puffin Books.

Smith, Frank. 1988. *Insult to Intelligence: The Bureaucratic Invasion of Our Classrooms*. Portsmouth, NH: Heinemann.

Smith, Lane. 2011. *Grandpa Green*. New York: Roaring Book Press.

Snowball, Diane, and Faye Bolton. 1999. *Spelling K–8: Planning and Teaching*. Portland, ME: Stenhouse.

Spinelli, Jerry. 1990. *Maniac Magee*. New York: Little, Brown Books for Young Readers.

———. 1996. *Crash*. New York: Dell Yearling.

Steig, William. 1986. *Brave Irene*. New York: Farrar, Straus and Giroux.

Stein, Sol. 1995. *Stein on Writing: A Master Editor of Some of the Most Successful Writers of Our Century Shares His Craft Techniques and Strategies*. New York: St. Martin's Press.

Strong, William. 1999. "Coaching Writing Development: Syntax Revisited, Options Explored." In *Evaluating Writing: The Role of Teachers' Knowledge About Text, Learning, and Culture,* edited by Charles R. Cooper and Lee Odell, 72–92. Urbana, IL: NCTE.

Strunk, William Jr., and E. B. White. 1999. *The Elements of Style*. 4th ed. London: Pearson.

Swados, Elizabeth. 2002. "Me." In *Hey You! C'Mere a Poetry Slam*. New York: Arthur A. Levine Books.

Taylor, Sarah Picard. 2008. *A Quick Guide to Teaching Persuasive Writing, K–2.* Portsmouth, NH: Heinemann.

Terban, Marvin. 1993. *It Figures! Fun Figures of Speech.* New York: Clarion Books.

Thimmesh, Cathcrine. 2006. *Team Moon: How 400,000 People Landed Apollo 11 on the Moon.* New York: Houghton Mifflin.

Thomas, P. L. 2016. "Student Choice, Engagement Keys to Higher Quality Writing." https://radicalscholarship.wordpress.com/2016/02/16/student-choice-engagement-keys-to-higher-quality-writing. Last accessed May 7, 2016.

Truss, Lynne. 2006. *Eats, Shoots & Leaves: Why, Commas Really Do Make a Difference!* New York: G.P. Putnam's Sons.

Twain, Mark. 1999. *The Wit and Wisdom of Mark Twain: A Book of Quotations.* Mineola, NY: Dover.

Vernali, Stephanie. 2000. *Eat It, Print It.* Oxford: Rigby Heinemann.

Vopat, Jim. 2007a. *Micro Lessons in Writing: Big Ideas for Getting Started.* Portsmouth, NH: Heinemann.

———. 2007b. *Micro Lessons in Writing: Big Ideas for Ideas for Revising.* Portsmouth, NH: Heinemann.

———. 2007c. *Micro Lessons in Writing: Big Ideas for Ideas for Editing and Publishing.* Portsmouth, NH: Heinemann.

Weeks, Sarah. 2008. *Oggie Cooder.* New York: Scholastic.

White, E. B. 1945. *Stuart Little.* New York: HarperCollins.

Wiggins, Grant, and Jay McTighe. 2011. *Understanding by Design, Expanded 2nd Edition.* Upper Saddle River, NJ: Pearson.

Willems, Mo. 2004. *Knuffle Bunny: A Cautionary Tale.* New York: Hyperion Books for Children.

———. Pigeon series. New York: Hyperion.

———. Piggy and Elephant series. New York: Hyperion.

Williams, William Carlos. 1962. "The Red Wheelbarrow." In *Spring and All.* New York: New Directions.

Wilson, N. D. 2015. *Boys of Blur.* New York: Yearling.

Woodson, Jacqueline. 2001. *The Other Side.* New York: G.P. Putnam's Sons.

Worth, Valerie. 1996. *All the Small Poems and Fourteen More.* Sunburst ed. Melbourne, FL: Sunburst Books.

Yamada, Kobi. 2014. *What Do You Do with an Idea?* Seattle, WA: Compendium.

Yolen, Jane. 1987. *Owl Moon.* New York: Putnam.

———. 1995. *Water Music: Poems for Children.* Honesdale, PA: Boyds Mills Press.

———. 1997. *Nocturne.* San Diego, CA: Harcourt Books.

Woodson, Jacqueline. 2012. *Each Kindness.* New York. Penguin.

Zagarenski, Pamela. 2015. *The Whisper.* New York: Houghton Mifflin Harcourt.

Zimmerman, Alicia. 2013. "Beyond the Publishing Party: Ten Ways to Celebrate Learning." www.scholastic.com/teachers/top-teaching/2013/03/beyond -publishing-party-ten-ways-celebrate-learning. Last accessed September 8, 2016.

Zinsser, William. 2001. *On Writing Well: The Classic Guide to Writing Nonfiction.* 25th Anniversary Edition. New York: HarperCollins.

Resources from Jen Serravallo
that help you across the literacy curriculum

JENNIFER SERRAVALLO

With **300** strategies

The
Reading Strategies Book

YOUR **EVERYTHING GUIDE** TO
DEVELOPING SKILLED READERS

Heinemann
DEDICATED TO TEACHERS

JENNIFER SERRAVALLO   *Foreword by Lucy Calkins*

TEACHING READING
in SMALL GROUPS

DIFFERENTIATED INSTRUCTION
FOR BUILDING STRATEGIC,
INDEPENDENT READERS

Heinemann
DEDICATED TO TEACHERS

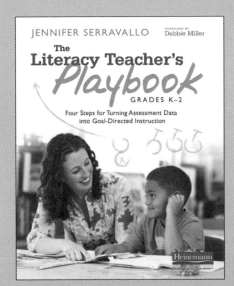

JENNIFER SERRAVALLO   FOREWORD BY
Debbie Miller

The
Literacy Teacher's
Playbook
GRADES K–2

Four Steps for Turning Assessment Data
into Goal-Directed Instruction

Heinemann
DEDICATED TO TEACHERS

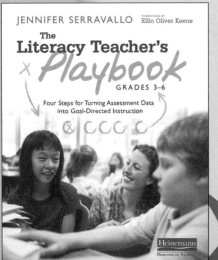

JENNIFER SERRAVALLO   FOREWORD BY
Ellin Oliver Keene

The
Literacy Teacher's
Playbook
GRADES 3–6

Four Steps for Turning Assessment Data
into Goal-Directed Instruction

Heinemann
DEDICATED TO TEACHERS